OCT   2017

BEP PRESENT

MASTERS OF THE SUN

WRITERS
will.i.am & BENJAMIN JACKENDOFF

PRODUCED BY
apl.de.ap
TABOO
will.i.am

EXECUTIVE PRODUCTION
POLO MOLINA
SARA RAMAKER

ARTIST
DAMION SCOTT

COLORIST
SIGMUND TORRE

LETTERS / DESIGN
A LARGER WORLD STUDIOS'
DAVE LANPHEAR

CONSULTANT
JIM KRUEGER

COLOR ASSISTS
TAKAKO SONO

BASED ON AN ORGINAL STORY BY
will.i.am & NIR STUDNITSKI

PACKAGE / LOGO DESIGN
EDDIE AXLEY
CODY ACHTER
PO WANG
MONIKA ARECHAVALA

COVER ART
will.i.am
PASHA SHAPIRO
ERIK WEBER
EDDIE AXLEY
CODY ACHTER

BLACK EYED PEAS PRESENTS: MASTERS OF THE SUN — THE ZOMBIE CHRONICLES. FIRST PRINTING 2017. ISBN# 978-1-302-91084-6. PUBLISHED BY MARVEL WORLDWIDE, INC., A SUBSIDIARY OF MARVEL ENTERTAINMENT, LLC. OFFICE OF PUBLICATION: 135 WEST 50TH STREET, NEW YORK, NY 10020. COPYRIGHT © 2017 i.am.bizzy, llc. NO SIMILARITY BETWEEN ANY OF THE NAMES, CHARACTERS, PERSONS, AND/OR INSTITUTIONS IN THIS MAGAZINE WITH THOSE OF ANY LIVING OR DEAD PERSON OR INSTITUTION IS INTENDED, AND ANY SUCH SIMILARITY WHICH MAY EXIST IS PURELY COINCIDENTAL. MARVEL AND ITS LOGOS ARE TM & © MARVEL CHARACTERS, INC. PRINTED IN USA. DAN BUCKLEY, PRESIDENT, MARVEL ENTERTAINMENT; JOE QUESADA, CHIEF CREATIVE OFFICER; TOM BREVOORT, SVP OF PUBLISHING; DAVID BOGART, SVP OF BUSINESS AFFAIRS & OPERATIONS, PUBLISHING & PARTNERSHIP; C.B. CEBULSKI, VP OF BRAND MANAGEMENT & DEVELOPMENT, ASIA; DAVID GABRIEL, SVP OF SALES & MARKETING, PUBLISHING; JEFF YOUNGQUIST, VP OF PRODUCTION & SPECIAL PROJECTS; DAN CARR, EXECUTIVE DIRECTOR OF PUBLISHING TECHNOLOGY; ALEX MORALES, DIRECTOR OF PUBLISHING OPERATIONS; SUSAN CRESPI, PRODUCTION MANAGER; STAN LEE, CHAIRMAN EMERITUS. FOR INFORMATION REGARDING ADVERTISING IN MARVEL COMICS OR ON MARVEL.COM, PLEASE CONTACT VIT DEBELLIS, INTEGRATED SALES MANAGER, AT VDEBELLIS@MARVEL.COM. FOR MARVEL SUBSCRIPTION INQUIRIES, PLEASE CALL 888-511-5480. MANUFACTURED BETWEEN 5/26/2017 AND 6/27/2017 BY GRAPHICOM, SANTA FE SPRINGS, CALIFORNIA, USA.
10 9 8 7 6 5 4 3 2 1

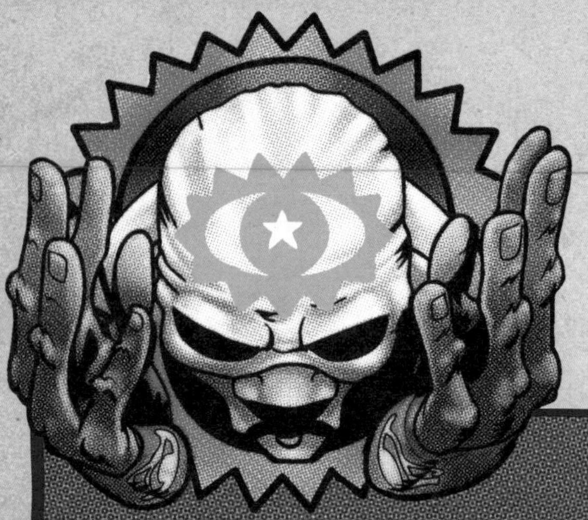

MASTER SUN'S VERSE 13:36

ONCE THERE WAS A TIME OF HARMONY
a time long before the Annunaki.
When Black was known as a powerful Word
One of Divine property, and that was always heard.

But then came the Creatures
dropped in from the sky.
"Gods" from above
Bearing a lie.

The Black were told that they were all Dark
And Dark is Evil and they bore the Mark.
The Mark of the Foulest most Wicked Beast
And that they would have to sacrifice in order to Feast.

The Feast was for them to become "gods"
to sell out their families
and put their People at odds.

-Masters of the Sun

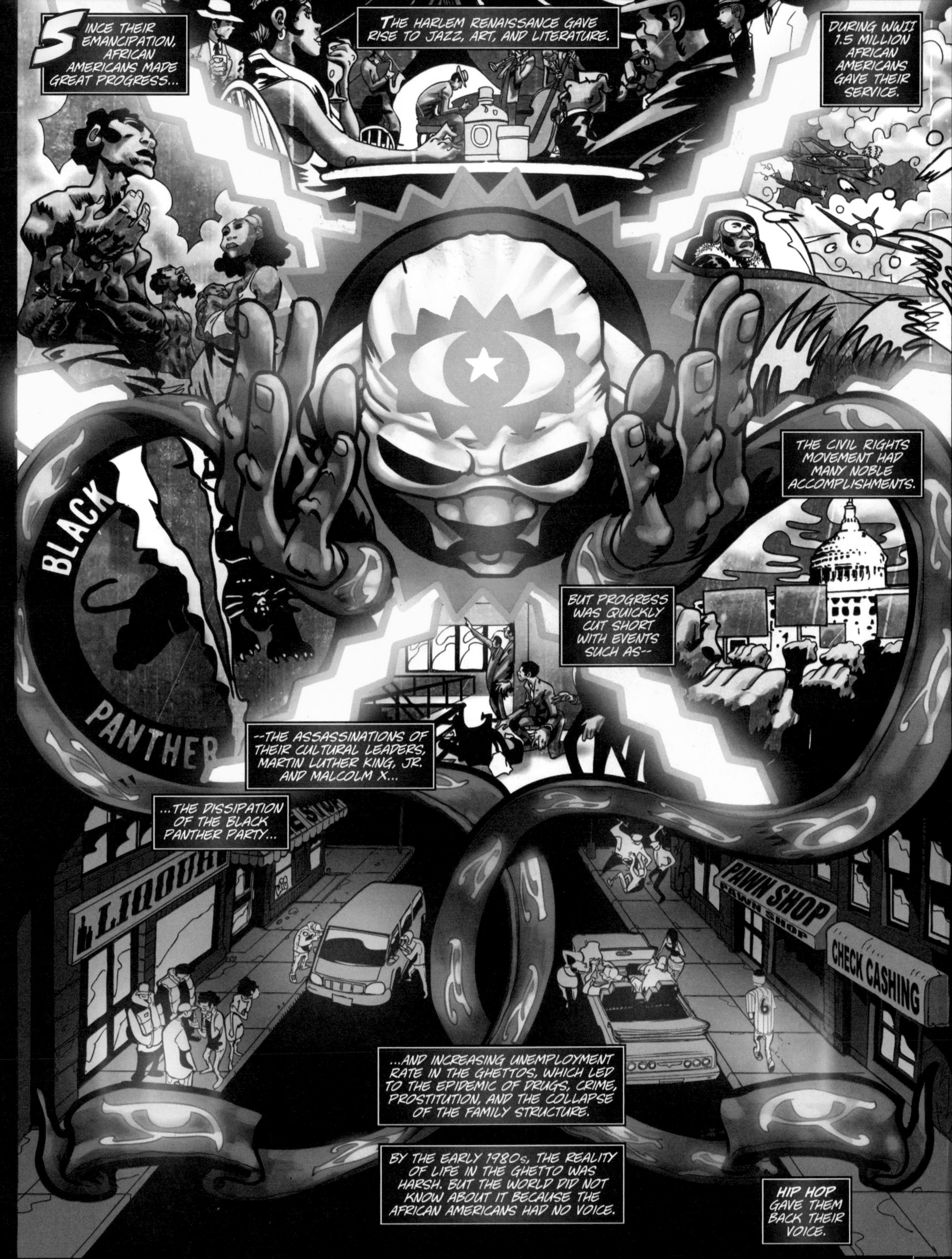
SINCE THEIR EMANCIPATION, AFRICAN AMERICANS MADE GREAT PROGRESS...
THE HARLEM RENAISSANCE GAVE RISE TO JAZZ, ART, AND LITERATURE.
DURING WWII 1.5 MILLION AFRICAN AMERICANS GAVE THEIR SERVICE.
THE CIVIL RIGHTS MOVEMENT HAD MANY NOBLE ACCOMPLISHMENTS.
BLACK PANTHER
BUT PROGRESS WAS QUICKLY CUT SHORT WITH EVENTS SUCH AS--
--THE ASSASSINATIONS OF THEIR CULTURAL LEADERS, MARTIN LUTHER KING, JR. AND MALCOLM X...
...THE DISSIPATION OF THE BLACK PANTHER PARTY...
LIQUOR
PAWN SHOP
PAWN SHOP
CHECK CASHING
...AND INCREASING UNEMPLOYMENT RATE IN THE GHETTOS, WHICH LED TO THE EPIDEMIC OF DRUGS, CRIME, PROSTITUTION, AND THE COLLAPSE OF THE FAMILY STRUCTURE.
BY THE EARLY 1980s, THE REALITY OF LIFE IN THE GHETTO WAS HARSH. BUT THE WORLD DID NOT KNOW ABOUT IT BECAUSE THE AFRICAN AMERICANS HAD NO VOICE.
HIP HOP GAVE THEM BACK THEIR VOICE.

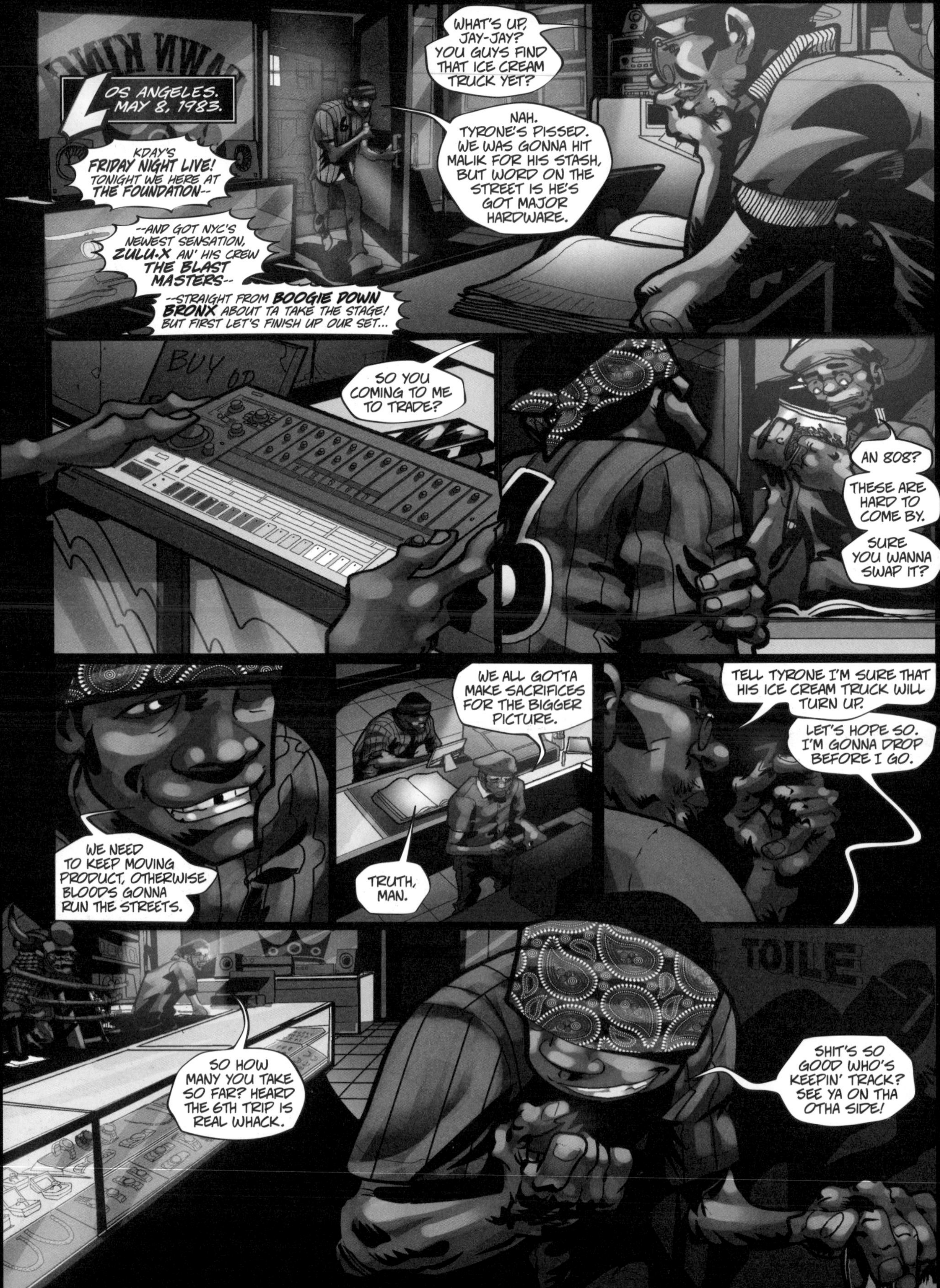
LOS ANGELES. MAY 8, 1983.
KDAY'S FRIDAY NIGHT LIVE! TONIGHT WE HERE AT THE FOUNDATION--
--AND GOT NYC'S NEWEST SENSATION, ZULU-X AN' HIS CREW THE BLAST MASTERS--
--STRAIGHT FROM BOOGIE DOWN BRONX ABOUT TA TAKE THE STAGE! BUT FIRST LET'S FINISH UP OUR SET...
WHAT'S UP, JAY-JAY? YOU GUYS FIND THAT ICE CREAM TRUCK YET?
NAH. TYRONE'S PISSED. WE WAS GONNA HIT MALIK FOR HIS STASH, BUT WORD ON THE STREET IS HE'S GOT MAJOR HARDWARE.
BUY
SO YOU COMING TO ME TO TRADE?
AN 808?
THESE ARE HARD TO COME BY.
SURE YOU WANNA SWAP IT?
WE NEED TO KEEP MOVING PRODUCT, OTHERWISE BLOODS GONNA RUN THE STREETS.
WE ALL GOTTA MAKE SACRIFICES FOR THE BIGGER PICTURE.
TRUTH, MAN.
TELL TYRONE I'M SURE THAT HIS ICE CREAM TRUCK WILL TURN UP.
LET'S HOPE SO. I'M GONNA DROP BEFORE I GO.
SO HOW MANY YOU TAKE SO FAR? HEARD THE 6TH TRIP IS REAL WHACK.
SHIT'S SO GOOD WHO'S KEEPIN' TRACK? SEE YA ON THA OTHA SIDE!
TOILE

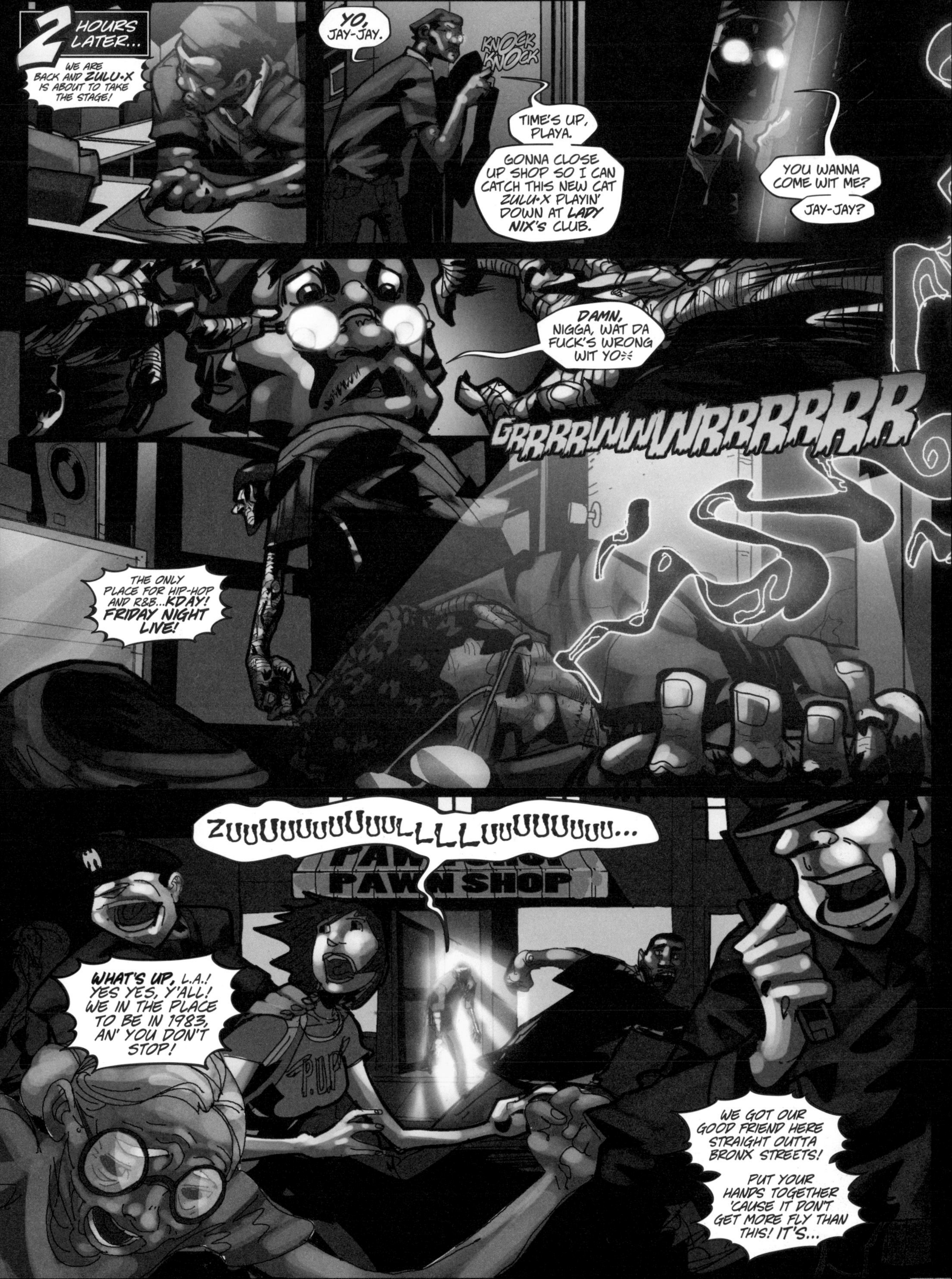
2 HOURS LATER...
WE ARE BACK AND ZULU-X IS ABOUT TO TAKE THE STAGE!
YO, JAY-JAY.
KNOCK KNOCK
TIME'S UP, PLAYA.
GONNA CLOSE UP SHOP SO I CAN CATCH THIS NEW CAT ZULU-X PLAYIN' DOWN AT LADY NIX'S CLUB.
YOU WANNA COME WIT ME?
JAY-JAY?
DAMN, NIGGA, WAT DA FUCK'S WRONG WIT YO--
GRRRRWWWRRRRRRR
THE ONLY PLACE FOR HIP-HOP AND R&B...KDAY! FRIDAY NIGHT LIVE!
ZUUUUUUUUUULLLUUUUUUUU...
PAWN SHOP
WHAT'S UP, L.A.! YES YES, Y'ALL! WE IN THE PLACE TO BE IN 1983, AN' YOU DON'T STOP!
WE GOT OUR GOOD FRIEND HERE STRAIGHT OUTTA BRONX STREETS!
PUT YOUR HANDS TOGETHER 'CAUSE IT DON'T GET MORE FLY THAN THIS! IT'S...

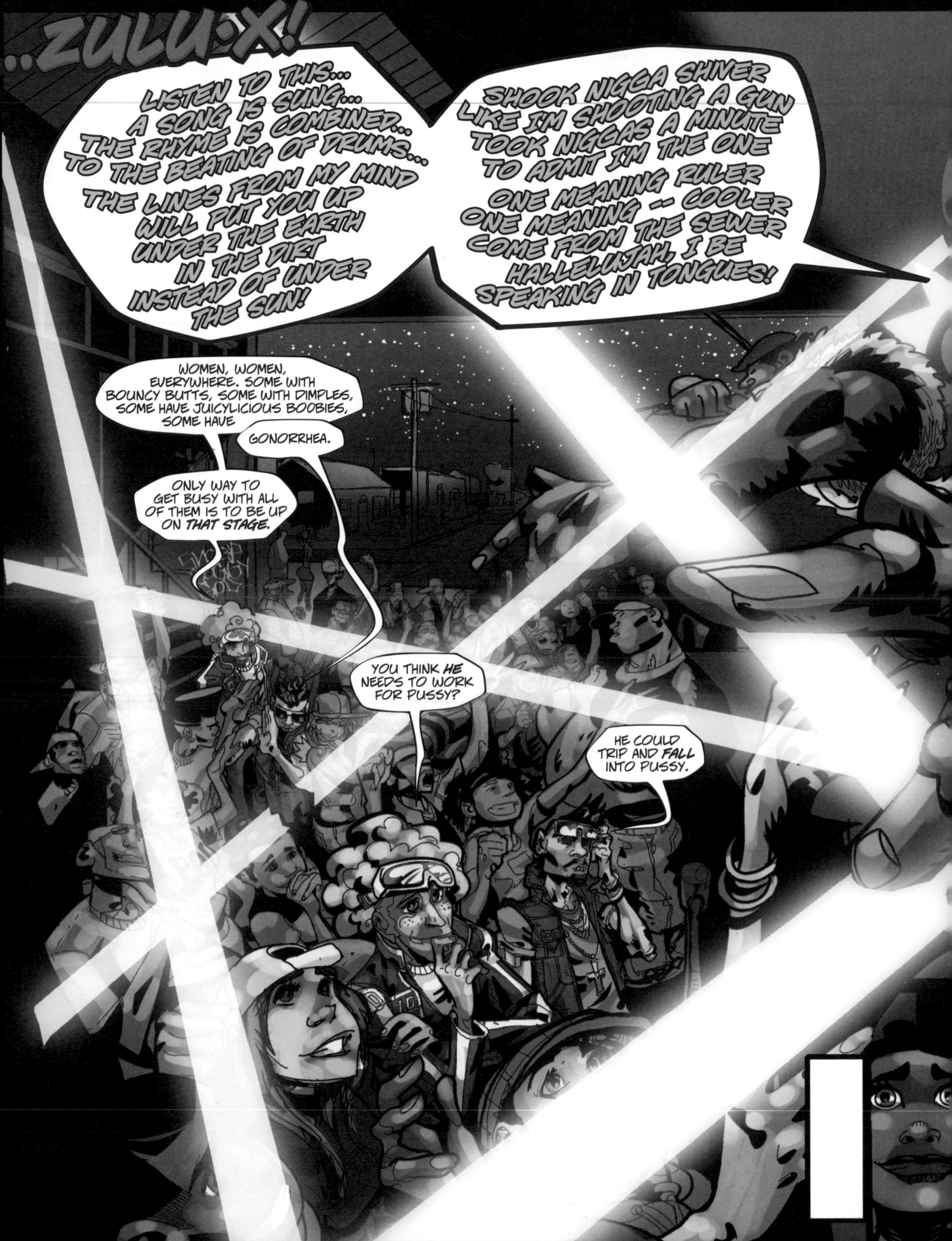
...ZULU-X!
LISTEN TO THIS... A SONG IS SUNG... THE RHYME IS COMBINED... TO THE BEATING OF DRUMS... THE LINES FROM MY MIND WILL PUT YOU UP UNDER THE EARTH IN THE DIRT INSTEAD OF UNDER THE SUN!
SHOOK NIGGA SHIVER LIKE I'M SHOOTING A GUN TOOK NIGGAS A MINUTE TO ADMIT I'M THE ONE ONE MEANING RULER ONE MEANING -- COOLER COME FROM THE SEWER HALLELUJAH, I BE SPEAKING IN TONGUES!
WOMEN, WOMEN, EVERYWHERE. SOME WITH BOUNCY BUTTS, SOME WITH DIMPLES, SOME HAVE JUICYLICIOUS BOOBIES, SOME HAVE
GONORRHEA.
ONLY WAY TO GET BUSY WITH ALL OF THEM IS TO BE UP ON THAT STAGE.
YOU THINK HE NEEDS TO WORK FOR PUSSY?
HE COULD TRIP AND FALL INTO PUSSY.

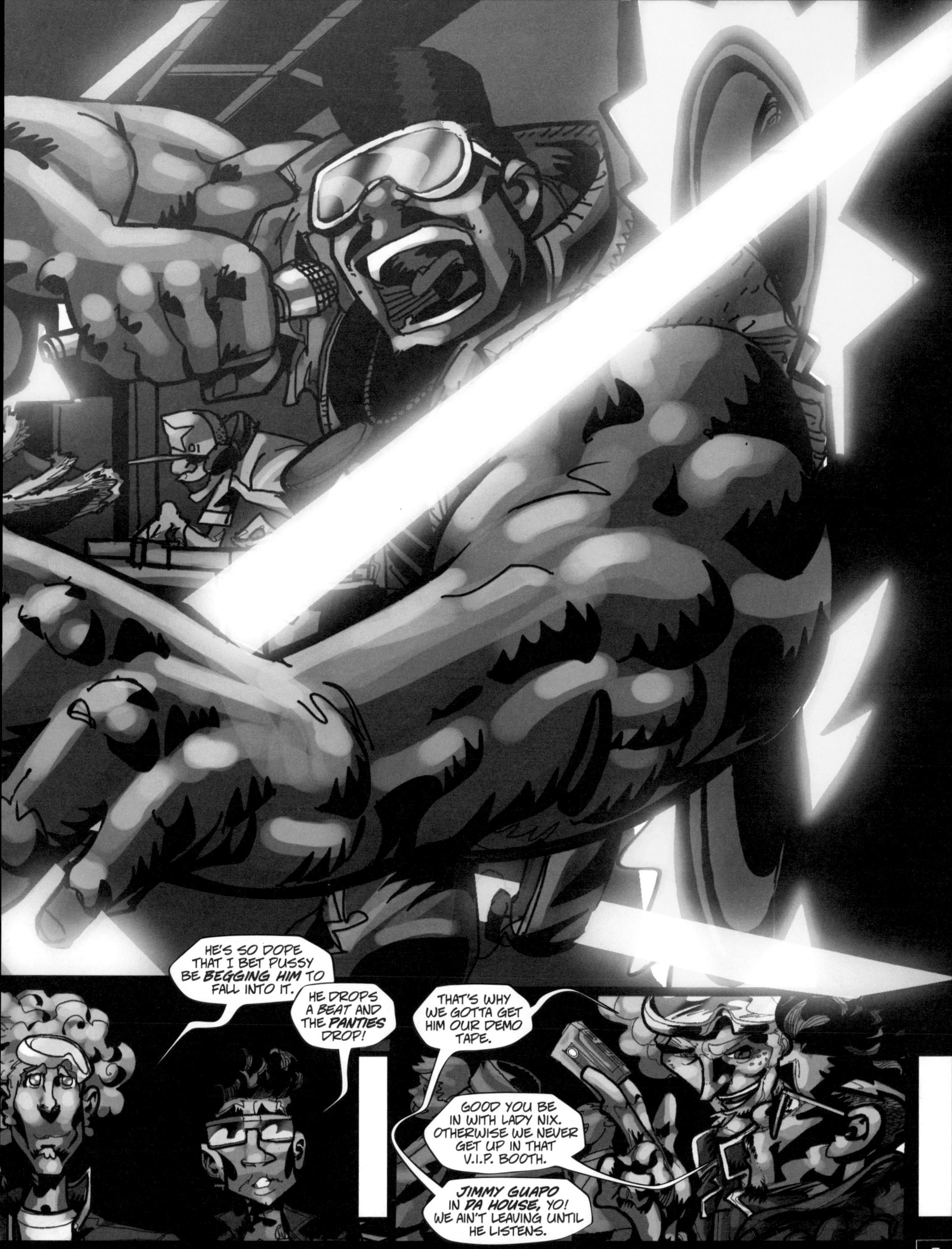
HE'S SO DOPE THAT I BET PUSSY BE BEGGING HIM TO FALL INTO IT.
HE DROPS A BEAT AND THE PANTIES DROP!
THAT'S WHY WE GOTTA GET HIM OUR DEMO TAPE.
GOOD YOU BE IN WITH LADY NIX. OTHERWISE WE NEVER GET UP IN THAT V.I.P. BOOTH.
JIMMY GUAPO IN DA HOUSE, YO! WE AIN'T LEAVING UNTIL HE LISTENS.

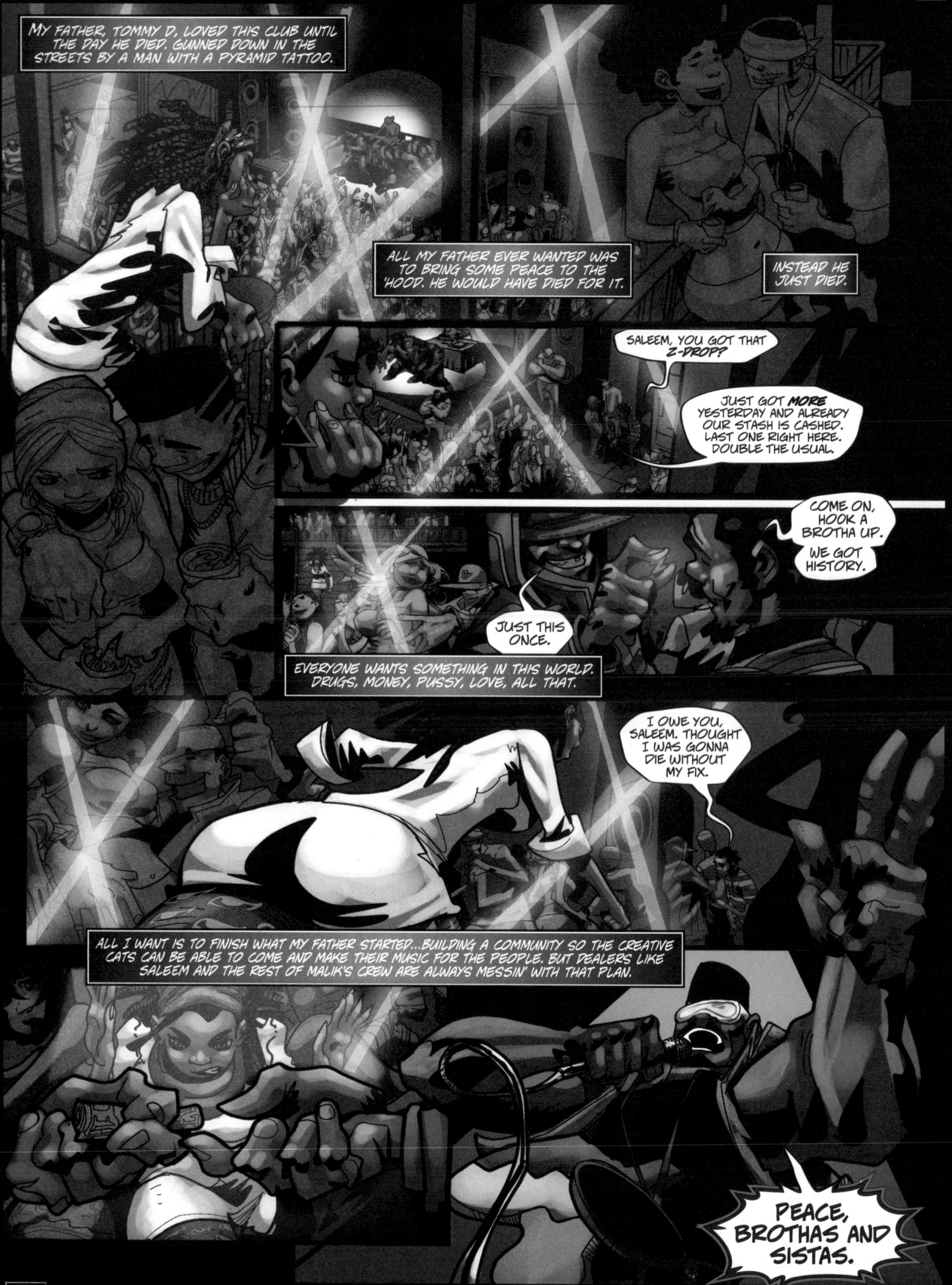
MY FATHER, TOMMY D, LOVED THIS CLUB UNTIL THE DAY HE DIED. GUNNED DOWN IN THE STREETS BY A MAN WITH A PYRAMID TATTOO.
ALL MY FATHER EVER WANTED WAS TO BRING SOME PEACE TO THE 'HOOD. HE WOULD HAVE DIED FOR IT.
INSTEAD HE JUST DIED.
SALEEM, YOU GOT THAT Z-DROP?
JUST GOT MORE YESTERDAY AND ALREADY OUR STASH IS CASHED. LAST ONE RIGHT HERE. DOUBLE THE USUAL.
COME ON, HOOK A BROTHA UP.
WE GOT HISTORY.
JUST THIS ONCE.
EVERYONE WANTS SOMETHING IN THIS WORLD. DRUGS, MONEY, PUSSY, LOVE, ALL THAT.
I OWE YOU, SALEEM. THOUGHT I WAS GONNA DIE WITHOUT MY FIX.
ALL I WANT IS TO FINISH WHAT MY FATHER STARTED...BUILDING A COMMUNITY SO THE CREATIVE CATS CAN BE ABLE TO COME AND MAKE THEIR MUSIC FOR THE PEOPLE. BUT DEALERS LIKE SALEEM AND THE REST OF MALIK'S CREW ARE ALWAYS MESSIN' WITH THAT PLAN.
PEACE, BROTHAS AND SISTAS.

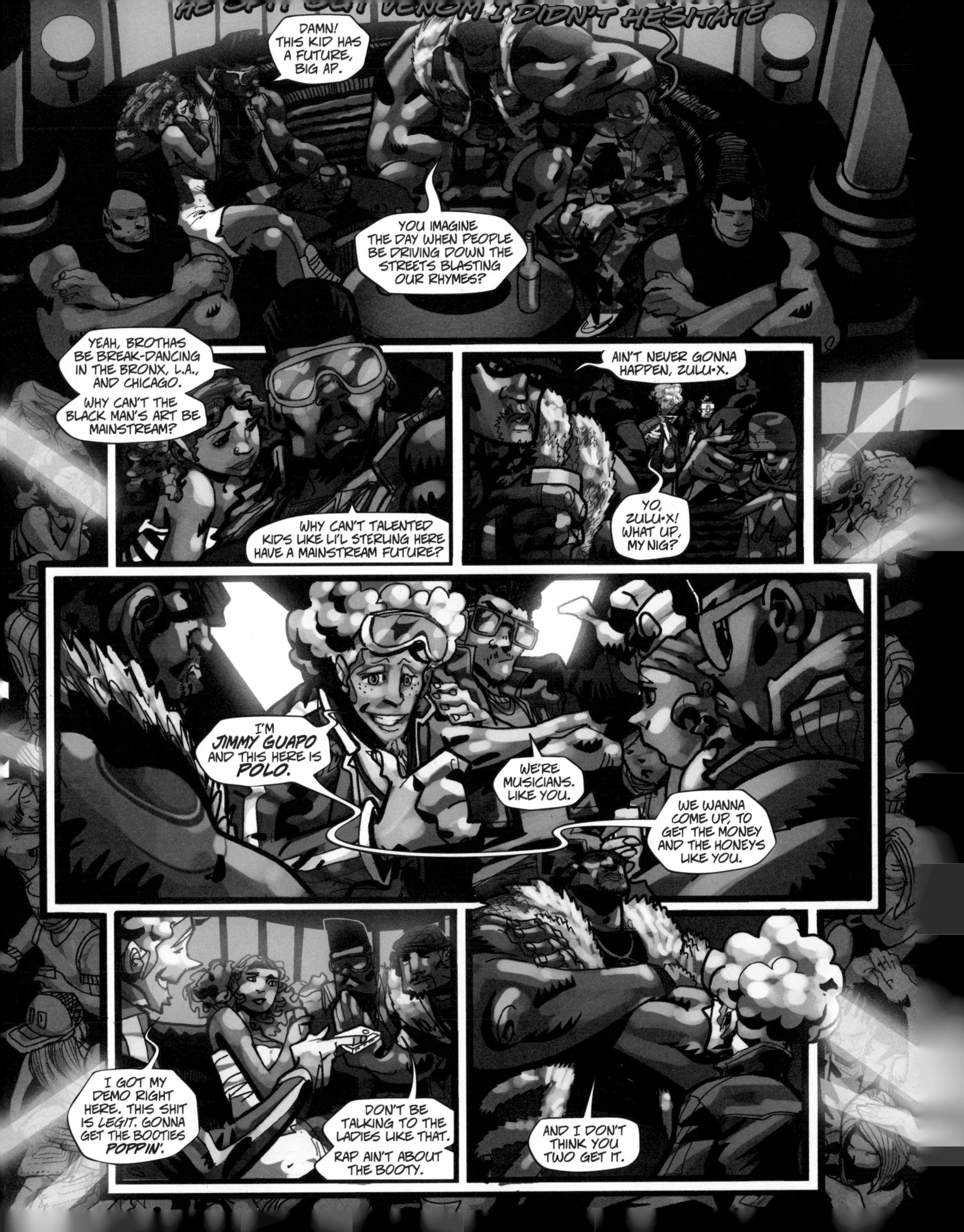
VENOM I DIDN'T HESITATE
DAMN! THIS KID HAS A FUTURE, BIG AP.
YOU IMAGINE THE DAY WHEN PEOPLE BE DRIVING DOWN THE STREETS BLASTING OUR RHYMES?
YEAH, BROTHAS BE BREAK-DANCING IN THE BRONX, L.A., AND CHICAGO.
WHY CAN'T THE BLACK MAN'S ART BE MAINSTREAM?
WHY CAN'T TALENTED KIDS LIKE LI'L STERLING HERE HAVE A MAINSTREAM FUTURE?
AIN'T NEVER GONNA HAPPEN, ZULU•X.
YO, ZULU•X! WHAT UP, MY NIG?
I'M JIMMY GUAPO AND THIS HERE IS POLO.
WE'RE MUSICIANS. LIKE YOU.
WE WANNA COME UP, TO GET THE MONEY AND THE HONEYS LIKE YOU.
I GOT MY DEMO RIGHT HERE. THIS SHIT IS LEGIT. GONNA GET THE BOOTIES POPPIN'.
DON'T BE TALKING TO THE LADIES LIKE THAT.
RAP AIN'T ABOUT THE BOOTY.
AND I DON'T THINK YOU TWO GET IT.

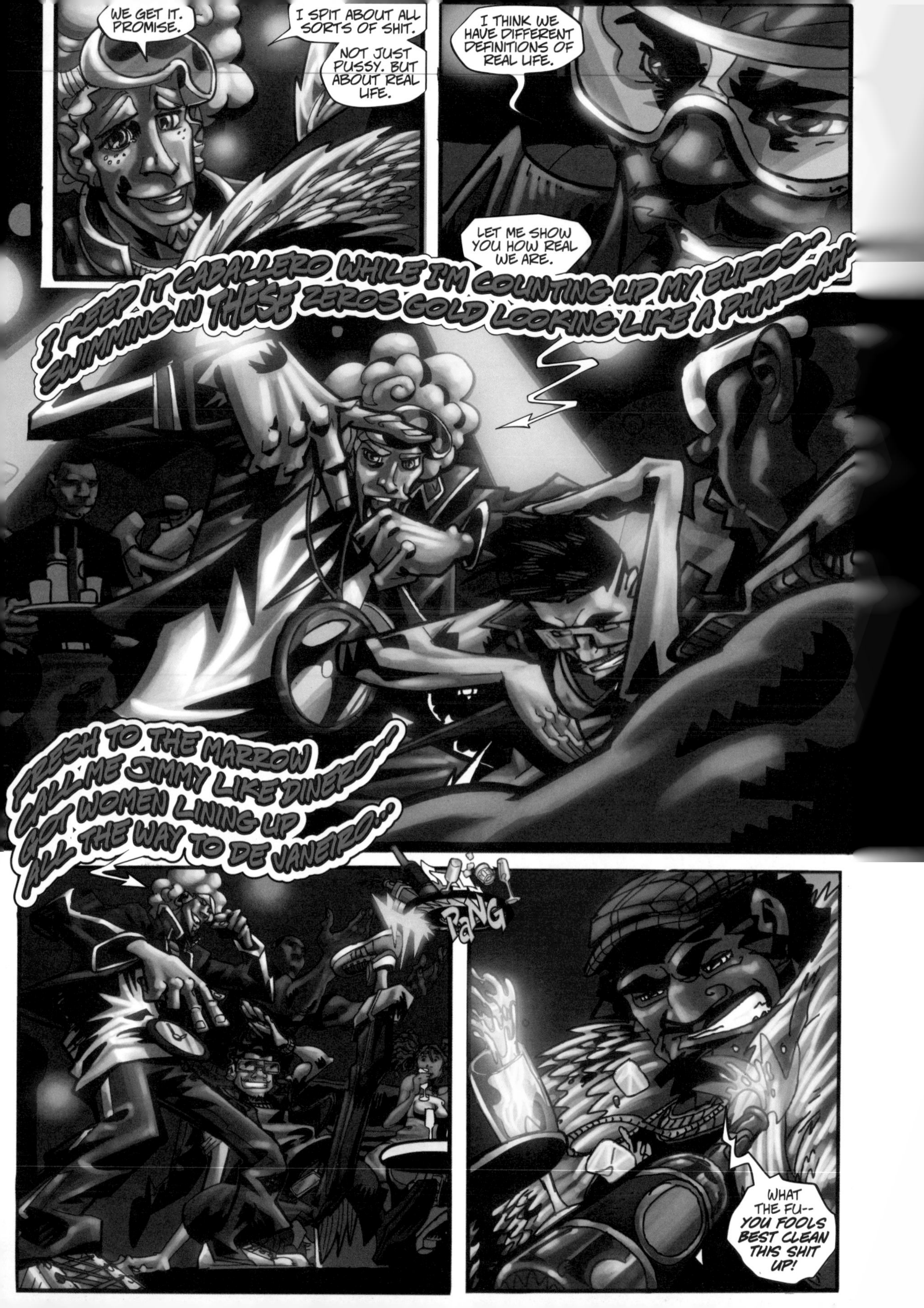

WE GET IT. PROMISE.
I SPIT ABOUT ALL SORTS OF SHIT.
NOT JUST PUSSY. BUT ABOUT REAL LIFE.
I THINK WE HAVE DIFFERENT DEFINITIONS OF REAL LIFE.
LET ME SHOW YOU HOW REAL WE ARE.
I KEEP IT CABALLERO WHILE I'M COUNTING UP MY EUROS-- SWIMMING IN THESE ZEROS GOLD LOOKING LIKE A PHAROAH--
FRESH TO THE MARROW CALL ME JIMMY LIKE DINERO-- GOT WOMEN LINING UP ALL THE WAY TO DE JANEIRO--
PANG
WHAT THE FU-- YOU FOOLS BEST CLEAN THIS SHIT UP!

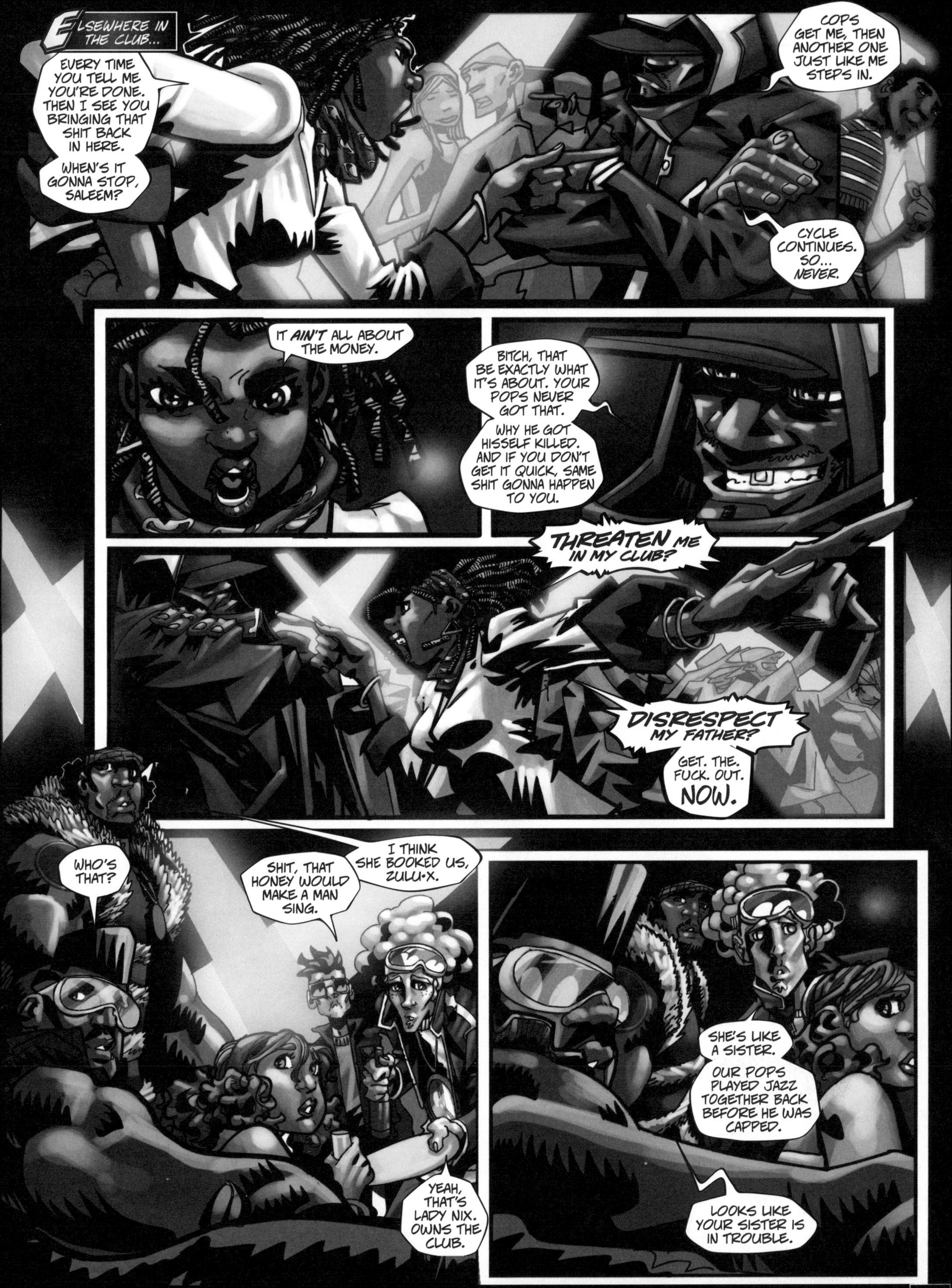
ELSEWHERE IN THE CLUB...
EVERY TIME YOU TELL ME YOU'RE DONE. THEN I SEE YOU BRINGING THAT SHIT BACK IN HERE.
WHEN'S IT GONNA STOP, SALEEM?
COPS GET ME, THEN ANOTHER ONE JUST LIKE ME STEPS IN.
CYCLE CONTINUES. SO... NEVER.
IT AIN'T ALL ABOUT THE MONEY.
BITCH, THAT BE EXACTLY WHAT IT'S ABOUT. YOUR POPS NEVER GOT THAT.
WHY HE GOT HISSELF KILLED. AND IF YOU DON'T GET IT QUICK, SAME SHIT GONNA HAPPEN TO YOU.
THREATEN ME IN MY CLUB?
DISRESPECT MY FATHER?
GET. THE. FUCK. OUT. NOW.
WHO'S THAT?
SHIT, THAT HONEY WOULD MAKE A MAN SING.
I THINK SHE BOOKED US, ZULU-X.
YEAH, THAT'S LADY NIX. OWNS THE CLUB.
SHE'S LIKE A SISTER.
OUR POPS PLAYED JAZZ TOGETHER BACK BEFORE HE WAS CAPPED.
LOOKS LIKE YOUR SISTER IS IN TROUBLE.

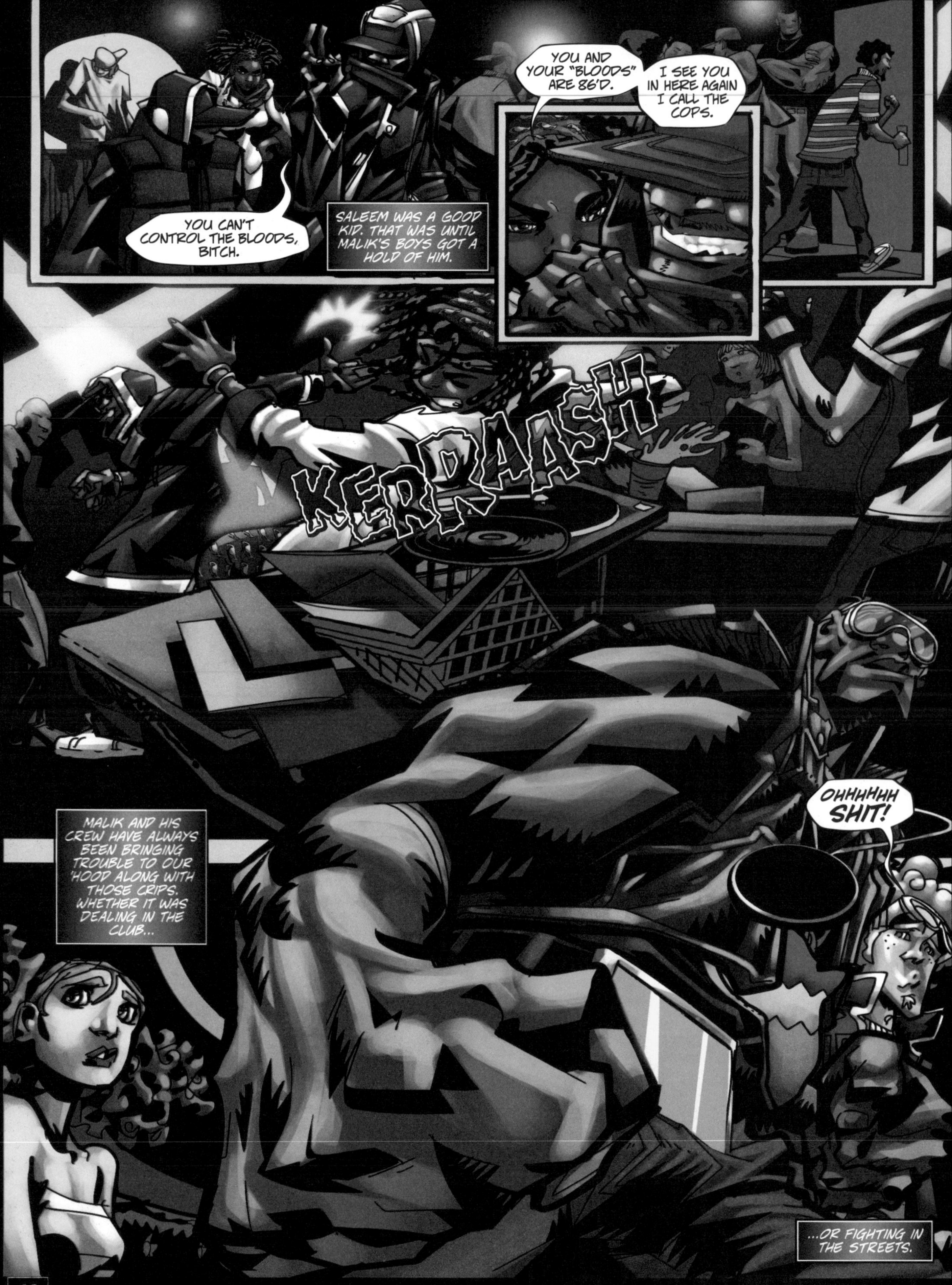
YOU CAN'T CONTROL THE BLOODS, BITCH.
SALEEM WAS A GOOD KID. THAT WAS UNTIL MALIK'S BOYS GOT A HOLD OF HIM.
YOU AND YOUR "BLOODS" ARE 86'D.
I SEE YOU IN HERE AGAIN I CALL THE COPS.
KERRAASH
MALIK AND HIS CREW HAVE ALWAYS BEEN BRINGING TROUBLE TO OUR 'HOOD ALONG WITH THOSE CRIPS. WHETHER IT WAS DEALING IN THE CLUB...
OHHHHHH SHIT!
...OR FIGHTING IN THE STREETS.

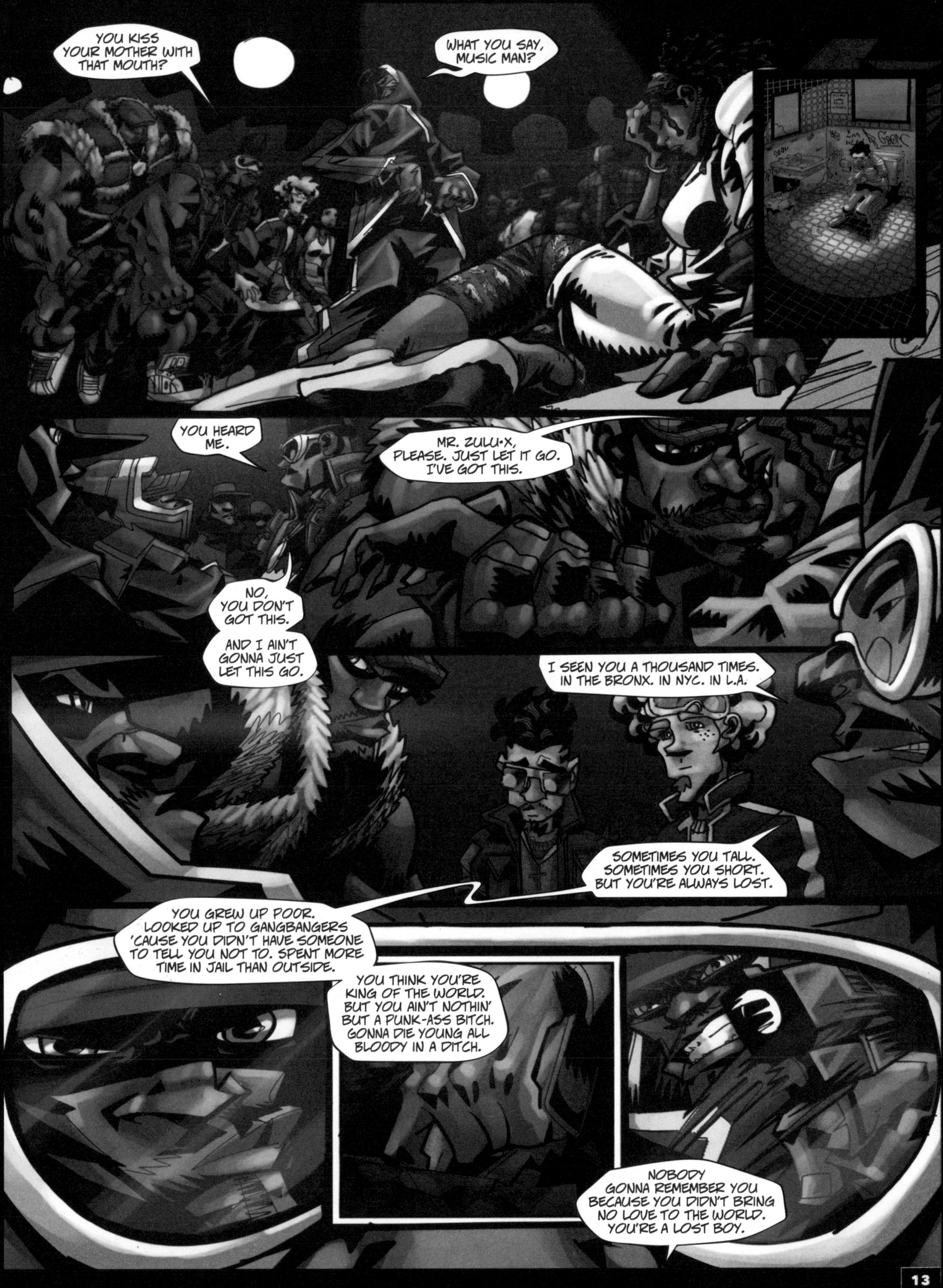
YOU KISS YOUR MOTHER WITH THAT MOUTH?
WHAT YOU SAY, MUSIC MAN?
YOU HEARD ME.
MR. ZULU-X, PLEASE. JUST LET IT GO. I'VE GOT THIS.
NO, YOU DON'T GOT THIS.
AND I AIN'T GONNA JUST LET THIS GO.
I SEEN YOU A THOUSAND TIMES. IN THE BRONX. IN NYC. IN L.A.
SOMETIMES YOU TALL. SOMETIMES YOU SHORT. BUT YOU'RE ALWAYS LOST.
YOU GREW UP POOR. LOOKED UP TO GANGBANGERS 'CAUSE YOU DIDN'T HAVE SOMEONE TO TELL YOU NOT TO. SPENT MORE TIME IN JAIL THAN OUTSIDE.
YOU THINK YOU'RE KING OF THE WORLD. BUT YOU AIN'T NOTHIN' BUT A PUNK-ASS BITCH. GONNA DIE YOUNG ALL BLOODY IN A DITCH.
NOBODY GONNA REMEMBER YOU BECAUSE YOU DIDN'T BRING NO LOVE TO THE WORLD. YOU'RE A LOST BOY.

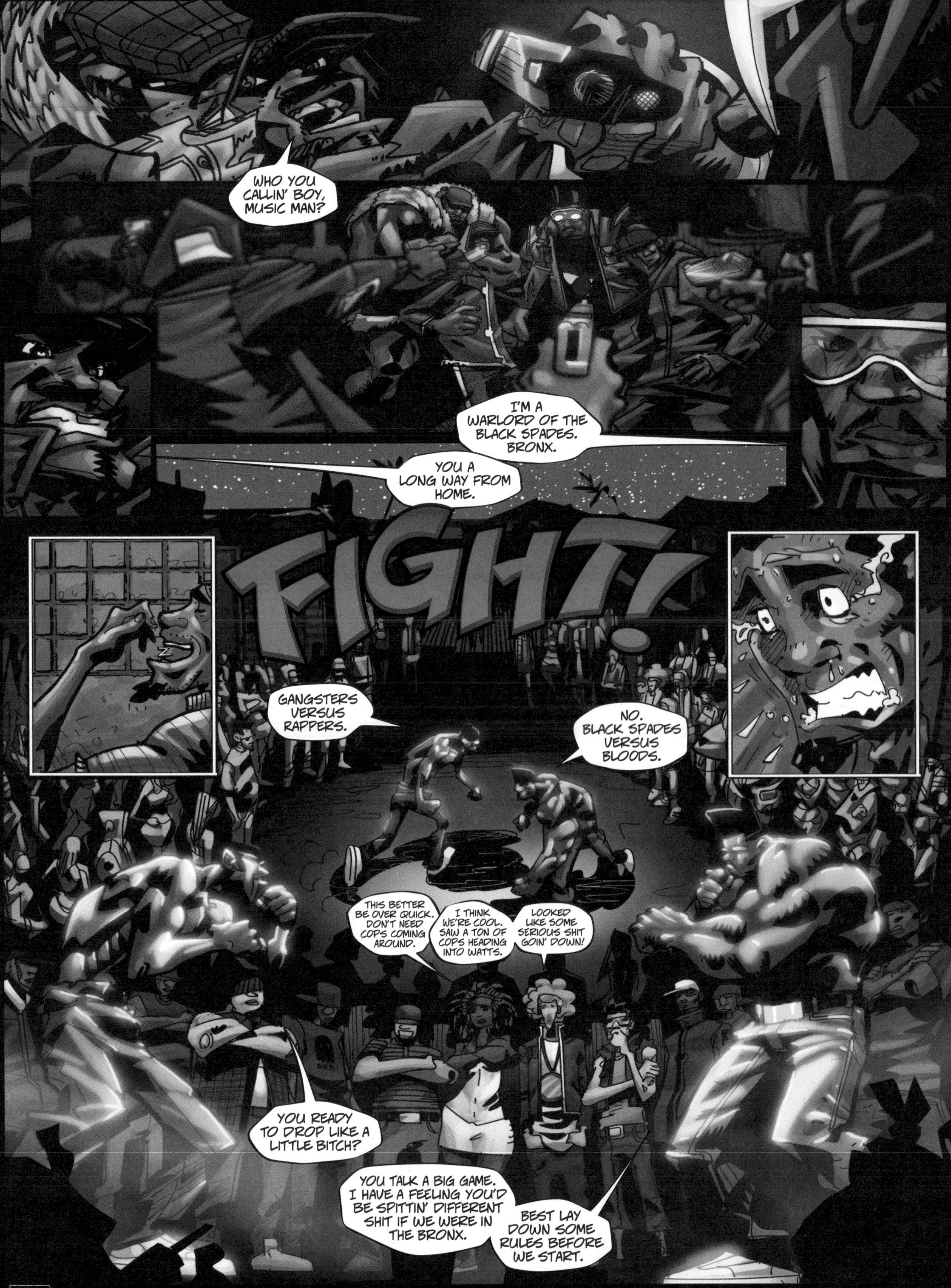
WHO YOU CALLIN' BOY, MUSIC MAN?
I'M A WARLORD OF THE BLACK SPADES. BRONX.
YOU A LONG WAY FROM HOME.
FIGHT!
GANGSTERS VERSUS RAPPERS.
NO. BLACK SPADES VERSUS BLOODS.
THIS BETTER BE OVER QUICK. DON'T NEED COPS COMING AROUND.
I THINK WE'RE COOL. SAW A TON OF COPS HEADING INTO WATTS.
LOOKED LIKE SOME SERIOUS SHIT GOIN' DOWN!
YOU READY TO DROP LIKE A LITTLE BITCH?
YOU TALK A BIG GAME. I HAVE A FEELING YOU'D BE SPITTIN' DIFFERENT SHIT IF WE WERE IN THE BRONX.
BEST LAY DOWN SOME RULES BEFORE WE START.

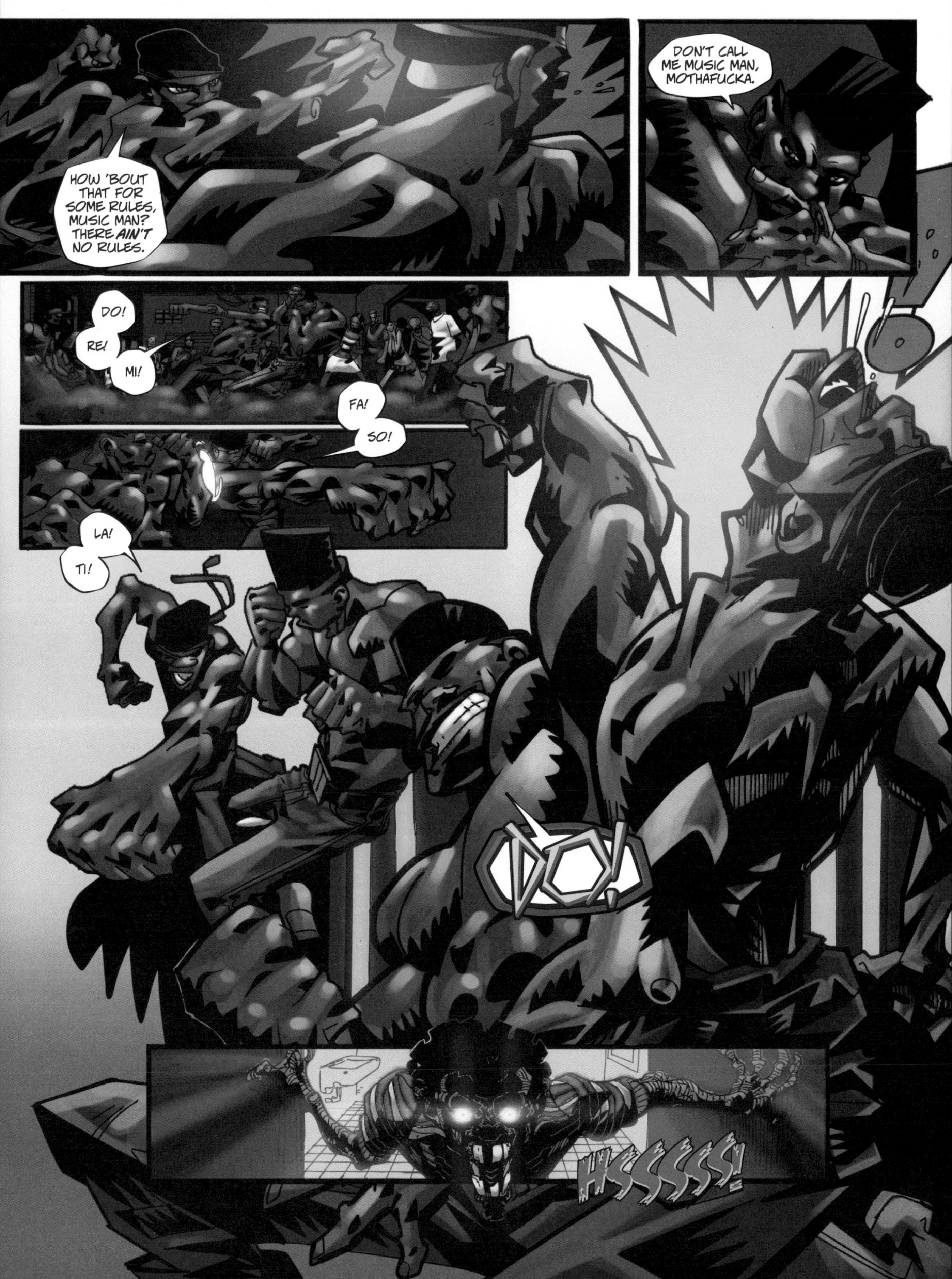
HOW 'BOUT THAT FOR SOME RULES, MUSIC MAN? THERE AIN'T NO RULES.
DON'T CALL ME MUSIC MAN, MOTHAFUCKA.
DO!
RE!
MI!
FA!
SO!
LA!
TI!
DO!
HSSSSSS!

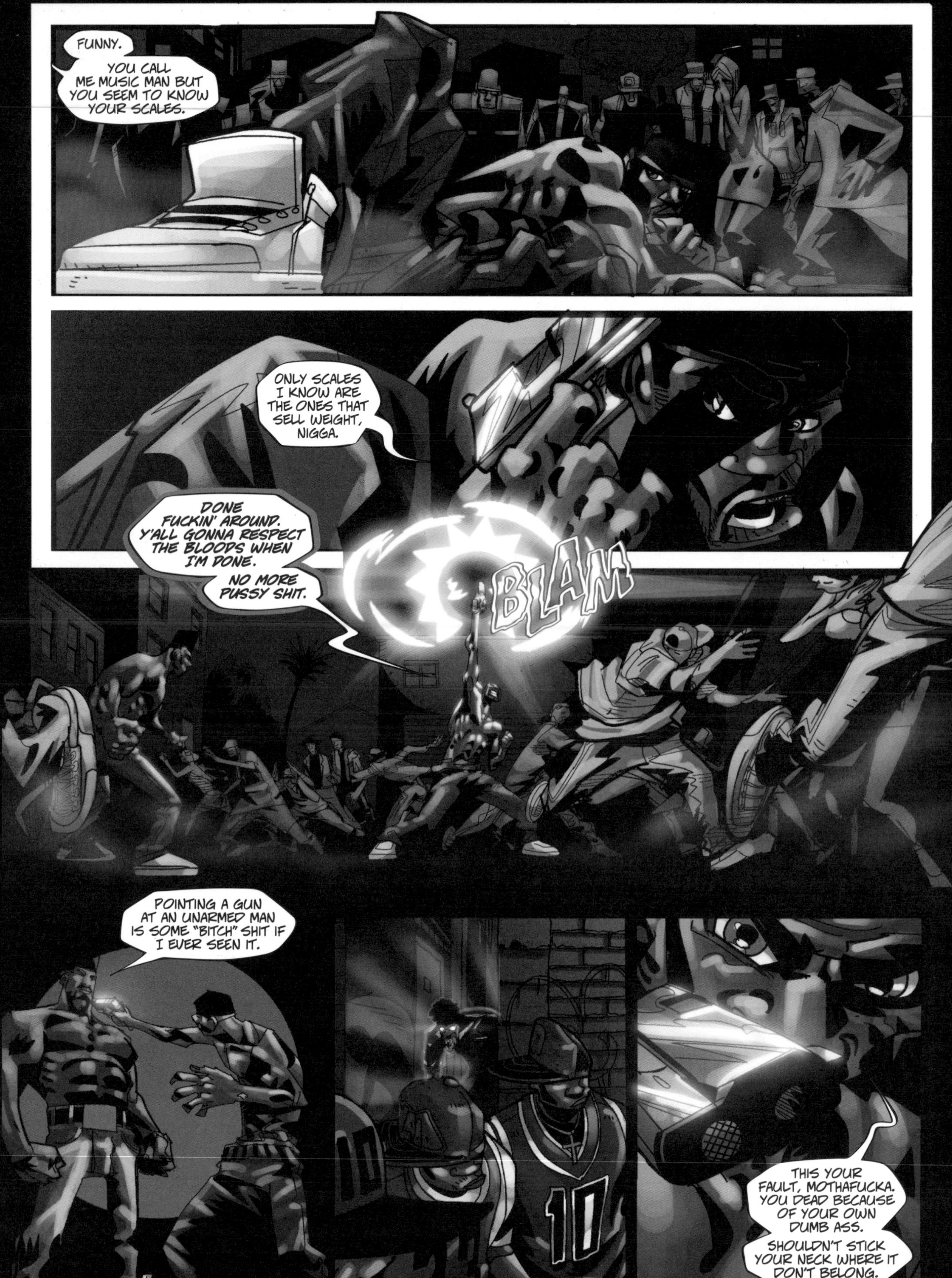

FUNNY.
YOU CALL ME MUSIC MAN BUT YOU SEEM TO KNOW YOUR SCALES.
ONLY SCALES I KNOW ARE THE ONES THAT SELL WEIGHT, NIGGA.
DONE FUCKIN' AROUND. Y'ALL GONNA RESPECT THE BLOODS WHEN I'M DONE.
NO MORE PUSSY SHIT.
BLAM
POINTING A GUN AT AN UNARMED MAN IS SOME "BITCH" SHIT IF I EVER SEEN IT.
THIS YOUR FAULT, MOTHAFUCKA. YOU DEAD BECAUSE OF YOUR OWN DUMB ASS.
SHOULDN'T STICK YOUR NECK WHERE IT DON'T BELONG.

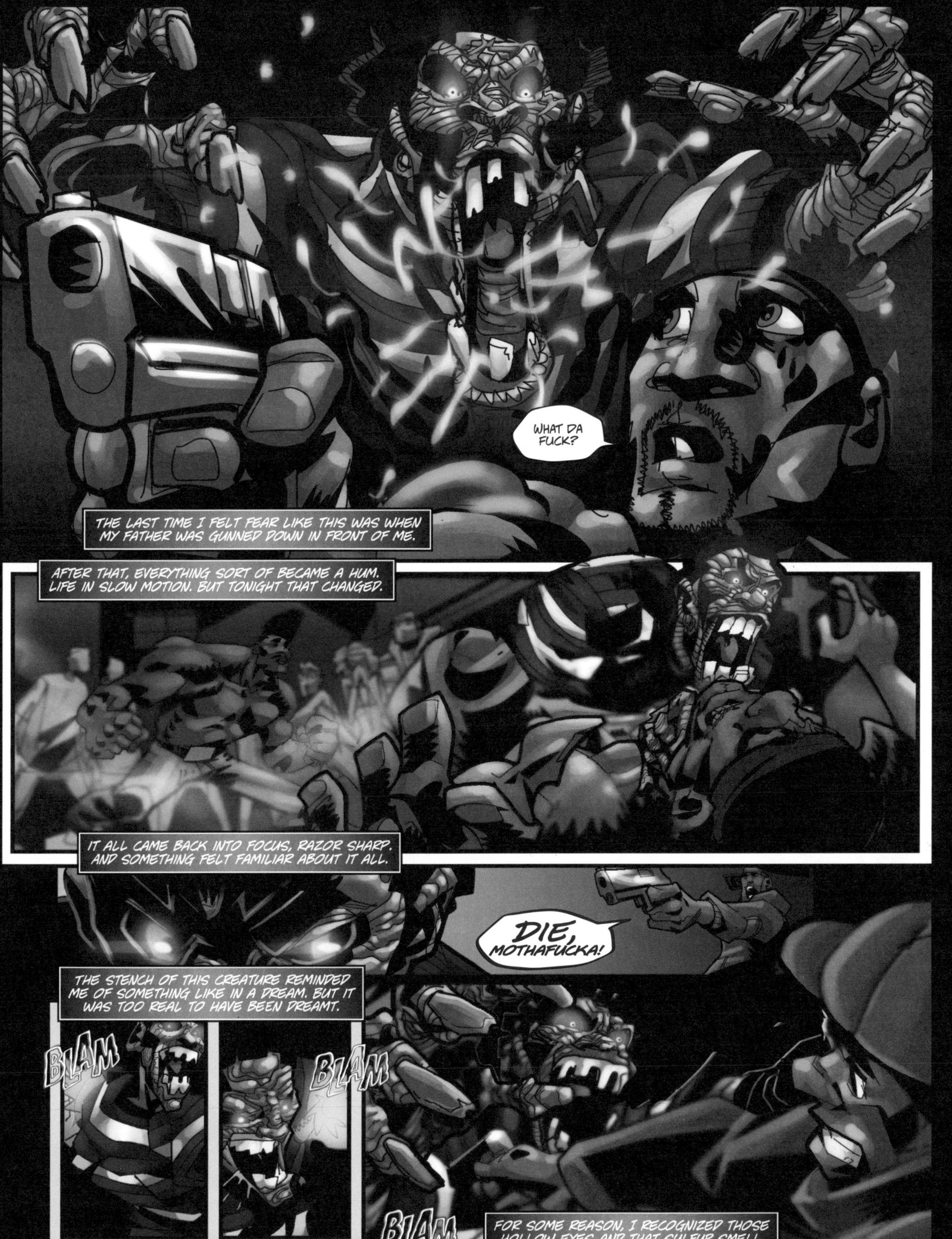
WHAT DA FUCK?
THE LAST TIME I FELT FEAR LIKE THIS WAS WHEN MY FATHER WAS GUNNED DOWN IN FRONT OF ME.
AFTER THAT, EVERYTHING SORT OF BECAME A HUM. LIFE IN SLOW MOTION. BUT TONIGHT THAT CHANGED.
IT ALL CAME BACK INTO FOCUS, RAZOR SHARP. AND SOMETHING FELT FAMILIAR ABOUT IT ALL.
DIE, MOTHAFUCKA!
THE STENCH OF THIS CREATURE REMINDED ME OF SOMETHING LIKE IN A DREAM. BUT IT WAS TOO REAL TO HAVE BEEN DREAMT.
BLAM
BLAM
BLAM
FOR SOME REASON, I RECOGNIZED THOSE HOLLOW EYES AND THAT SULFUR SMELL.

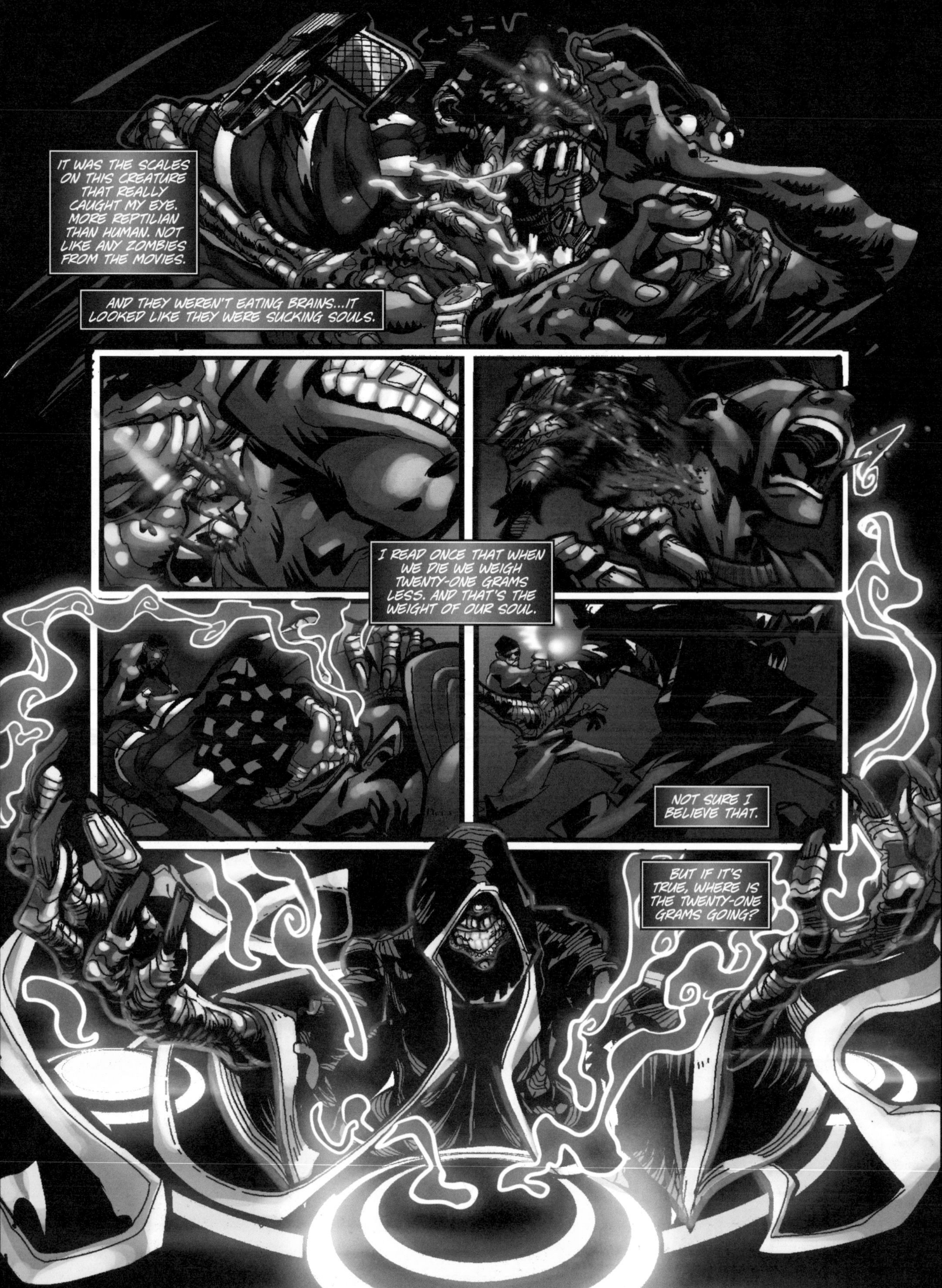
IT WAS THE SCALES ON THIS CREATURE THAT REALLY CAUGHT MY EYE. MORE REPTILIAN THAN HUMAN. NOT LIKE ANY ZOMBIES FROM THE MOVIES.
AND THEY WEREN'T EATING BRAINS...IT LOOKED LIKE THEY WERE SUCKING SOULS.
I READ ONCE THAT WHEN WE DIE WE WEIGH TWENTY-ONE GRAMS LESS. AND THAT'S THE WEIGHT OF OUR SOUL.
NOT SURE I BELIEVE THAT.
BUT IF IT'S TRUE, WHERE IS THE TWENTY-ONE GRAMS GOING?

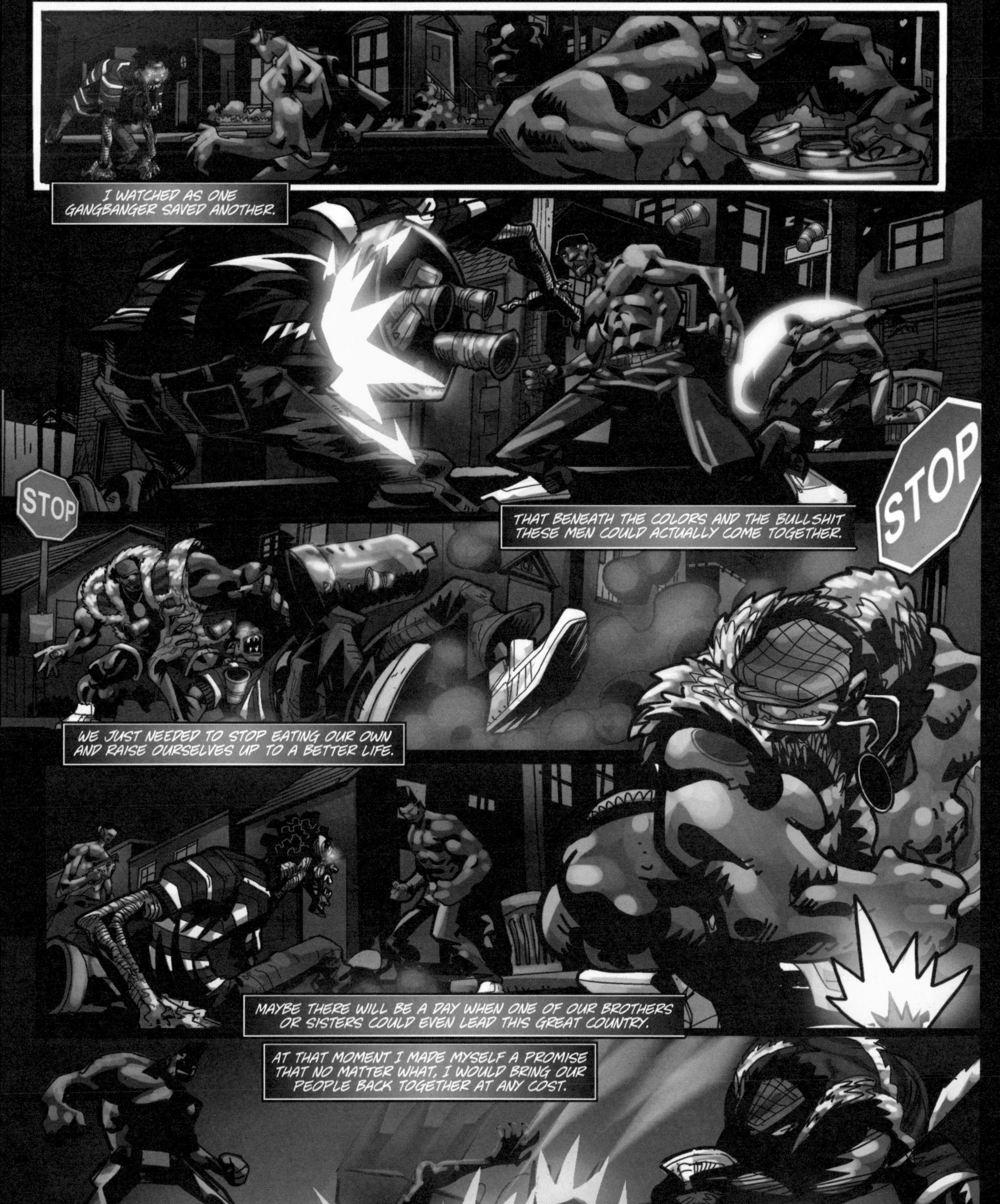
I WATCHED AS ONE GANGBANGER SAVED ANOTHER.
STOP
THAT BENEATH THE COLORS AND THE BULLSHIT THESE MEN COULD ACTUALLY COME TOGETHER.
STOP
WE JUST NEEDED TO STOP EATING OUR OWN AND RAISE OURSELVES UP TO A BETTER LIFE.
MAYBE THERE WILL BE A DAY WHEN ONE OF OUR BROTHERS OR SISTERS COULD EVEN LEAD THIS GREAT COUNTRY.
AT THAT MOMENT I MADE MYSELF A PROMISE THAT NO MATTER WHAT, I WOULD BRING OUR PEOPLE BACK TOGETHER AT ANY COST.

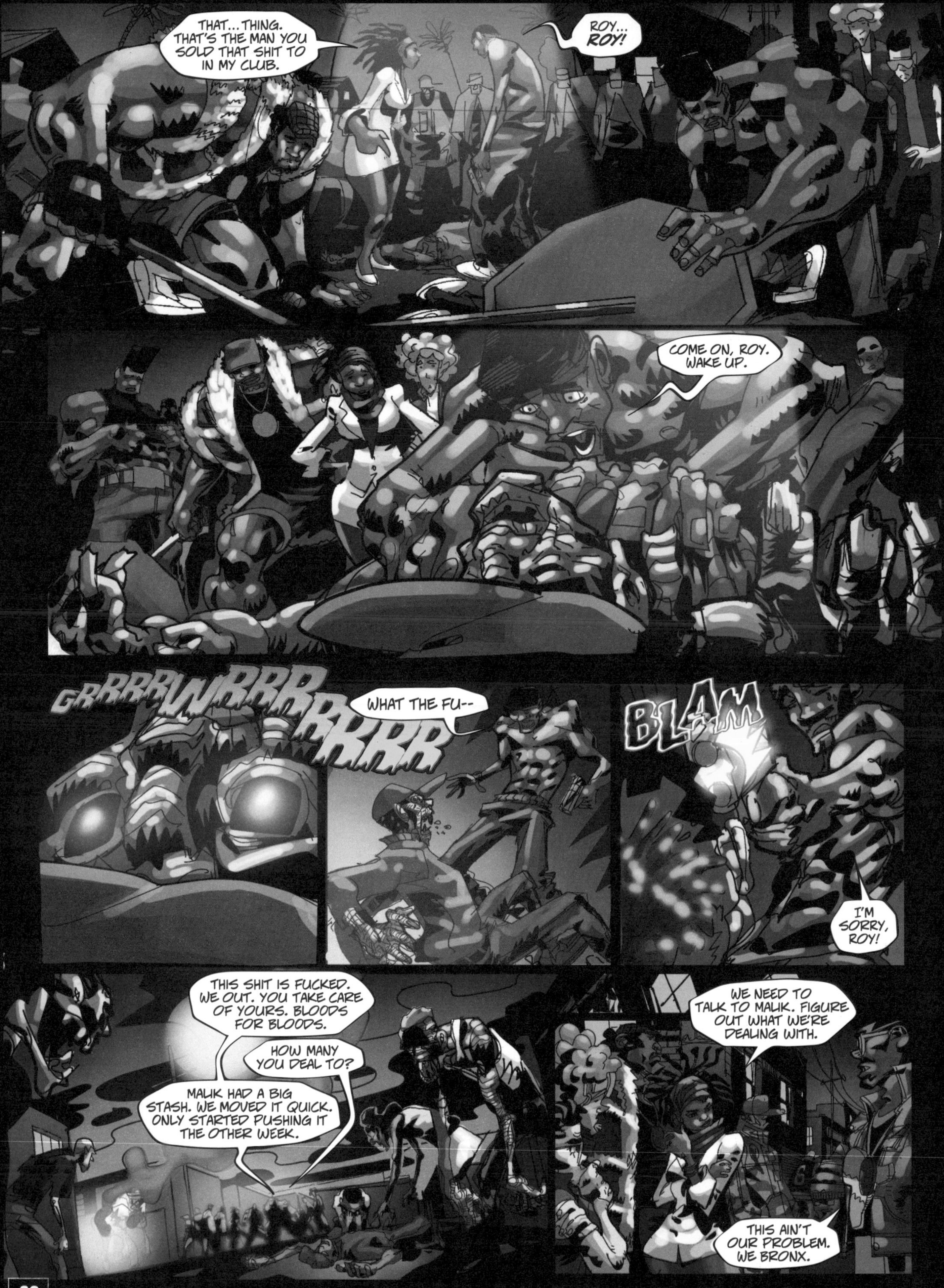
THAT... THING. THAT'S THE MAN YOU SOLD THAT SHIT TO IN MY CLUB.
ROY... ROY!
COME ON, ROY. WAKE UP.
GRRRRWRRRRRRRR
WHAT THE FU--
BLAM
I'M SORRY, ROY!
THIS SHIT IS FUCKED. WE OUT. YOU TAKE CARE OF YOURS. BLOODS FOR BLOODS.
HOW MANY YOU DEAL TO?
MALIK HAD A BIG STASH. WE MOVED IT QUICK. ONLY STARTED PUSHING IT THE OTHER WEEK.
WE NEED TO TALK TO MALIK. FIGURE OUT WHAT WE'RE DEALING WITH.
THIS AIN'T OUR PROBLEM. WE BRONX.

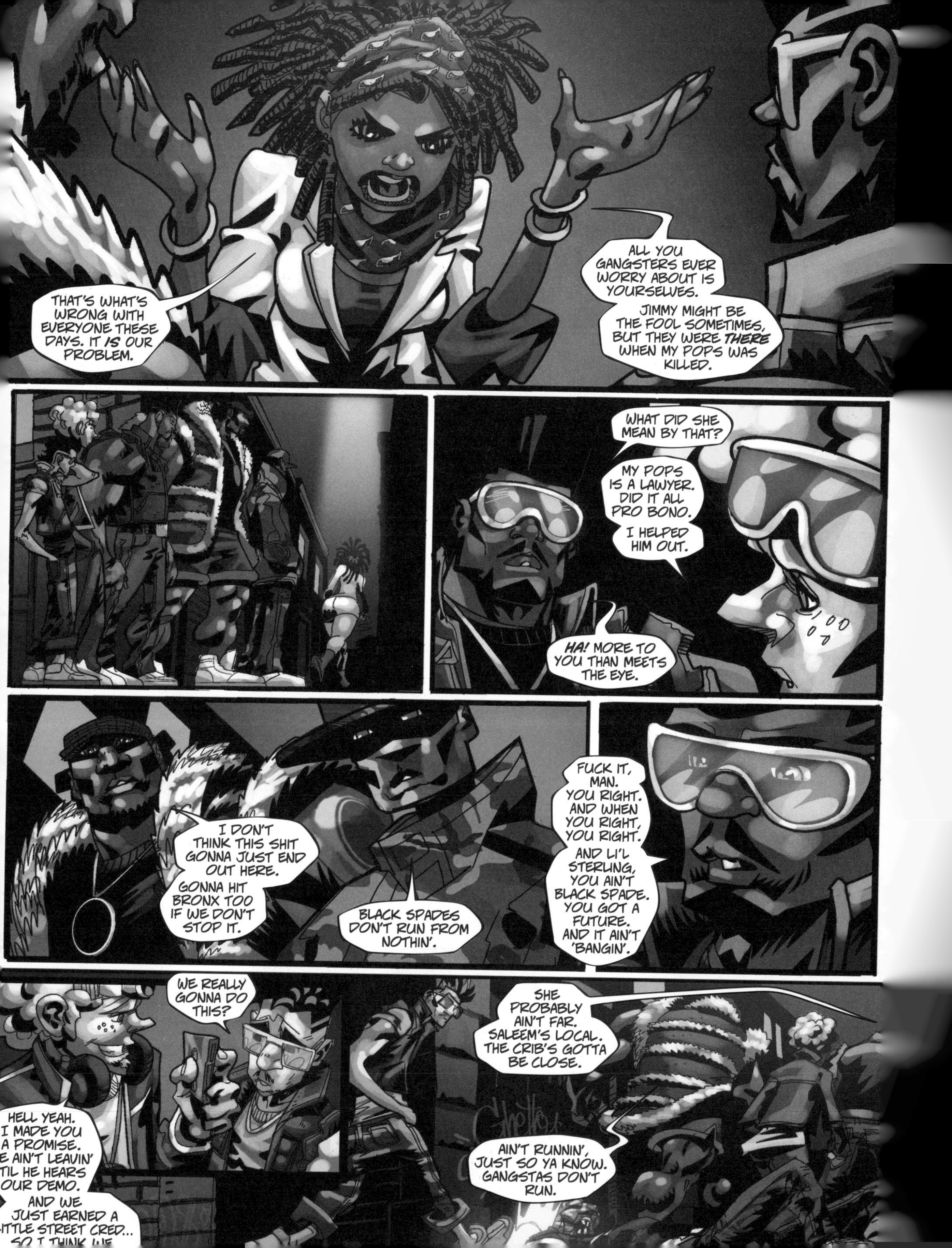

THAT'S WHAT'S WRONG WITH EVERYONE THESE DAYS. IT *IS* OUR PROBLEM.
ALL YOU GANGSTERS EVER WORRY ABOUT IS YOURSELVES.
JIMMY MIGHT BE THE FOOL SOMETIMES, BUT THEY WERE *THERE* WHEN MY POPS WAS KILLED.
WHAT DID SHE MEAN BY THAT?
MY POPS IS A LAWYER. DID IT ALL PRO BONO.
I HELPED HIM OUT.
HA! MORE TO YOU THAN MEETS THE EYE.
I DON'T THINK THIS SHIT GONNA JUST END OUT HERE.
GONNA HIT BRONX TOO IF WE DON'T STOP IT.
BLACK SPADES DON'T RUN FROM NOTHIN'.
FUCK IT, MAN. YOU RIGHT. AND WHEN YOU RIGHT, YOU RIGHT.
AND LI'L STERLING, YOU AIN'T BLACK SPADE. YOU GOT A FUTURE. AND IT AIN'T 'BANGIN'.
WE REALLY GONNA DO THIS?
HELL YEAH. I MADE YOU A PROMISE.
E AIN'T LEAVIN' TIL HE HEARS OUR DEMO.
AND WE JUST EARNED A ITTLE STREET CRED...
SHE PROBABLY AIN'T FAR. SALEEM'S LOCAL. THE CRIB'S GOTTA BE CLOSE.
AIN'T RUNNIN', JUST SO YA KNOW. GANGSTAS DON'T RUN.

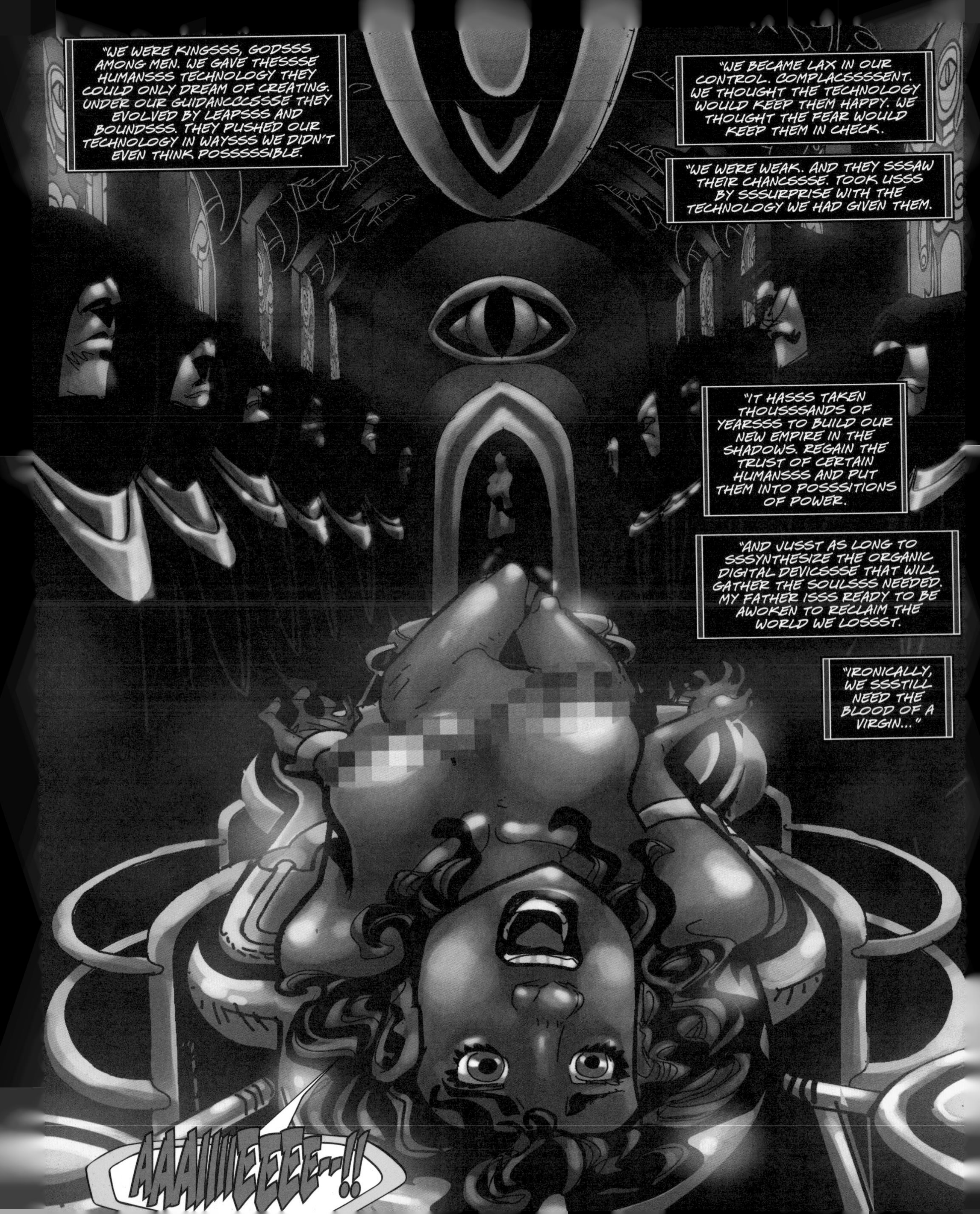
"WE WERE KINGSSS, GODSSS AMONG MEN. WE GAVE THESSSE HUMANSSS TECHNOLOGY THEY COULD ONLY DREAM OF CREATING. UNDER OUR GUIDANCCCSSSE THEY EVOLVED BY LEAPSSS AND BOUNDSSS. THEY PUSHED OUR TECHNOLOGY IN WAYSSS WE DIDN'T EVEN THINK POSSSSSIBLE.
"WE BECAME LAX IN OUR CONTROL. COMPLACSSSSENT. WE THOUGHT THE TECHNOLOGY WOULD KEEP THEM HAPPY. WE THOUGHT THE FEAR WOULD KEEP THEM IN CHECK.
"WE WERE WEAK. AND THEY SSSAW THEIR CHANCSSSE. TOOK USSS BY SSSURPRISE WITH THE TECHNOLOGY WE HAD GIVEN THEM.
"IT HASSS TAKEN THOUSSSANDS OF YEARSSS TO BUILD OUR NEW EMPIRE IN THE SHADOWS. REGAIN THE TRUST OF CERTAIN HUMANSSS AND PUT THEM INTO POSSSITIONS OF POWER.
"AND JUSST AS LONG TO SSSYNTHESIZE THE ORGANIC DIGITAL DEVICSSSE THAT WILL GATHER THE SOULSSS NEEDED. MY FATHER ISSS READY TO BE AWOKEN TO RECLAIM THE WORLD WE LOSSST.
"IRONICALLY, WE SSSTILL NEED THE BLOOD OF A VIRGIN..."
AAAIIIIEEEE--!!

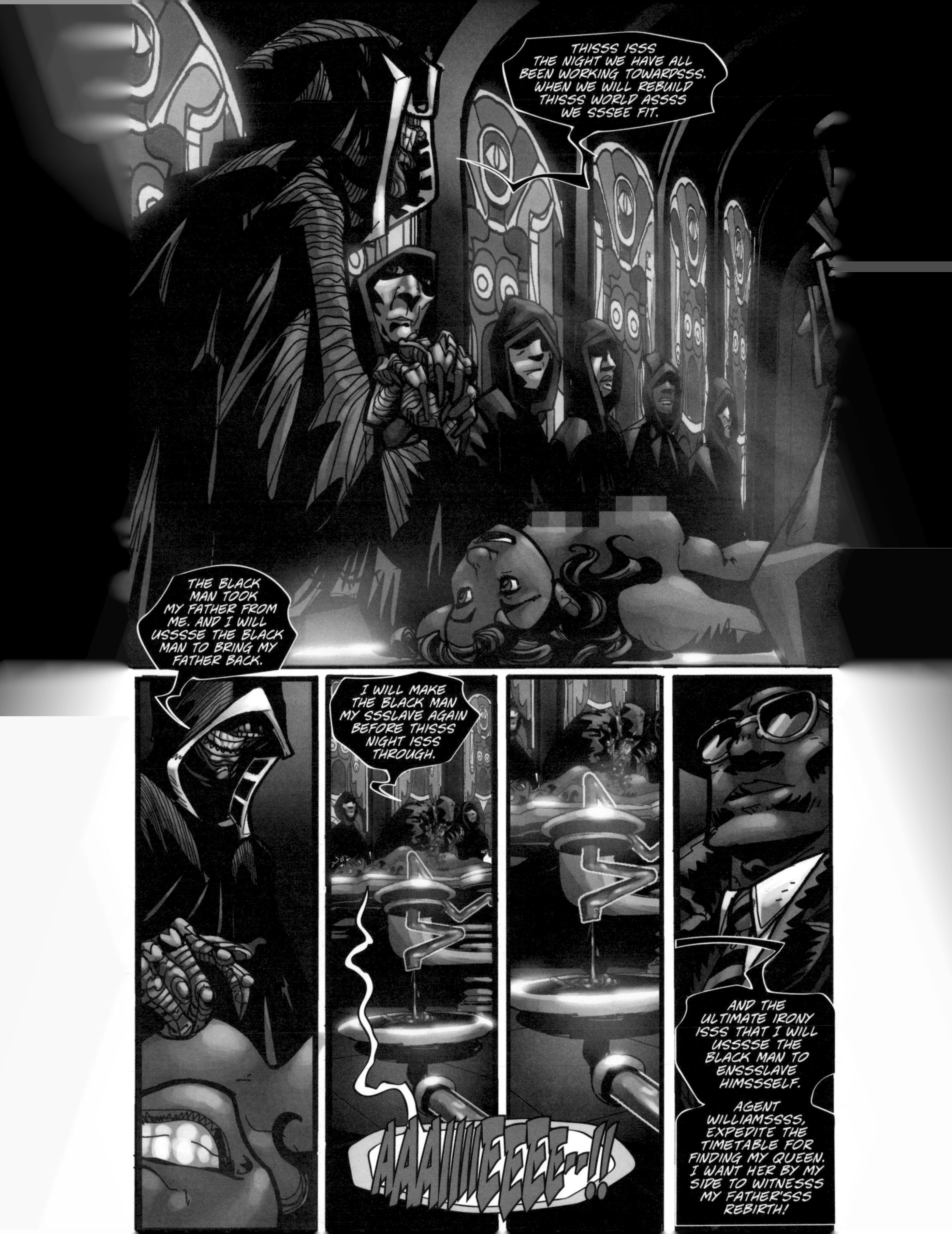
THISSS ISSS THE NIGHT WE HAVE ALL BEEN WORKING TOWARDSSS. WHEN WE WILL REBUILD THISSS WORLD ASSSS WE SSSEE FIT.
THE BLACK MAN TOOK MY FATHER FROM ME. AND I WILL USSSSE THE BLACK MAN TO BRING MY FATHER BACK.
I WILL MAKE THE BLACK MAN MY SSSLAVE AGAIN BEFORE THISSS NIGHT ISSS THROUGH.
AAAIIIIEEEE--!!
AND THE ULTIMATE IRONY ISSS THAT I WILL USSSSE THE BLACK MAN TO ENSSSLAVE HIMSSSELF.
AGENT WILLIAMSSSS, EXPEDITE THE TIMETABLE FOR FINDING MY QUEEN. I WANT HER BY MY SIDE TO WITNESSS MY FATHER'SSS REBIRTH!

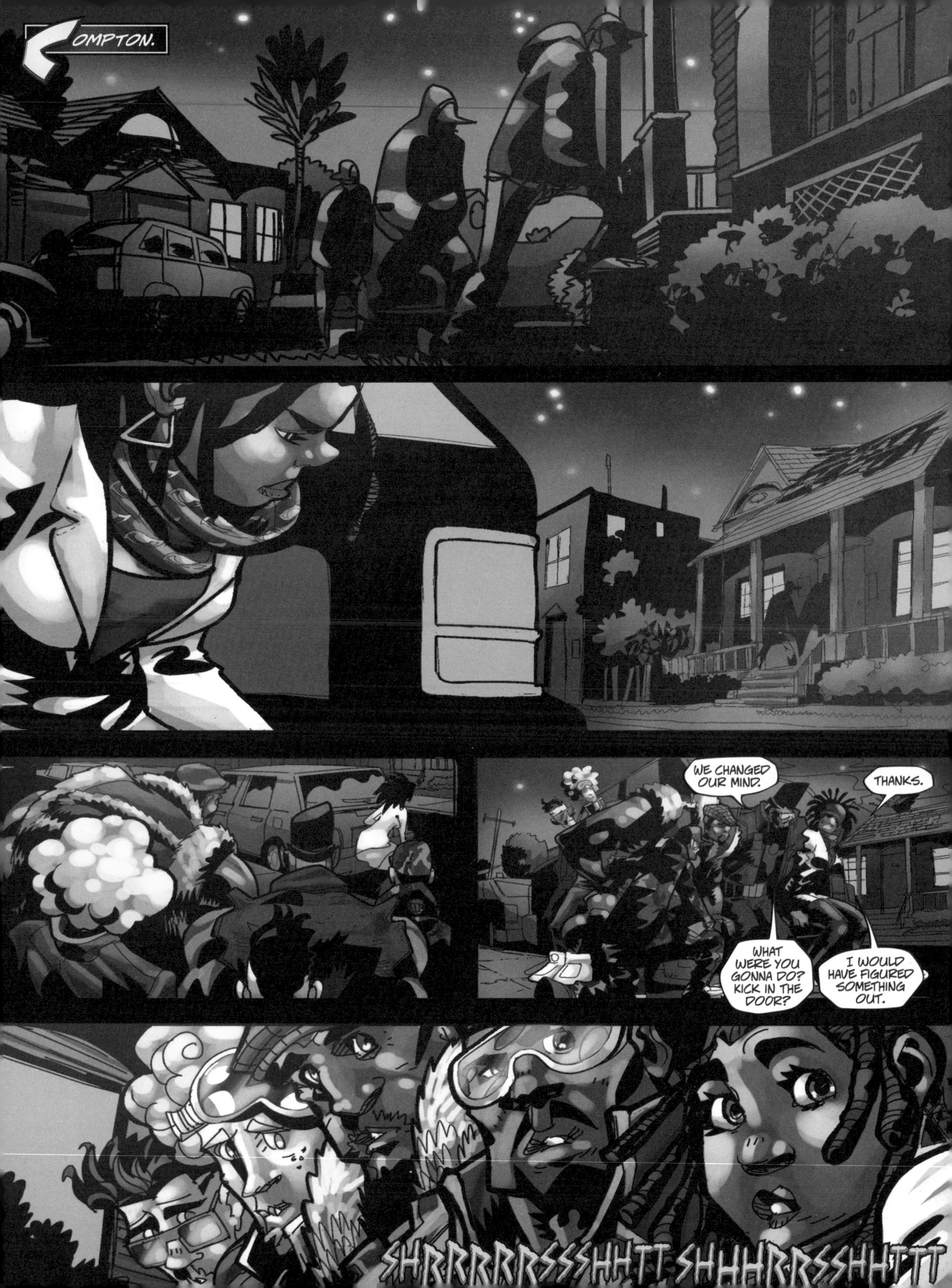
COMPTON.
WE CHANGED OUR MIND.
THANKS.
WHAT WERE YOU GONNA DO? KICK IN THE DOOR?
I WOULD HAVE FIGURED SOMETHING OUT.
SHRRRRRSSSHHTT SHHHRRSSHHTTT

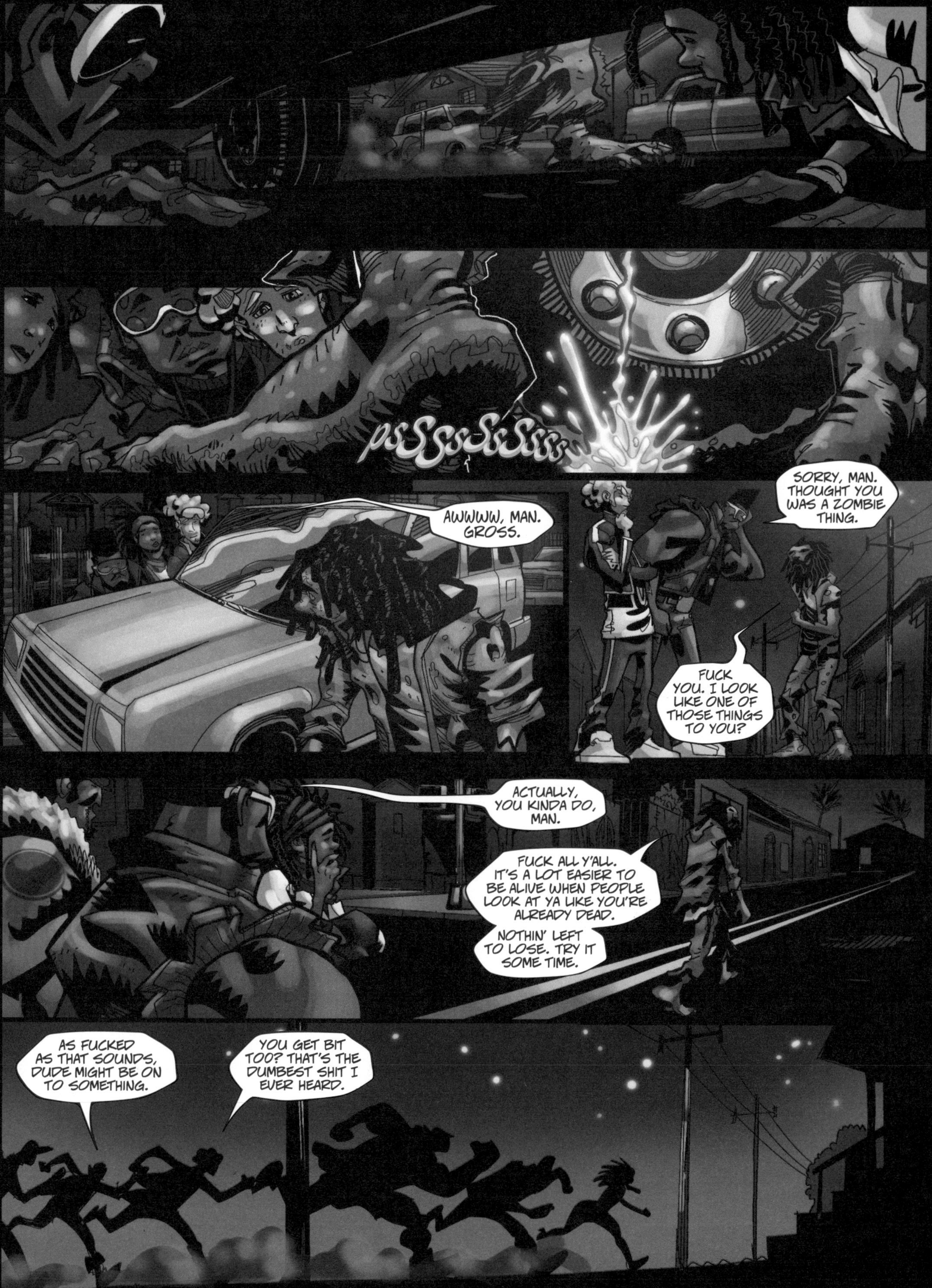

PSSSSSSSSSSS
AWWWW, MAN. GROSS.
SORRY, MAN. THOUGHT YOU WAS A ZOMBIE THING.
FUCK YOU. I LOOK LIKE ONE OF THOSE THINGS TO YOU?
ACTUALLY, YOU KINDA DO, MAN.
FUCK ALL Y'ALL. IT'S A LOT EASIER TO BE ALIVE WHEN PEOPLE LOOK AT YA LIKE YOU'RE ALREADY DEAD.
NOTHIN' LEFT TO LOSE. TRY IT SOME TIME.
AS FUCKED AS THAT SOUNDS, DUDE MIGHT BE ON TO SOMETHING.
YOU GET BIT TOO? THAT'S THE DUMBEST SHIT I EVER HEARD.

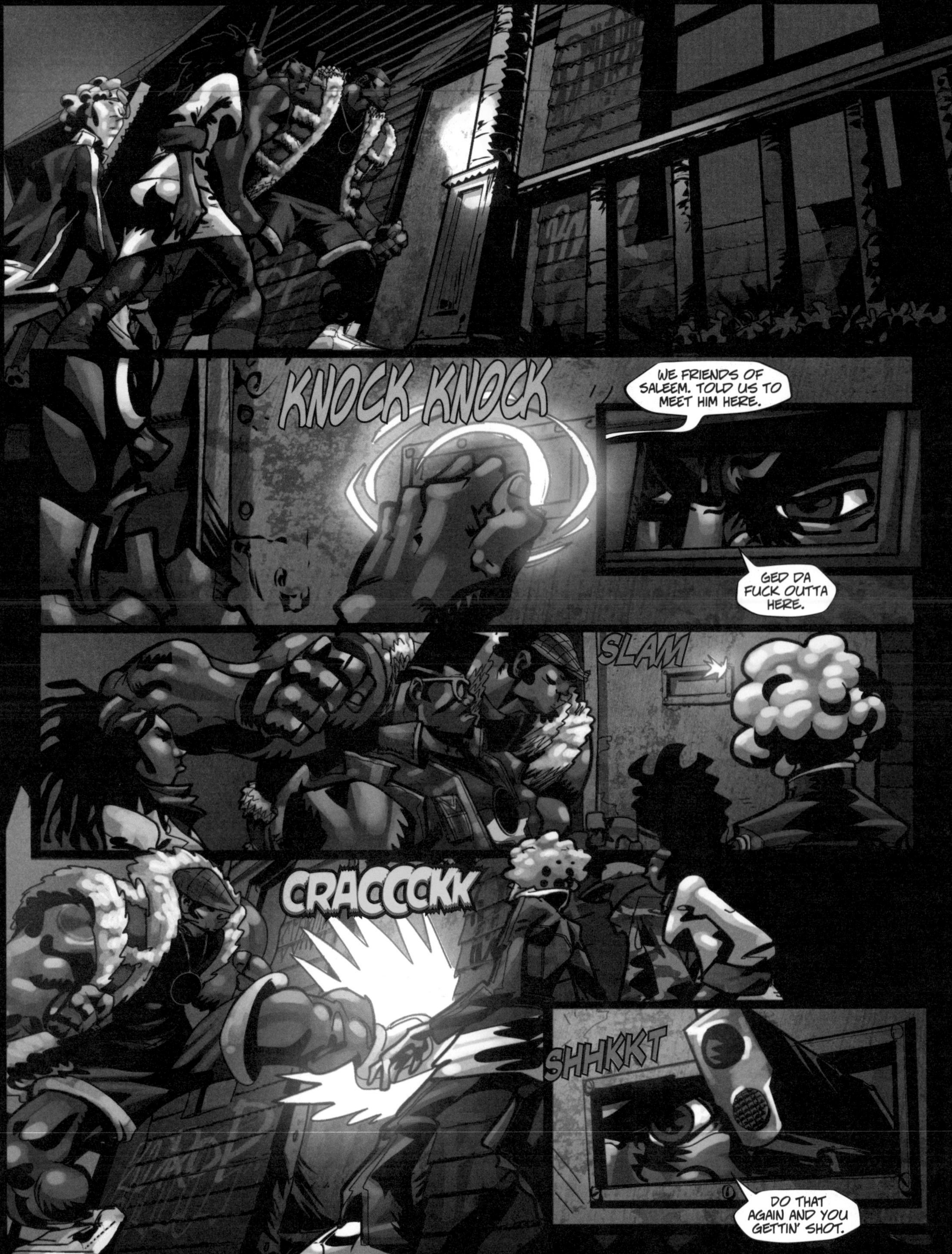
KNOCK KNOCK
WE FRIENDS OF SALEEM. TOLD US TO MEET HIM HERE.
GED DA FUCK OUTTA HERE.
SLAM
CRACCCKK
SHHKKT
DO THAT AGAIN AND YOU GETTIN' SHOT.

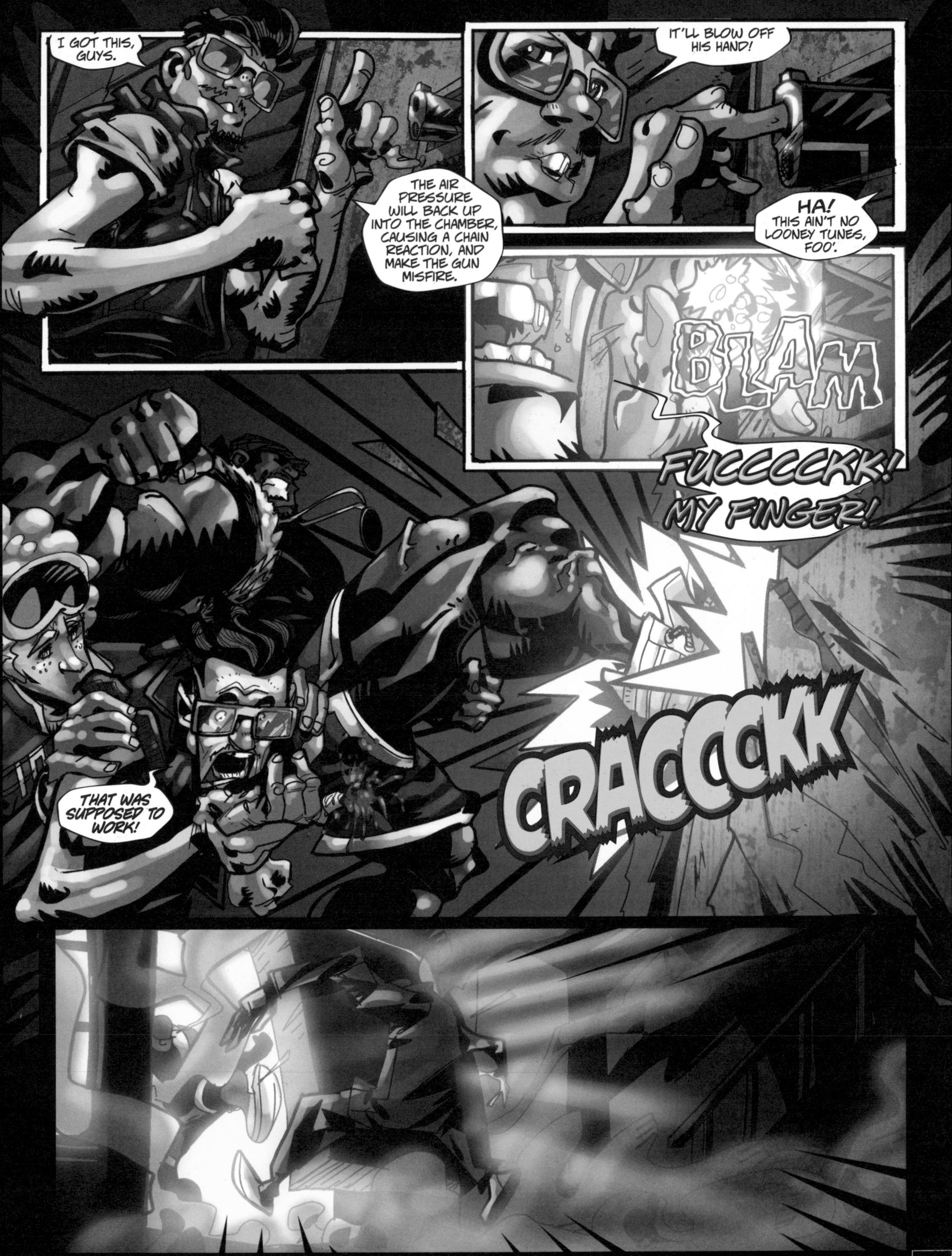

I GOT THIS, GUYS.
IT'LL BLOW OFF HIS HAND!
THE AIR PRESSURE WILL BACK UP INTO THE CHAMBER, CAUSING A CHAIN REACTION, AND MAKE THE GUN MISFIRE.
HA! THIS AIN'T NO LOONEY TUNES, FOO'.
BLAM
FUCCCCKK! MY FINGER!
CRACCCKK
THAT WAS SUPPOSED TO WORK!

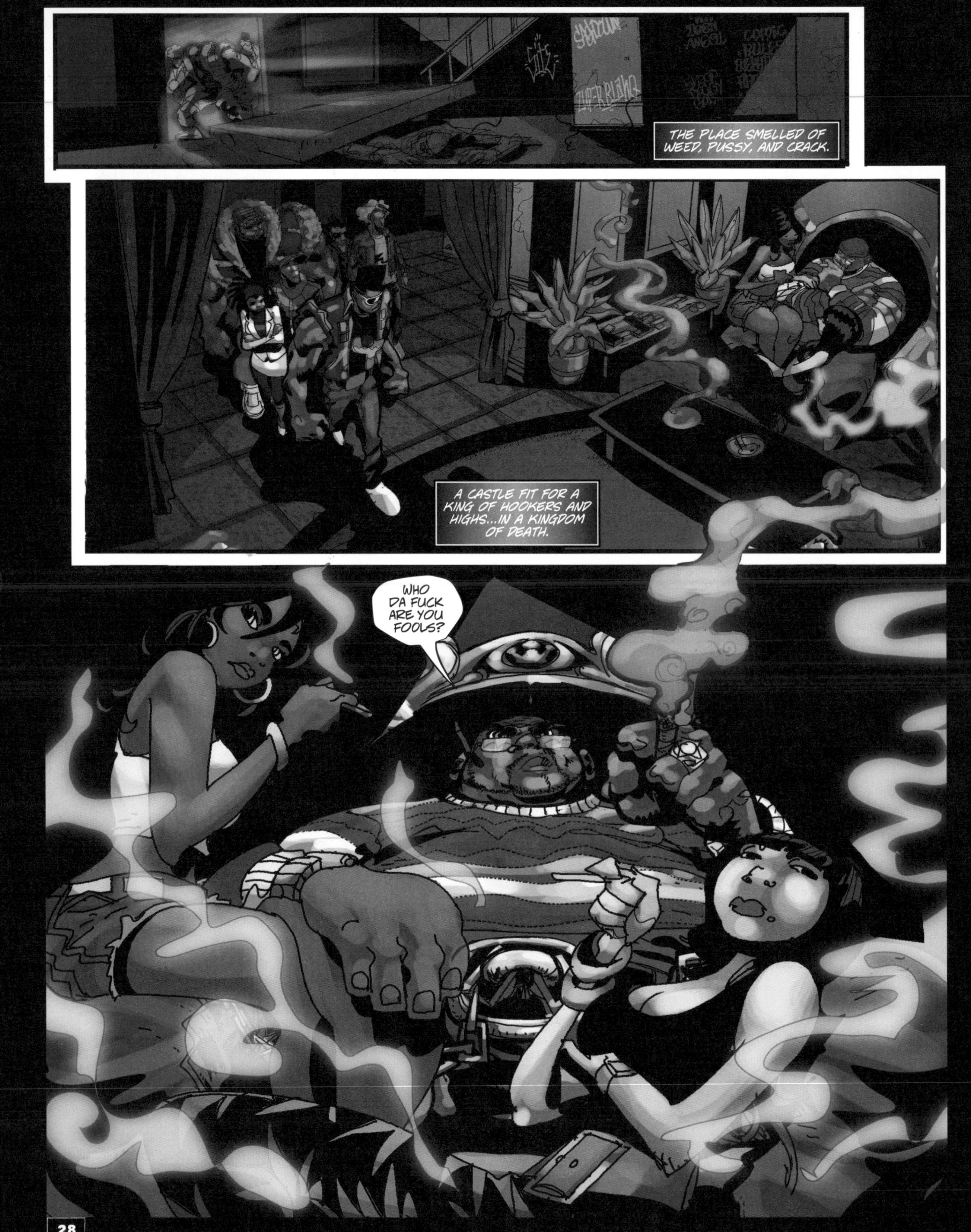
THE PLACE SMELLED OF WEED, PUSSY, AND CRACK.
A CASTLE FIT FOR A KING OF HOOKERS AND HIGHS...IN A KINGDOM OF DEATH.
WHO DA FUCK ARE YOU FOOLS?

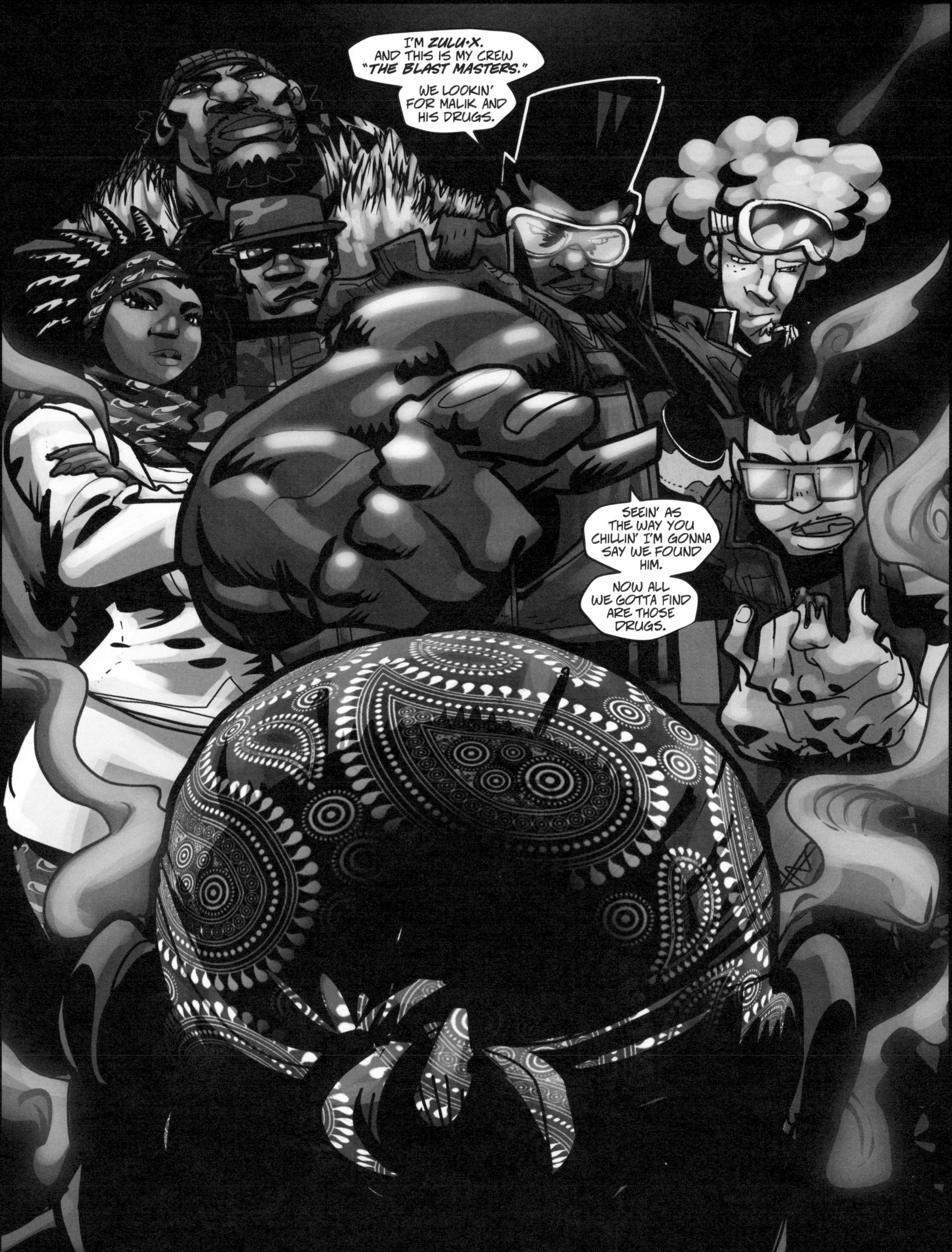
I'M ZULU-X. AND THIS IS MY CREW "THE BLAST MASTERS."
WE LOOKIN' FOR MALIK AND HIS DRUGS.
SEEIN' AS THE WAY YOU CHILLIN' I'M GONNA SAY WE FOUND HIM.
NOW ALL WE GOTTA FIND ARE THOSE DRUGS.

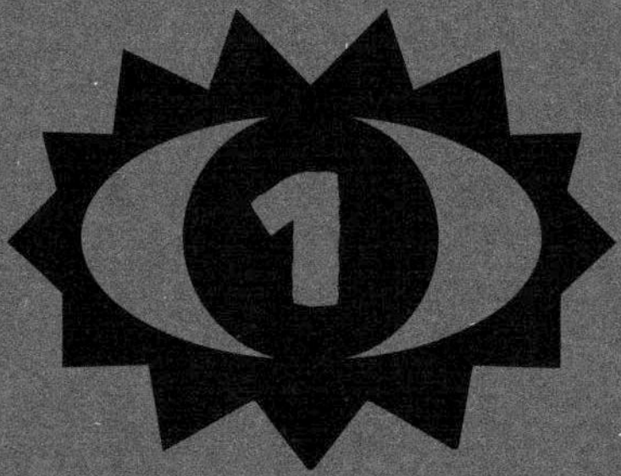
1

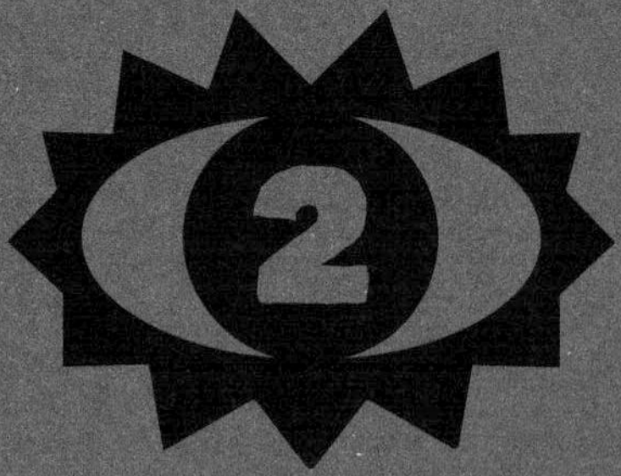
2

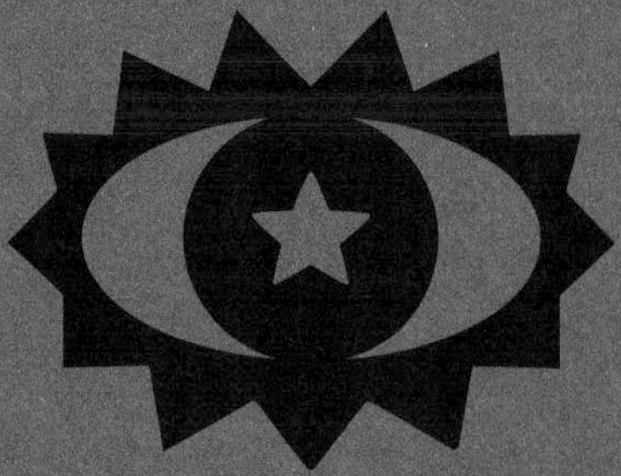

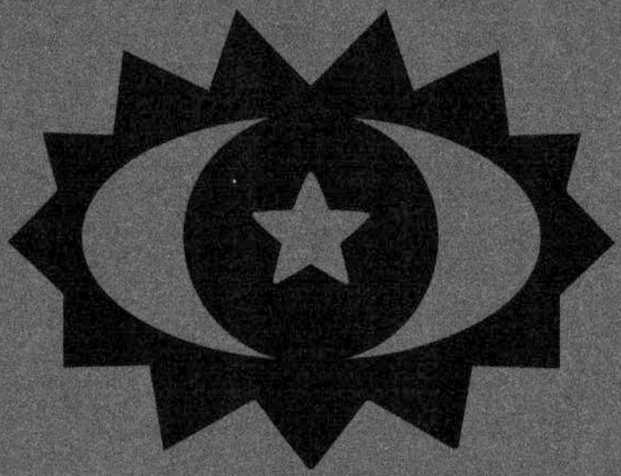

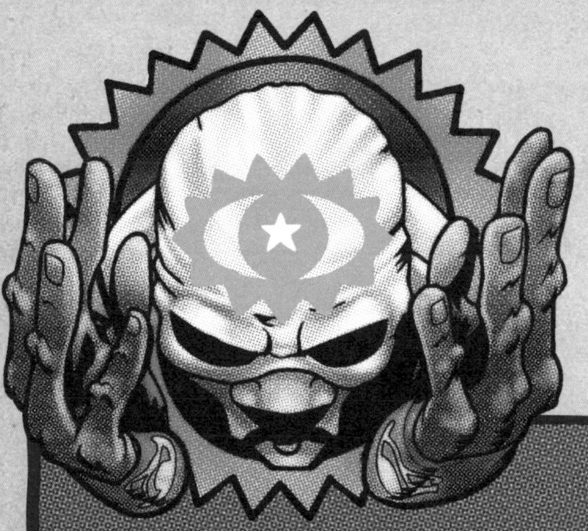

MASTER SUN'S VERSE 15:01

I WILL TELL YOU A STORY ABOUT
the power of the Word,
How your wings can be clipped or you can fly like a Bird.
When the Creatures took Black and made it a Neg
They subtracted history and culture so that all Black will beg.

Latin, the language of the Church built in Rome
Created Niger and Nigrum for the word Black
So that Wars were created to force them from home
And made Neg unbalanced by pushing Black back.

Neglect, Negotiate, Negro, and Negative
All words built on Neg that made Black derivative.
The words Nega, or Nigga, or Nigger came later
These Words were the doing of the Creature, the Traitor.

But now a time is coming to thrive
when we will rise up
and sing as one Tribe.

-Masters of the Sun

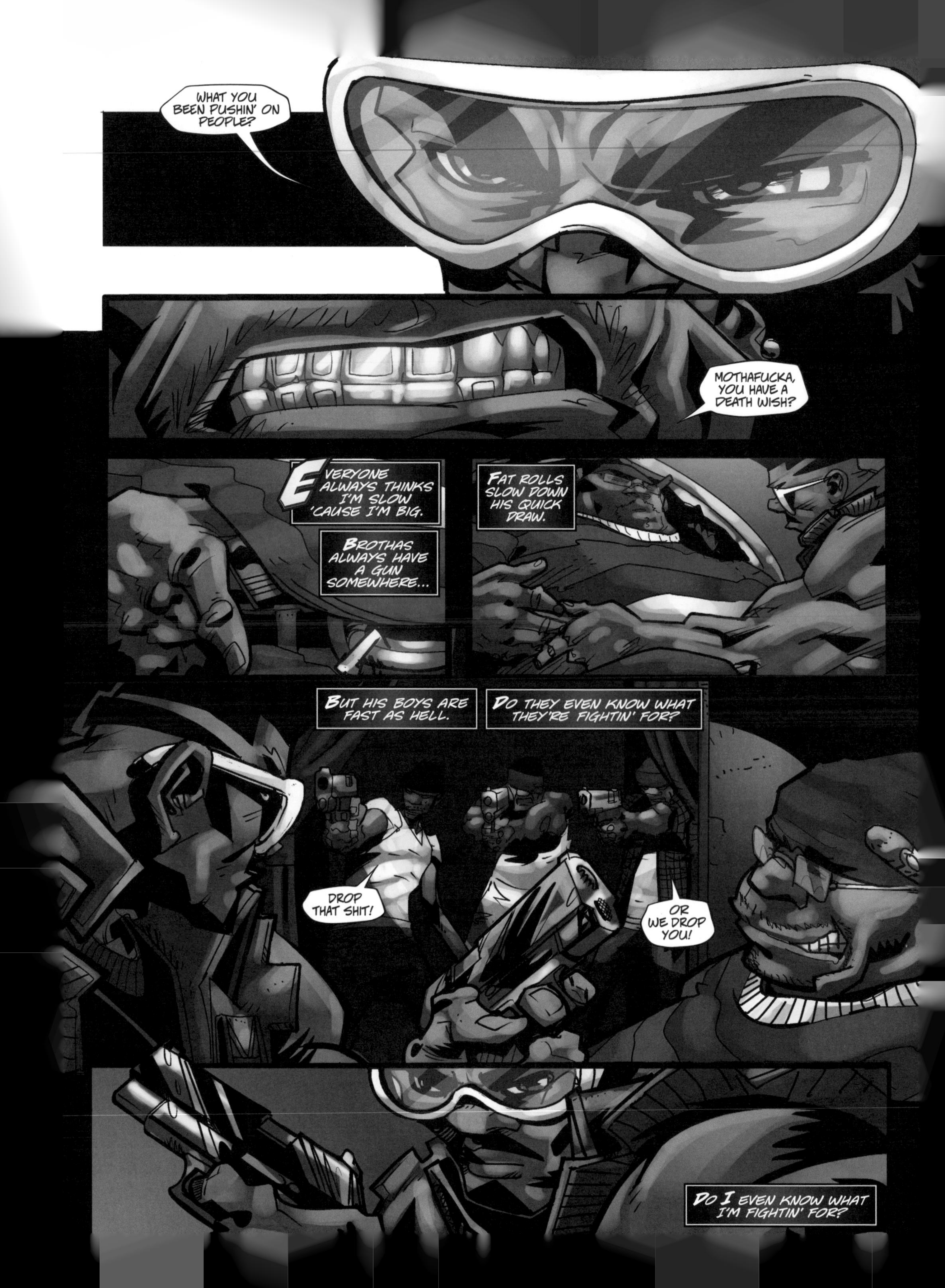
WHAT YOU BEEN PUSHIN' ON PEOPLE?
MOTHAFUCKA, YOU HAVE A DEATH WISH?
EVERYONE ALWAYS THINKS I'M SLOW 'CAUSE I'M BIG.
BROTHAS ALWAYS HAVE A GUN SOMEWHERE...
FAT ROLLS SLOW DOWN HIS QUICK DRAW.
BUT HIS BOYS ARE FAST AS HELL.
DO THEY EVEN KNOW WHAT THEY'RE FIGHTIN' FOR?
DROP THAT SHIT!
OR WE DROP YOU!
DO I EVEN KNOW WHAT I'M FIGHTIN' FOR?

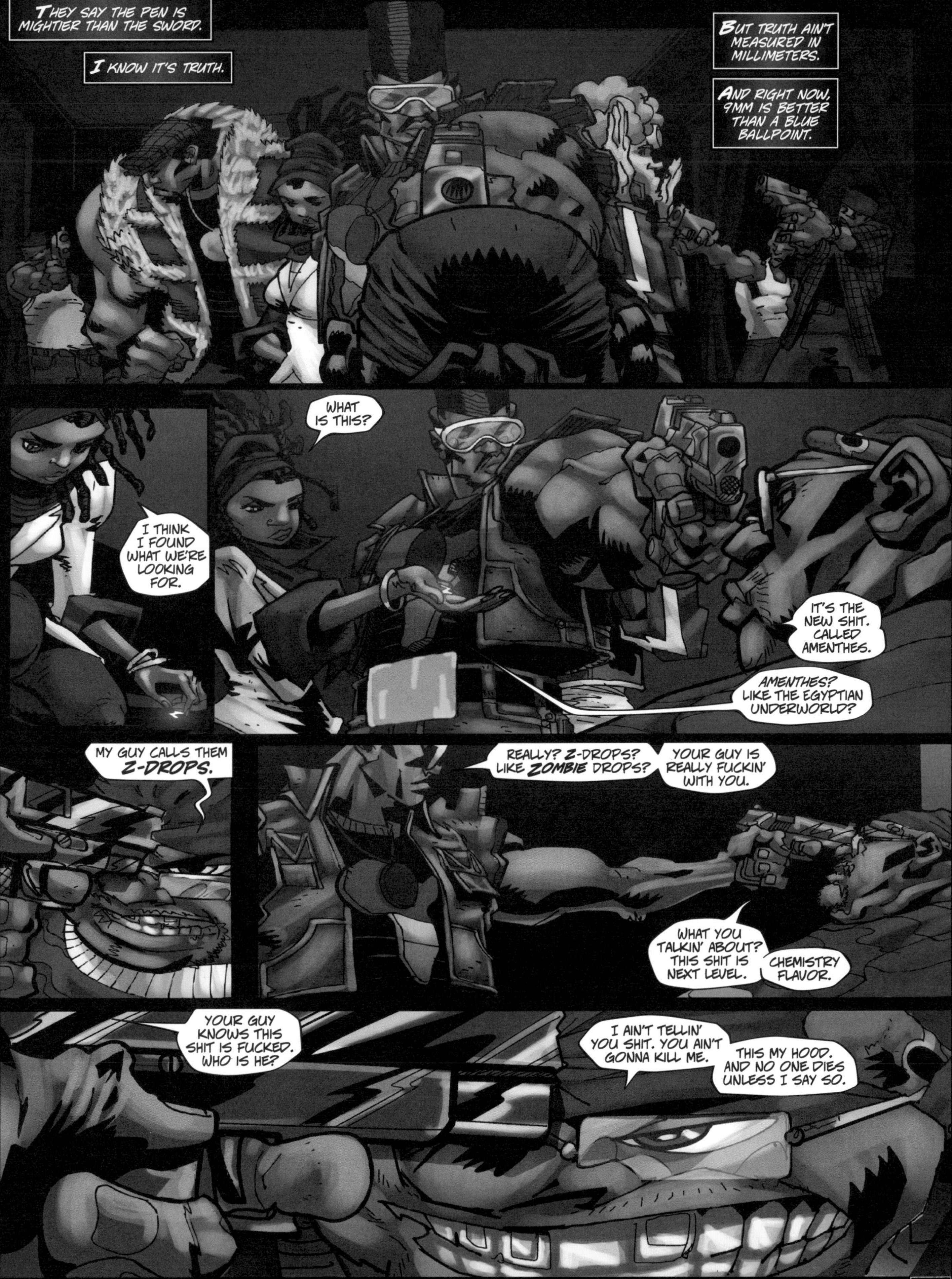
THEY SAY THE PEN IS MIGHTIER THAN THE SWORD.
I KNOW IT'S TRUTH.
BUT TRUTH AIN'T MEASURED IN MILLIMETERS.
AND RIGHT NOW, 9MM IS BETTER THAN A BLUE BALLPOINT.
I THINK I FOUND WHAT WE'RE LOOKING FOR.
WHAT IS THIS?
IT'S THE NEW SHIT. CALLED AMENTHES.
AMENTHES? LIKE THE EGYPTIAN UNDERWORLD?
MY GUY CALLS THEM Z-DROPS.
REALLY? Z-DROPS? LIKE ZOMBIE DROPS?
YOUR GUY IS REALLY FUCKIN' WITH YOU.
WHAT YOU TALKIN' ABOUT? THIS SHIT IS NEXT LEVEL.
CHEMISTRY FLAVOR.
YOUR GUY KNOWS THIS SHIT IS FUCKED. WHO IS HE?
I AIN'T TELLIN' YOU SHIT. YOU AIN'T GONNA KILL ME.
THIS MY HOOD. AND NO ONE DIES UNLESS I SAY SO.

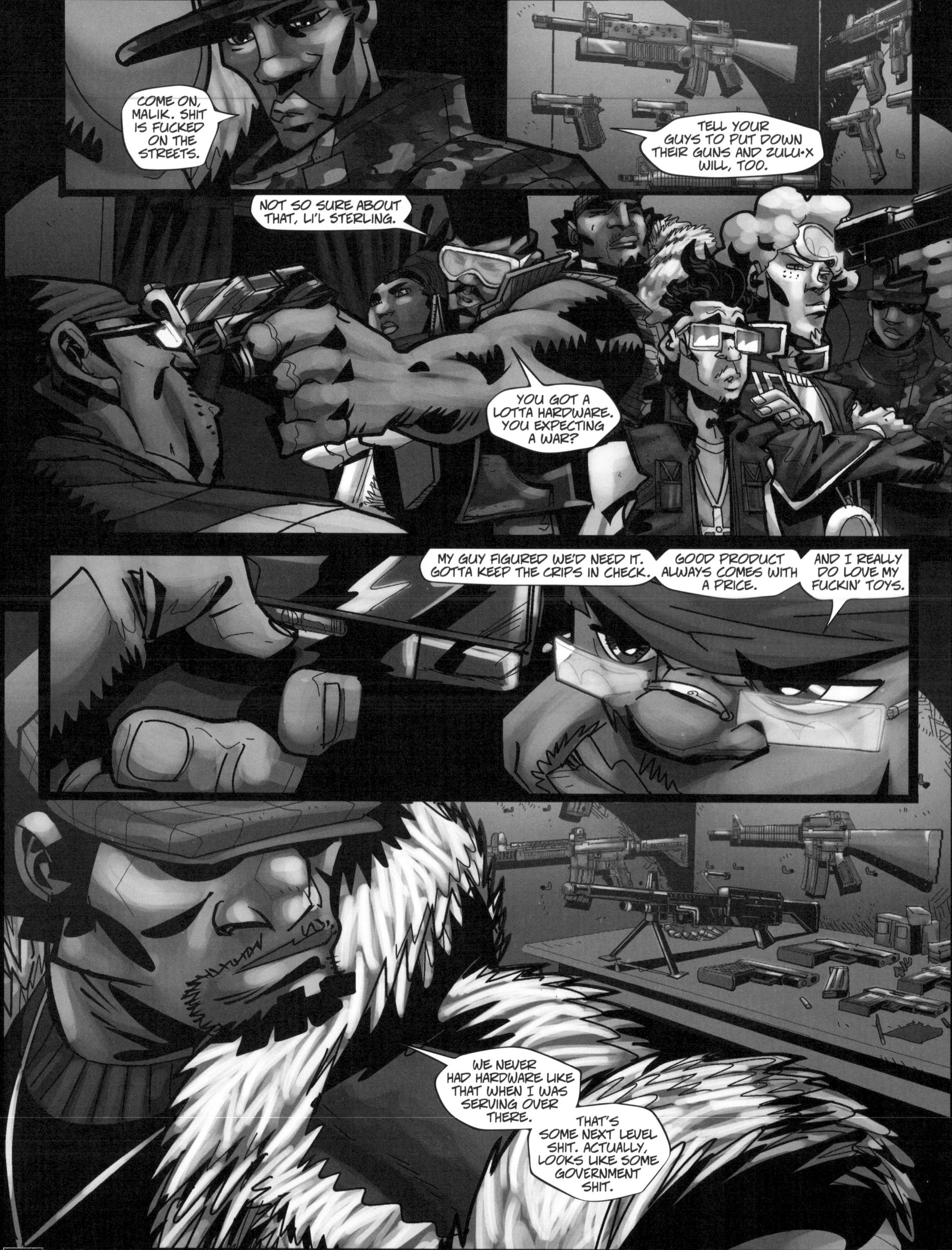

COME ON, MALIK. SHIT IS FUCKED ON THE STREETS.
TELL YOUR GUYS TO PUT DOWN THEIR GUNS AND ZULU-X WILL, TOO.
NOT SO SURE ABOUT THAT, LI'L STERLING.
YOU GOT A LOTTA HARDWARE. YOU EXPECTING A WAR?
MY GUY FIGURED WE'D NEED IT. GOTTA KEEP THE CRIPS IN CHECK.
GOOD PRODUCT ALWAYS COMES WITH A PRICE.
AND I REALLY DO LOVE MY FUCKIN' TOYS.
WE NEVER HAD HARDWARE LIKE THAT WHEN I WAS SERVING OVER THERE.
THAT'S SOME NEXT LEVEL SHIT. ACTUALLY, LOOKS LIKE SOME GOVERNMENT SHIT.

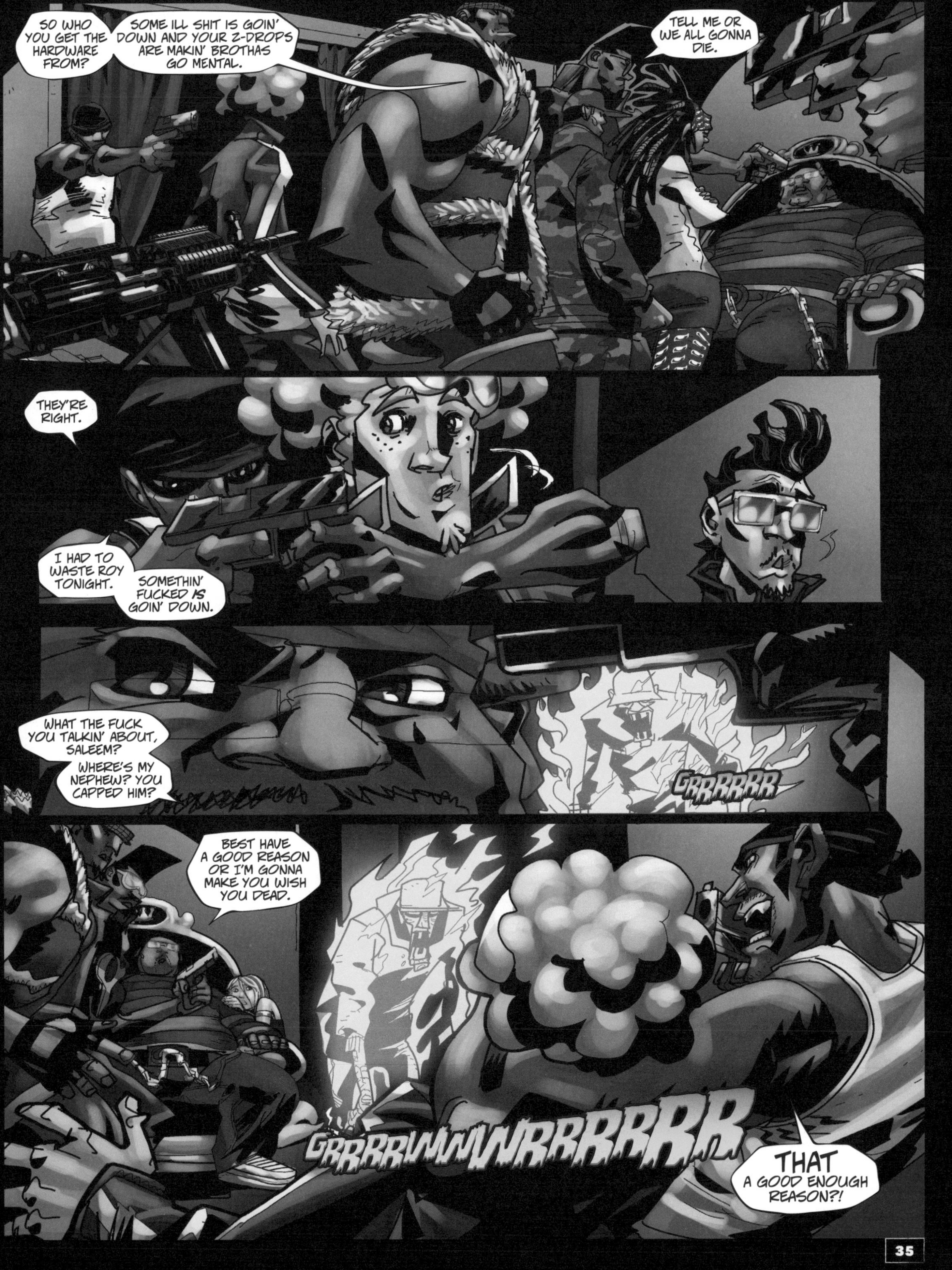
SO WHO YOU GET THE HARDWARE FROM?
SOME ILL SHIT IS GOIN' DOWN AND YOUR Z-DROPS ARE MAKIN' BROTHAS GO MENTAL.
TELL ME OR WE ALL GONNA DIE.
THEY'RE RIGHT.
I HAD TO WASTE ROY TONIGHT.
SOMETHIN' FUCKED IS GOIN' DOWN.
WHAT THE FUCK YOU TALKIN' ABOUT, SALEEM?
WHERE'S MY NEPHEW? YOU CAPPED HIM?
GRRRRRR
BEST HAVE A GOOD REASON OR I'M GONNA MAKE YOU WISH YOU DEAD.
GRRRRWWWWRRRRRRR
THAT A GOOD ENOUGH REASON?!

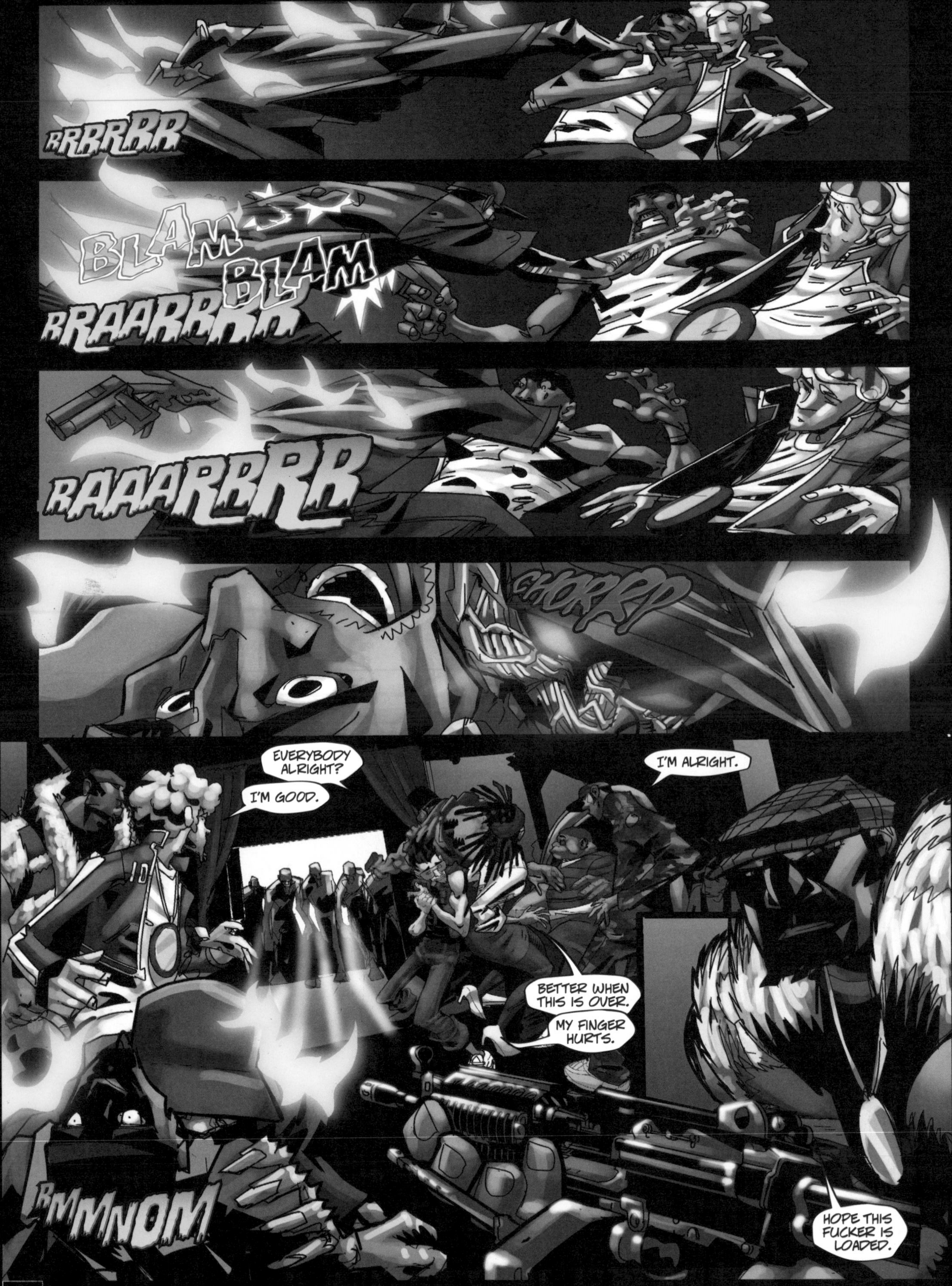
RRRRRR
BLAM
BLAM
RRAARRRR
RAAARRRR
CHORRP
EVERYBODY ALRIGHT?
I'M GOOD.
I'M ALRIGHT.
BETTER WHEN THIS IS OVER.
MY FINGER HURTS.
RMMNOM
HOPE THIS FUCKER IS LOADED.

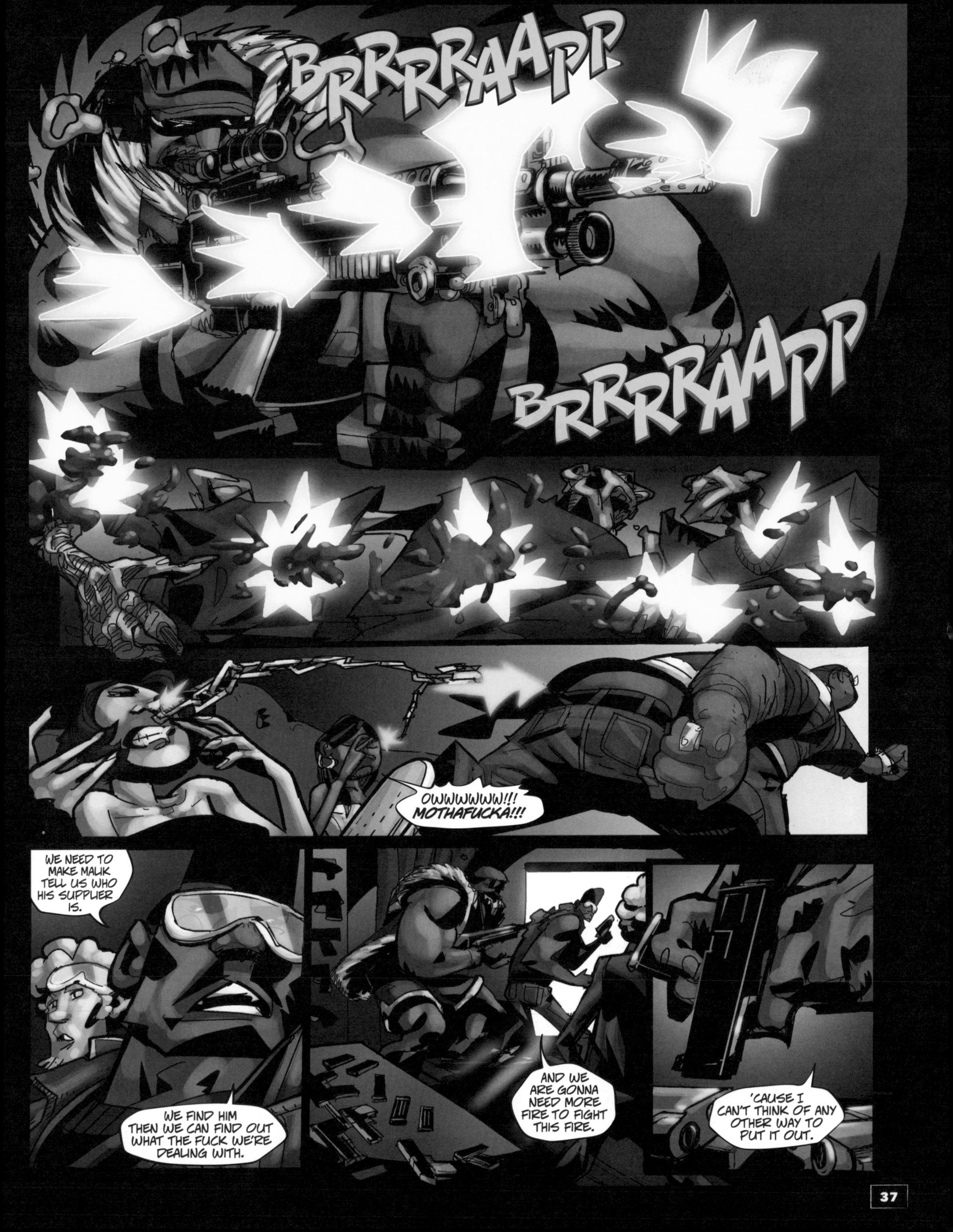

BRRRRAAPP
BRRRRAAPP
OWWWWWW!!! MOTHAFUCKA!!!
WE NEED TO MAKE MALIK TELL US WHO HIS SUPPLIER IS.
WE FIND HIM THEN WE CAN FIND OUT WHAT THE FUCK WE'RE DEALING WITH.
AND WE ARE GONNA NEED MORE FIRE TO FIGHT THIS FIRE.
'CAUSE I CAN'T THINK OF ANY OTHER WAY TO PUT IT OUT.

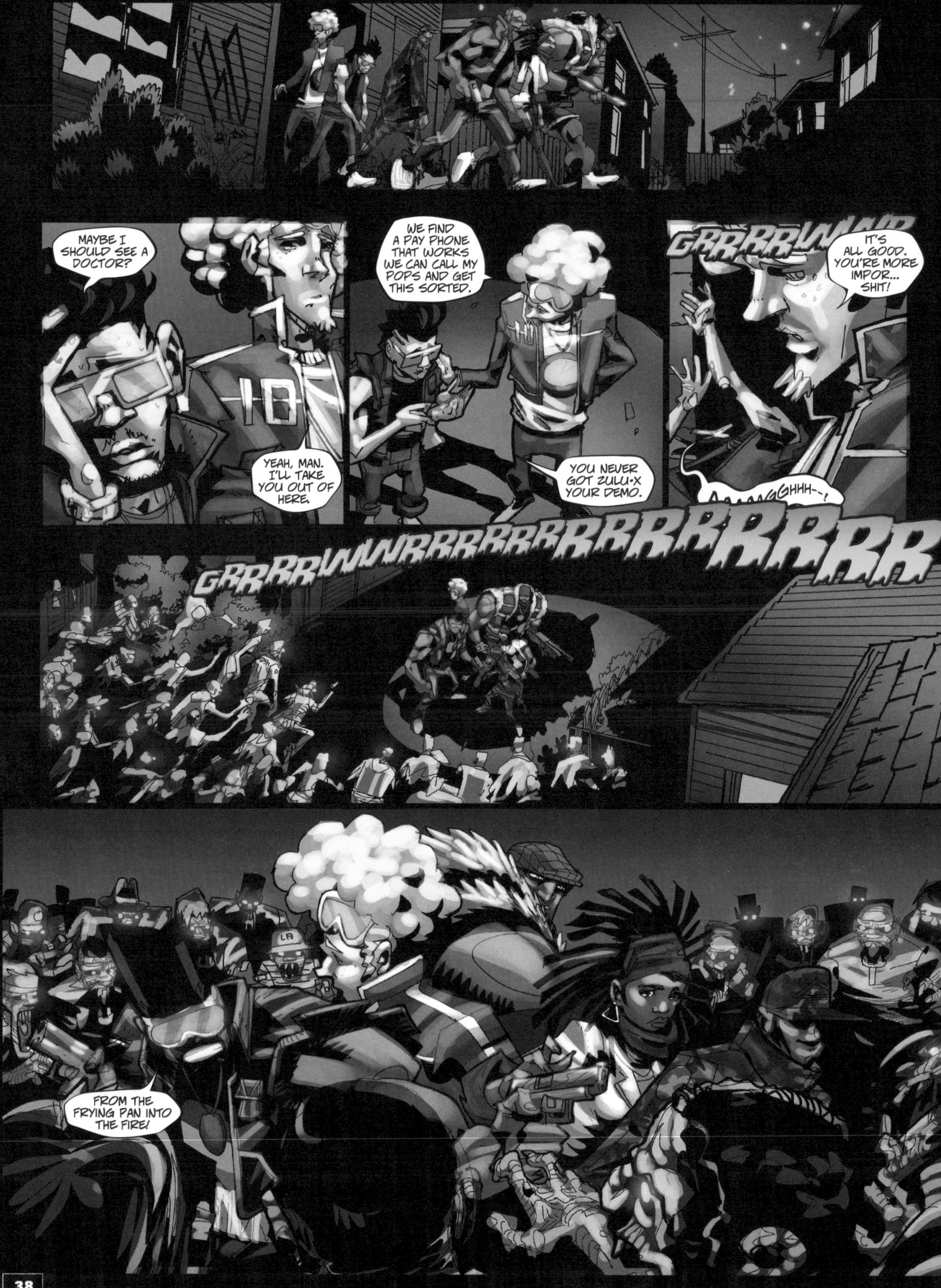
MAYBE I SHOULD SEE A DOCTOR?
YEAH, MAN. I'LL TAKE YOU OUT OF HERE.
WE FIND A PAY PHONE THAT WORKS WE CAN CALL MY POPS AND GET THIS SORTED.
YOU NEVER GOT ZULU-X YOUR DEMO.
GRRRRWWAR
IT'S ALL GOOD. YOU'RE MORE IMPOR... SHIT!
AAAAAGGHHH--!
GRRRRWWWRRRRRRRRRRRRRRRR
FROM THE FRYING PAN INTO THE FIRE!

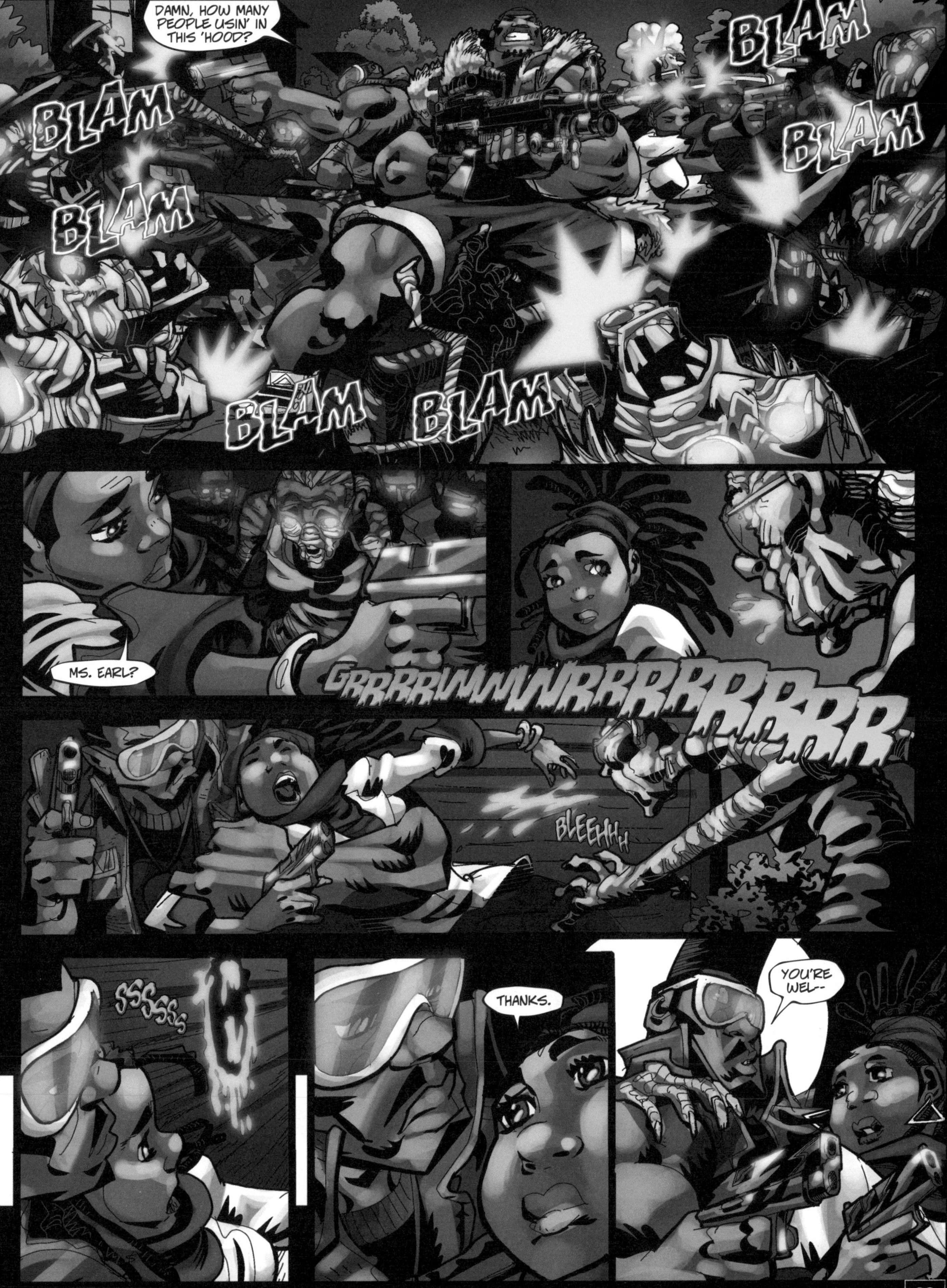

DAMN, HOW MANY PEOPLE USIN' IN THIS 'HOOD?
BLAM
BLAM
BLAM
BLAM
BLAM
BLAM
MS. EARL?
GRRRRWWWWRRRRRRRRRR
BLEEHHH
SSSSSSS
THANKS.
YOU'RE WEL--

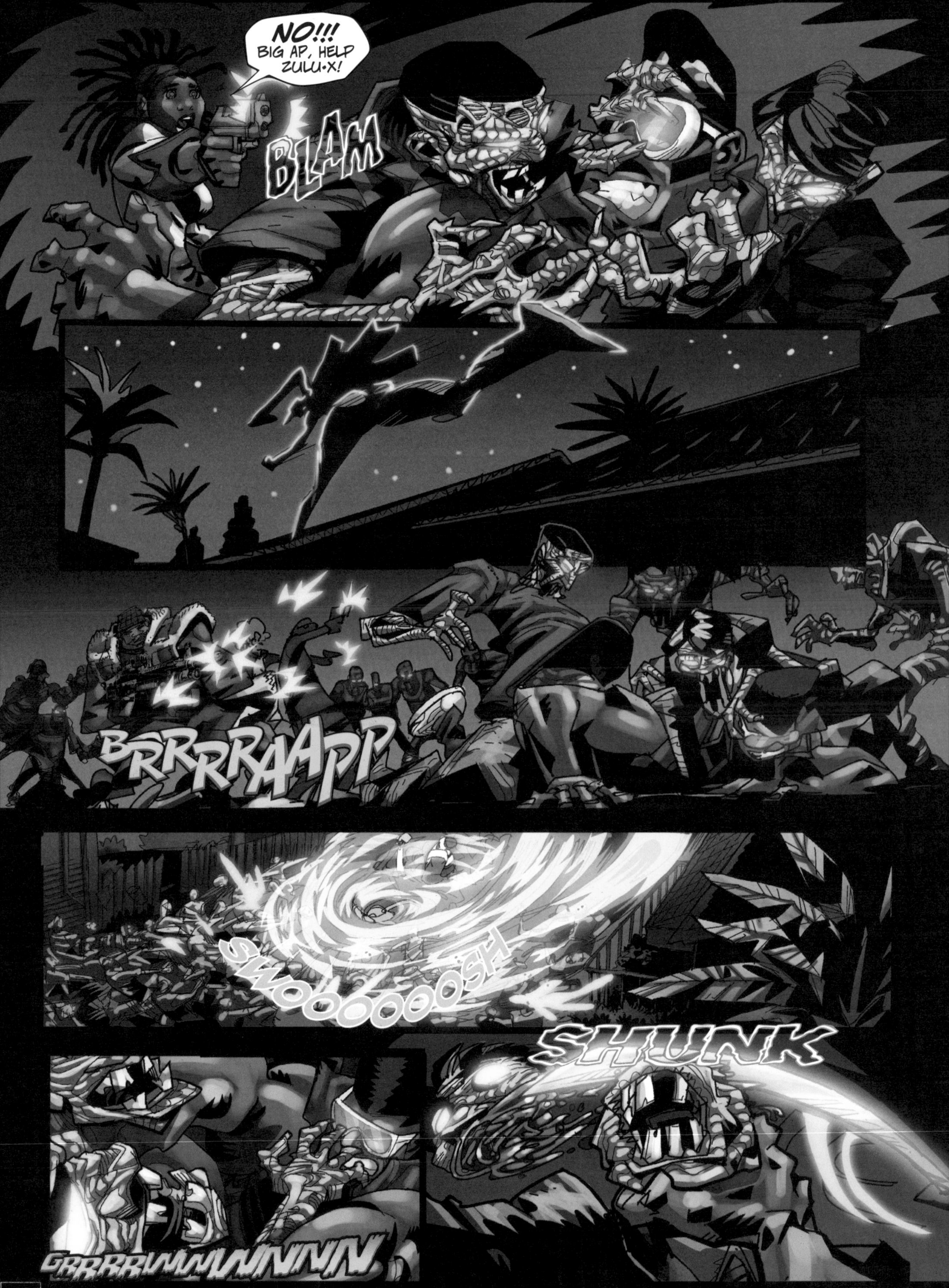
NO!!! BIG AP, HELP ZULU-X!
BLAM
BRRRRAAPP
SWOOOOOOOSH
SHUNK
GRRRRWWWNNNN

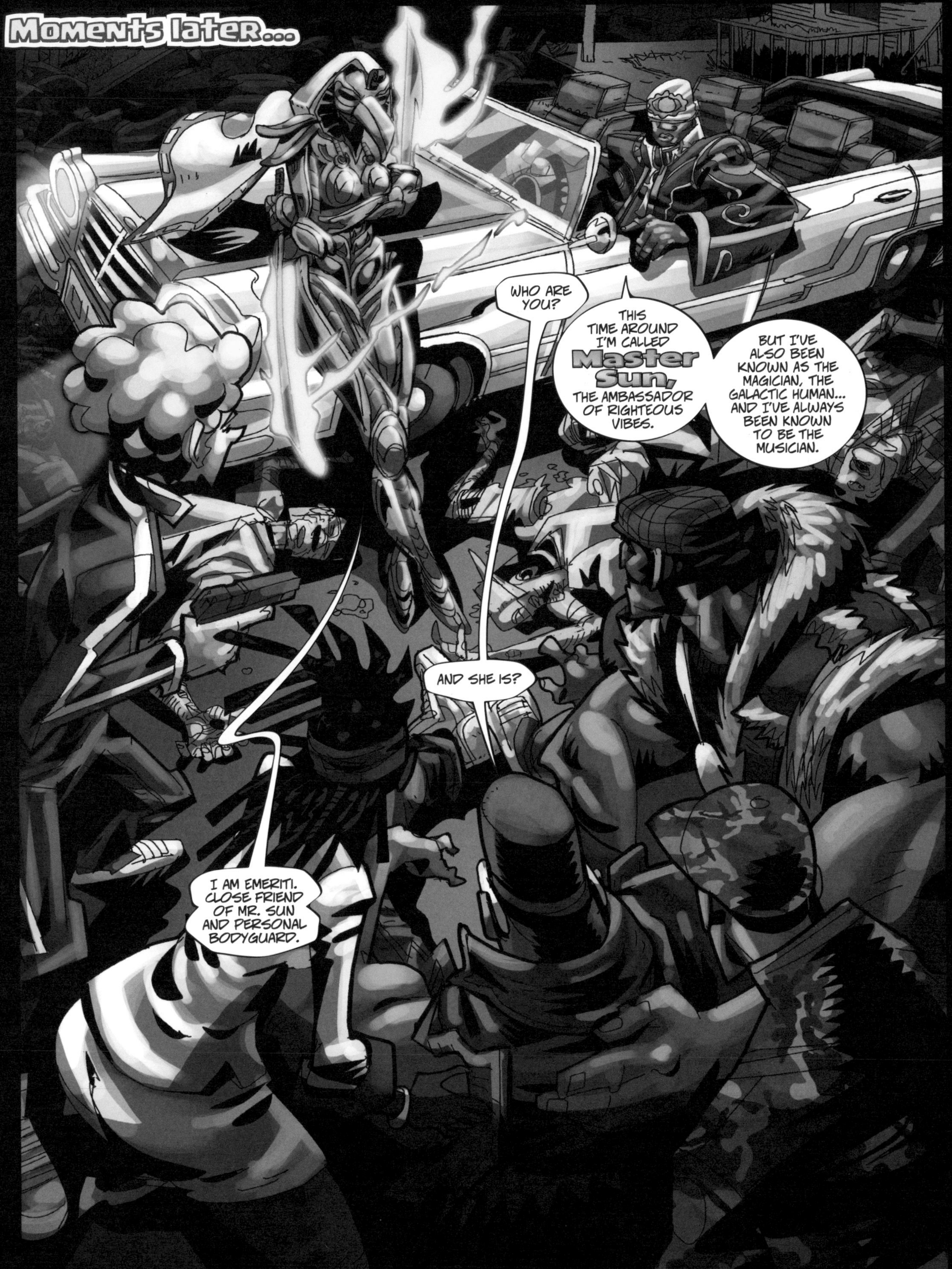

Moments later...
WHO ARE YOU?
THIS TIME AROUND I'M CALLED Master Sun, THE AMBASSADOR OF RIGHTEOUS VIBES.
BUT I'VE ALSO BEEN KNOWN AS THE MAGICIAN, THE GALACTIC HUMAN... AND I'VE ALWAYS BEEN KNOWN TO BE THE MUSICIAN.
AND SHE IS?
I AM EMERITI. CLOSE FRIEND OF MR. SUN AND PERSONAL BODYGUARD.

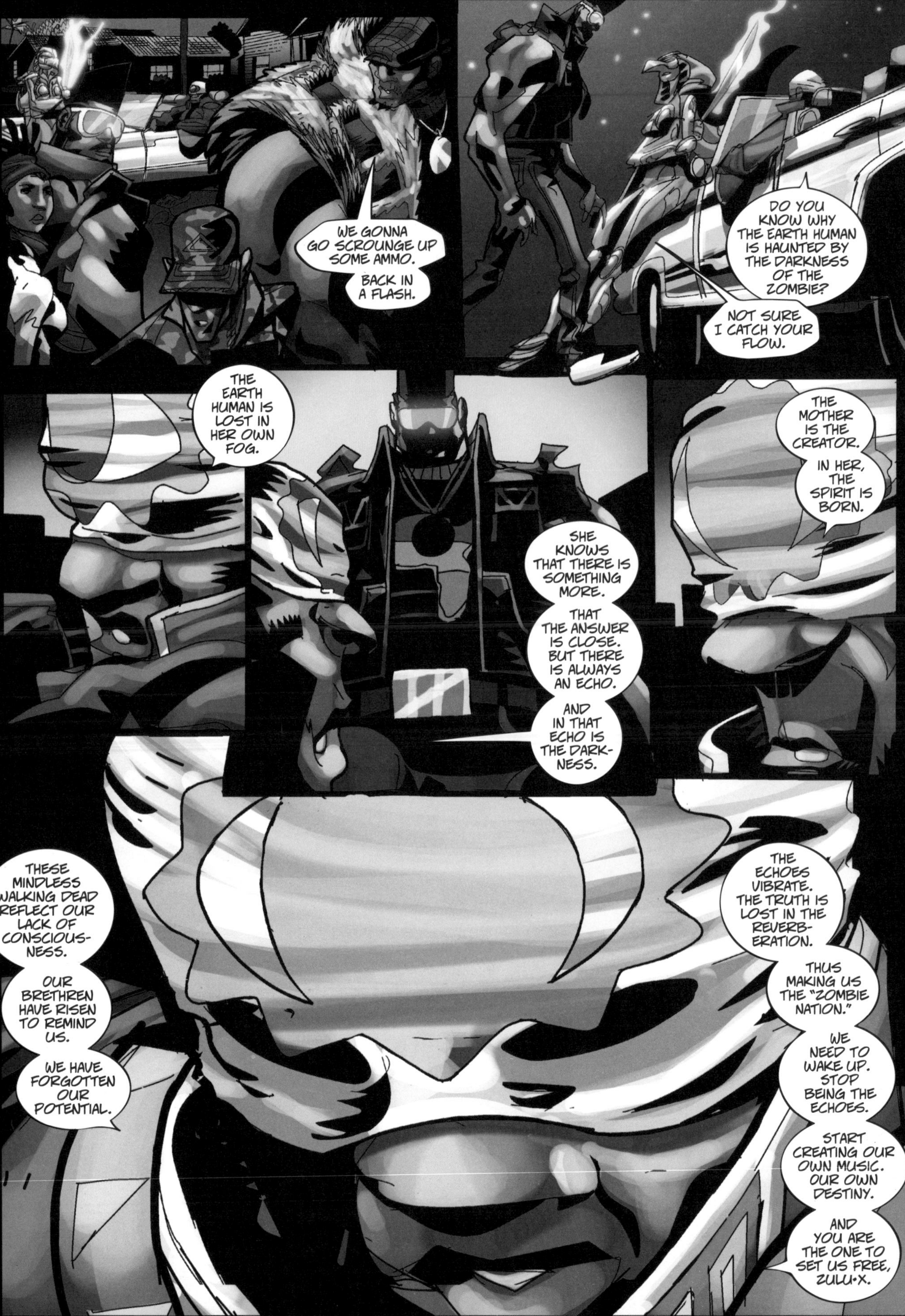
WE GONNA GO SCROUNGE UP SOME AMMO.
BACK IN A FLASH.
DO YOU KNOW WHY THE EARTH HUMAN IS HAUNTED BY THE DARKNESS OF THE ZOMBIE?
NOT SURE I CATCH YOUR FLOW.
THE EARTH HUMAN IS LOST IN HER OWN FOG.
SHE KNOWS THAT THERE IS SOMETHING MORE.
THAT THE ANSWER IS CLOSE. BUT THERE IS ALWAYS AN ECHO.
AND IN THAT ECHO IS THE DARK-NESS.
THE MOTHER IS THE CREATOR.
IN HER, THE SPIRIT IS BORN.
THESE MINDLESS WALKING DEAD REFLECT OUR LACK OF CONSCIOUS-NESS.
OUR BRETHREN HAVE RISEN TO REMIND US.
WE HAVE FORGOTTEN OUR POTENTIAL.
THE ECHOES VIBRATE. THE TRUTH IS LOST IN THE REVERB-ERATION.
THUS MAKING US THE "ZOMBIE NATION."
WE NEED TO WAKE UP. STOP BEING THE ECHOES.
START CREATING OUR OWN MUSIC. OUR OWN DESTINY.
AND YOU ARE THE ONE TO SET US FREE, ZULU•X.

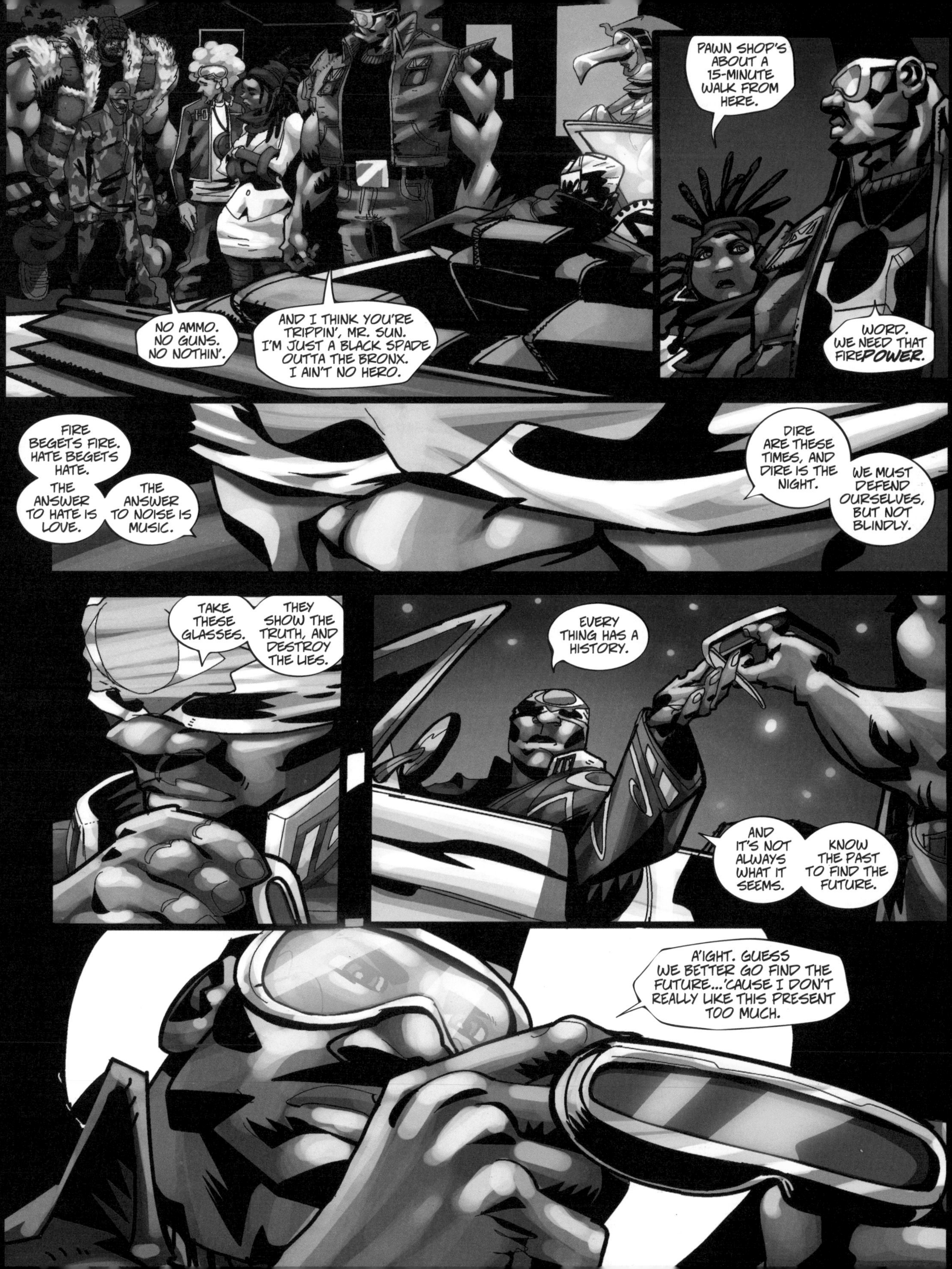
NO AMMO. NO GUNS. NO NOTHIN'.
AND I THINK YOU'RE TRIPPIN', MR. SUN. I'M JUST A BLACK SPADE OUTTA THE BRONX. I AIN'T NO HERO.
PAWN SHOP'S ABOUT A 15-MINUTE WALK FROM HERE.
WORD. WE NEED THAT FIREPOWER.
FIRE BEGETS FIRE. HATE BEGETS HATE.
THE ANSWER TO HATE IS LOVE.
THE ANSWER TO NOISE IS MUSIC.
DIRE ARE THESE TIMES, AND DIRE IS THE NIGHT.
WE MUST DEFEND OURSELVES, BUT NOT BLINDLY.
TAKE THESE GLASSES.
THEY SHOW THE TRUTH, AND DESTROY THE LIES.
EVERY THING HAS A HISTORY.
AND IT'S NOT ALWAYS WHAT IT SEEMS.
KNOW THE PAST TO FIND THE FUTURE.
A'IGHT. GUESS WE BETTER GO FIND THE FUTURE...'CAUSE I DON'T REALLY LIKE THIS PRESENT TOO MUCH.

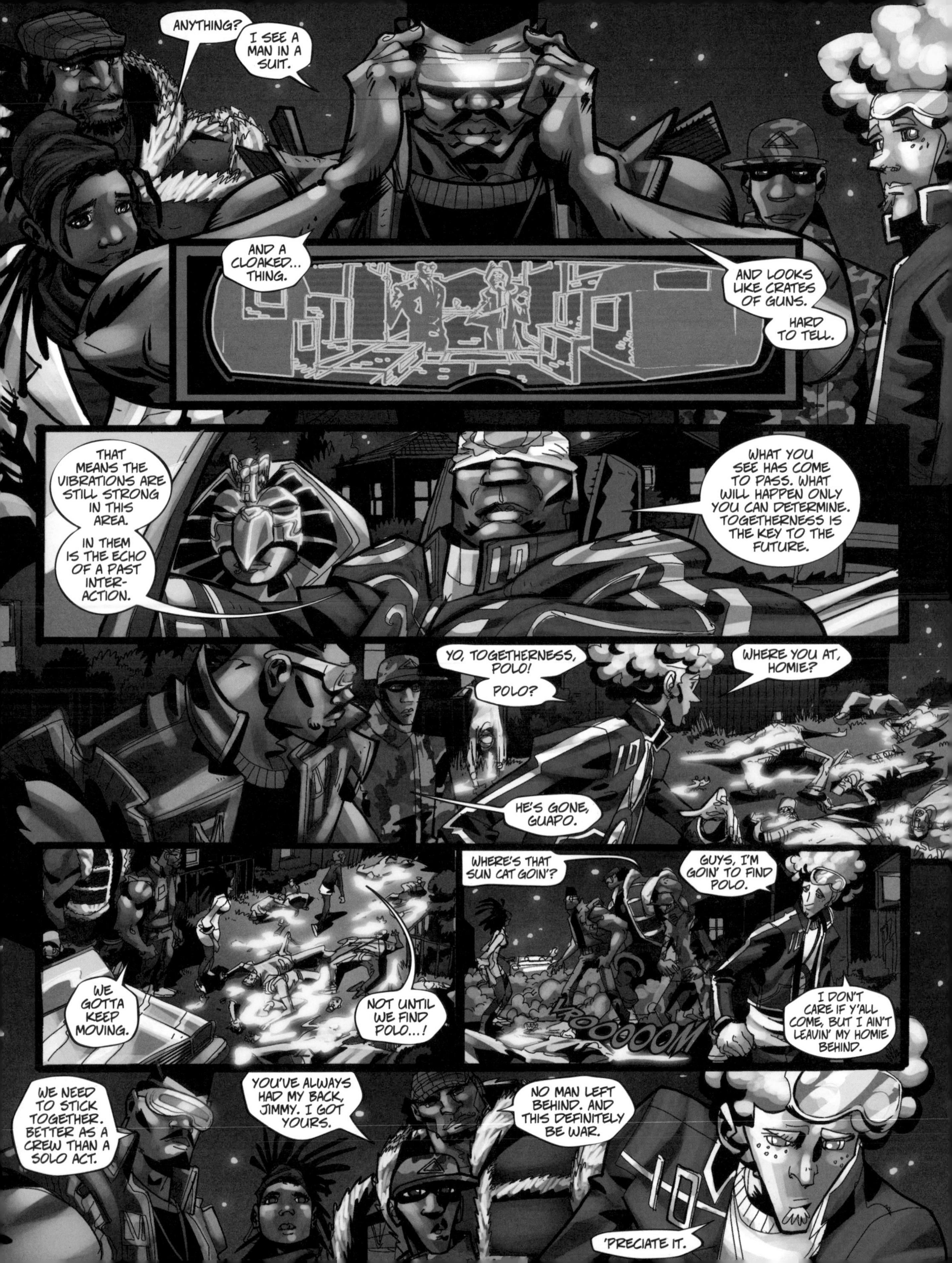

ANYTHING?
I SEE A MAN IN A SUIT.
AND A CLOAKED... THING.
AND LOOKS LIKE CRATES OF GUNS.
HARD TO TELL.
THAT MEANS THE VIBRATIONS ARE STILL STRONG IN THIS AREA.
IN THEM IS THE ECHO OF A PAST INTER-ACTION.
WHAT YOU SEE HAS COME TO PASS. WHAT WILL HAPPEN ONLY YOU CAN DETERMINE. TOGETHERNESS IS THE KEY TO THE FUTURE.
YO, TOGETHERNESS, POLO!
POLO?
WHERE YOU AT, HOMIE?
HE'S GONE, GUAPO.
WE GOTTA KEEP MOVING.
NOT UNTIL WE FIND POLO...!
WHERE'S THAT SUN CAT GOIN'?
GUYS, I'M GOIN' TO FIND POLO.
VROOOOOM
I DON'T CARE IF Y'ALL COME, BUT I AIN'T LEAVIN' MY HOMIE BEHIND.
WE NEED TO STICK TOGETHER. BETTER AS A CREW THAN A SOLO ACT.
YOU'VE ALWAYS HAD MY BACK, JIMMY. I GOT YOURS.
NO MAN LEFT BEHIND. AND THIS DEFINITELY BE WAR.
'PRECIATE IT.

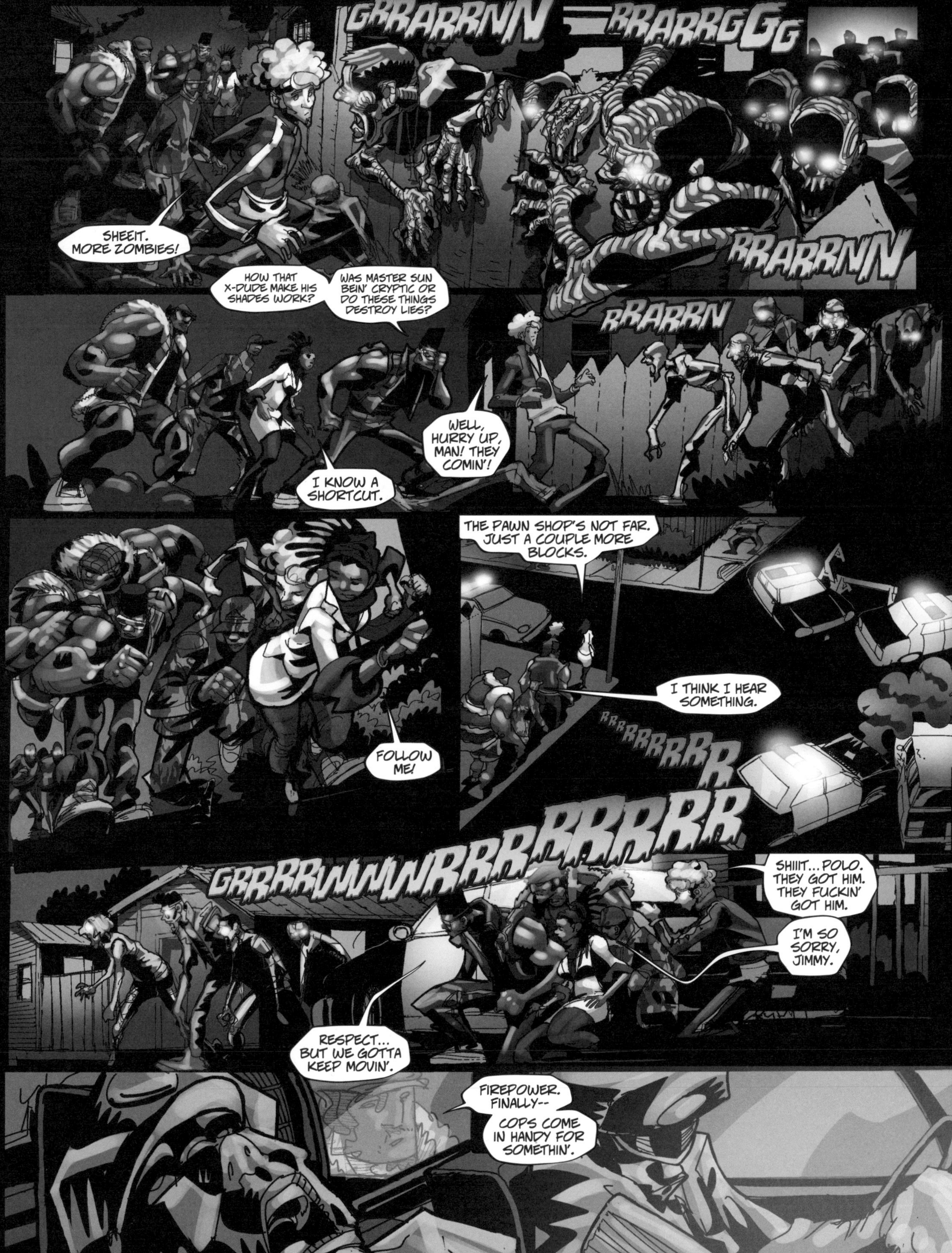
GRRARRNN
RRARRGGG
SHEEIT. MORE ZOMBIES!
RRARRNN
HOW THAT X-DUDE MAKE HIS SHADES WORK?
WAS MASTER SUN BEIN' CRYPTIC OR DO THESE THINGS DESTROY LIES?
RRARRN
WELL, HURRY UP, MAN! THEY COMIN'!
I KNOW A SHORTCUT.
FOLLOW ME!
THE PAWN SHOP'S NOT FAR. JUST A COUPLE MORE BLOCKS.
I THINK I HEAR SOMETHING.
RRRRRRRRR
GRRRRWWWWRRRRRRRRR
SHIIIT... POLO. THEY GOT HIM. THEY FUCKIN' GOT HIM.
I'M SO SORRY, JIMMY.
RESPECT... BUT WE GOTTA KEEP MOVIN'.
FIREPOWER. FINALLY--
COPS COME IN HANDY FOR SOMETHIN'.

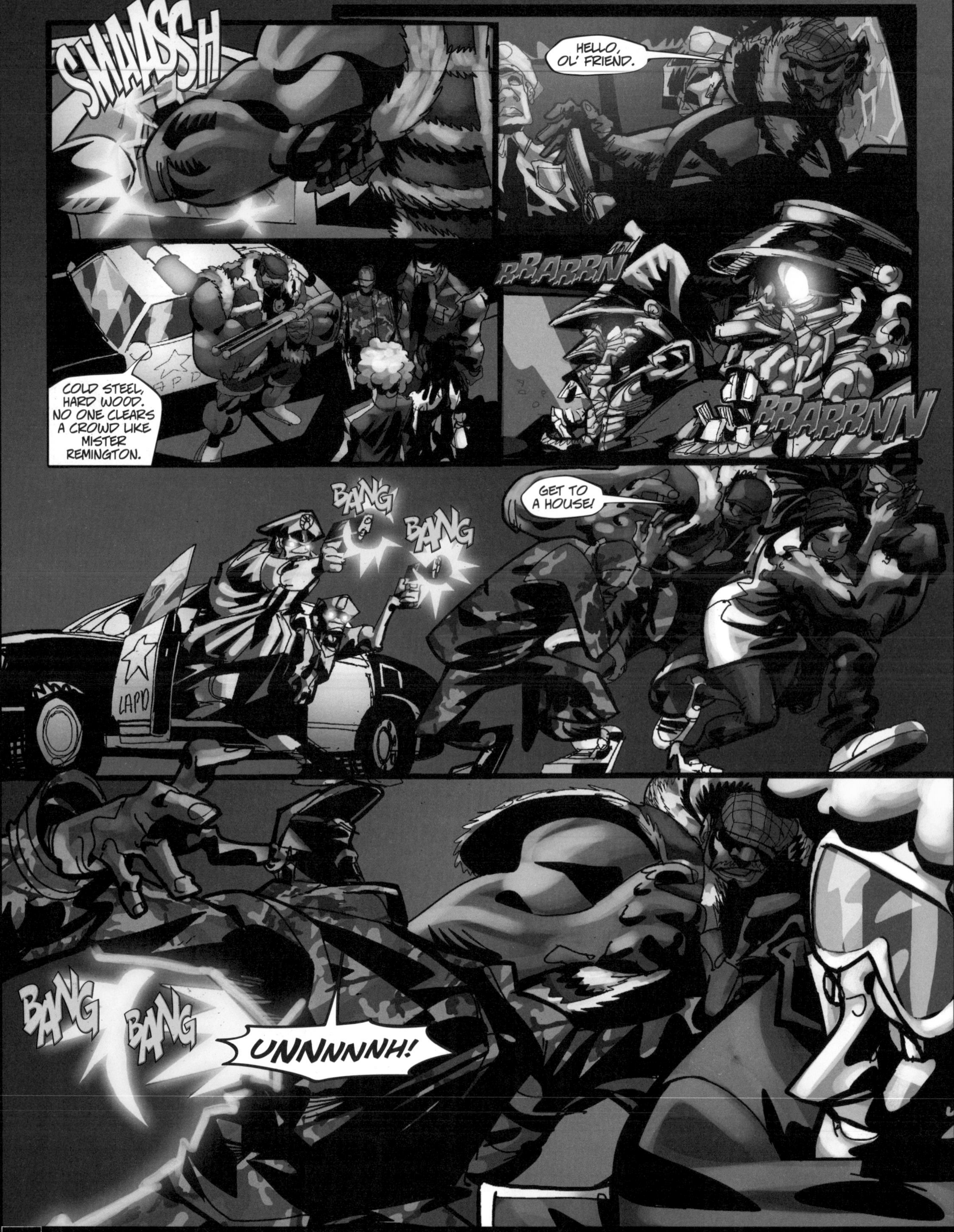
SWAASSH
HELLO, OL' FRIEND.
COLD STEEL, HARD WOOD. NO ONE CLEARS A CROWD LIKE MISTER REMINGTON.
RRARRN
RRARRNN
BANG
BANG
GET TO A HOUSE!
BANG
BANG
UNNNNNH!

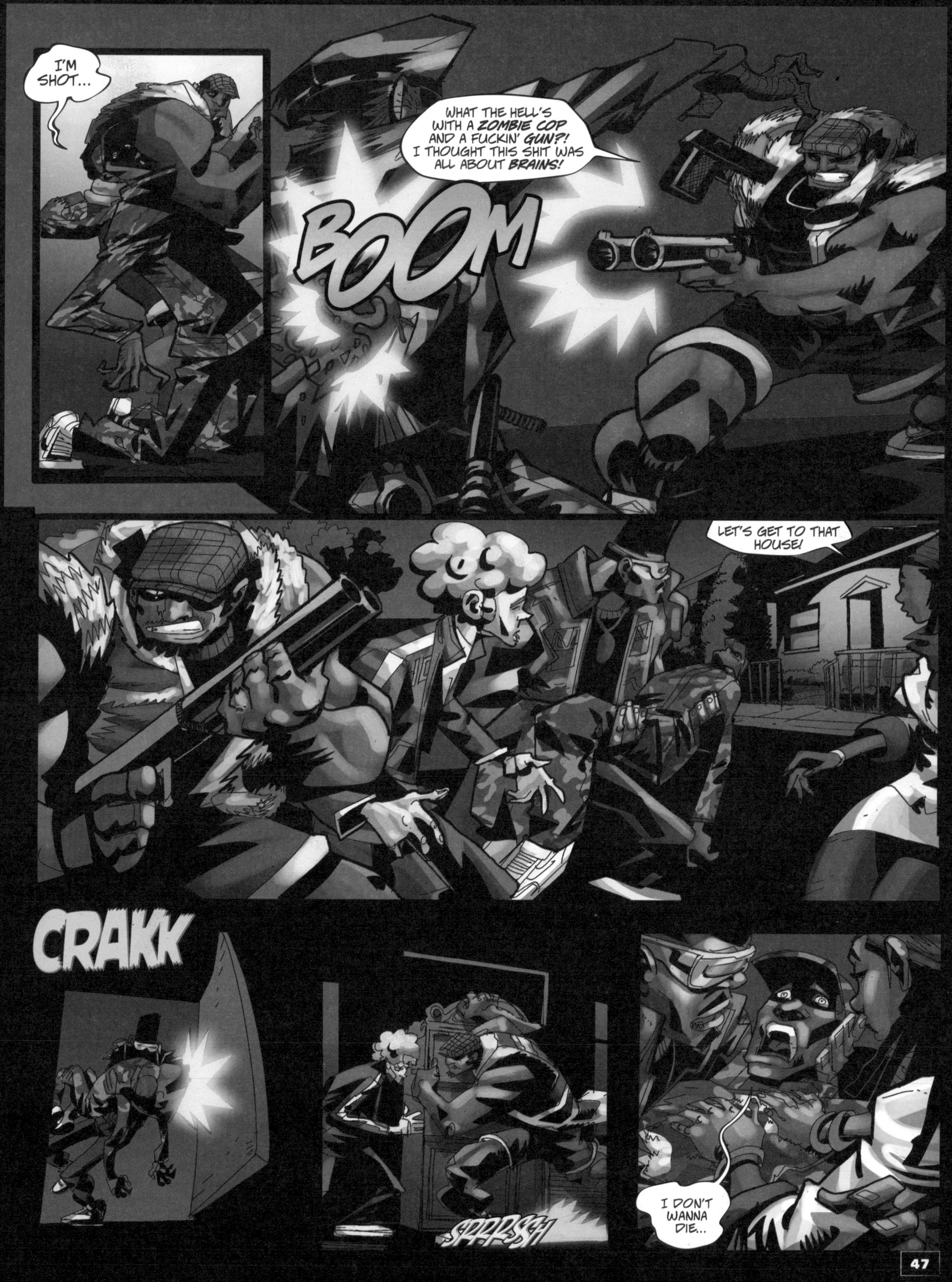

I'M SHOT...
WHAT THE HELL'S WITH A ZOMBIE COP AND A FUCKIN' GUN?! I THOUGHT THIS SHIT WAS ALL ABOUT BRAINS!
BOOM
LET'S GET TO THAT HOUSE!
CRAKK
SRRRSH
I DON'T WANNA DIE...

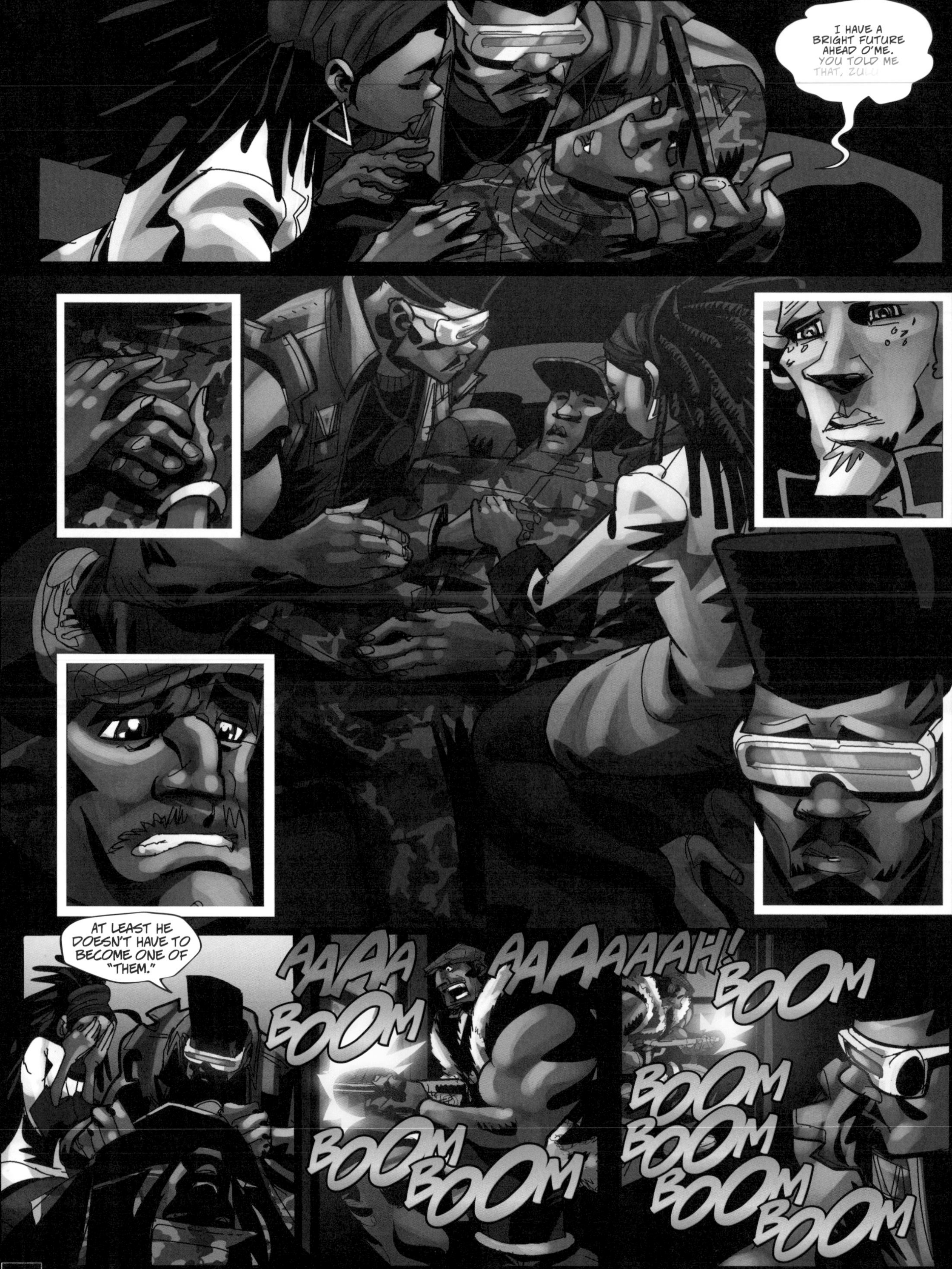
I HAVE A BRIGHT FUTURE AHEAD O'ME. YOU TOLD ME THAT, ZU
AT LEAST HE DOESN'T HAVE TO BECOME ONE OF "THEM."
AAAAAAAAAAH!
BOOM
BOOM
BOOM
BOOM
BOOM
BOOM
BOOM
BOOM
BOOM
BOOM

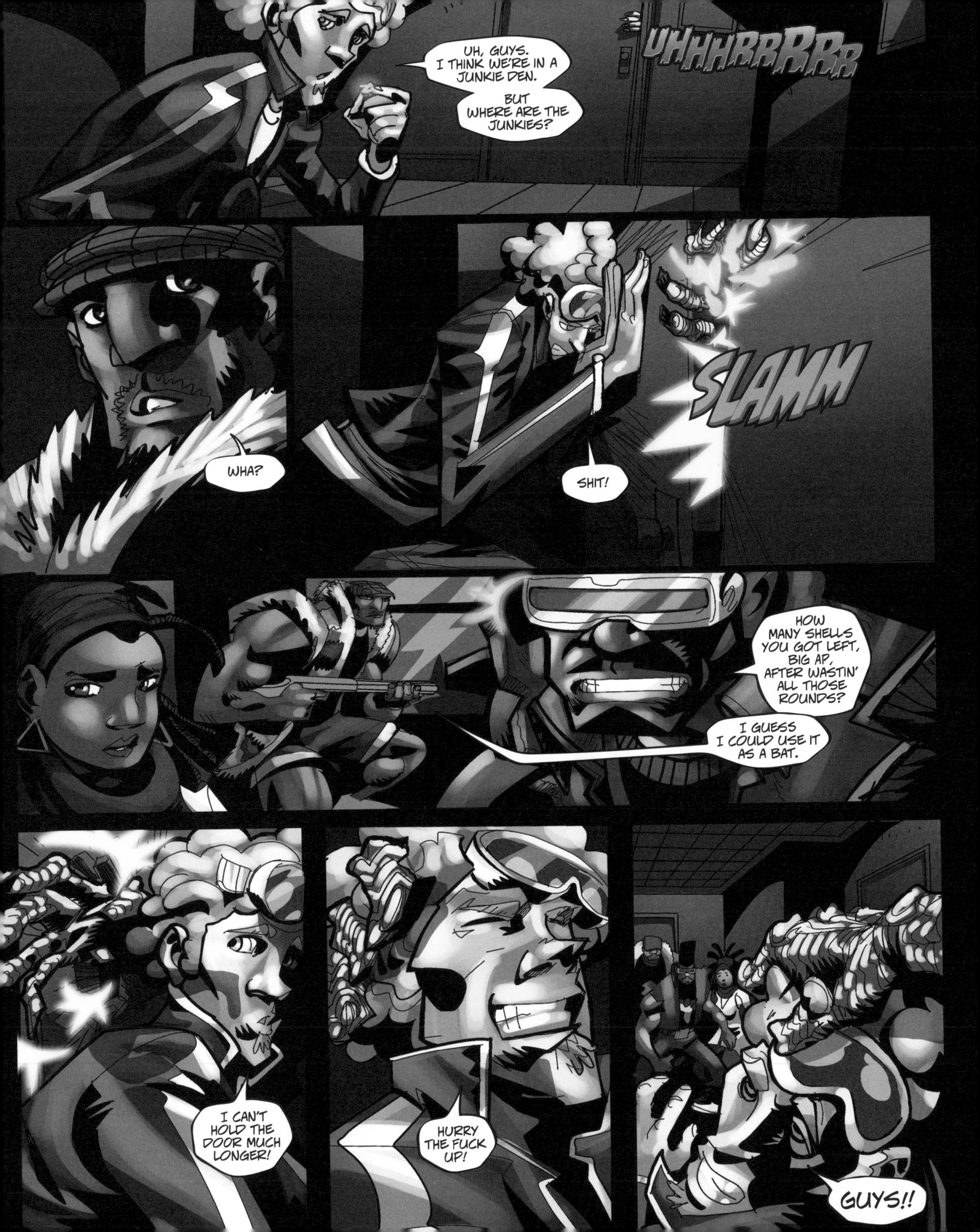
UH, GUYS. I THINK WE'RE IN A JUNKIE DEN.
BUT WHERE ARE THE JUNKIES?
UHHHRRRRR
WHA?
SHIT!
SLAMM
HOW MANY SHELLS YOU GOT LEFT, BIG AP, AFTER WASTIN' ALL THOSE ROUNDS?
I GUESS I COULD USE IT AS A BAT.
I CAN'T HOLD THE DOOR MUCH LONGER!
HURRY THE FUCK UP!
GUYS!!

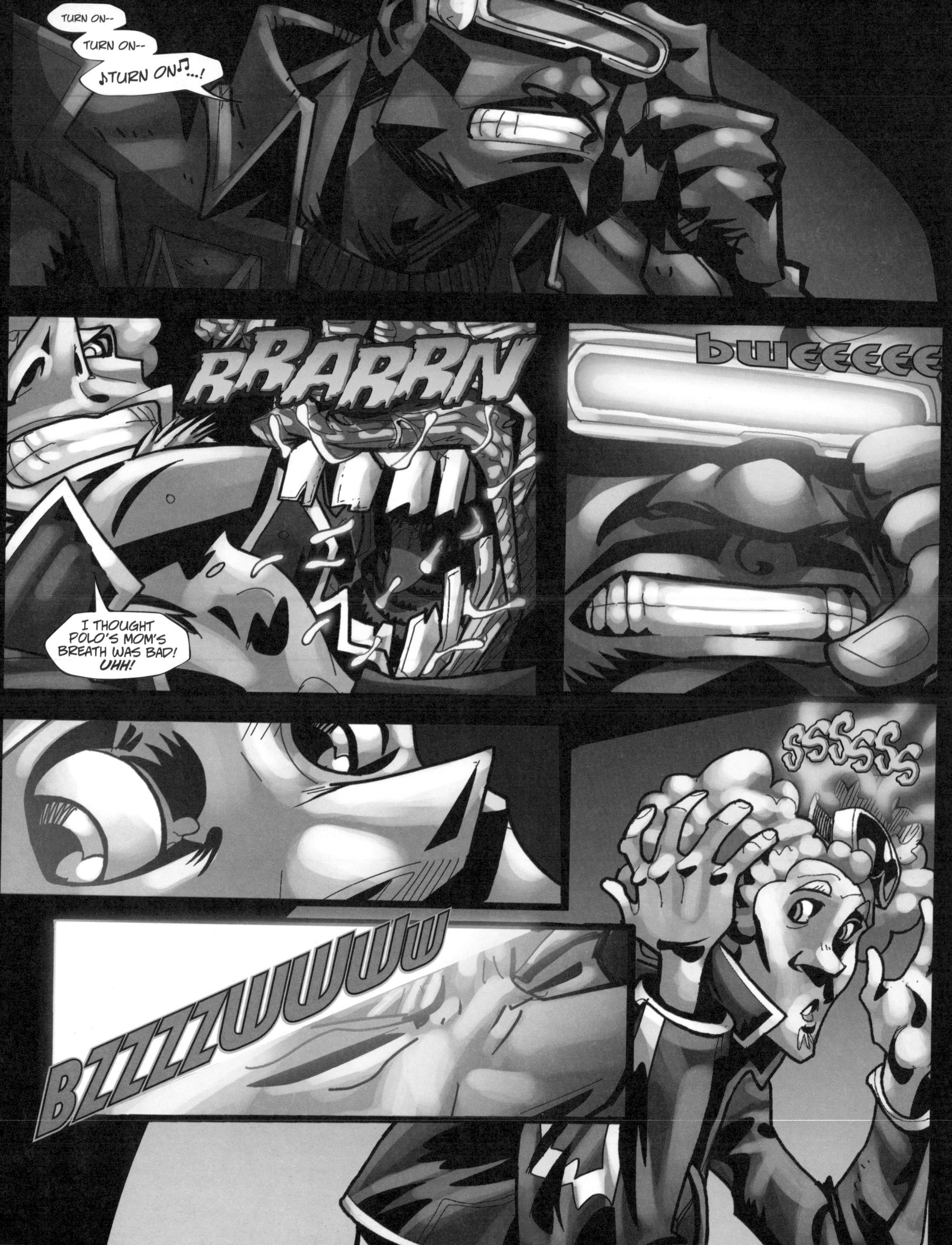
TURN ON--
TURN ON--
♪TURN ON♫...!
RRARRN
bweeeee
I THOUGHT POLO'S MOM'S BREATH WAS BAD! UHH!
SSSSSS
BZZZWWWW

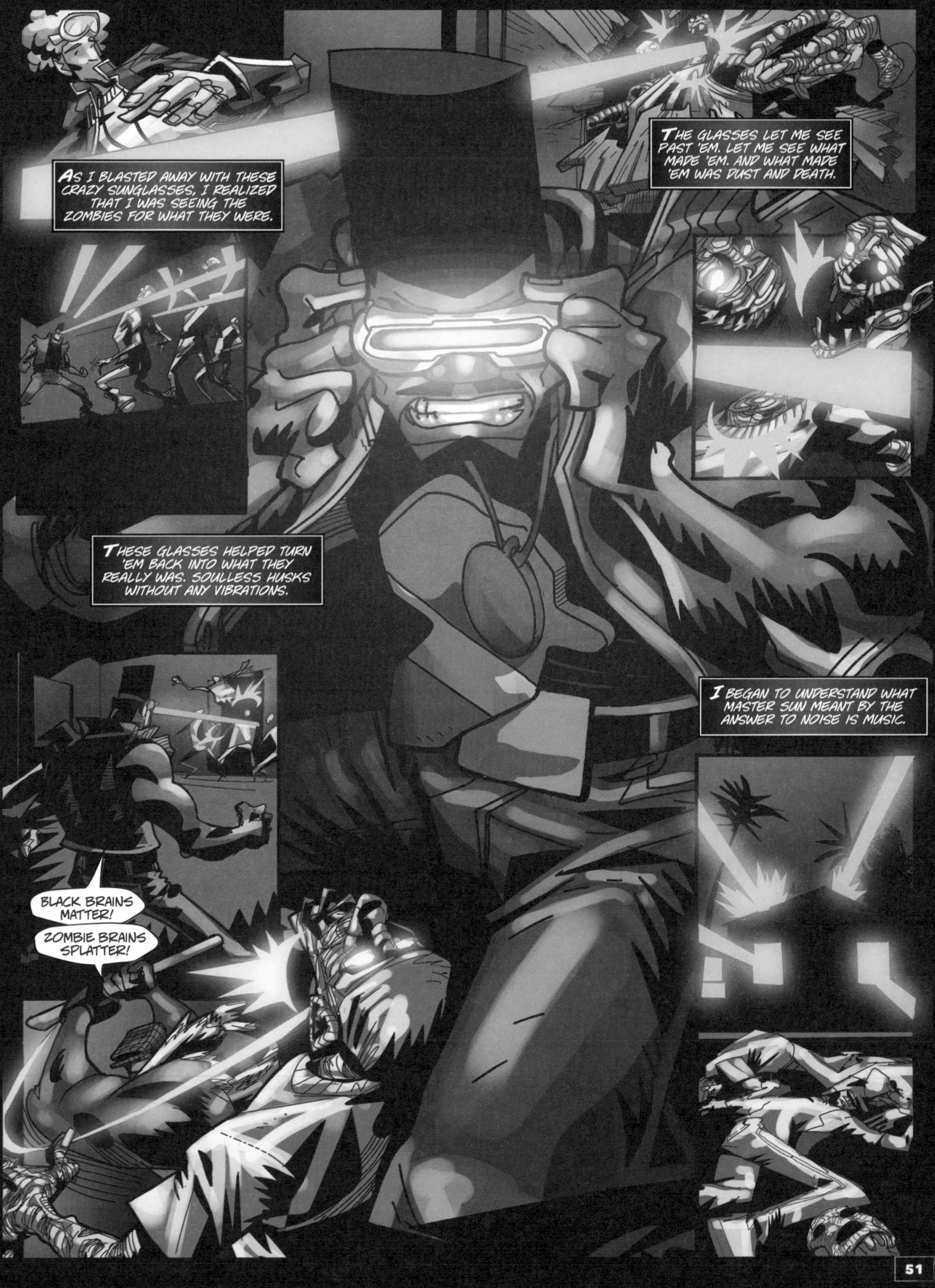

AS I BLASTED AWAY WITH THESE CRAZY SUNGLASSES, I REALIZED THAT I WAS SEEING THE ZOMBIES FOR WHAT THEY WERE.
THE GLASSES LET ME SEE PAST 'EM. LET ME SEE WHAT MADE 'EM. AND WHAT MADE 'EM WAS DUST AND DEATH.
THESE GLASSES HELPED TURN 'EM BACK INTO WHAT THEY REALLY WAS. SOULLESS HUSKS WITHOUT ANY VIBRATIONS.
I BEGAN TO UNDERSTAND WHAT MASTER SUN MEANT BY THE ANSWER TO NOISE IS MUSIC.
BLACK BRAINS MATTER!
ZOMBIE BRAINS SPLATTER!

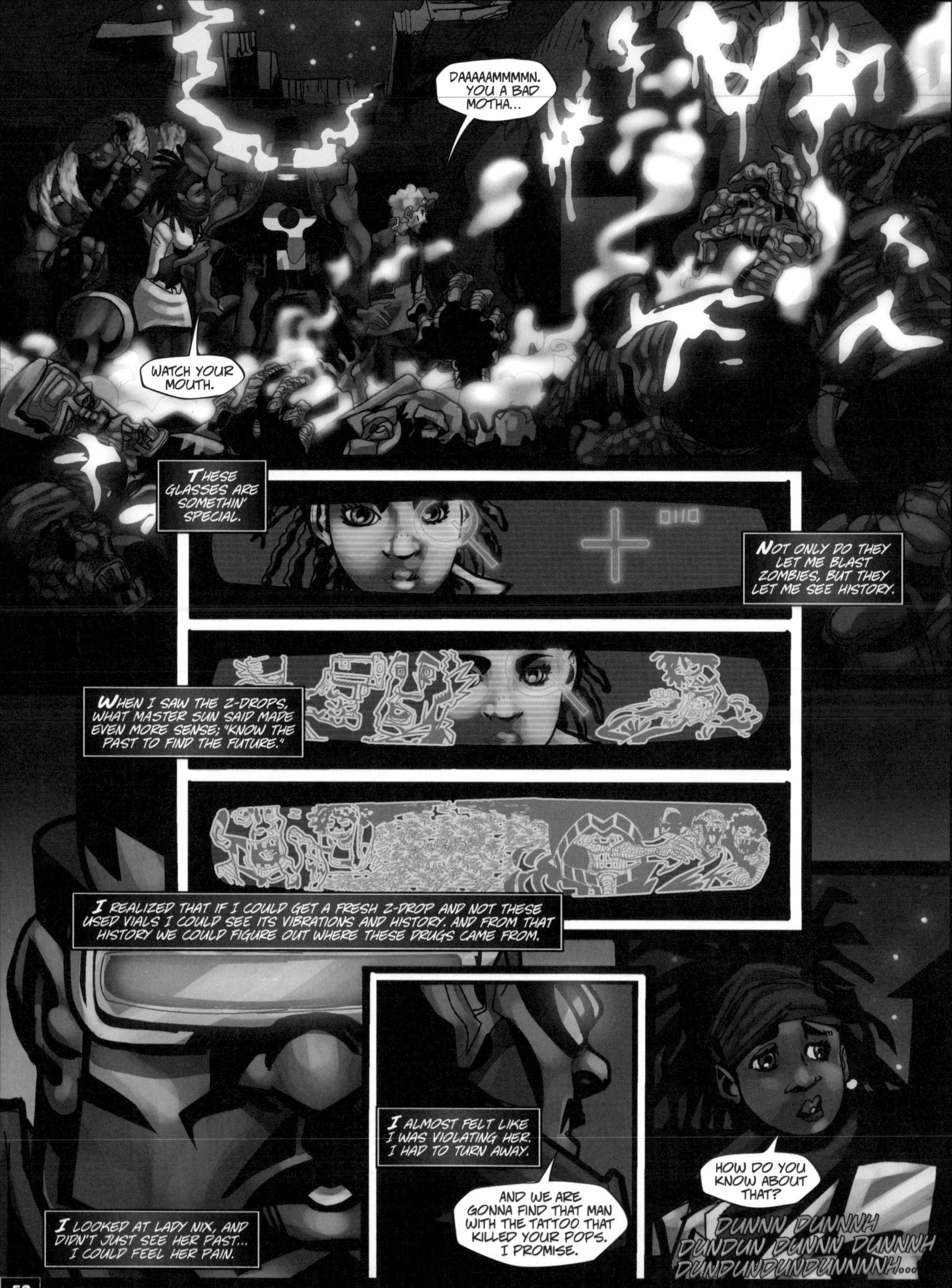

DAAAAAMMMMN. YOU A BAD MOTHA...
WATCH YOUR MOUTH.
THESE GLASSES ARE SOMETHIN' SPECIAL.
NOT ONLY DO THEY LET ME BLAST ZOMBIES, BUT THEY LET ME SEE HISTORY.
WHEN I SAW THE Z-DROPS, WHAT MASTER SUN SAID MADE EVEN MORE SENSE; "KNOW THE PAST TO FIND THE FUTURE."
I REALIZED THAT IF I COULD GET A FRESH Z-DROP AND NOT THESE USED VIALS I COULD SEE ITS VIBRATIONS AND HISTORY. AND FROM THAT HISTORY WE COULD FIGURE OUT WHERE THESE DRUGS CAME FROM.
I LOOKED AT LADY NIX, AND DIDN'T JUST SEE HER PAST... I COULD FEEL HER PAIN.
I ALMOST FELT LIKE I WAS VIOLATING HER. I HAD TO TURN AWAY.
AND WE ARE GONNA FIND THAT MAN WITH THE TATTOO THAT KILLED YOUR POPS. I PROMISE.
HOW DO YOU KNOW ABOUT THAT?
DUNNN DUNNNH DUNDUN DUNNN DUNNNH DUNDUNDUNDUNNNNH...

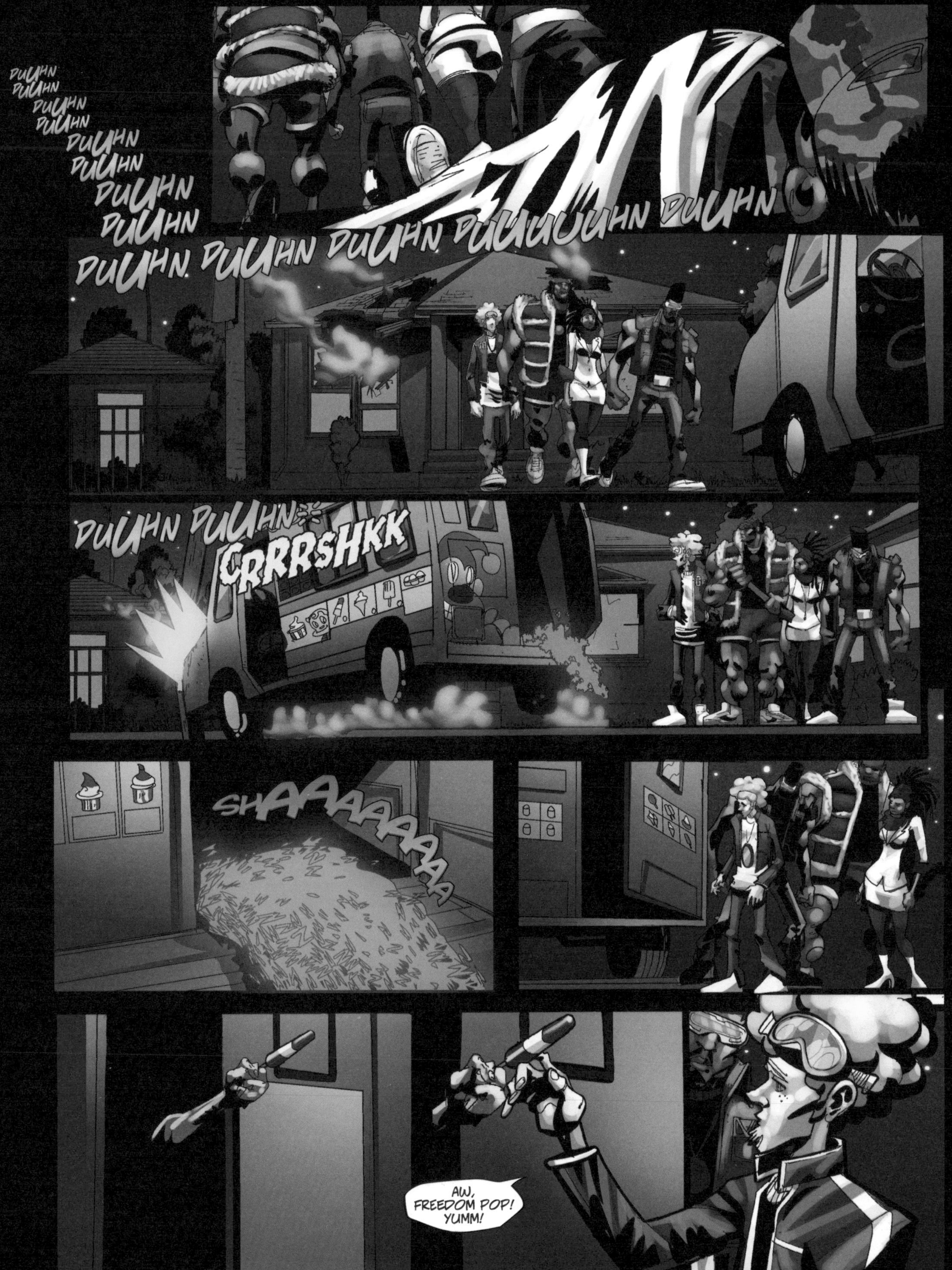
DUUHN
DUUHN
DUUHN
DUUHN
DUUHN
DUUHN
DUUHN
DUUHN
DUUHN DUUHN DUUHN DUUUUUUHN DUUHN
DUUHN DUUHN
CRRRSHKK
SHAAAAAAAA
AW, FREEDOM POP! YUMM!

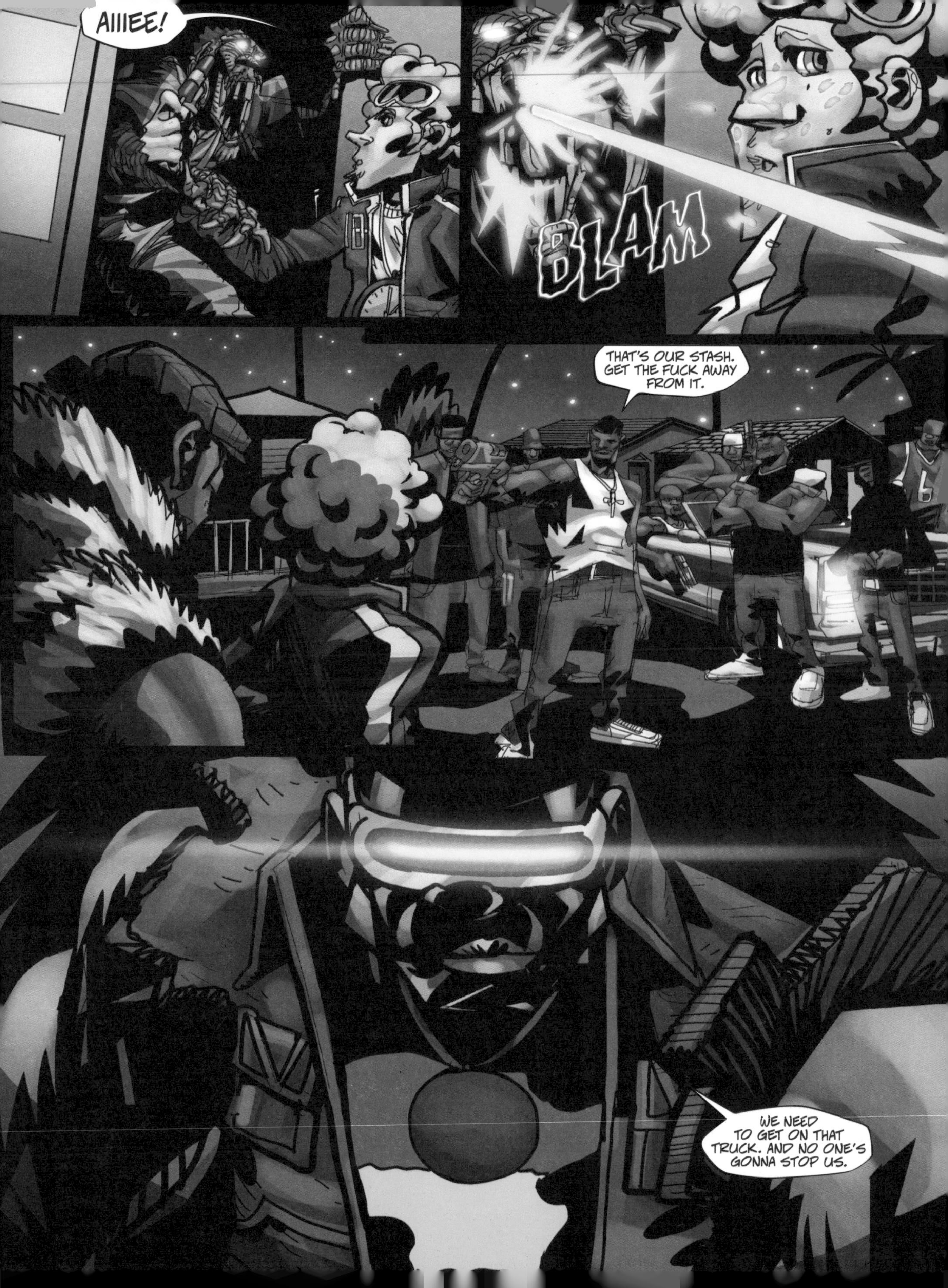
AIIIEE!
BLAM
THAT'S OUR STASH. GET THE FUCK AWAY FROM IT.
WE NEED TO GET ON THAT TRUCK. AND NO ONE'S GONNA STOP US.

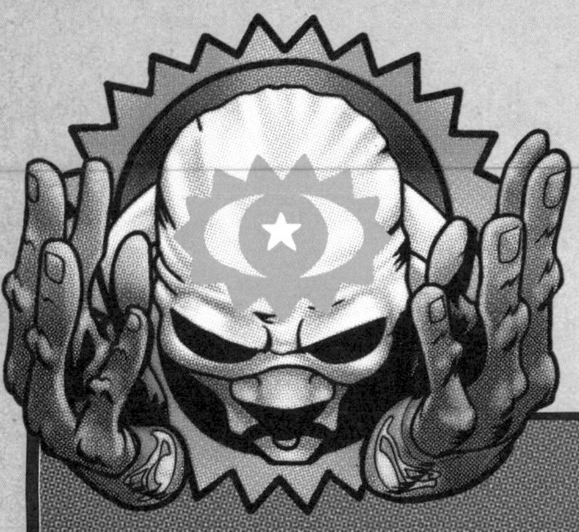

MASTER SUN'S VERSE 20:12

IT IS A TIME OF BALANCE,
a time for Energy and Flow
Where Vibrations make Rhythms and Harmonies show
That Words have Power and that Black is the One
Which came before Time with the Birth of the Sun.

Negative is not Bad and Positive is not Good
Since these are words of Balance from a Musical Master
Who's put us on a Circle of Fifths so that we should
Keep Composing our Spirits to avoid imminent Disaster.

Remember that Black are the Keys raised above
That sound Wave Sines of Light that emanate Love.
Harmony and Melody can't exist without Semitone
A Master of Sun needs all notes for the Throne.

And here we now find the World in Spiritual shift
an opportunity to be embraced
to heal this Ancient Rift.

-Masters of the Sun

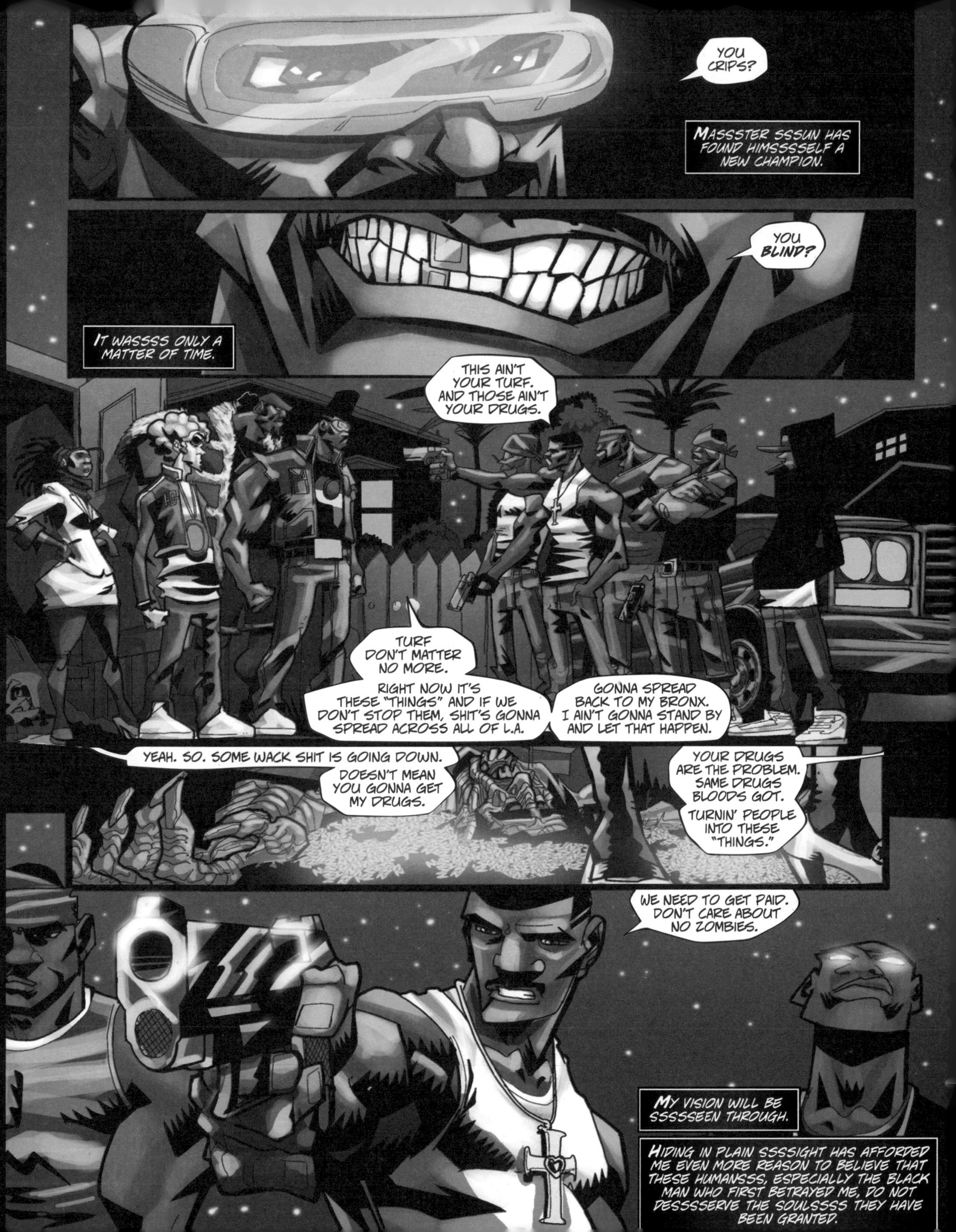
YOU CRIPS?
MASSSTER SSSUN HAS FOUND HIMSSSSELF A NEW CHAMPION.
YOU BLIND?
IT WASSSS ONLY A MATTER OF TIME.
THIS AIN'T YOUR TURF. AND THOSE AIN'T YOUR DRUGS.
TURF DON'T MATTER NO MORE.
RIGHT NOW IT'S THESE "THINGS" AND IF WE DON'T STOP THEM, SHIT'S GONNA SPREAD ACROSS ALL OF L.A.
GONNA SPREAD BACK TO MY BRONX. I AIN'T GONNA STAND BY AND LET THAT HAPPEN.
YEAH. SO. SOME WACK SHIT IS GOING DOWN.
DOESN'T MEAN YOU GONNA GET MY DRUGS.
YOUR DRUGS ARE THE PROBLEM. SAME DRUGS BLOODS GOT.
TURNIN' PEOPLE INTO THESE "THINGS."
WE NEED TO GET PAID. DON'T CARE ABOUT NO ZOMBIES.
MY VISION WILL BE SSSSSEEN THROUGH.
HIDING IN PLAIN SSSSIGHT HAS AFFORDED ME EVEN MORE REASON TO BELIEVE THAT THESE HUMANSSS, ESPECIALLY THE BLACK MAN WHO FIRST BETRAYED ME, DO NOT DESSSSERVE THE SOULSSSS THEY HAVE BEEN GRANTED.

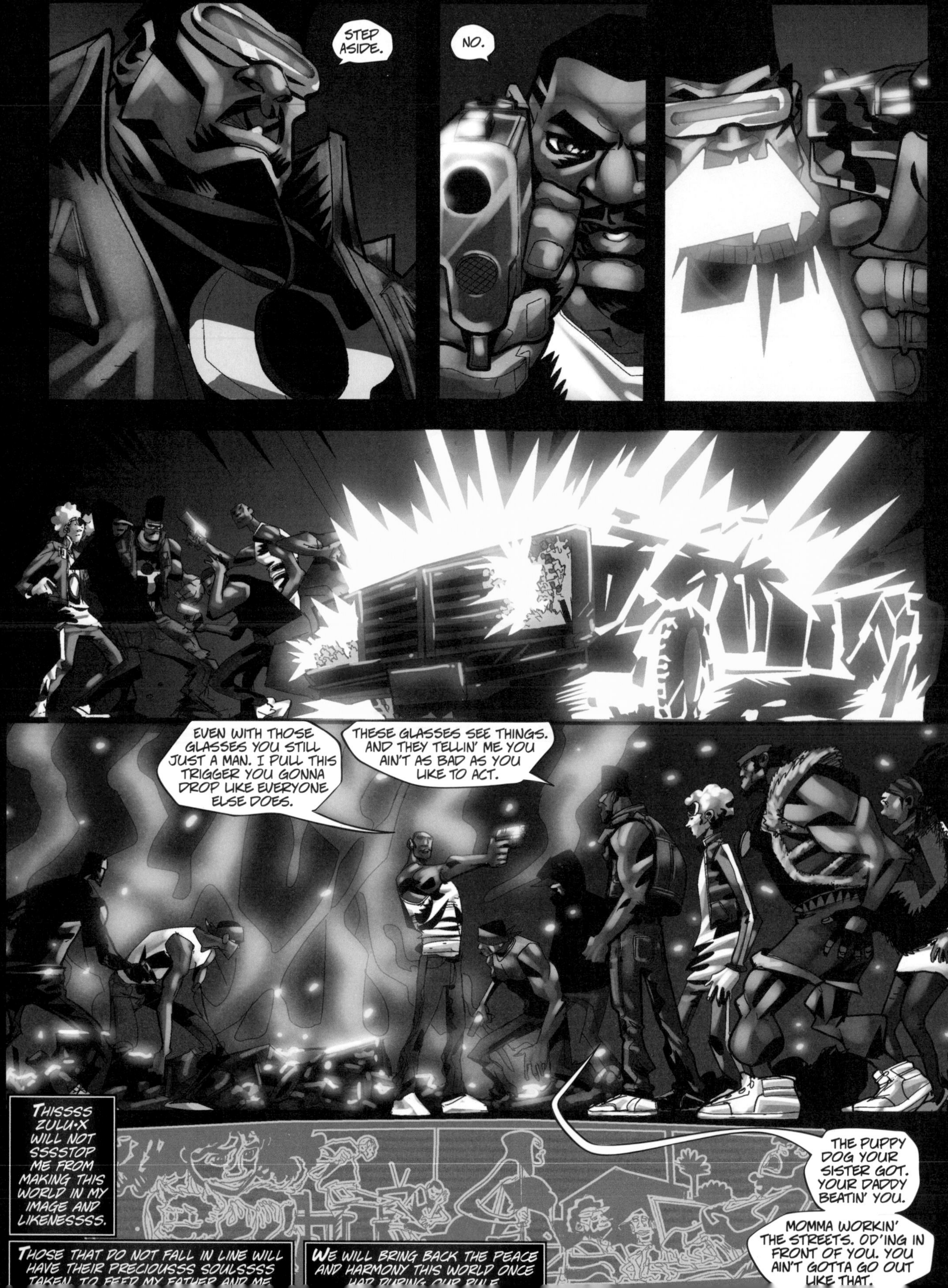
STEP ASIDE.
NO.
EVEN WITH THOSE GLASSES YOU STILL JUST A MAN. I PULL THIS TRIGGER YOU GONNA DROP LIKE EVERYONE ELSE DOES.
THESE GLASSES SEE THINGS. AND THEY TELLIN' ME YOU AIN'T AS BAD AS YOU LIKE TO ACT.
THISSSS ZULU•X WILL NOT SSSSTOP ME FROM MAKING THIS WORLD IN MY IMAGE AND LIKENESSSS.
THE PUPPY DOG YOUR SISTER GOT. YOUR DADDY BEATIN' YOU.
MOMMA WORKIN' THE STREETS. OD'ING IN FRONT OF YOU. YOU AIN'T GOTTA GO OUT LIKE THAT.
THOSE THAT DO NOT FALL IN LINE WILL HAVE THEIR PRECIOUSSS SOULSSSS
WE WILL BRING BACK THE PEACE AND HARMONY THIS WORLD ONCE

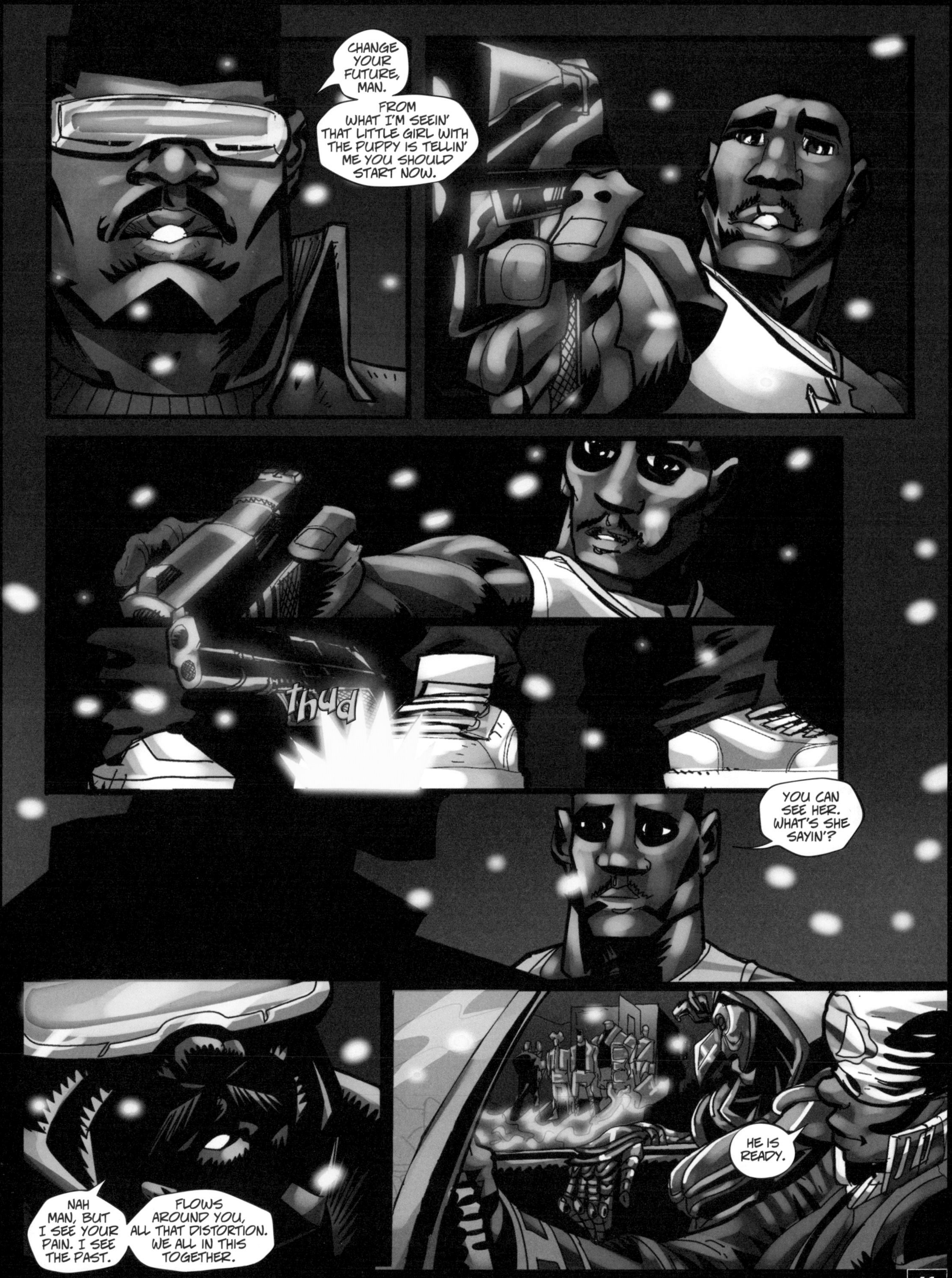
CHANGE YOUR FUTURE, MAN.
FROM WHAT I'M SEEIN' THAT LITTLE GIRL WITH THE PUPPY IS TELLIN' ME YOU SHOULD START NOW.
thud
YOU CAN SEE HER. WHAT'S SHE SAYIN'?
NAH MAN, BUT I SEE YOUR PAIN. I SEE THE PAST.
FLOWS AROUND YOU, ALL THAT DISTORTION. WE ALL IN THIS TOGETHER.
HE IS READY.

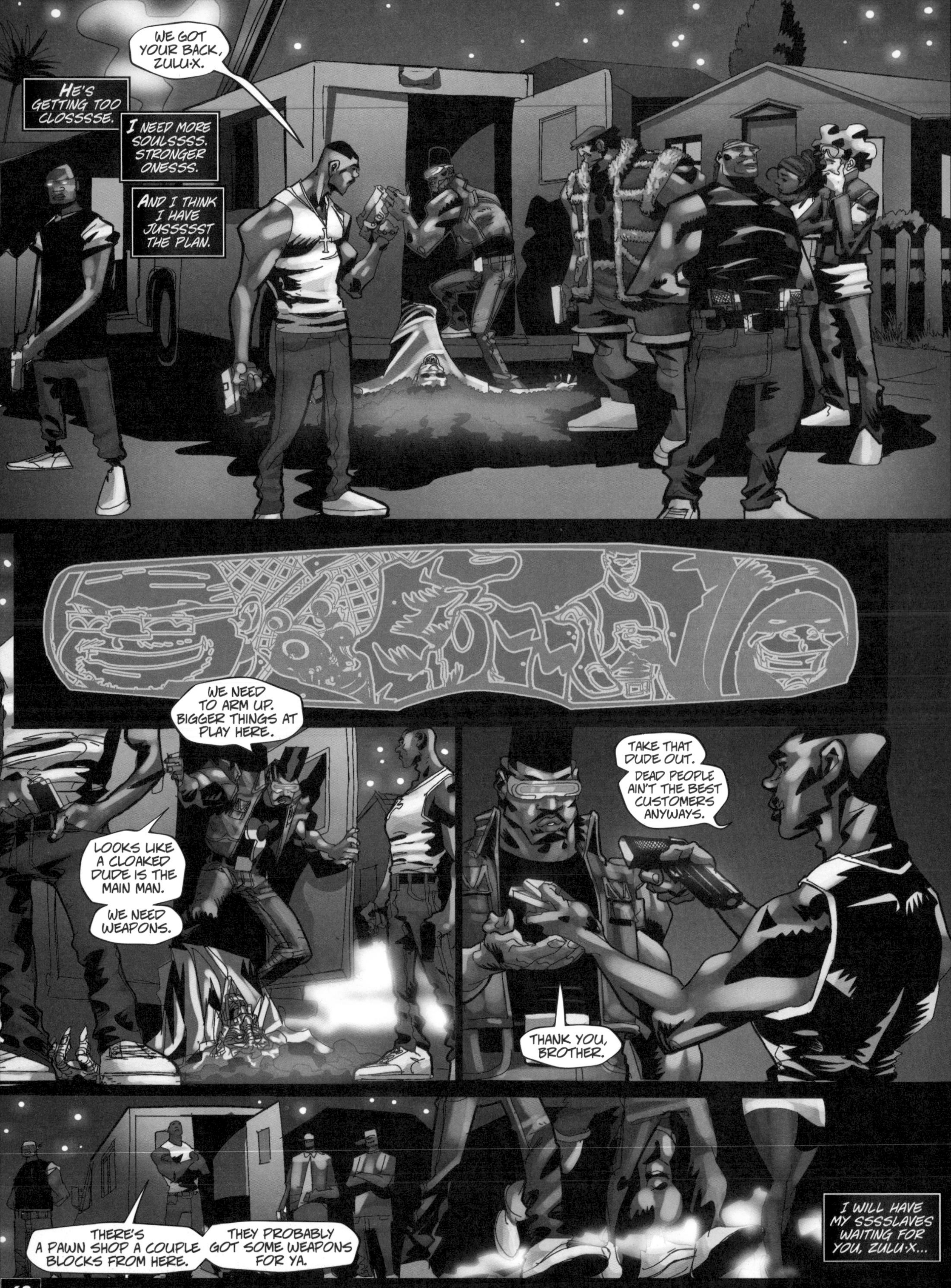
HE'S GETTING TOO CLOSSSSE.
WE GOT YOUR BACK, ZULU-X.
I NEED MORE SOULSSSS. STRONGER ONESSS.
AND I THINK I HAVE JUSSSSST THE PLAN.
WE NEED TO ARM UP. BIGGER THINGS AT PLAY HERE.
LOOKS LIKE A CLOAKED DUDE IS THE MAIN MAN.
WE NEED WEAPONS.
TAKE THAT DUDE OUT.
DEAD PEOPLE AIN'T THE BEST CUSTOMERS ANYWAYS.
THANK YOU, BROTHER.
THERE'S A PAWN SHOP A COUPLE BLOCKS FROM HERE.
THEY PROBABLY GOT SOME WEAPONS FOR YA.
I WILL HAVE MY SSSSLAVES WAITING FOR YOU, ZULU-X...

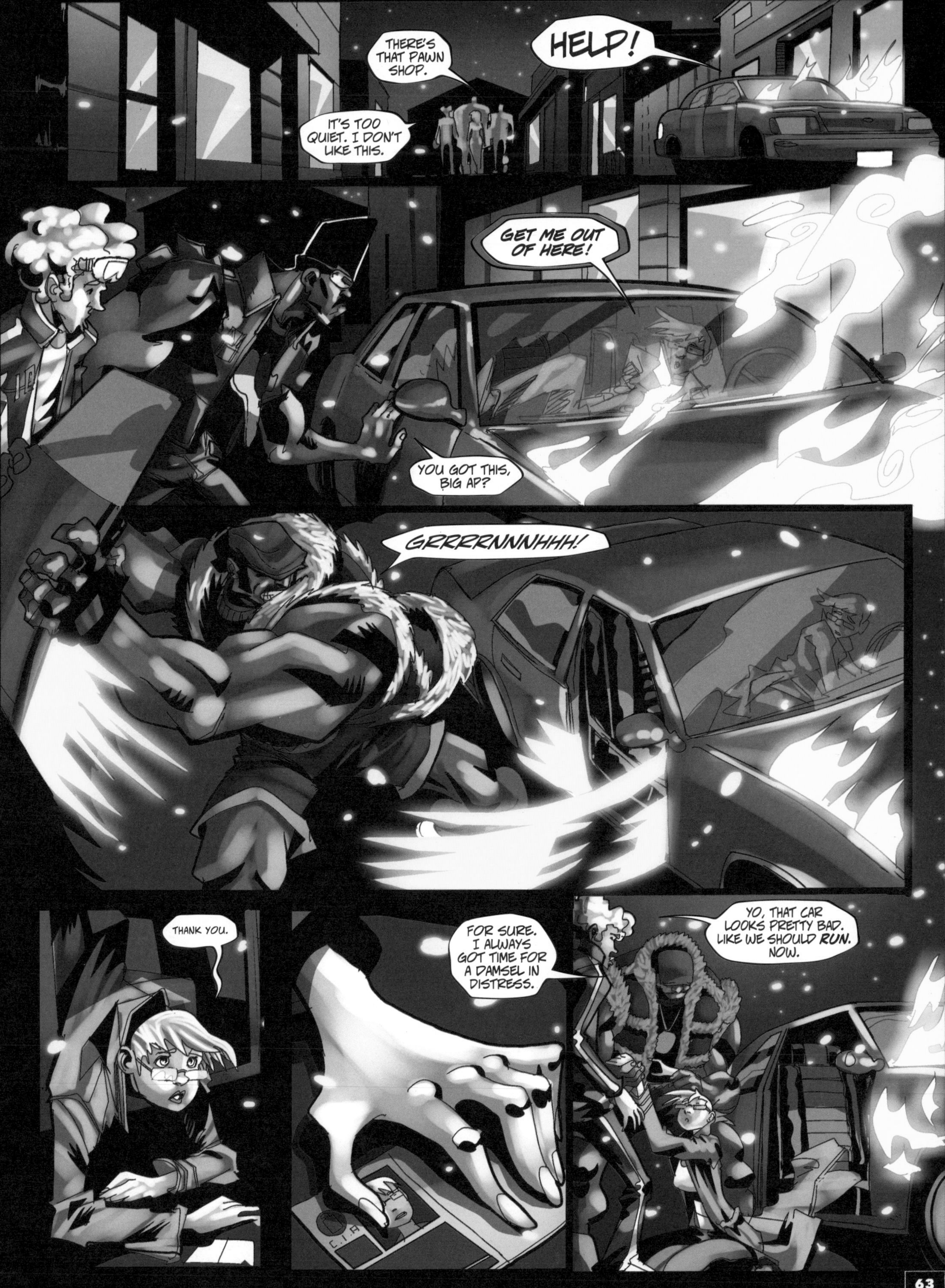
THERE'S THAT PAWN SHOP.
HELP!
IT'S TOO QUIET. I DON'T LIKE THIS.
GET ME OUT OF HERE!
YOU GOT THIS, BIG AP?
GRRRRNNNHHH!
THANK YOU.
FOR SURE. I ALWAYS GOT TIME FOR A DAMSEL IN DISTRESS.
YO, THAT CAR LOOKS PRETTY BAD. LIKE WE SHOULD RUN. NOW.

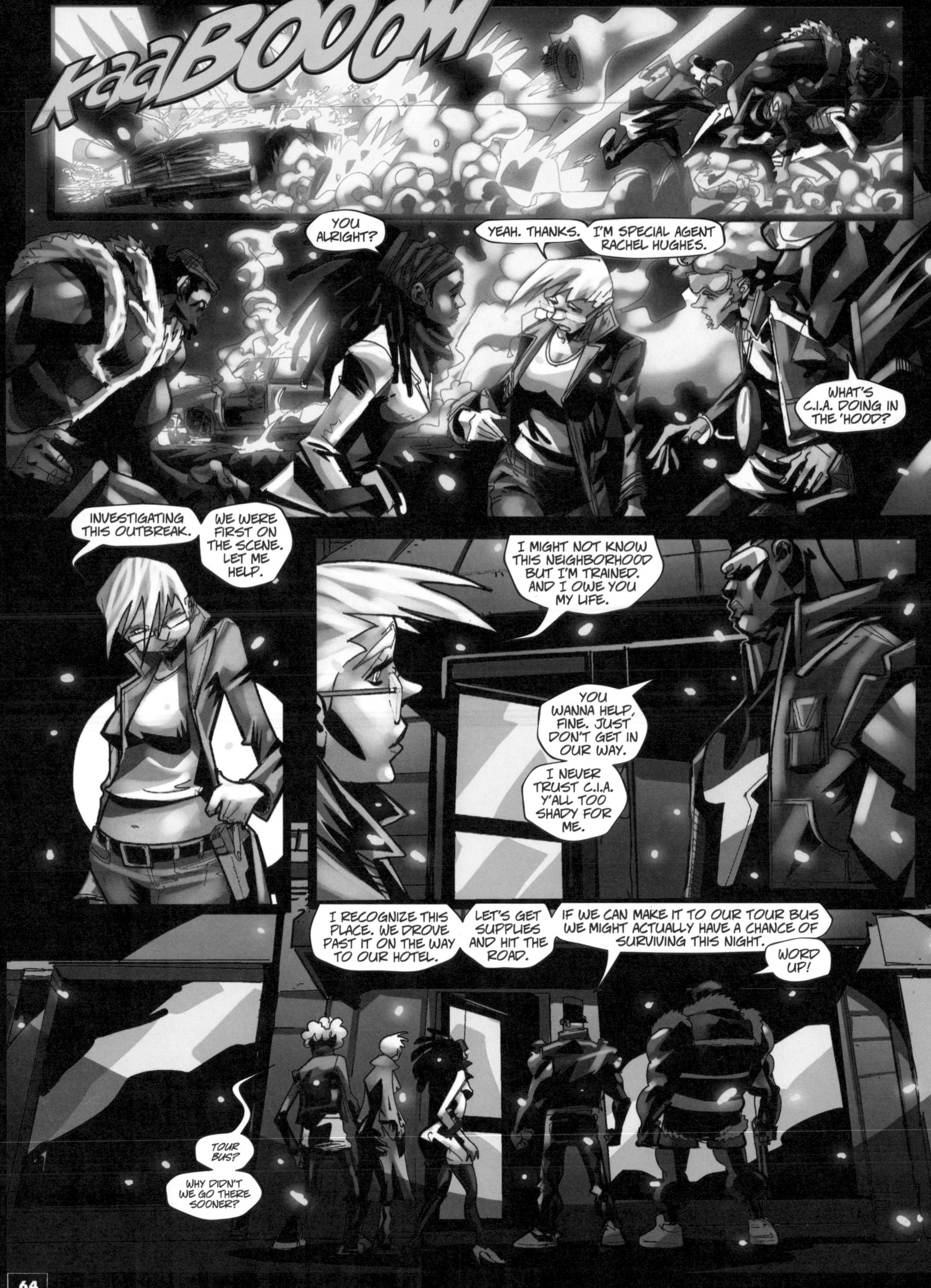
KAABOOOM
YOU ALRIGHT?
YEAH. THANKS.
I'M SPECIAL AGENT RACHEL HUGHES.
WHAT'S C.I.A. DOING IN THE 'HOOD?
INVESTIGATING THIS OUTBREAK.
WE WERE FIRST ON THE SCENE. LET ME HELP.
I MIGHT NOT KNOW THIS NEIGHBORHOOD BUT I'M TRAINED. AND I OWE YOU MY LIFE.
YOU WANNA HELP, FINE. JUST DON'T GET IN OUR WAY.
I NEVER TRUST C.I.A. Y'ALL TOO SHADY FOR ME.
I RECOGNIZE THIS PLACE. WE DROVE PAST IT ON THE WAY TO OUR HOTEL.
LET'S GET SUPPLIES AND HIT THE ROAD.
IF WE CAN MAKE IT TO OUR TOUR BUS WE MIGHT ACTUALLY HAVE A CHANCE OF SURVIVING THIS NIGHT.
WORD UP!
TOUR BUS?
WHY DIDN'T WE GO THERE SOONER?

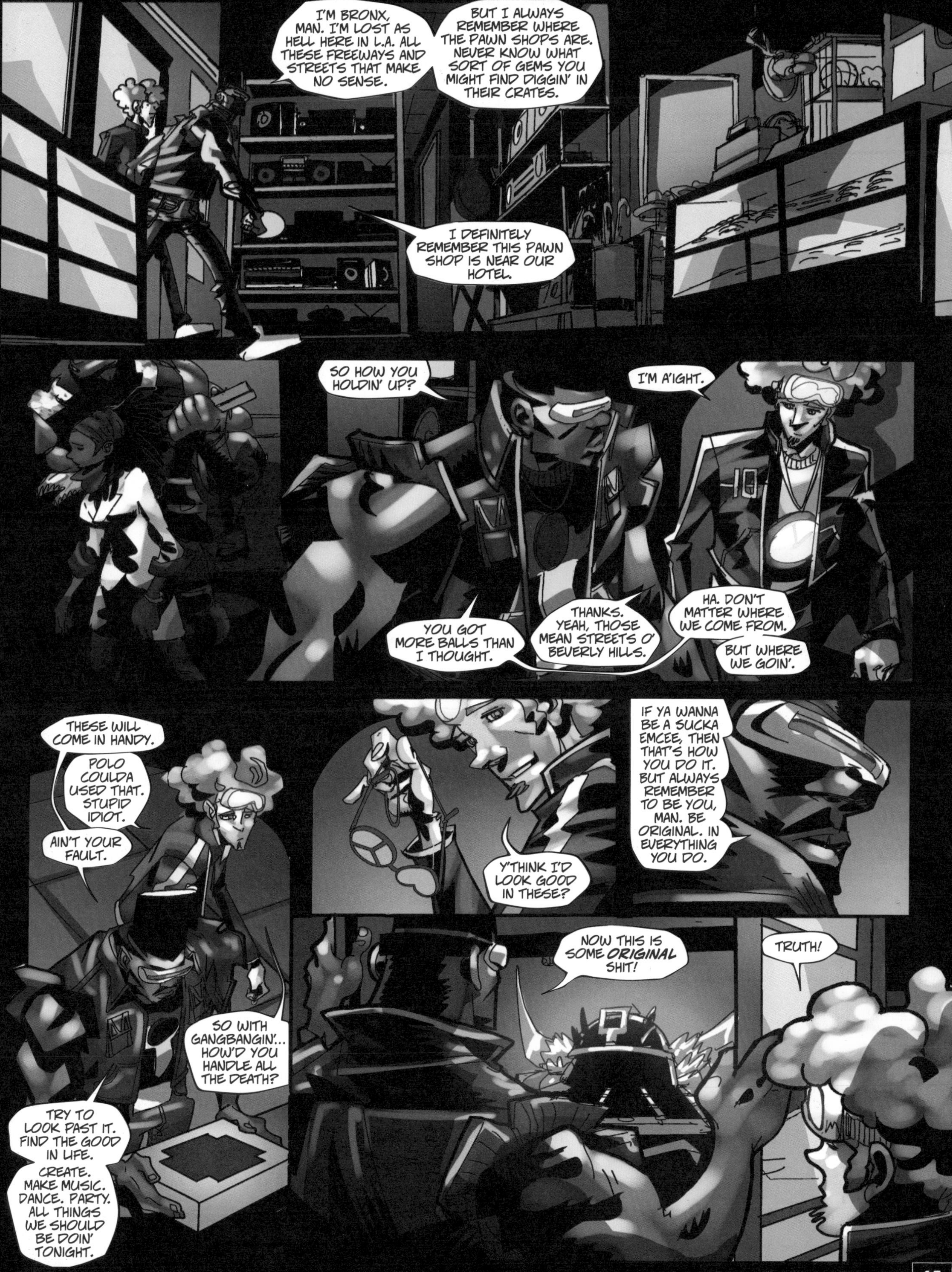

I'M BRONX, MAN. I'M LOST AS HELL HERE IN L.A. ALL THESE FREEWAYS AND STREETS THAT MAKE NO SENSE.
BUT I ALWAYS REMEMBER WHERE THE PAWN SHOPS ARE. NEVER KNOW WHAT SORT OF GEMS YOU MIGHT FIND DIGGIN' IN THEIR CRATES.
I DEFINITELY REMEMBER THIS PAWN SHOP IS NEAR OUR HOTEL.
SO HOW YOU HOLDIN' UP?
I'M A'IGHT.
YOU GOT MORE BALLS THAN I THOUGHT.
THANKS. YEAH, THOSE MEAN STREETS O' BEVERLY HILLS.
HA. DON'T MATTER WHERE WE COME FROM.
BUT WHERE WE GOIN'.
THESE WILL COME IN HANDY.
POLO COULDA USED THAT. STUPID IDIOT.
AIN'T YOUR FAULT.
Y'THINK I'D LOOK GOOD IN THESE?
IF YA WANNA BE A SUCKA EMCEE, THEN THAT'S HOW YOU DO IT. BUT ALWAYS REMEMBER TO BE YOU, MAN. BE ORIGINAL. IN EVERYTHING YOU DO.
SO WITH GANGBANGIN'... HOW'D YOU HANDLE ALL THE DEATH?
TRY TO LOOK PAST IT. FIND THE GOOD IN LIFE.
CREATE. MAKE MUSIC. DANCE. PARTY. ALL THINGS WE SHOULD BE DOIN' TONIGHT.
NOW THIS IS SOME ORIGINAL SHIT!
TRUTH!

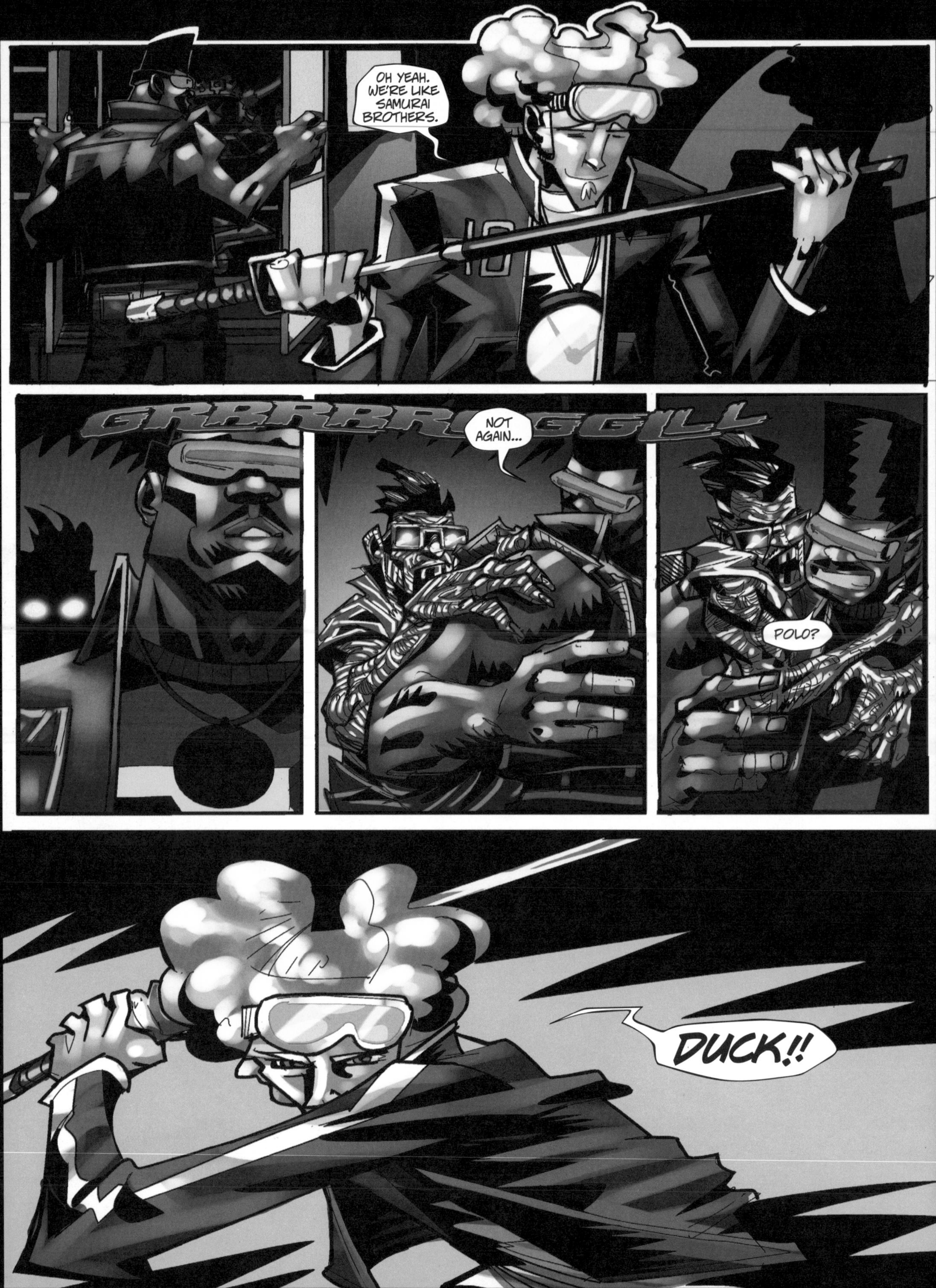

OH YEAH. WE'RE LIKE SAMURAI BROTHERS.
GRRRRRGGILL
NOT AGAIN...
POLO?
DUCK!!

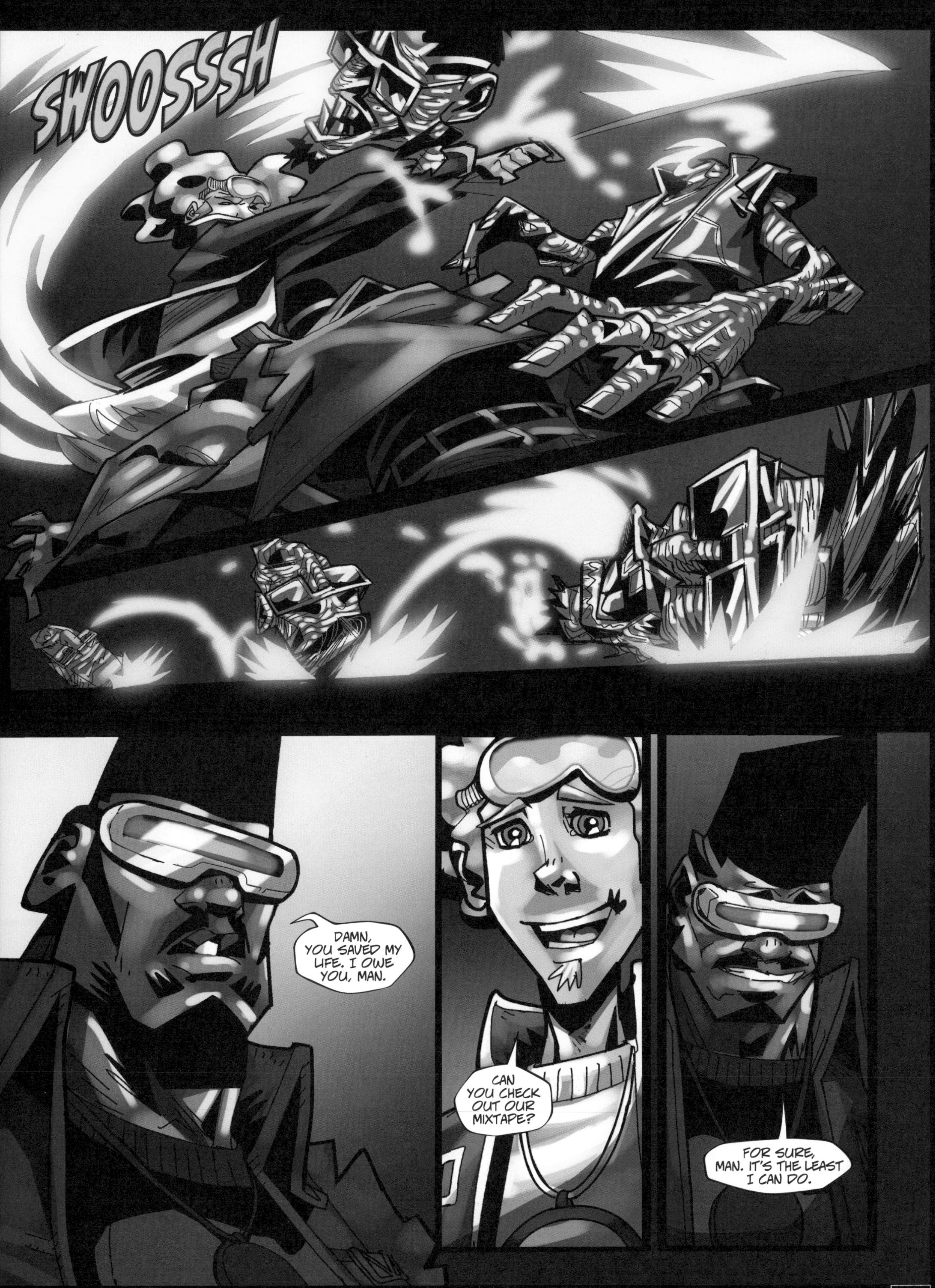
SWOOSSSH
DAMN, YOU SAVED MY LIFE. I OWE YOU, MAN.
CAN YOU CHECK OUT OUR MIXTAPE?
FOR SURE, MAN. IT'S THE LEAST I CAN DO.

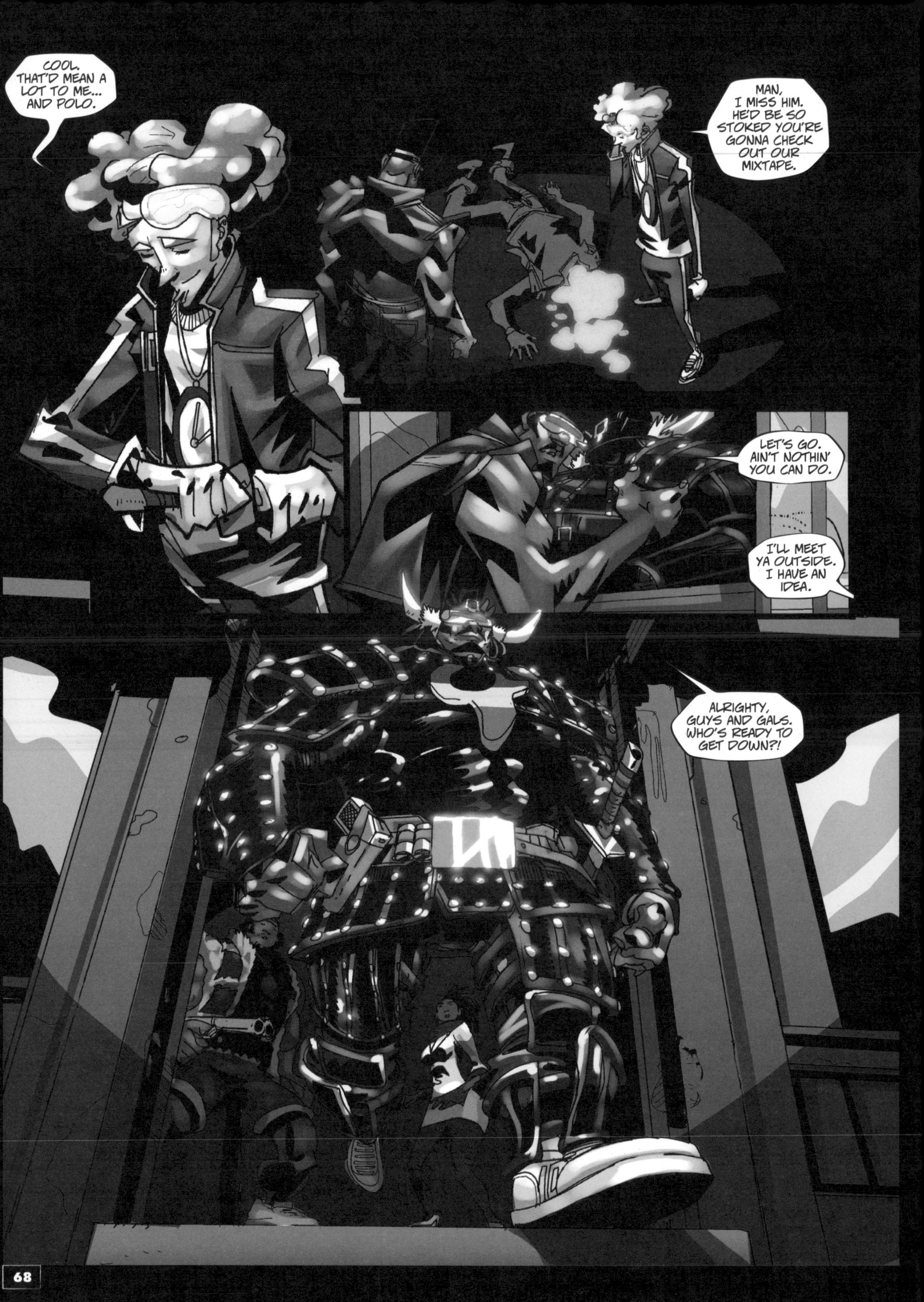
COOL. THAT'D MEAN A LOT TO ME... AND POLO.
MAN, I MISS HIM. HE'D BE SO STOKED YOU'RE GONNA CHECK OUT OUR MIXTAPE.
LET'S GO. AIN'T NOTHIN' YOU CAN DO.
I'LL MEET YA OUTSIDE. I HAVE AN IDEA.
ALRIGHTY, GUYS AND GALS. WHO'S READY TO GET DOWN?!

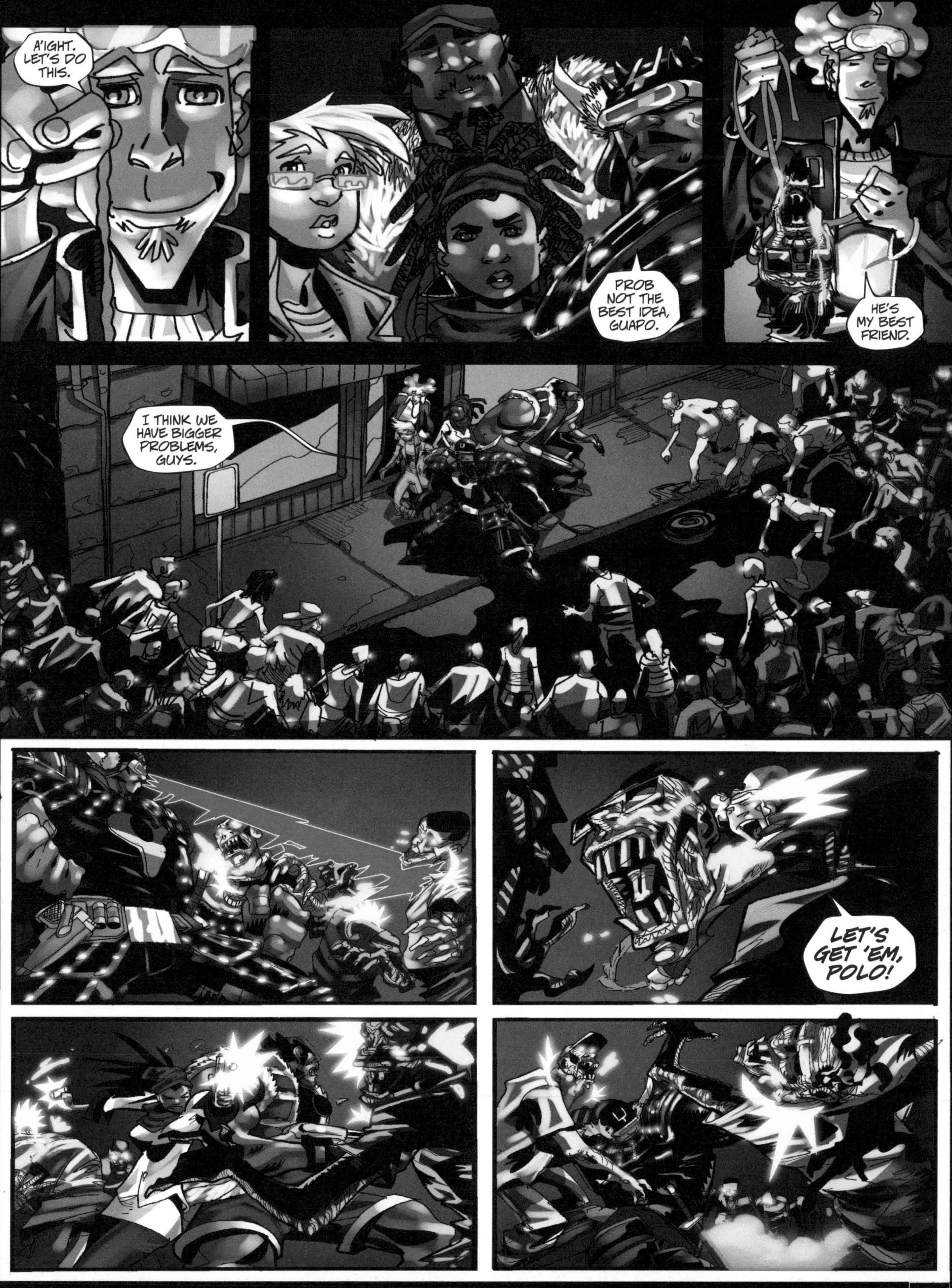
A'IGHT. LET'S DO THIS.
PROB NOT THE BEST IDEA, GUAPO.
HE'S MY BEST FRIEND.
I THINK WE HAVE BIGGER PROBLEMS, GUYS.
LET'S GET 'EM, POLO!

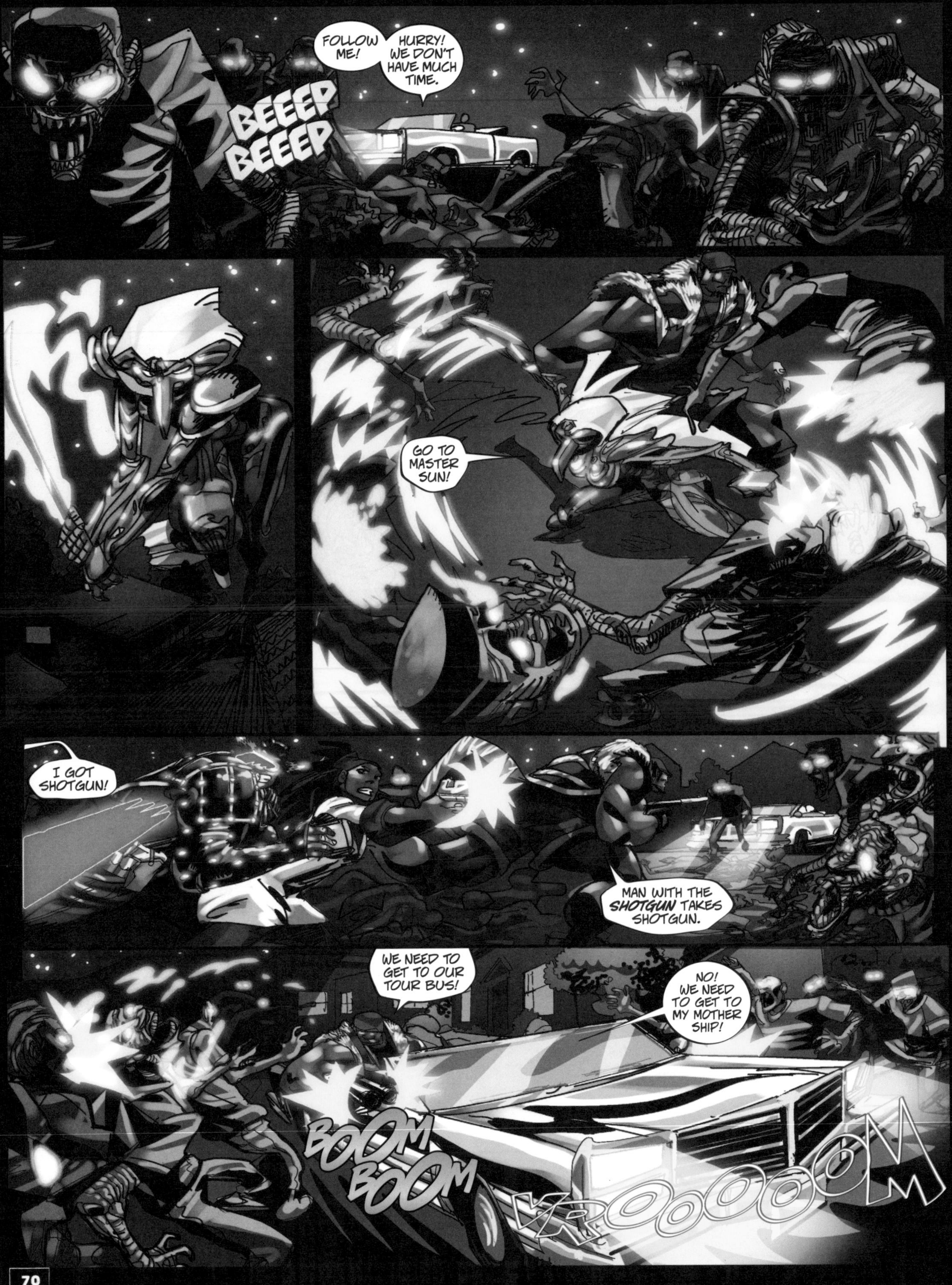
FOLLOW ME!
HURRY! WE DON'T HAVE MUCH TIME.
BEEEP BEEEP
GO TO MASTER SUN!
I GOT SHOTGUN!
MAN WITH THE SHOTGUN TAKES SHOTGUN.
WE NEED TO GET TO OUR TOUR BUS!
NO! WE NEED TO GET TO MY MOTHER SHIP!
BOOM BOOM
VROOOOOOOM

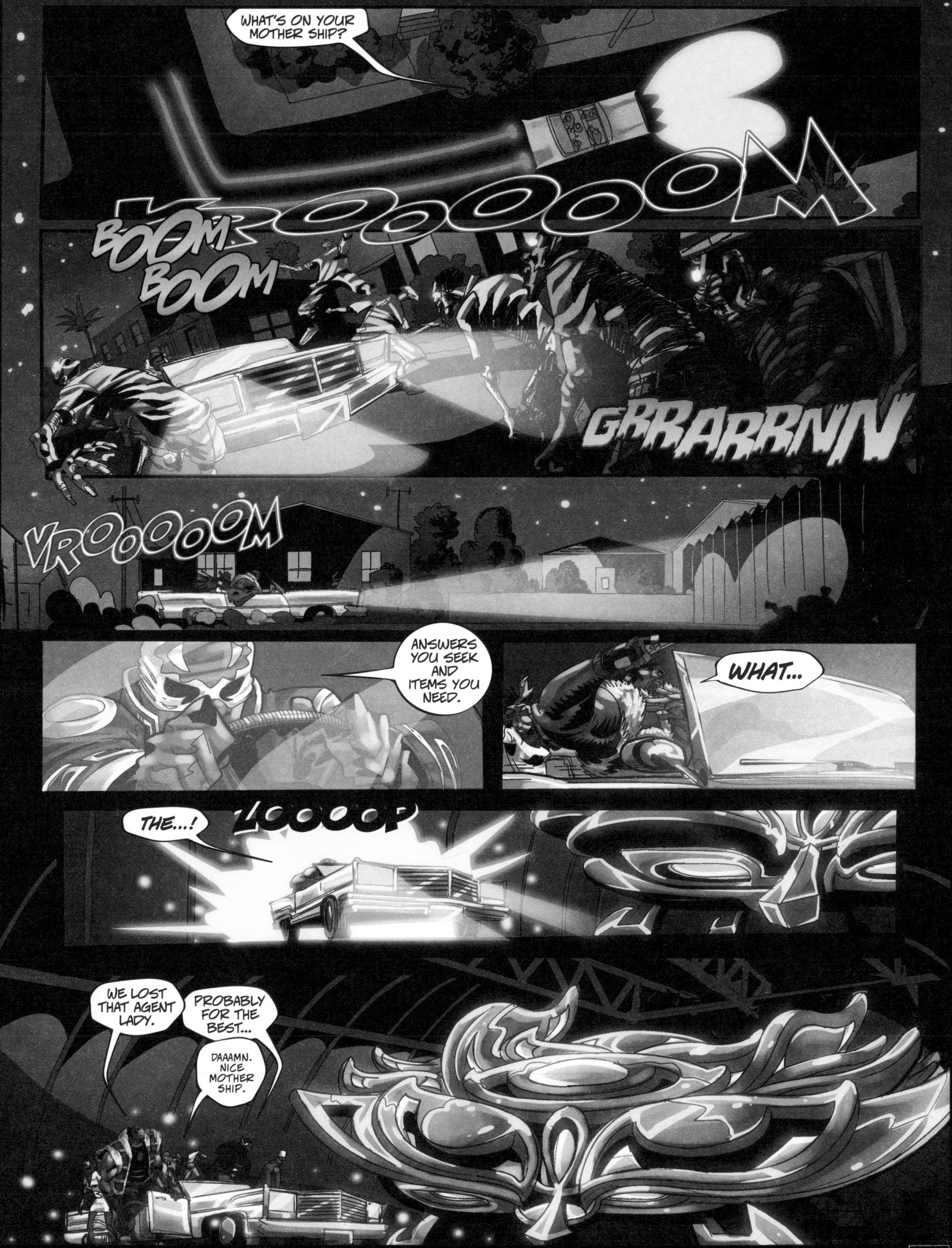
WHAT'S ON YOUR MOTHER SHIP?
VROOOOOOM
BOOM BOOM
GRRARRNN
VROOOOOM
ANSWERS YOU SEEK AND ITEMS YOU NEED.
WHAT...
THE...!
ZOOOOOP
WE LOST THAT AGENT LADY.
PROBABLY FOR THE BEST...
DAAAMN. NICE MOTHER SHIP.

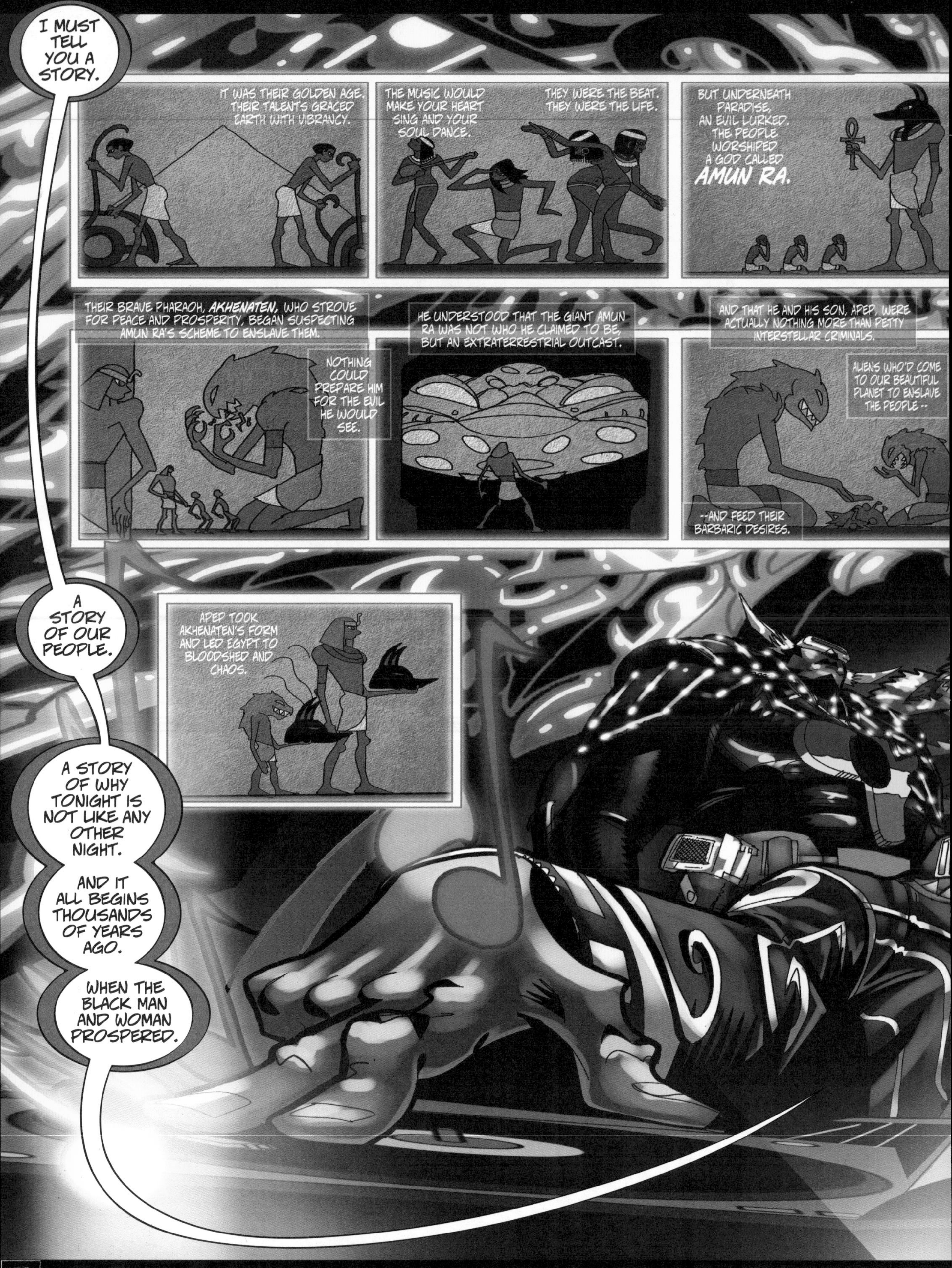
I MUST TELL YOU A STORY.
IT WAS THEIR GOLDEN AGE. THEIR TALENTS GRACED EARTH WITH VIBRANCY.
THE MUSIC WOULD MAKE YOUR HEART SING AND YOUR SOUL DANCE.
THEY WERE THE BEAT. THEY WERE THE LIFE.
BUT UNDERNEATH PARADISE, AN EVIL LURKED. THE PEOPLE WORSHIPED A GOD CALLED AMUN RA.
THEIR BRAVE PHARAOH, AKHENATEN, WHO STROVE FOR PEACE AND PROSPERITY, BEGAN SUSPECTING AMUN RA'S SCHEME TO ENSLAVE THEM.
NOTHING COULD PREPARE HIM FOR THE EVIL HE WOULD SEE.
HE UNDERSTOOD THAT THE GIANT AMUN RA WAS NOT WHO HE CLAIMED TO BE, BUT AN EXTRATERRESTRIAL OUTCAST.
AND THAT HE AND HIS SON, APEP, WERE ACTUALLY NOTHING MORE THAN PETTY INTERSTELLAR CRIMINALS.
ALIENS WHO'D COME TO OUR BEAUTIFUL PLANET TO ENSLAVE THE PEOPLE --
--AND FEED THEIR BARBARIC DESIRES.
A STORY OF OUR PEOPLE.
APEP TOOK AKHENATEN'S FORM AND LED EGYPT TO BLOODSHED AND CHAOS.
A STORY OF WHY TONIGHT IS NOT LIKE ANY OTHER NIGHT.
AND IT ALL BEGINS THOUSANDS OF YEARS AGO.
WHEN THE BLACK MAN AND WOMAN PROSPERED.

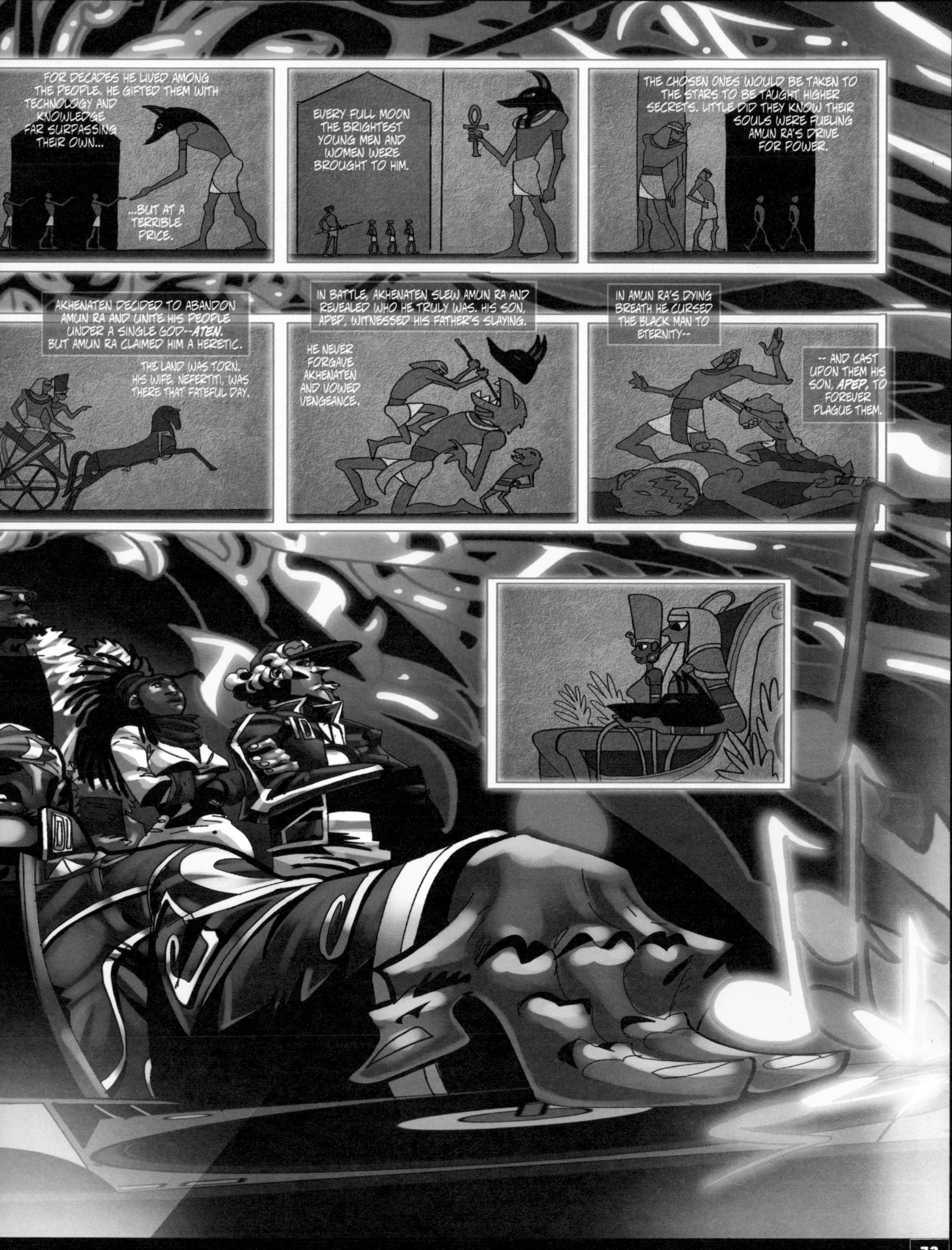

FOR DECADES HE LIVED AMONG THE PEOPLE. HE GIFTED THEM WITH TECHNOLOGY AND KNOWLEDGE FAR SURPASSING THEIR OWN...
...BUT AT A TERRIBLE PRICE.
EVERY FULL MOON THE BRIGHTEST YOUNG MEN AND WOMEN WERE BROUGHT TO HIM.
THE CHOSEN ONES WOULD BE TAKEN TO THE STARS TO BE TAUGHT HIGHER SECRETS. LITTLE DID THEY KNOW THEIR SOULS WERE FUELING AMUN RA'S DRIVE FOR POWER.
AKHENATEN DECIDED TO ABANDON AMUN RA AND UNITE HIS PEOPLE UNDER A SINGLE GOD--ATEN. BUT AMUN RA CLAIMED HIM A HERETIC.
THE LAND WAS TORN. HIS WIFE, NEFERTITI, WAS THERE THAT FATEFUL DAY.
IN BATTLE, AKHENATEN SLEW AMUN RA AND REVEALED WHO HE TRULY WAS. HIS SON, APEP, WITNESSED HIS FATHER'S SLAYING.
HE NEVER FORGAVE AKHENATEN AND VOWED VENGEANCE.
IN AMUN RA'S DYING BREATH HE CURSED THE BLACK MAN TO ETERNITY--
-- AND CAST UPON THEM HIS SON, APEP, TO FOREVER PLAGUE THEM.

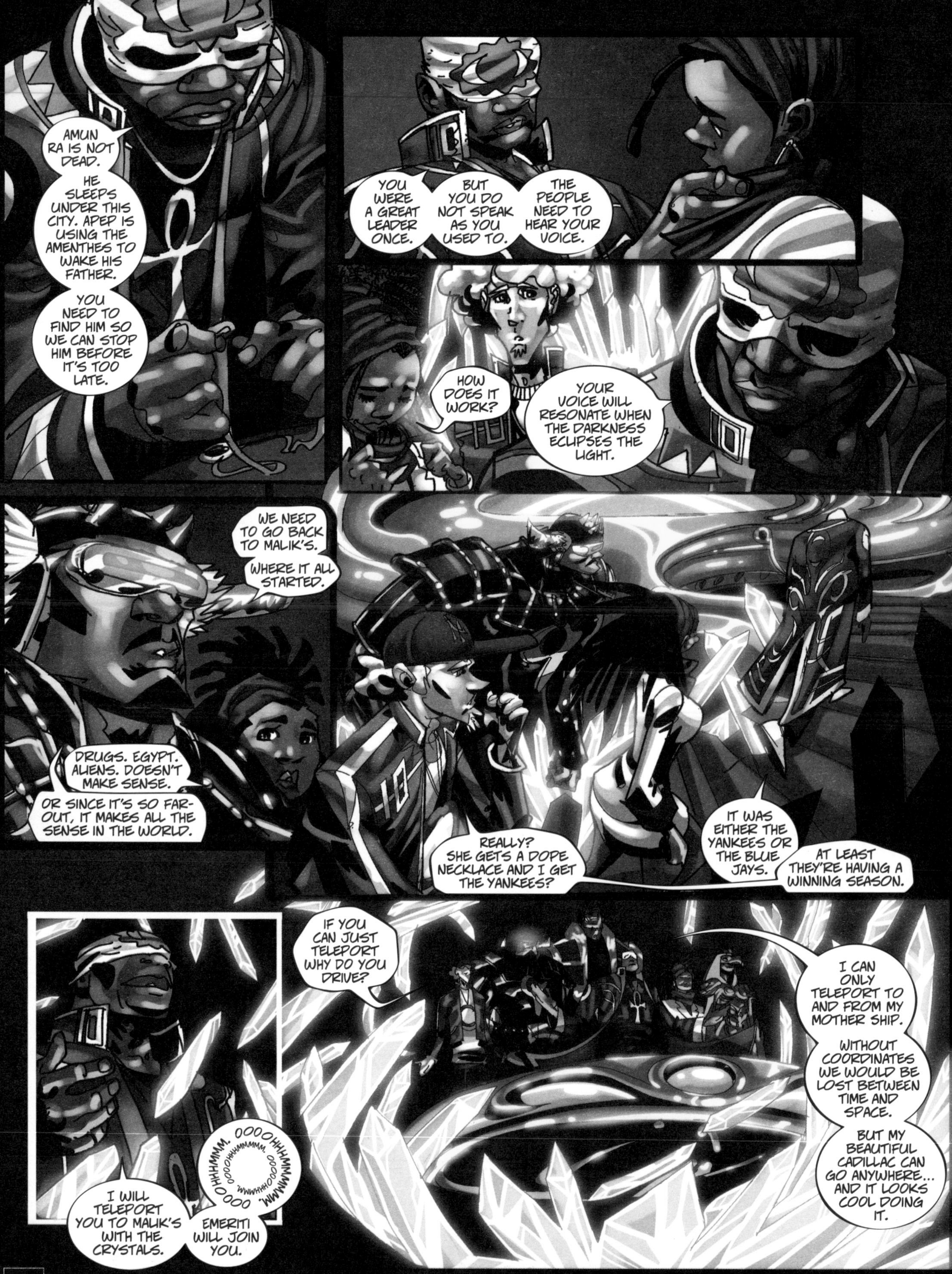
AMUN RA IS NOT DEAD.
HE SLEEPS UNDER THIS CITY. APEP IS USING THE AMENTHES TO WAKE HIS FATHER.
YOU NEED TO FIND HIM SO WE CAN STOP HIM BEFORE IT'S TOO LATE.
YOU WERE A GREAT LEADER ONCE.
BUT YOU DO NOT SPEAK AS YOU USED TO.
THE PEOPLE NEED TO HEAR YOUR VOICE.
HOW DOES IT WORK?
YOUR VOICE WILL RESONATE WHEN THE DARKNESS ECLIPSES THE LIGHT.
WE NEED TO GO BACK TO MALIK'S.
WHERE IT ALL STARTED.
DRUGS. EGYPT. ALIENS. DOESN'T MAKE SENSE.
OR SINCE IT'S SO FAR-OUT, IT MAKES ALL THE SENSE IN THE WORLD.
REALLY? SHE GETS A DOPE NECKLACE AND I GET THE YANKEES?
IT WAS EITHER THE YANKEES OR THE BLUE JAYS.
AT LEAST THEY'RE HAVING A WINNING SEASON.
I WILL TELEPORT YOU TO MALIK'S WITH THE CRYSTALS.
EMERITI WILL JOIN YOU.
OOOOHHHMMMM. OOOOHHHMMMM. OOOOHHHMMMM. OOOOHHHMMMM.
IF YOU CAN JUST TELEPORT WHY DO YOU DRIVE?
I CAN ONLY TELEPORT TO AND FROM MY MOTHER SHIP.
WITHOUT COORDINATES WE WOULD BE LOST BETWEEN TIME AND SPACE.
BUT MY BEAUTIFUL CADILLAC CAN GO ANYWHERE... AND IT LOOKS COOL DOING IT.

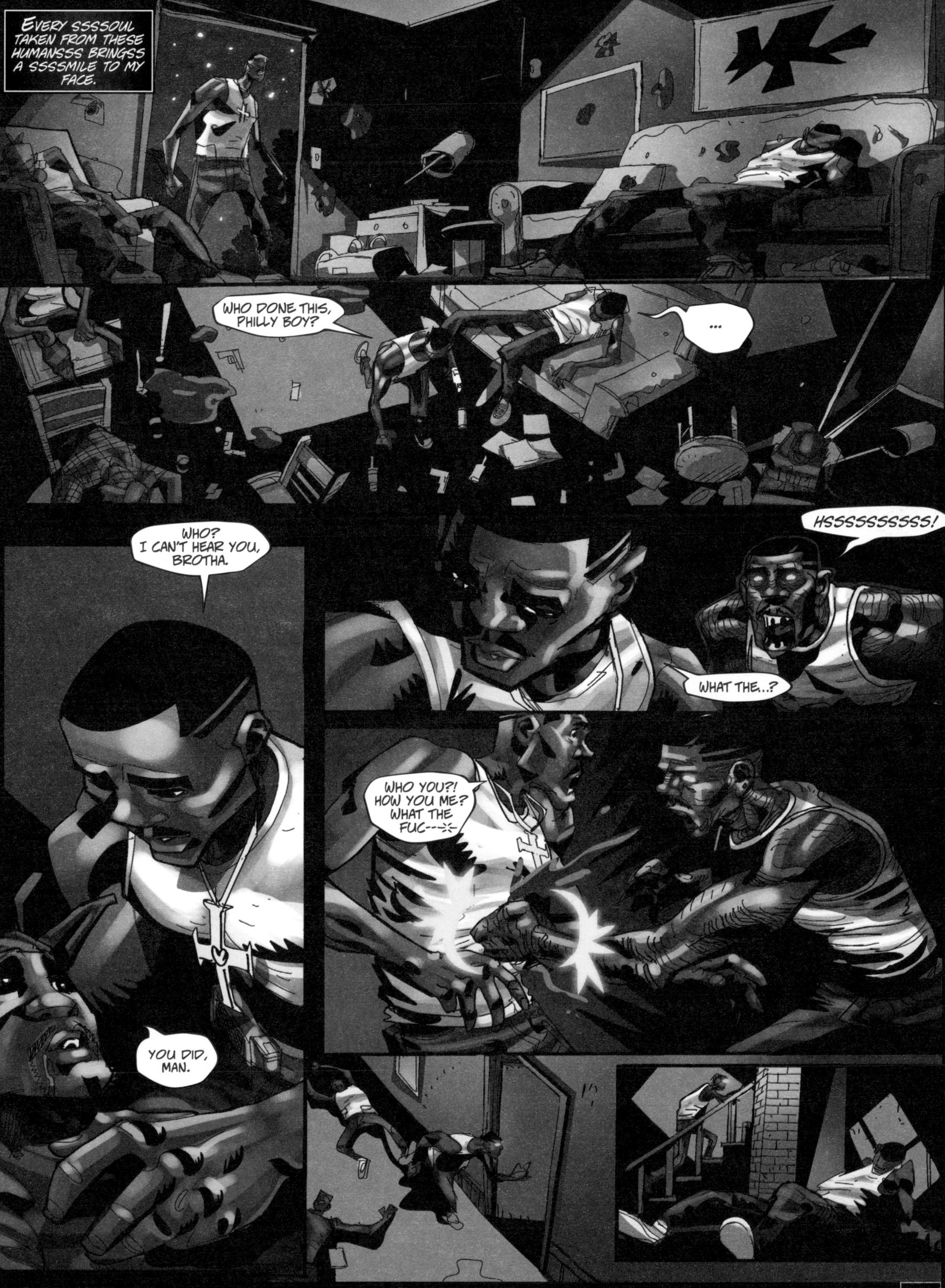
EVERY SSSSOUL TAKEN FROM THESE HUMANSSS BRINGSS A SSSSMILE TO MY FACE.
WHO DONE THIS, PHILLY BOY?
...
WHO? I CAN'T HEAR YOU, BROTHA.
YOU DID, MAN.
HSSSSSSSSSS!
WHAT THE...?
WHO YOU?! HOW YOU ME? WHAT THE FUC--

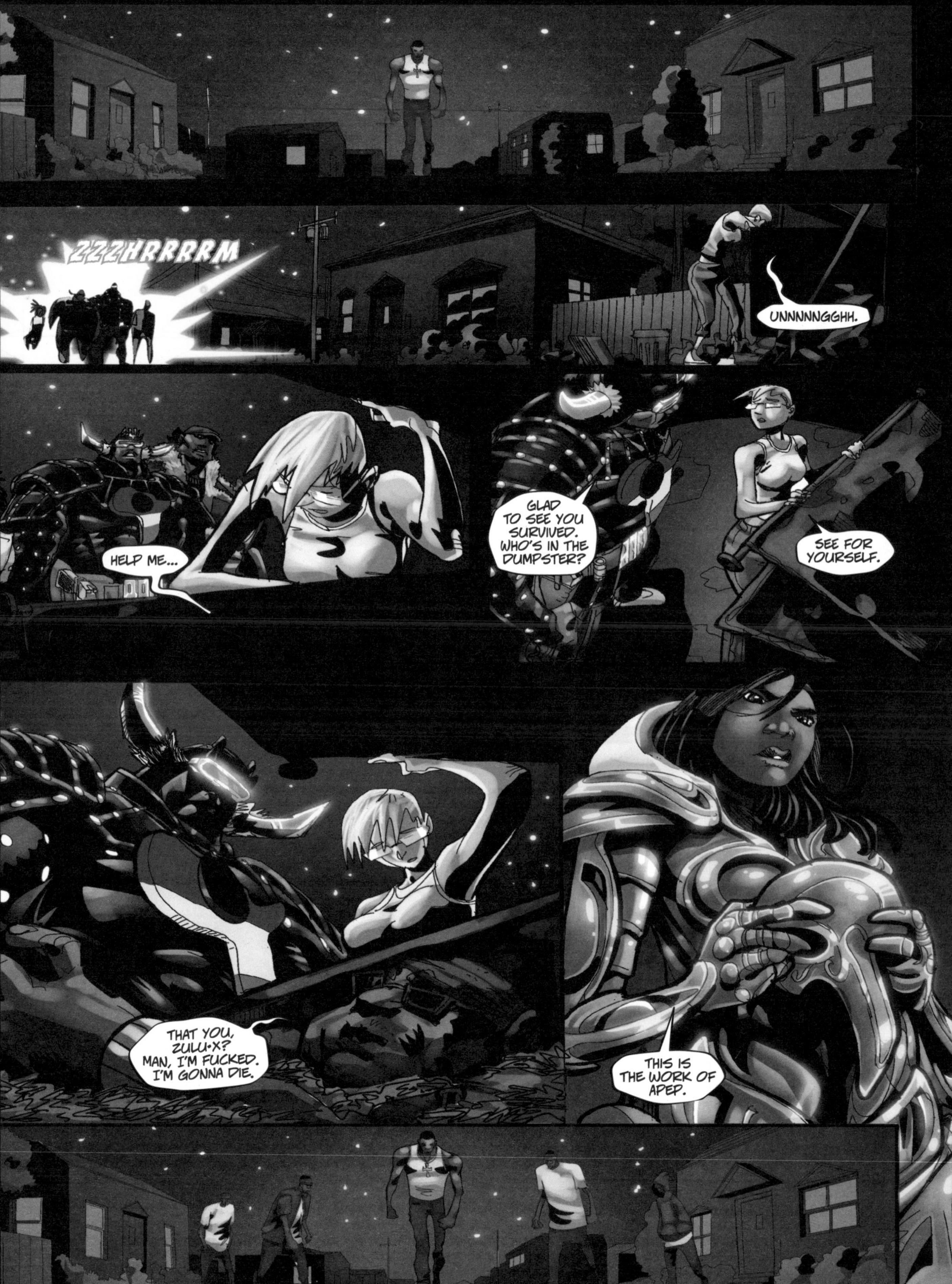
ZZZHRRRRM
UNNNNNGGHH.
HELP ME...
GLAD TO SEE YOU SURVIVED. WHO'S IN THE DUMPSTER?
SEE FOR YOURSELF.
THAT YOU, ZULU•X? MAN, I'M FUCKED. I'M GONNA DIE.
THIS IS THE WORK OF APEP.

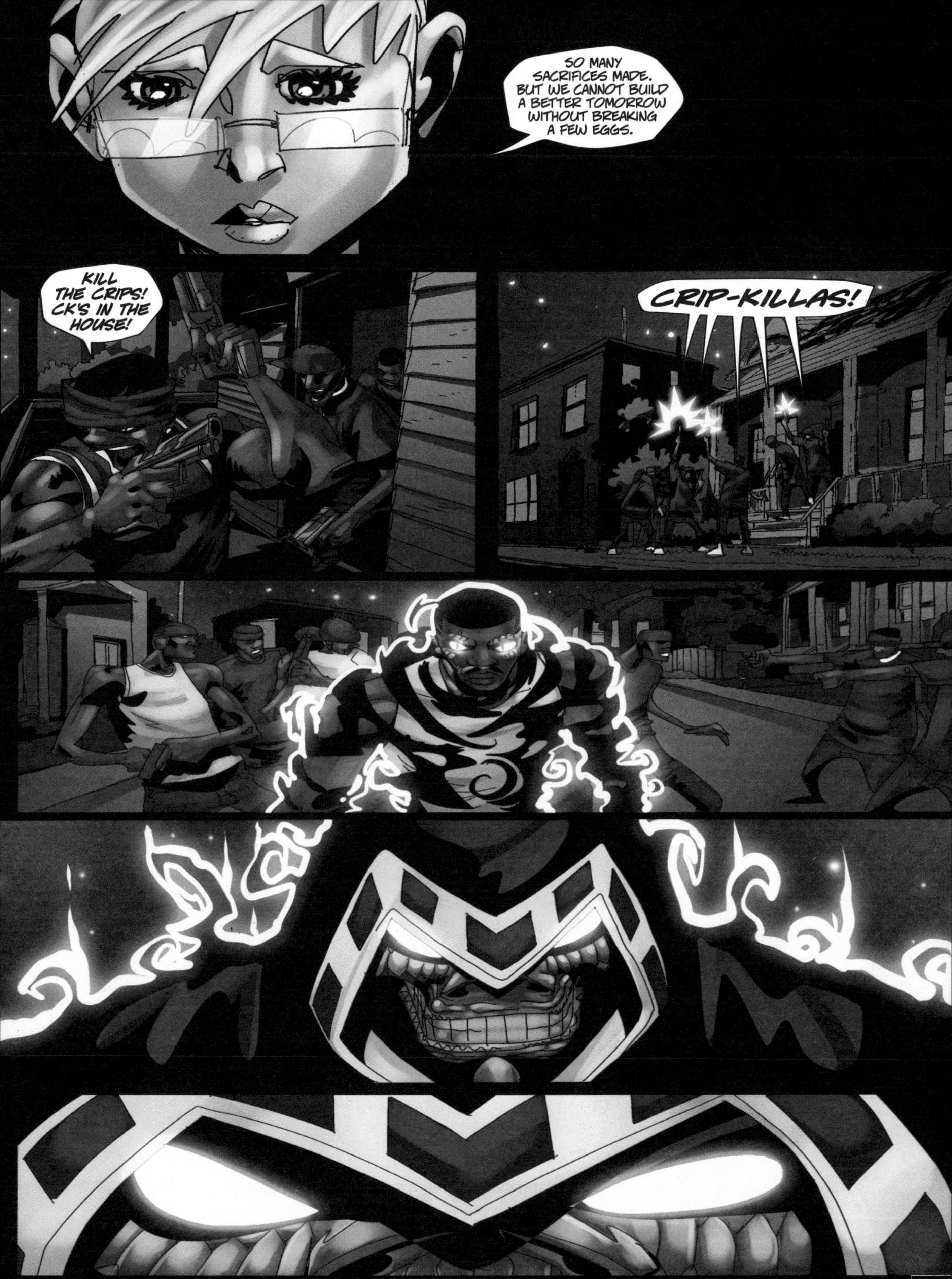

SO MANY SACRIFICES MADE. BUT WE CANNOT BUILD A BETTER TOMORROW WITHOUT BREAKING A FEW EGGS.
KILL THE CRIPS! CK'S IN THE HOUSE!
CRIP-KILLAS!

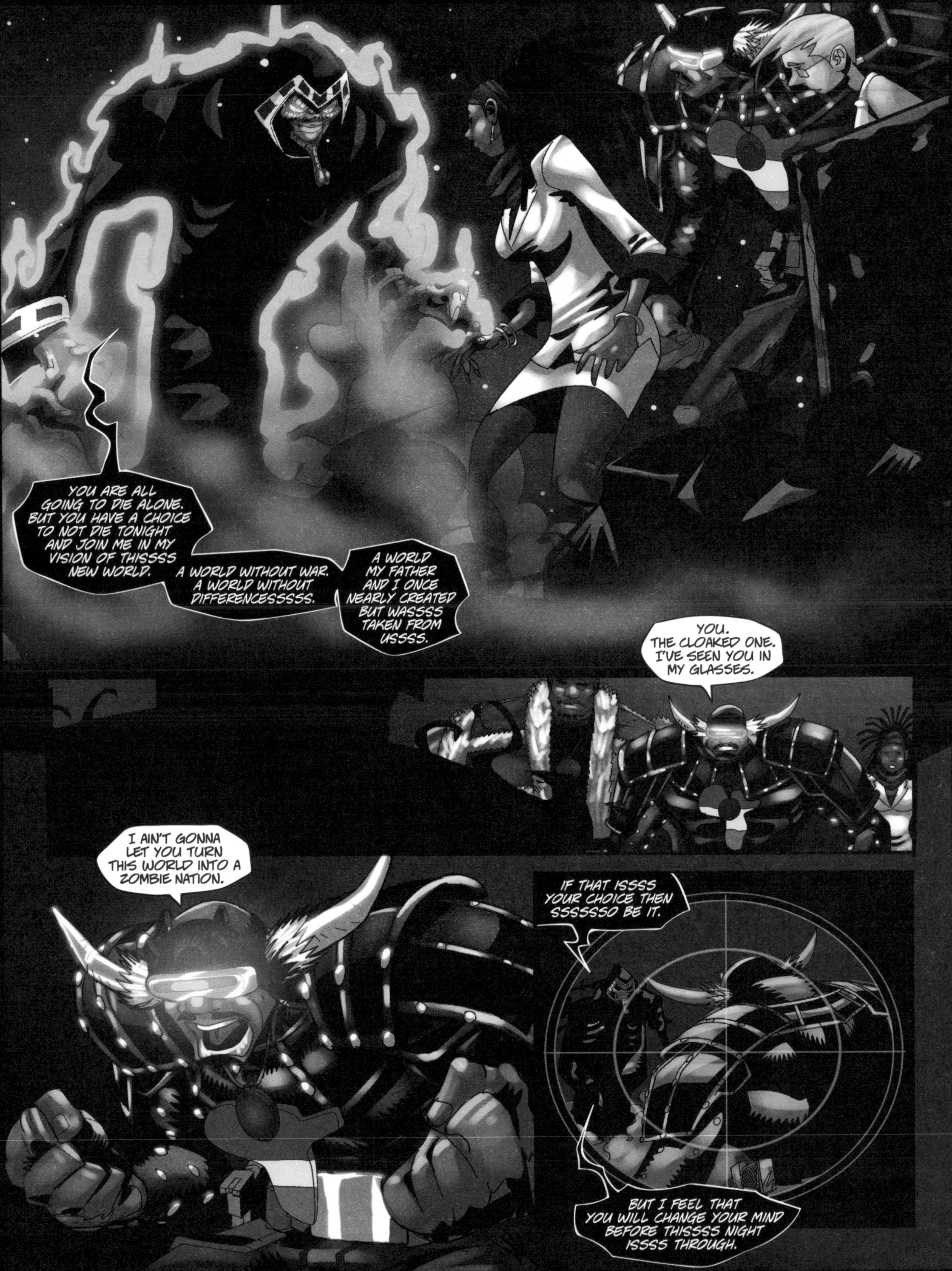
YOU ARE ALL GOING TO DIE ALONE. BUT YOU HAVE A CHOICE TO NOT DIE TONIGHT AND JOIN ME IN MY VISION OF THISSS NEW WORLD.
A WORLD WITHOUT WAR. A WORLD WITHOUT DIFFERENCESSSSS.
A WORLD MY FATHER AND I ONCE NEARLY CREATED BUT WASSSS TAKEN FROM USSSS.
YOU. THE CLOAKED ONE. I'VE SEEN YOU IN MY GLASSES.
I AIN'T GONNA LET YOU TURN THIS WORLD INTO A ZOMBIE NATION.
IF THAT ISSSS YOUR CHOICE THEN SSSSSSO BE IT.
BUT I FEEL THAT YOU WILL CHANGE YOUR MIND BEFORE THISSSS NIGHT ISSSS THROUGH.

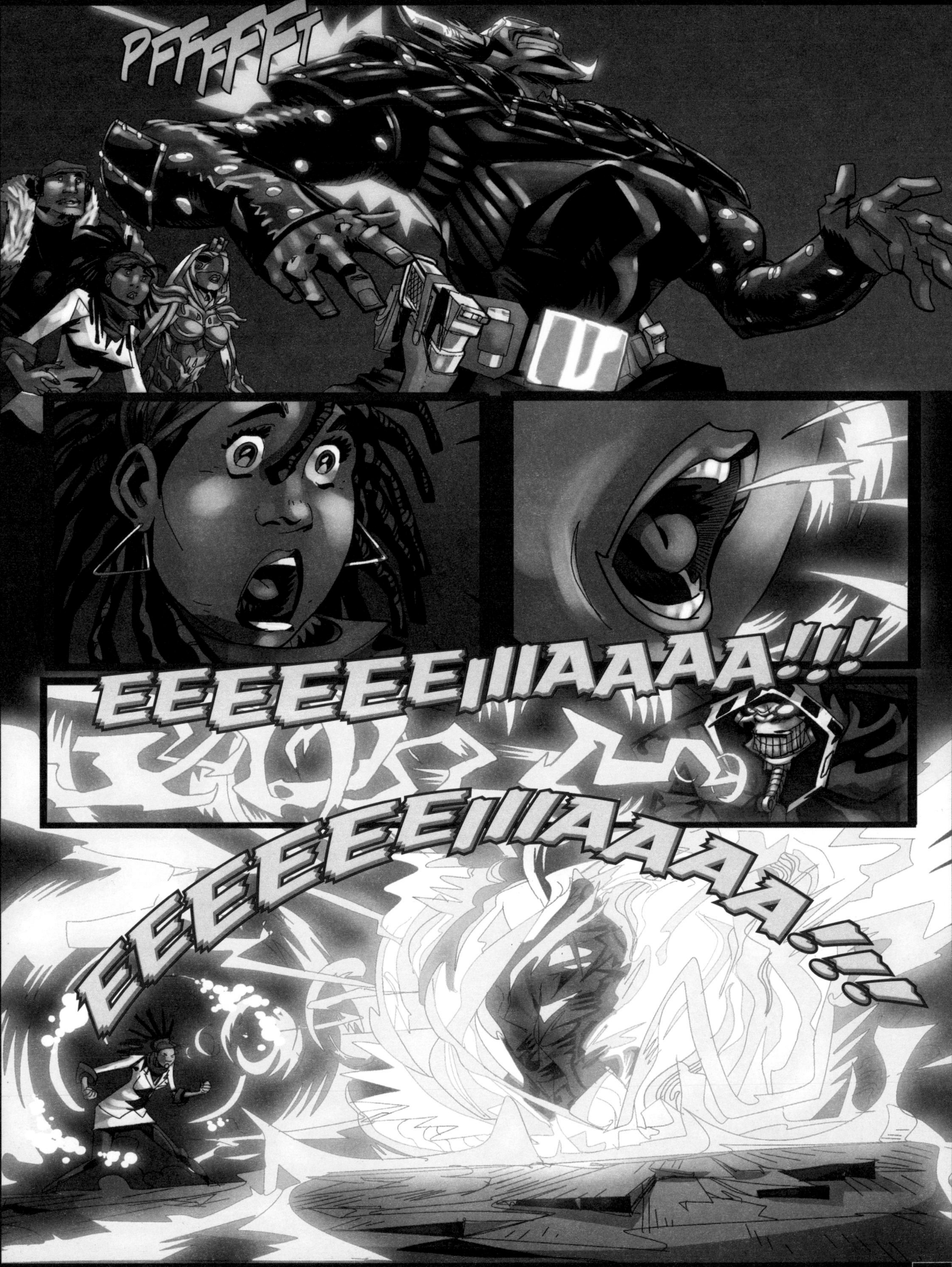
PFFFFFT
EEEEEEIIIIAAAAA!!!
EEEEEEIIIIAAAAA!!!!

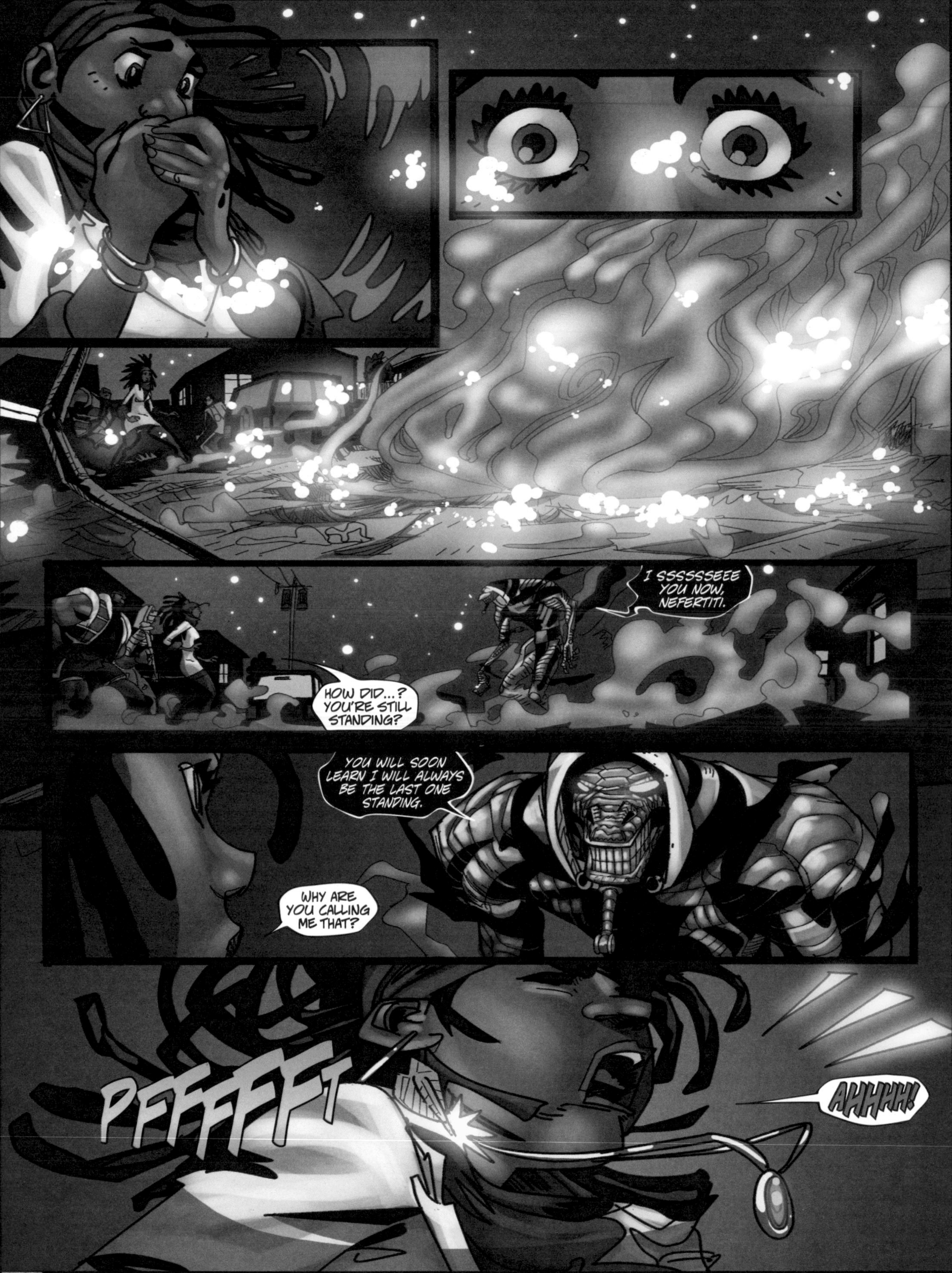
I SSSSSSEEE YOU NOW, NEFERTITI.
HOW DID...? YOU'RE STILL STANDING?
YOU WILL SOON LEARN I WILL ALWAYS BE THE LAST ONE STANDING.
WHY ARE YOU CALLING ME THAT?
PFFFFFT
AHHHH!

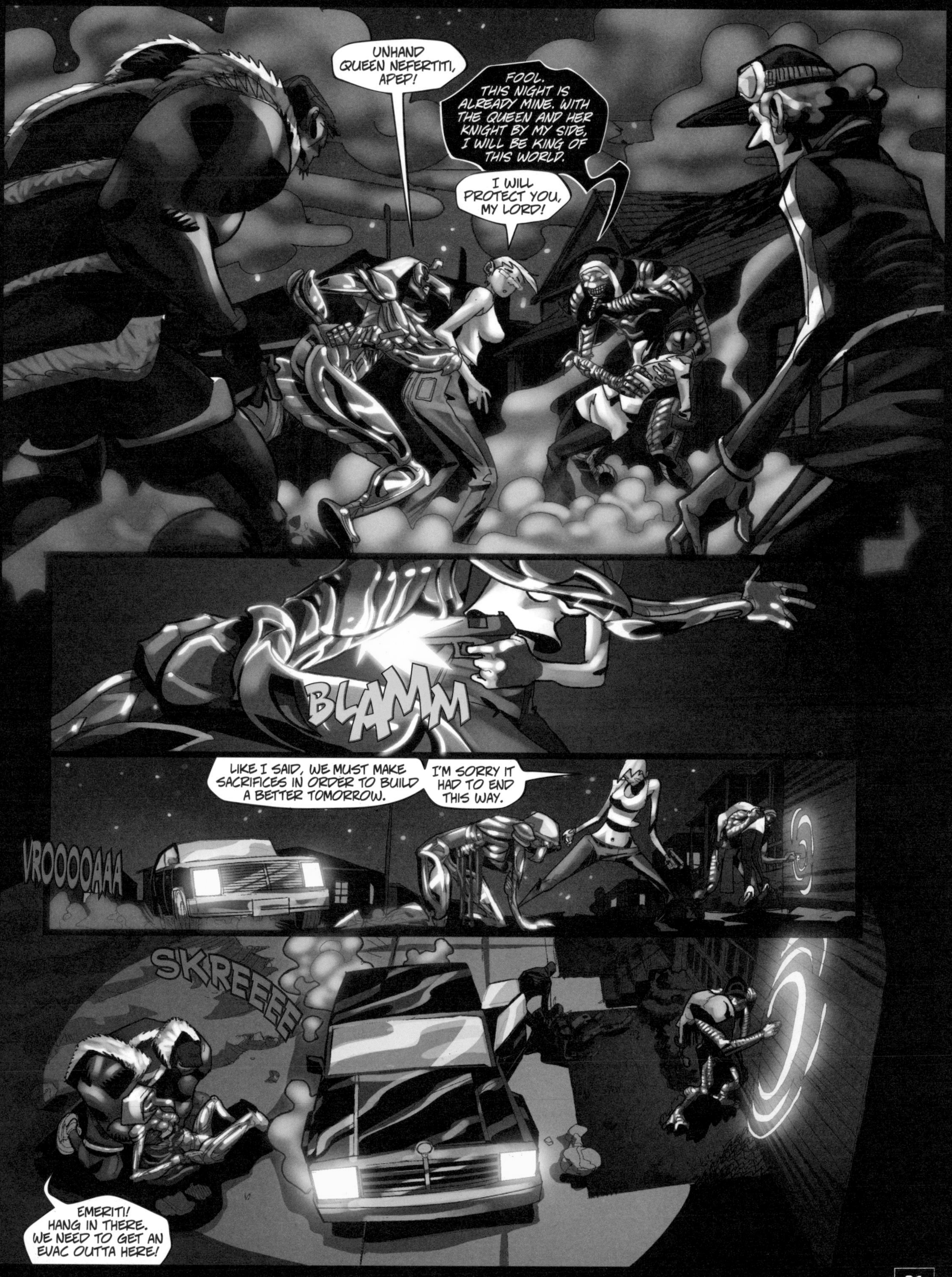
UNHAND QUEEN NEFERTITI, APEP!
FOOL. THIS NIGHT IS ALREADY MINE. WITH THE QUEEN AND HER KNIGHT BY MY SIDE, I WILL BE KING OF THIS WORLD.
I WILL PROTECT YOU, MY LORD!
BLAMM
LIKE I SAID, WE MUST MAKE SACRIFICES IN ORDER TO BUILD A BETTER TOMORROW.
I'M SORRY IT HAD TO END THIS WAY.
VROOOOAAA
SKREEEEE
EMERITI! HANG IN THERE. WE NEED TO GET AN EVAC OUTTA HERE!

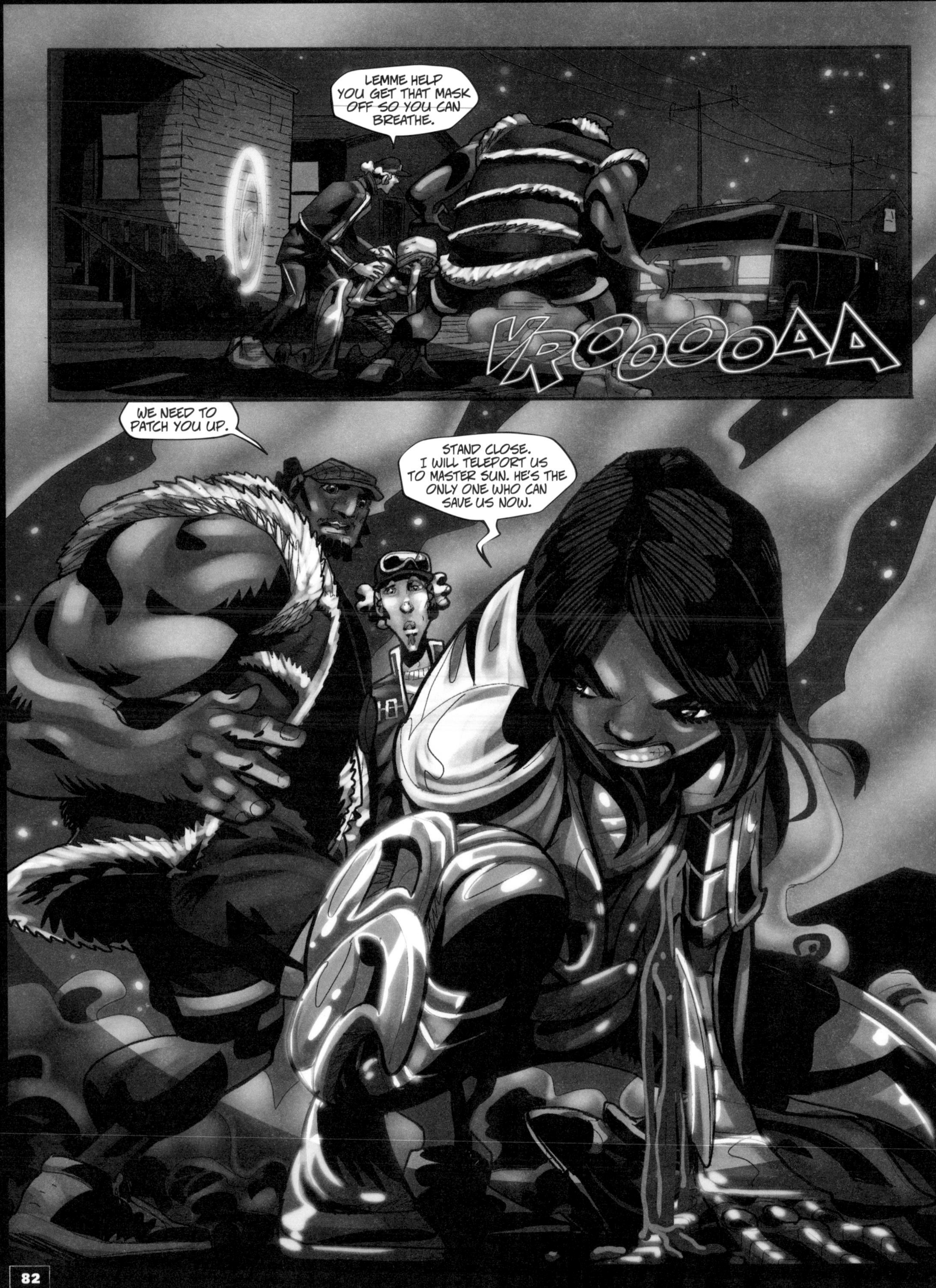
LEMME HELP YOU GET THAT MASK OFF SO YOU CAN BREATHE.
VROOOOOAA
WE NEED TO PATCH YOU UP.
STAND CLOSE. I WILL TELEPORT US TO MASTER SUN. HE'S THE ONLY ONE WHO CAN SAVE US NOW.

MASTER SUN'S VERSE 20:17

EVERY EYE HAS A PUPIL
in the centre...
And that centre in
every eye is black...

Light does not mean good...
White light is a brain wash...
It means nothing...
Like a white lie isn't
innocent...
Every lie is foul...

Light is information, energy,
knowledge...

Black beckons light...
Black is the entity
that captures light...
The sun is in
a void of blackness...
That blackness is how
a star can exist.

A black hole can swallow all
knowledge and any amount of
energy and light...

What's on the other side of
a black hole is a brain...

Every healthy human
is connected
to a black hole...

Since every black hole is
connected
to a brain...

Don't let the zombies suck
your brain by infecting you
with ignorance and distortion...

The word used for black holes
in the eye is: "pupils"

Black eyed Pupils

The word for student who is in
search of knowledge is: "Pupil"

The absorber of light
and the pupil
to the cosmos

-Masters of the Sun

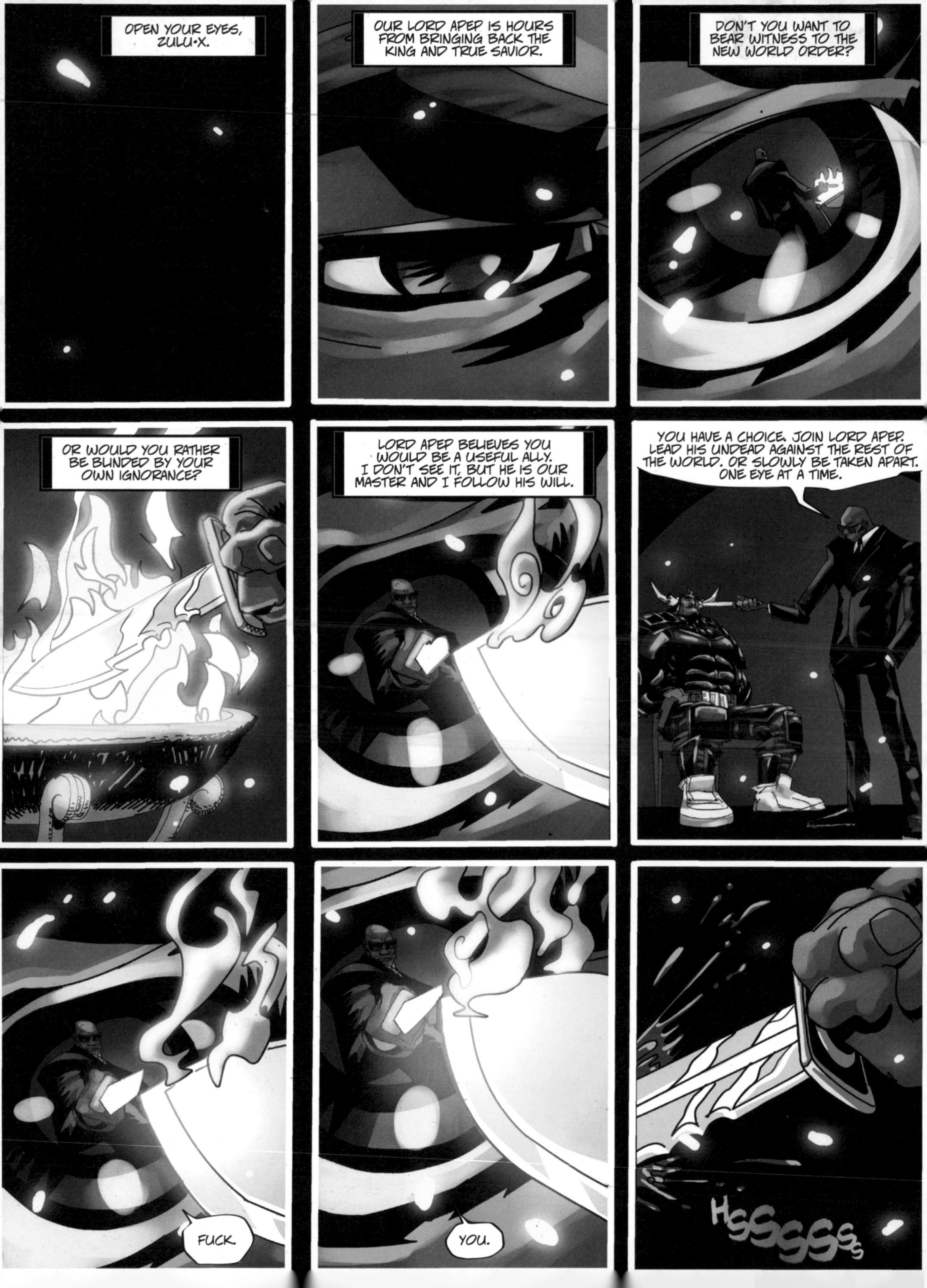
OPEN YOUR EYES, ZULU•X.
OUR LORD APEP IS HOURS FROM BRINGING BACK THE KING AND TRUE SAVIOR.
DON'T YOU WANT TO BEAR WITNESS TO THE NEW WORLD ORDER?
OR WOULD YOU RATHER BE BLINDED BY YOUR OWN IGNORANCE?
LORD APEP BELIEVES YOU WOULD BE A USEFUL ALLY. I DON'T SEE IT, BUT HE IS OUR MASTER AND I FOLLOW HIS WILL.
YOU HAVE A CHOICE. JOIN LORD APEP. LEAD HIS UNDEAD AGAINST THE REST OF THE WORLD. OR SLOWLY BE TAKEN APART. ONE EYE AT A TIME.
FUCK.
YOU.
HSSSSSS

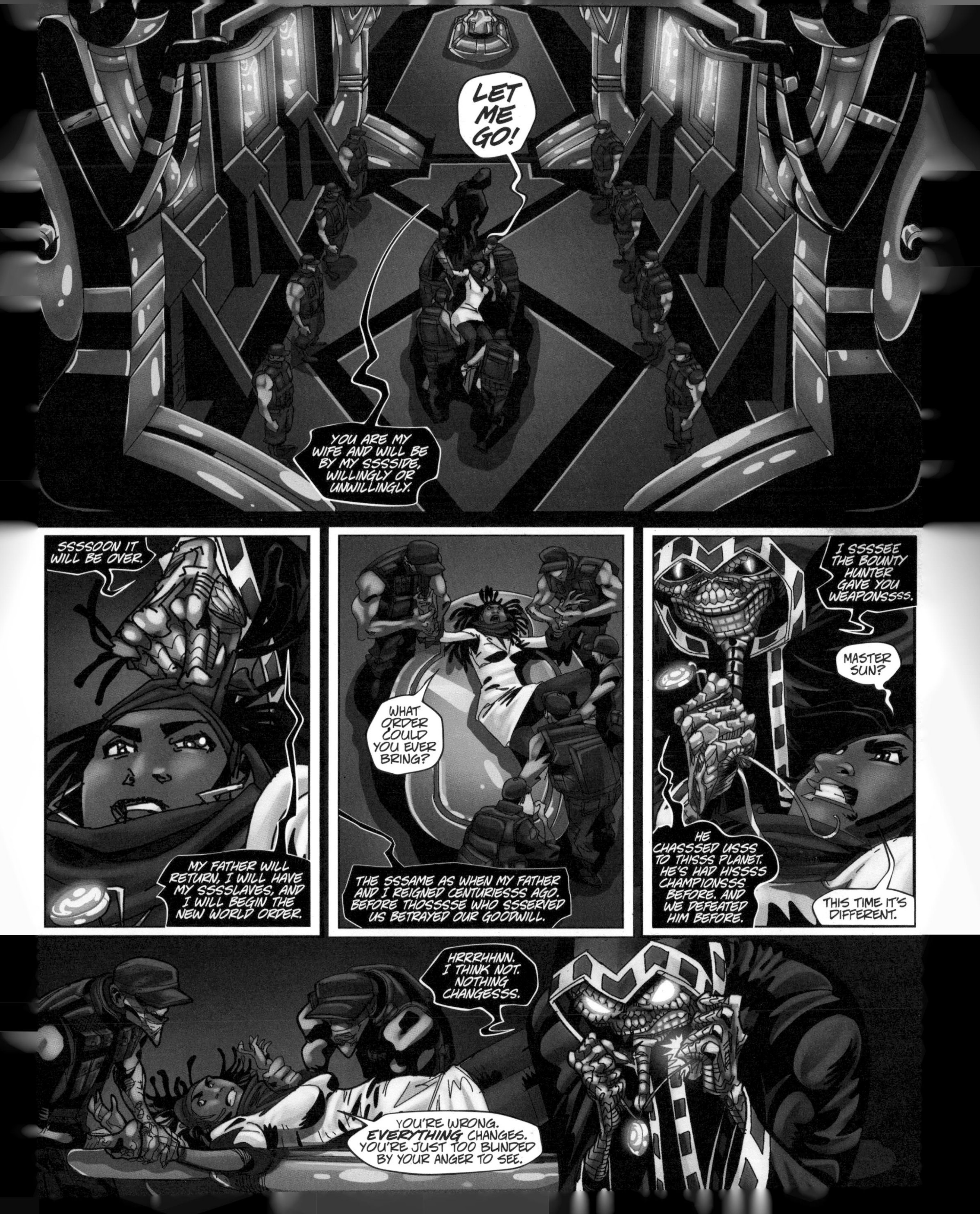
LET ME GO!
YOU ARE MY WIFE AND WILL BE BY MY SSSSIDE, WILLINGLY OR UNWILLINGLY.
SSSSOON IT WILL BE OVER.
MY FATHER WILL RETURN, I WILL HAVE MY SSSSLAVES, AND I WILL BEGIN THE NEW WORLD ORDER.
WHAT ORDER COULD YOU EVER BRING?
THE SSSAME AS WHEN MY FATHER AND I REIGNED CENTURIESSS AGO. BEFORE THOSSSSE WHO SSSERVED US BETRAYED OUR GOODWILL.
I SSSSEE THE BOUNTY HUNTER GAVE YOU WEAPONSSSS.
MASTER SUN?
HE CHASSSED USSS TO THISSS PLANET. HE'S HAD HISSSS CHAMPIONSSS BEFORE. AND WE DEFEATED HIM BEFORE.
THIS TIME IT'S DIFFERENT.
HRRRHHNN. I THINK NOT. NOTHING CHANGESSS.
YOU'RE WRONG. EVERYTHING CHANGES. YOU'RE JUST TOO BLINDED BY YOUR ANGER TO SEE.

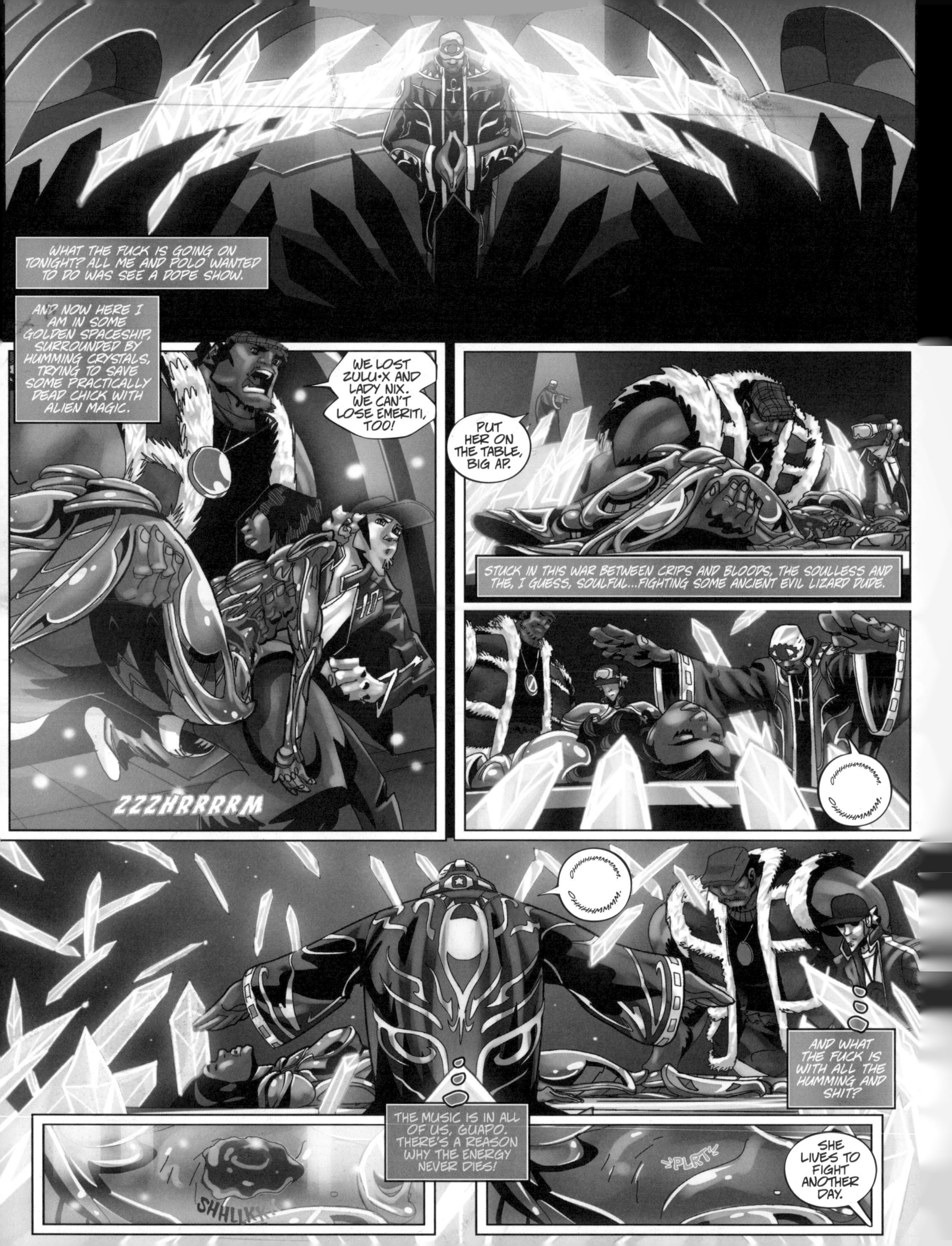
WHAT THE FUCK IS GOING ON TONIGHT? ALL ME AND POLO WANTED TO DO WAS SEE A DOPE SHOW.
AND NOW HERE I AM IN SOME GOLDEN SPACESHIP, SURROUNDED BY HUMMING CRYSTALS, TRYING TO SAVE SOME PRACTICALLY DEAD CHICK WITH ALIEN MAGIC.
WE LOST ZULU•X AND LADY NIX. WE CAN'T LOSE EMERITI, TOO!
ZZZHRRRRM
PUT HER ON THE TABLE, BIG AP.
STUCK IN THIS WAR BETWEEN CRIPS AND BLOODS, THE SOULLESS AND THE, I GUESS, SOULFUL...FIGHTING SOME ANCIENT EVIL LIZARD DUDE.
OHHHHHMMMMM.
OHHHHHMMMM.
OHHHHHMMMMM.
OHHHHHMMMM.
AND WHAT THE FUCK IS WITH ALL THE HUMMING AND SHIT?
THE MUSIC IS IN ALL OF US, GUAPO. THERE'S A REASON WHY THE ENERGY NEVER DIES!
SHHLIKK
PLRT
SHE LIVES TO FIGHT ANOTHER DAY.

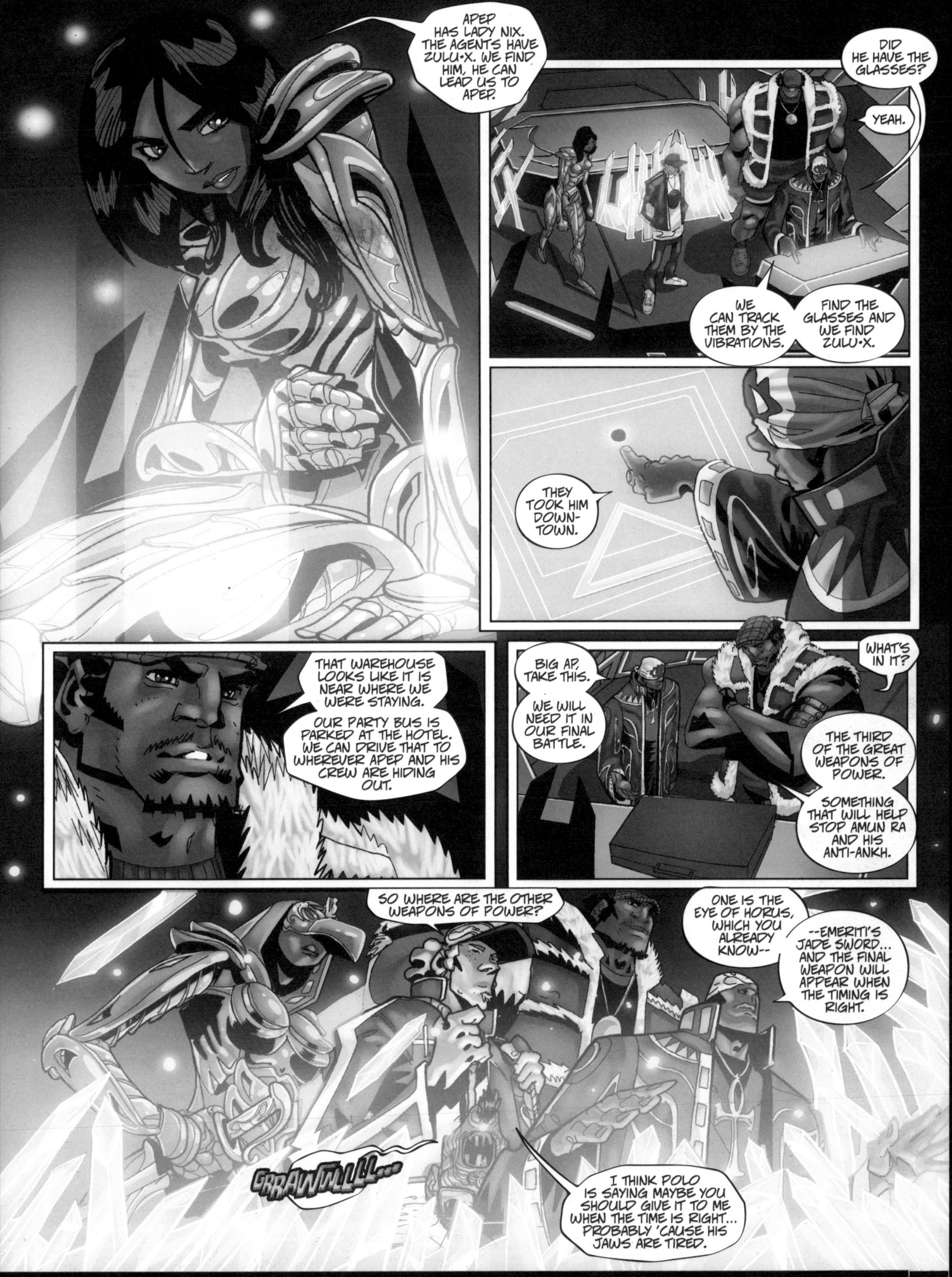
APEP HAS LADY NIX. THE AGENTS HAVE ZULU•X. WE FIND HIM, HE CAN LEAD US TO APEP.
DID HE HAVE THE GLASSES?
YEAH.
WE CAN TRACK THEM BY THE VIBRATIONS.
FIND THE GLASSES AND WE FIND ZULU•X.
THEY TOOK HIM DOWN-TOWN.
THAT WAREHOUSE LOOKS LIKE IT IS NEAR WHERE WE WERE STAYING.
OUR PARTY BUS IS PARKED AT THE HOTEL. WE CAN DRIVE THAT TO WHEREVER APEP AND HIS CREW ARE HIDING OUT.
BIG AP, TAKE THIS.
WE WILL NEED IT IN OUR FINAL BATTLE.
WHAT'S IN IT?
THE THIRD OF THE GREAT WEAPONS OF POWER.
SOMETHING THAT WILL HELP STOP AMUN RA AND HIS ANTI-ANKH.
SO WHERE ARE THE OTHER WEAPONS OF POWER?
ONE IS THE EYE OF HORUS, WHICH YOU ALREADY KNOW--
--EMERITI'S JADE SWORD... AND THE FINAL WEAPON WILL APPEAR WHEN THE TIMING IS RIGHT.
GRRAWWLLLL...
I THINK POLO IS SAYING MAYBE YOU SHOULD GIVE IT TO ME WHEN THE TIME IS RIGHT... PROBABLY 'CAUSE HIS JAWS ARE TIRED.

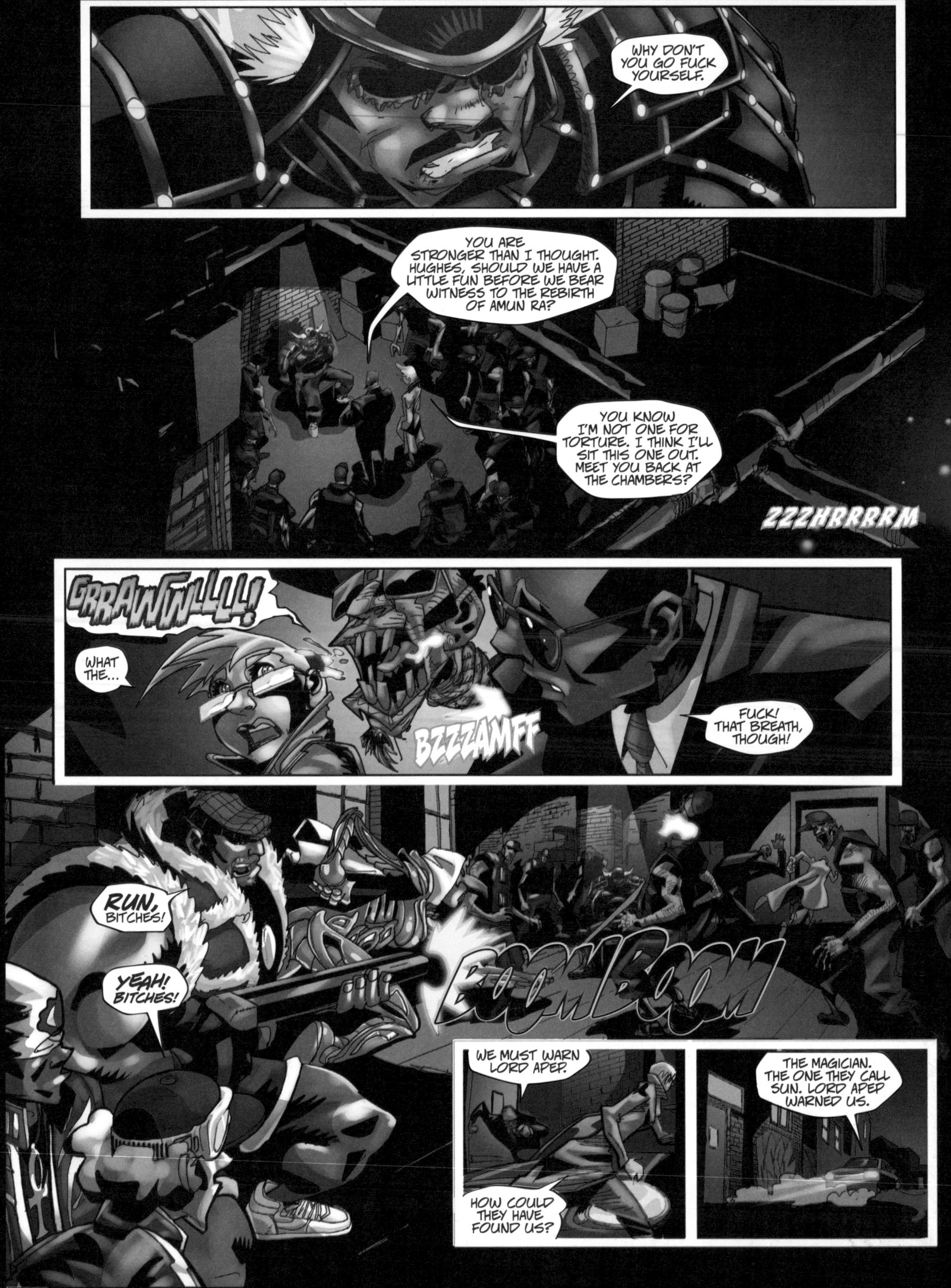
WHY DON'T YOU GO FUCK YOURSELF.
YOU ARE STRONGER THAN I THOUGHT. HUGHES, SHOULD WE HAVE A LITTLE FUN BEFORE WE BEAR WITNESS TO THE REBIRTH OF AMUN RA?
YOU KNOW I'M NOT ONE FOR TORTURE. I THINK I'LL SIT THIS ONE OUT. MEET YOU BACK AT THE CHAMBERS?
ZZZHRRRRM
GRRAWWLLLL!
WHAT THE...
BZZZAMFF
FUCK! THAT BREATH, THOUGH!
RUN, BITCHES!
YEAH! BITCHES!
BOOMBOOM
WE MUST WARN LORD APEP.
HOW COULD THEY HAVE FOUND US?
THE MAGICIAN. THE ONE THEY CALL SUN. LORD APEP WARNED US.

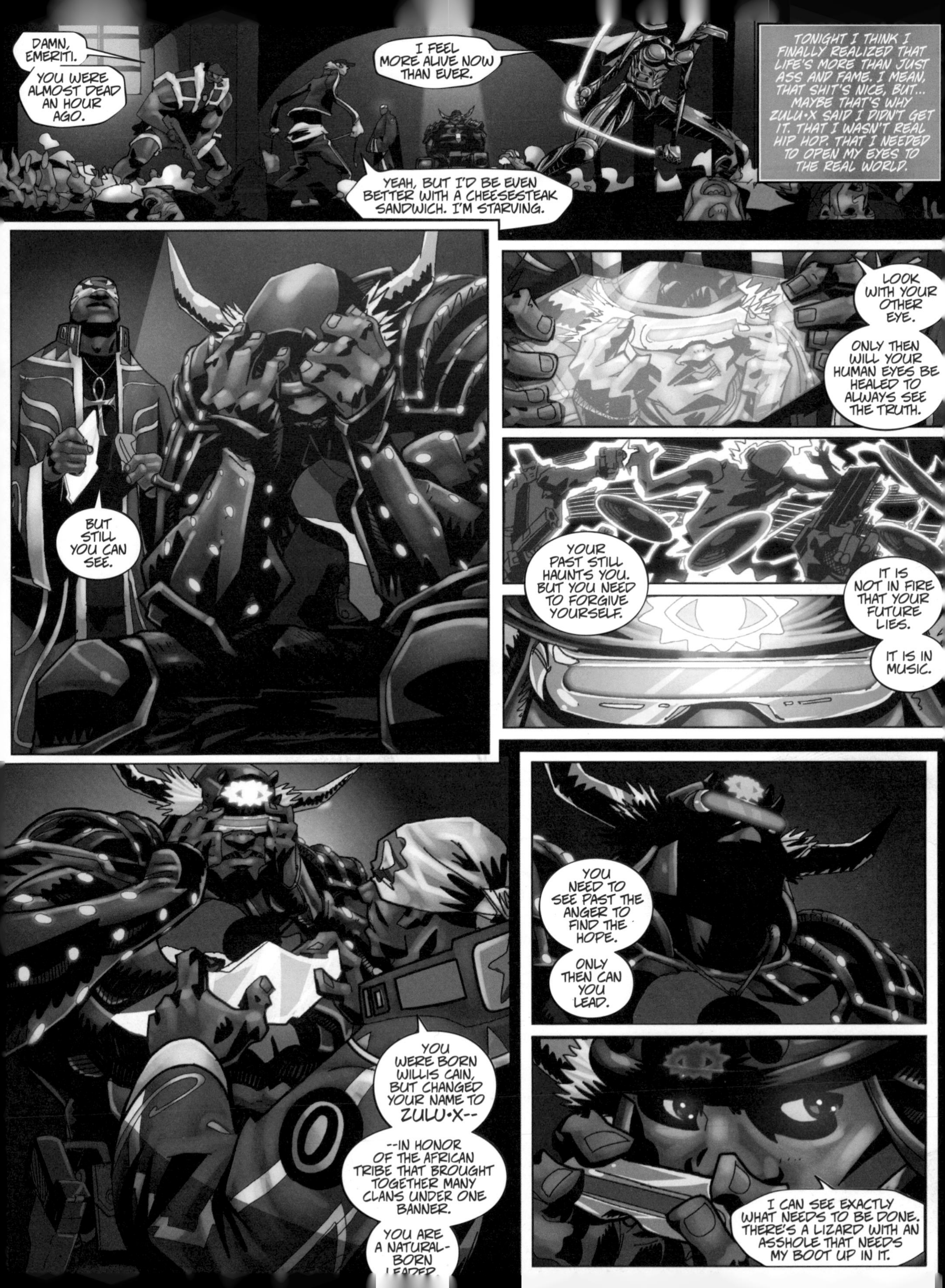
DAMN, EMERITI.
YOU WERE ALMOST DEAD AN HOUR AGO.
I FEEL MORE ALIVE NOW THAN EVER.
YEAH, BUT I'D BE EVEN BETTER WITH A CHEESESTEAK SANDWICH. I'M STARVING.
TONIGHT I THINK I FINALLY REALIZED THAT LIFE'S MORE THAN JUST ASS AND FAME. I MEAN, THAT SHIT'S NICE, BUT... MAYBE THAT'S WHY ZULU•X SAID I DIDN'T GET IT. THAT I WASN'T REAL HIP HOP. THAT I NEEDED TO OPEN MY EYES TO THE REAL WORLD.
BUT STILL YOU CAN SEE.
LOOK WITH YOUR OTHER EYE.
ONLY THEN WILL YOUR HUMAN EYES BE HEALED TO ALWAYS SEE THE TRUTH.
YOUR PAST STILL HAUNTS YOU. BUT YOU NEED TO FORGIVE YOURSELF.
IT IS NOT IN FIRE THAT YOUR FUTURE LIES.
IT IS IN MUSIC.
YOU WERE BORN WILLIS CAIN, BUT CHANGED YOUR NAME TO ZULU•X--
--IN HONOR OF THE AFRICAN TRIBE THAT BROUGHT TOGETHER MANY CLANS UNDER ONE BANNER.
YOU ARE A NATURAL-BORN LEADER.
YOU NEED TO SEE PAST THE ANGER TO FIND THE HOPE.
ONLY THEN CAN YOU LEAD.
I CAN SEE EXACTLY WHAT NEEDS TO BE DONE. THERE'S A LIZARD WITH AN ASSHOLE THAT NEEDS MY BOOT UP IN IT.

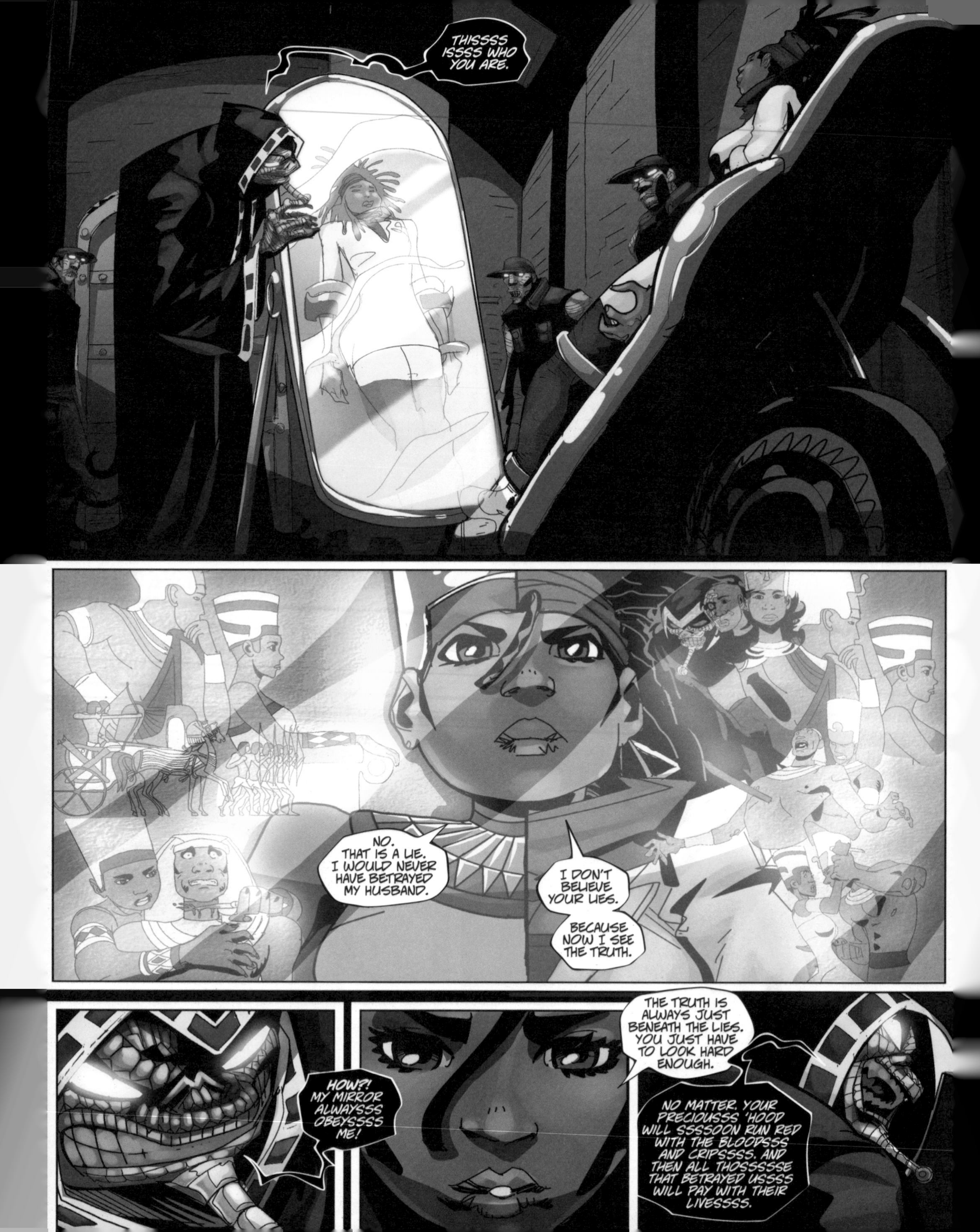

THISSSS ISSSS WHO YOU ARE.
NO. THAT IS A LIE. I WOULD NEVER HAVE BETRAYED MY HUSBAND.
I DON'T BELIEVE YOUR LIES.
BECAUSE NOW I SEE THE TRUTH.
HOW?! MY MIRROR ALWAYSSS OBEYSSSS ME!
THE TRUTH IS ALWAYS JUST BENEATH THE LIES. YOU JUST HAVE TO LOOK HARD ENOUGH.
NO MATTER. YOUR PRECIOUSSS 'HOOD WILL SSSSOON RUN RED WITH THE BLOODSSS AND CRIPSSSS. AND THEN ALL THOSSSSSE THAT BETRAYED USSSS WILL PAY WITH THEIR LIVESSSS.

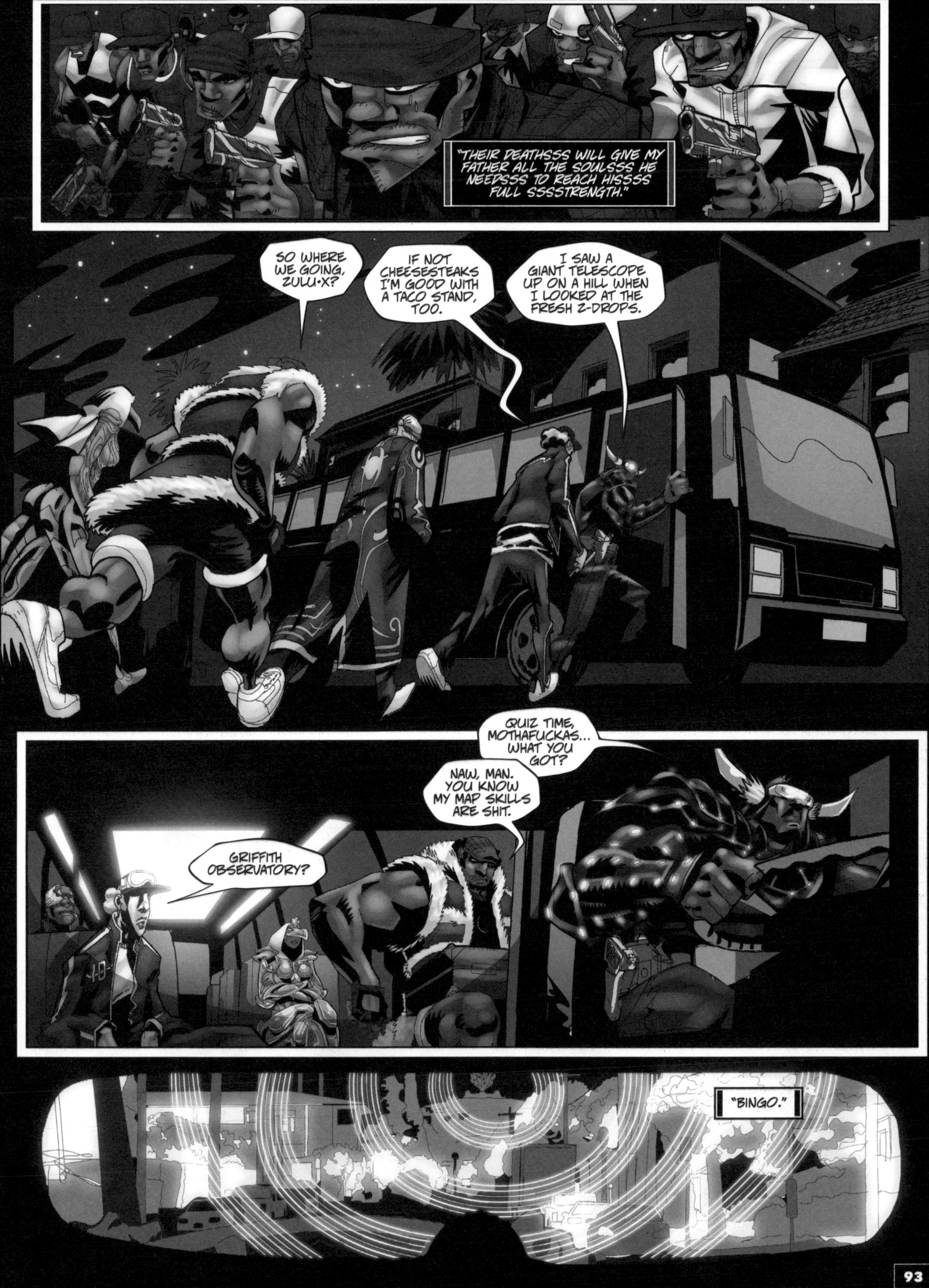
"THEIR DEATHSSS WILL GIVE MY FATHER ALL THE SOULSSS HE NEEDSSS TO REACH HISSSS FULL SSSSTRENGTH."
SO WHERE WE GOING, ZULU•X?
IF NOT CHEESESTEAKS I'M GOOD WITH A TACO STAND, TOO.
I SAW A GIANT TELESCOPE UP ON A HILL WHEN I LOOKED AT THE FRESH Z-DROPS.
QUIZ TIME, MOTHAFUCKAS... WHAT YOU GOT?
NAW, MAN. YOU KNOW MY MAP SKILLS ARE SHIT.
GRIFFITH OBSERVATORY?
"BINGO."

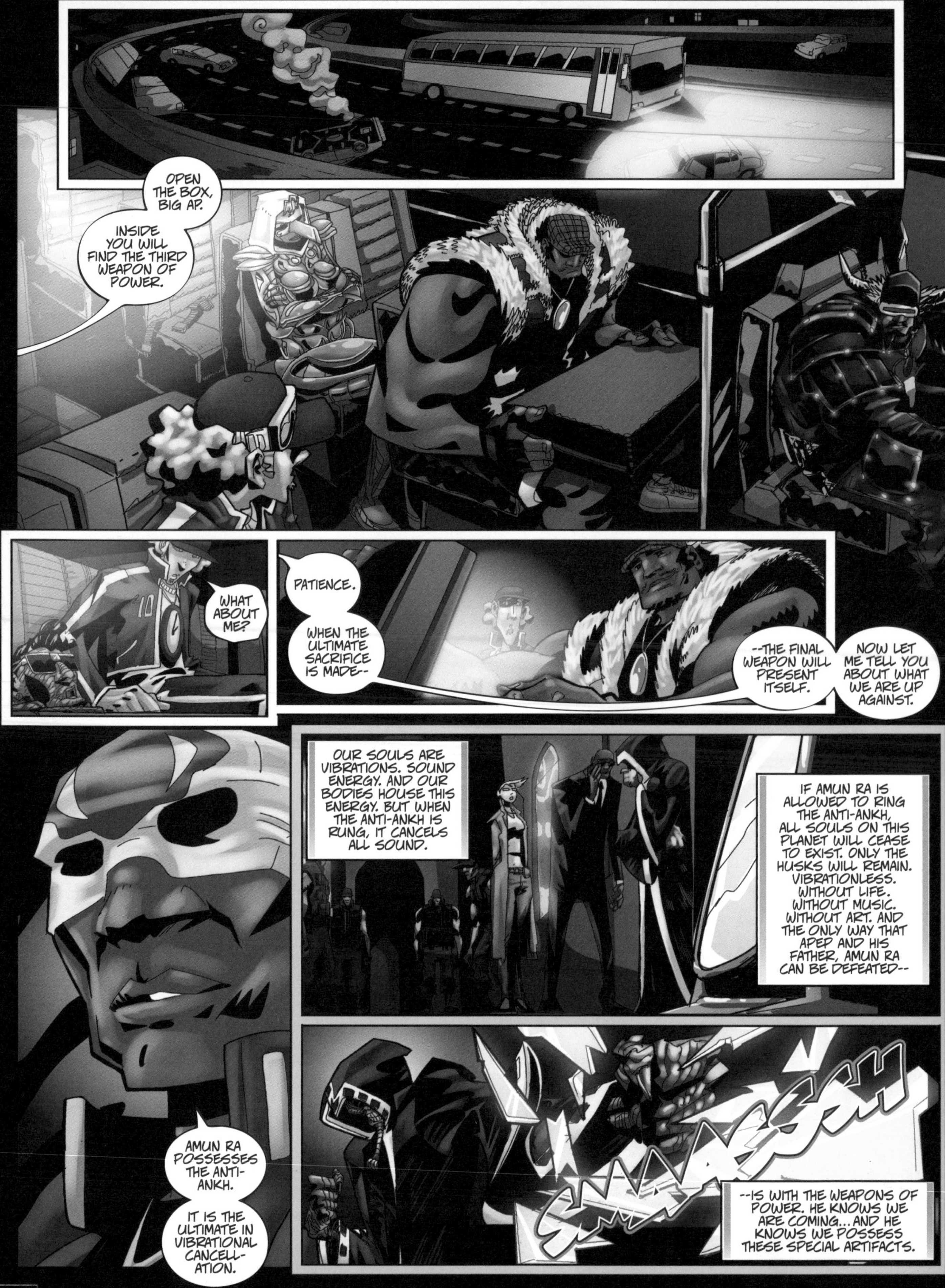

OPEN THE BOX, BIG AP.
INSIDE YOU WILL FIND THE THIRD WEAPON OF POWER.
WHAT ABOUT ME?
PATIENCE.
WHEN THE ULTIMATE SACRIFICE IS MADE--
--THE FINAL WEAPON WILL PRESENT ITSELF.
NOW LET ME TELL YOU ABOUT WHAT WE ARE UP AGAINST.
AMUN RA POSSESSES THE ANTI-ANKH.
IT IS THE ULTIMATE IN VIBRATIONAL CANCELL-ATION.
OUR SOULS ARE VIBRATIONS. SOUND ENERGY. AND OUR BODIES HOUSE THIS ENERGY. BUT WHEN THE ANTI-ANKH IS RUNG, IT CANCELS ALL SOUND.
IF AMUN RA IS ALLOWED TO RING THE ANTI-ANKH, ALL SOULS ON THIS PLANET WILL CEASE TO EXIST. ONLY THE HUSKS WILL REMAIN. VIBRATIONLESS. WITHOUT LIFE. WITHOUT MUSIC. WITHOUT ART. AND THE ONLY WAY THAT APEP AND HIS FATHER, AMUN RA CAN BE DEFEATED--
SMAAASSH
--IS WITH THE WEAPONS OF POWER. HE KNOWS WE ARE COMING... AND HE KNOWS WE POSSESS THESE SPECIAL ARTIFACTS.

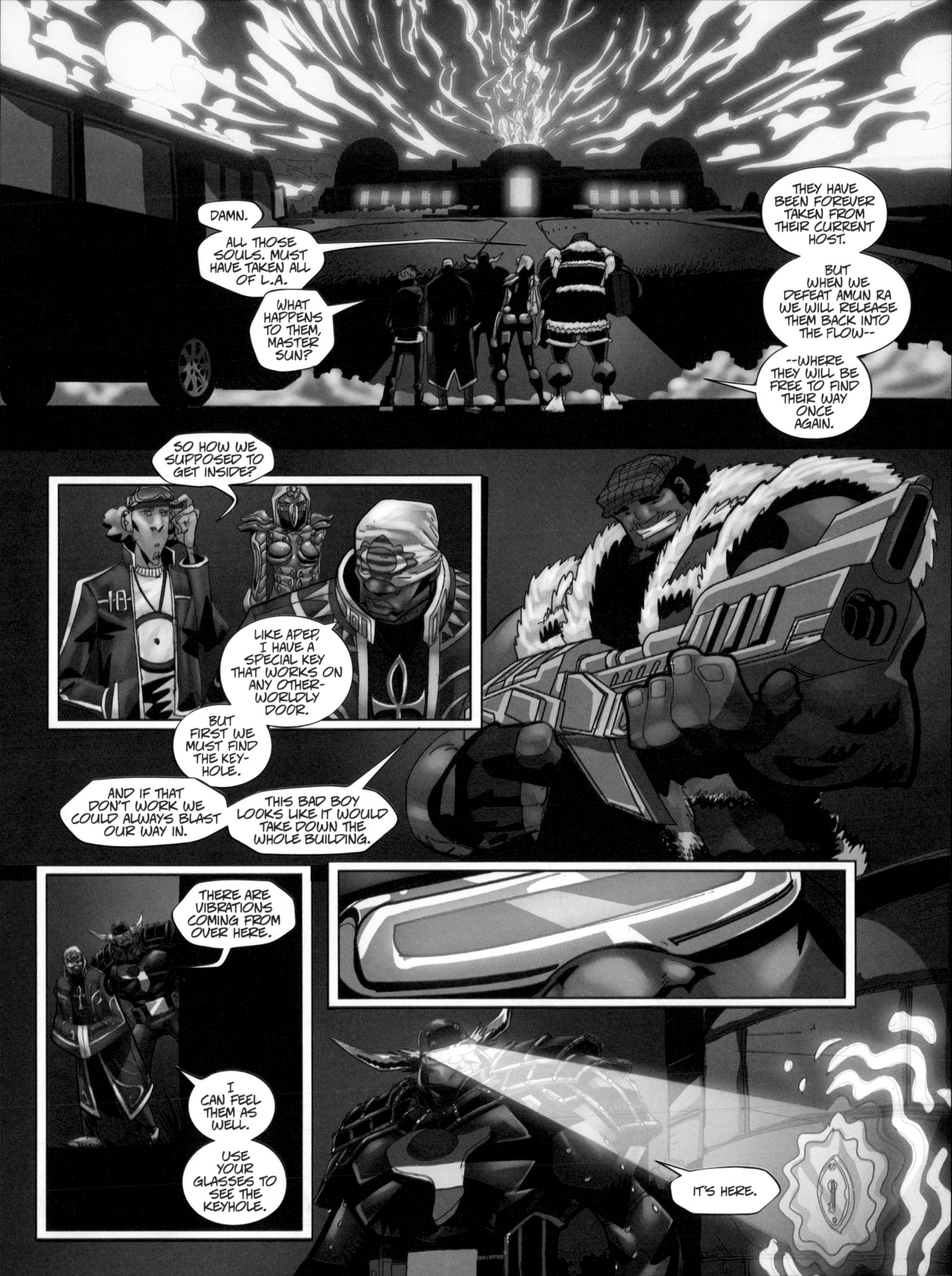
DAMN.
ALL THOSE SOULS. MUST HAVE TAKEN ALL OF L.A.
WHAT HAPPENS TO THEM, MASTER SUN?
THEY HAVE BEEN FOREVER TAKEN FROM THEIR CURRENT HOST.
BUT WHEN WE DEFEAT AMUN RA WE WILL RELEASE THEM BACK INTO THE FLOW--
--WHERE THEY WILL BE FREE TO FIND THEIR WAY ONCE AGAIN.
SO HOW WE SUPPOSED TO GET INSIDE?
LIKE APEP, I HAVE A SPECIAL KEY THAT WORKS ON ANY OTHER-WORLDLY DOOR.
BUT FIRST WE MUST FIND THE KEY-HOLE.
AND IF THAT DON'T WORK WE COULD ALWAYS BLAST OUR WAY IN.
THIS BAD BOY LOOKS LIKE IT WOULD TAKE DOWN THE WHOLE BUILDING.
THERE ARE VIBRATIONS COMING FROM OVER HERE.
I CAN FEEL THEM AS WELL.
USE YOUR GLASSES TO SEE THE KEYHOLE.
IT'S HERE.

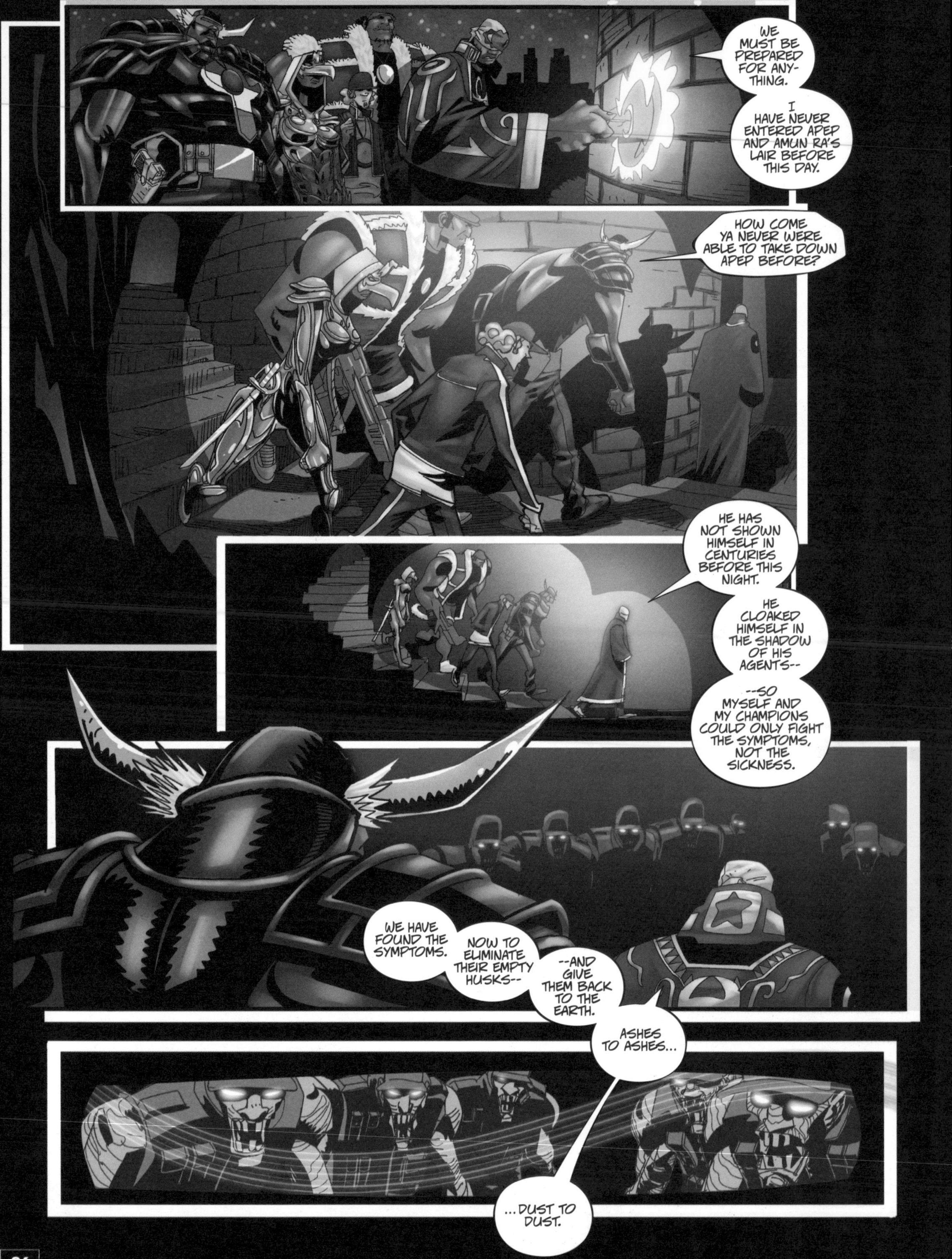
WE MUST BE PREPARED FOR ANY-THING.
I HAVE NEVER ENTERED APEP AND AMUN RA'S LAIR BEFORE THIS DAY.
HOW COME YA NEVER WERE ABLE TO TAKE DOWN APEP BEFORE?
HE HAS NOT SHOWN HIMSELF IN CENTURIES BEFORE THIS NIGHT.
HE CLOAKED HIMSELF IN THE SHADOW OF HIS AGENTS--
--SO MYSELF AND MY CHAMPIONS COULD ONLY FIGHT THE SYMPTOMS, NOT THE SICKNESS.
WE HAVE FOUND THE SYMPTOMS.
NOW TO ELIMINATE THEIR EMPTY HUSKS--
--AND GIVE THEM BACK TO THE EARTH.
ASHES TO ASHES...
...DUST TO DUST.

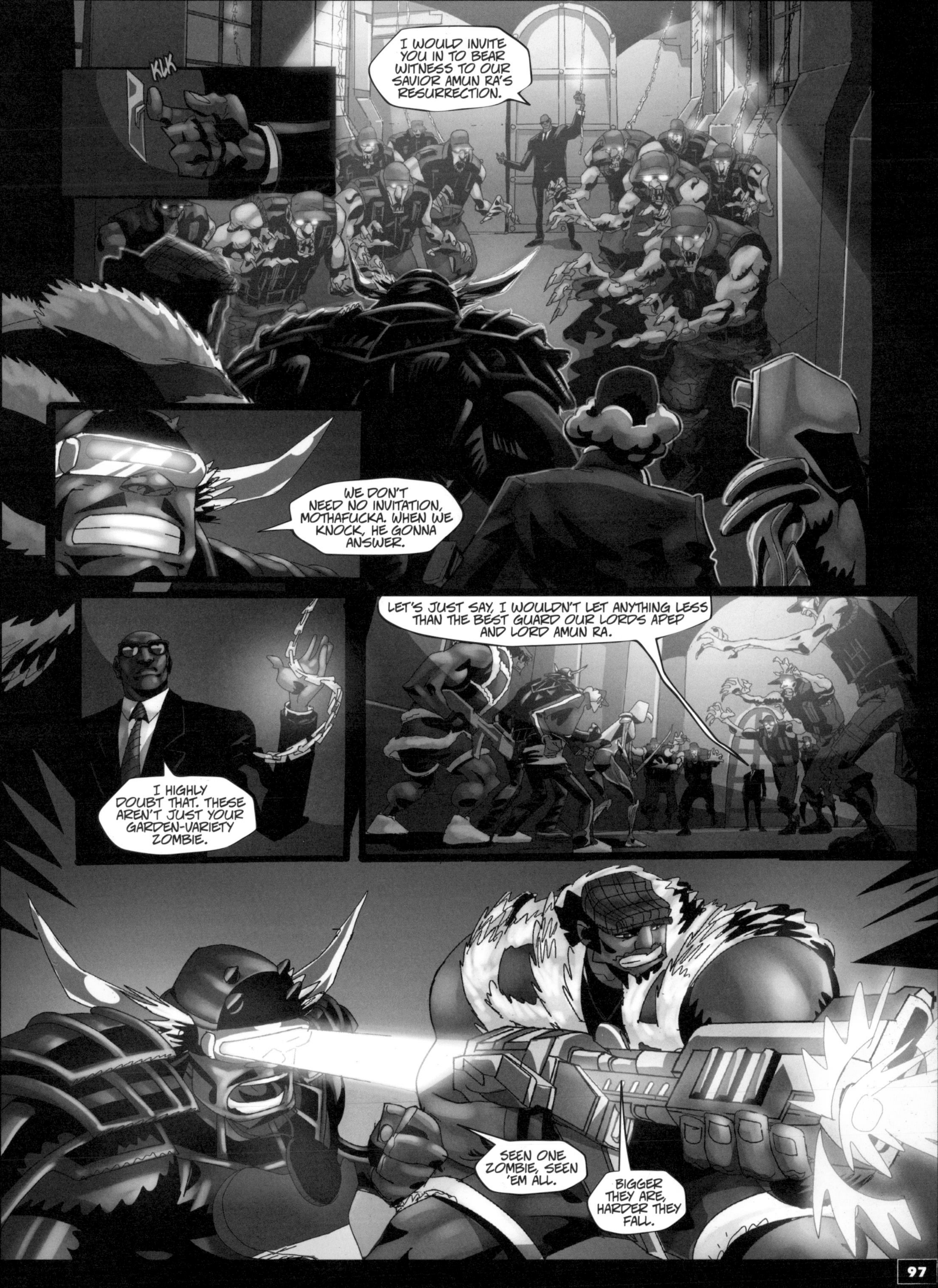

KLIK
I WOULD INVITE YOU IN TO BEAR WITNESS TO OUR SAVIOR AMUN RA'S RESURRECTION.
WE DON'T NEED NO INVITATION, MOTHAFUCKA. WHEN WE KNOCK, HE GONNA ANSWER.
I HIGHLY DOUBT THAT. THESE AREN'T JUST YOUR GARDEN-VARIETY ZOMBIE.
LET'S JUST SAY, I WOULDN'T LET ANYTHING LESS THAN THE BEST GUARD OUR LORDS APEP AND LORD AMUN RA.
SEEN ONE ZOMBIE, SEEN 'EM ALL.
BIGGER THEY ARE, HARDER THEY FALL.

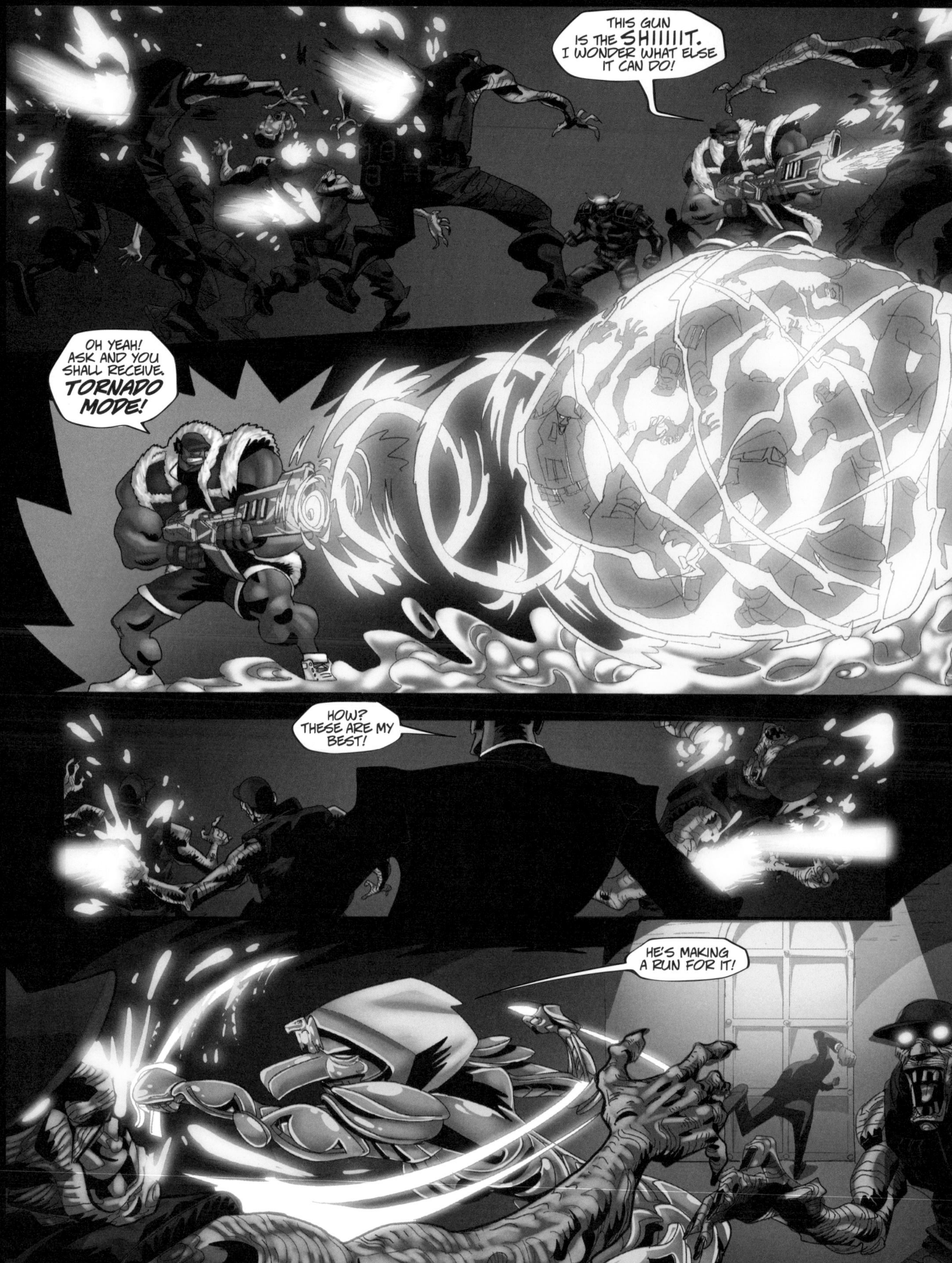
THIS GUN IS THE SHIIIIIIT. I WONDER WHAT ELSE IT CAN DO!
OH YEAH! ASK AND YOU SHALL RECEIVE. TORNADO MODE!
HOW? THESE ARE MY BEST!
HE'S MAKING A RUN FOR IT!

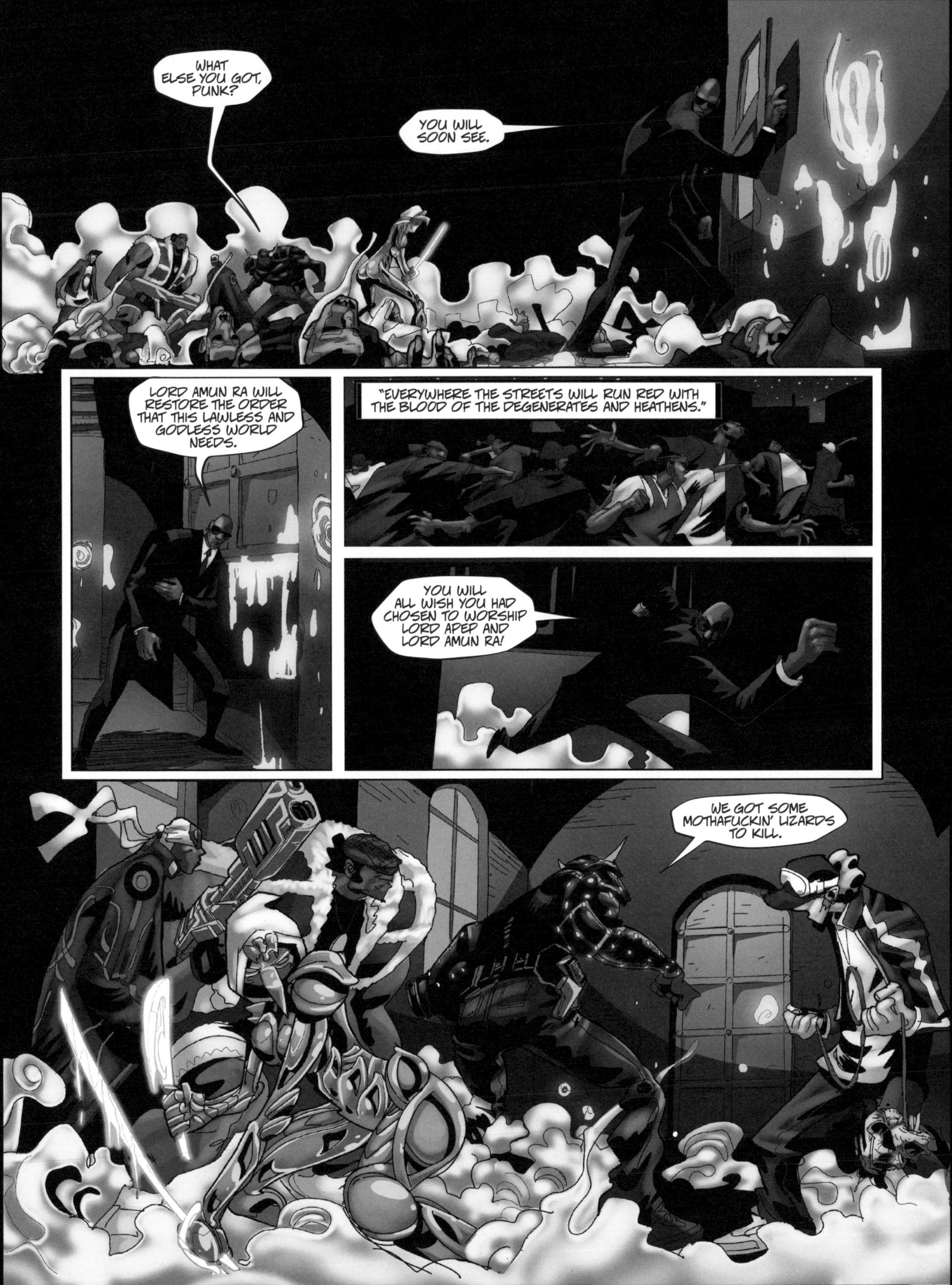
WHAT ELSE YOU GOT, PUNK?
YOU WILL SOON SEE.
LORD AMUN RA WILL RESTORE THE ORDER THAT THIS LAWLESS AND GODLESS WORLD NEEDS.
"EVERYWHERE THE STREETS WILL RUN RED WITH THE BLOOD OF THE DEGENERATES AND HEATHENS."
YOU WILL ALL WISH YOU HAD CHOSEN TO WORSHIP LORD APEP AND LORD AMUN RA!
WE GOT SOME MOTHAFUCKIN' LIZARDS TO KILL.

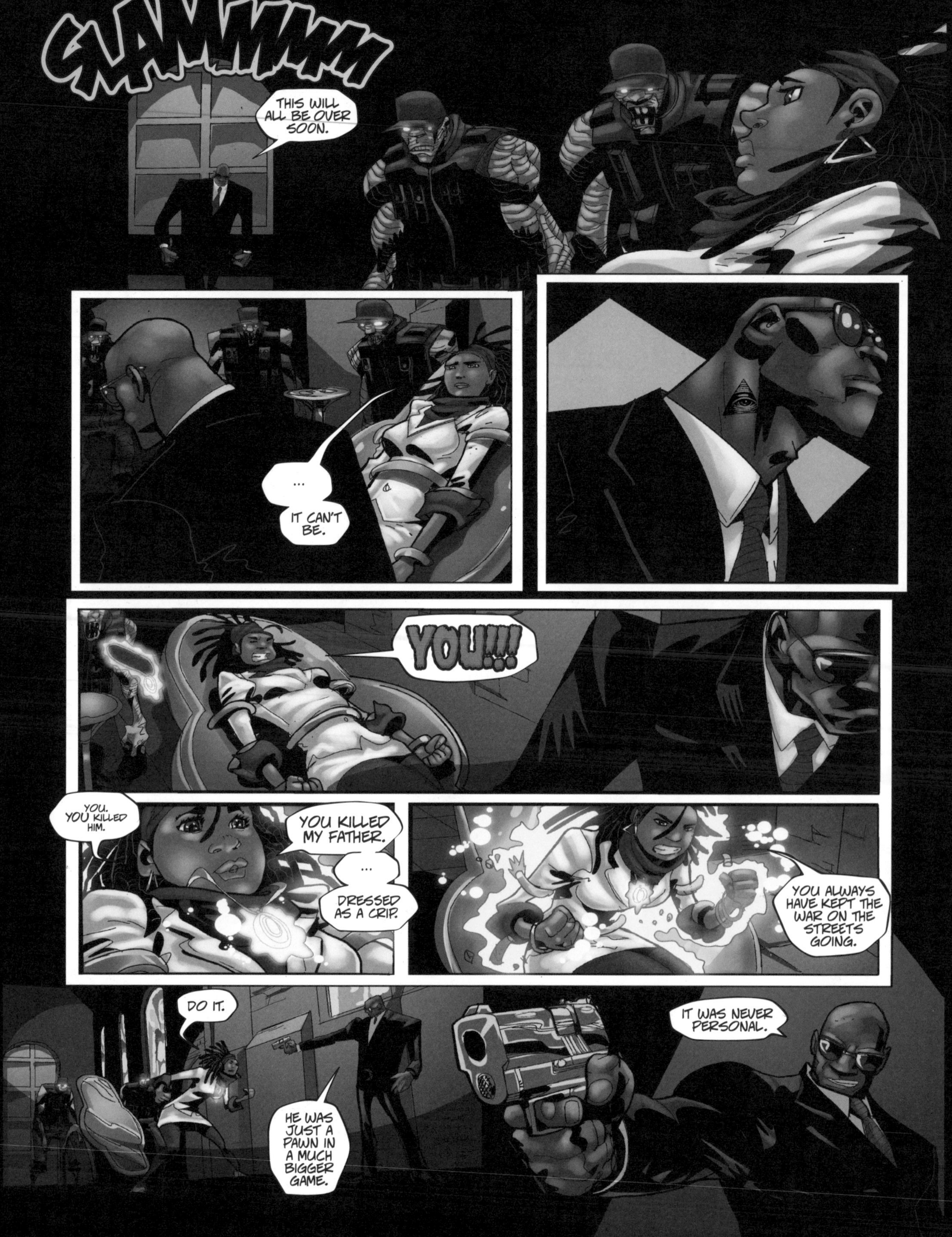

SLAMMMMM
THIS WILL ALL BE OVER SOON.
...
IT CAN'T BE.
YOU!!!
YOU. YOU KILLED HIM.
YOU KILLED MY FATHER.
...
DRESSED AS A CRIP.
YOU ALWAYS HAVE KEPT THE WAR ON THE STREETS GOING.
DO IT.
HE WAS JUST A PAWN IN A MUCH BIGGER GAME.
IT WAS NEVER PERSONAL.

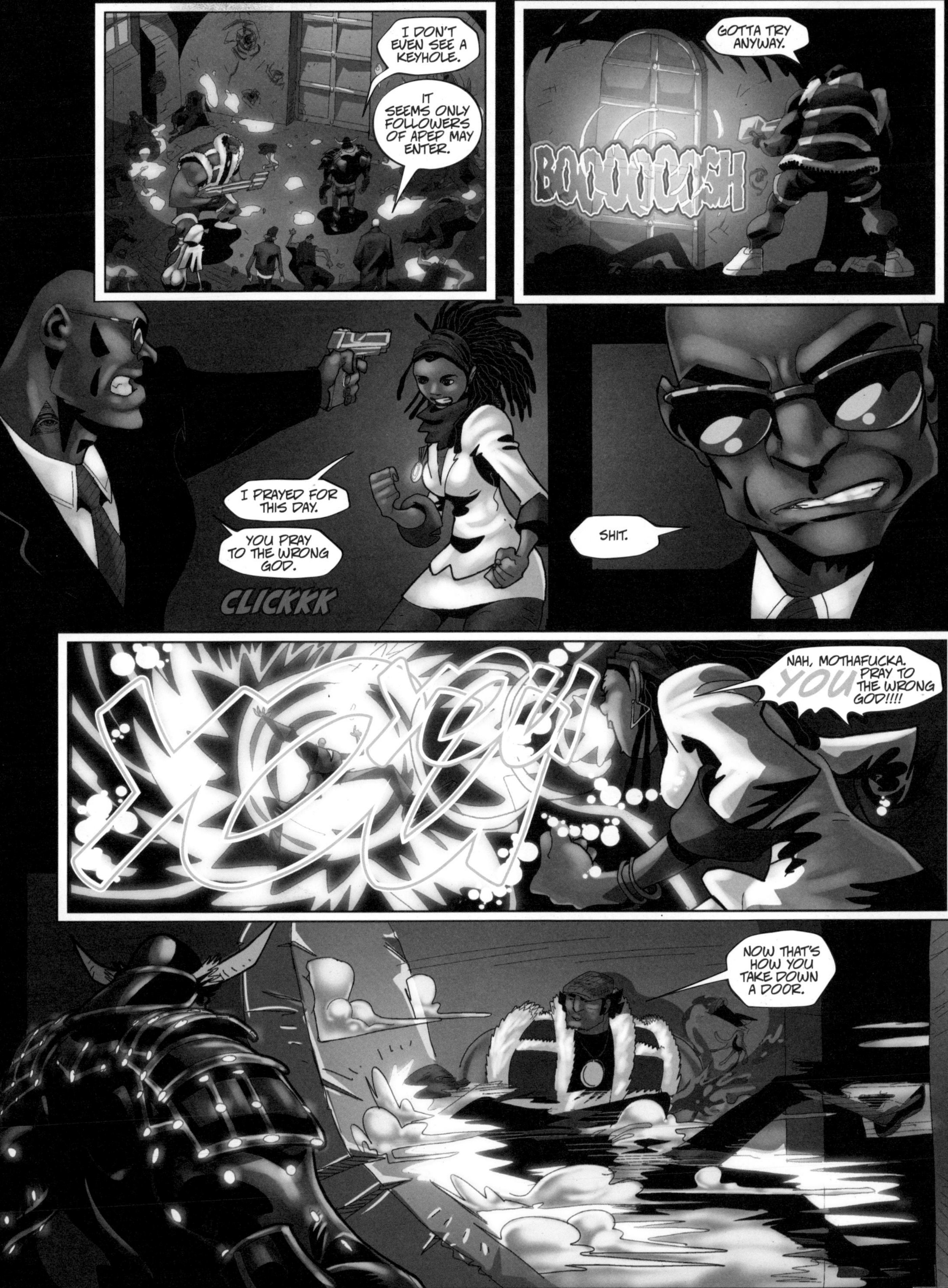

I DON'T EVEN SEE A KEYHOLE.
IT SEEMS ONLY FOLLOWERS OF APEP MAY ENTER.
GOTTA TRY ANYWAY.
BOOOOOOSH
I PRAYED FOR THIS DAY.
YOU PRAY TO THE WRONG GOD.
CLICKKK
SHIT.
NAH, MOTHAFUCKA. YOU PRAY TO THE WRONG GOD!!!!
NOW THAT'S HOW YOU TAKE DOWN A DOOR.

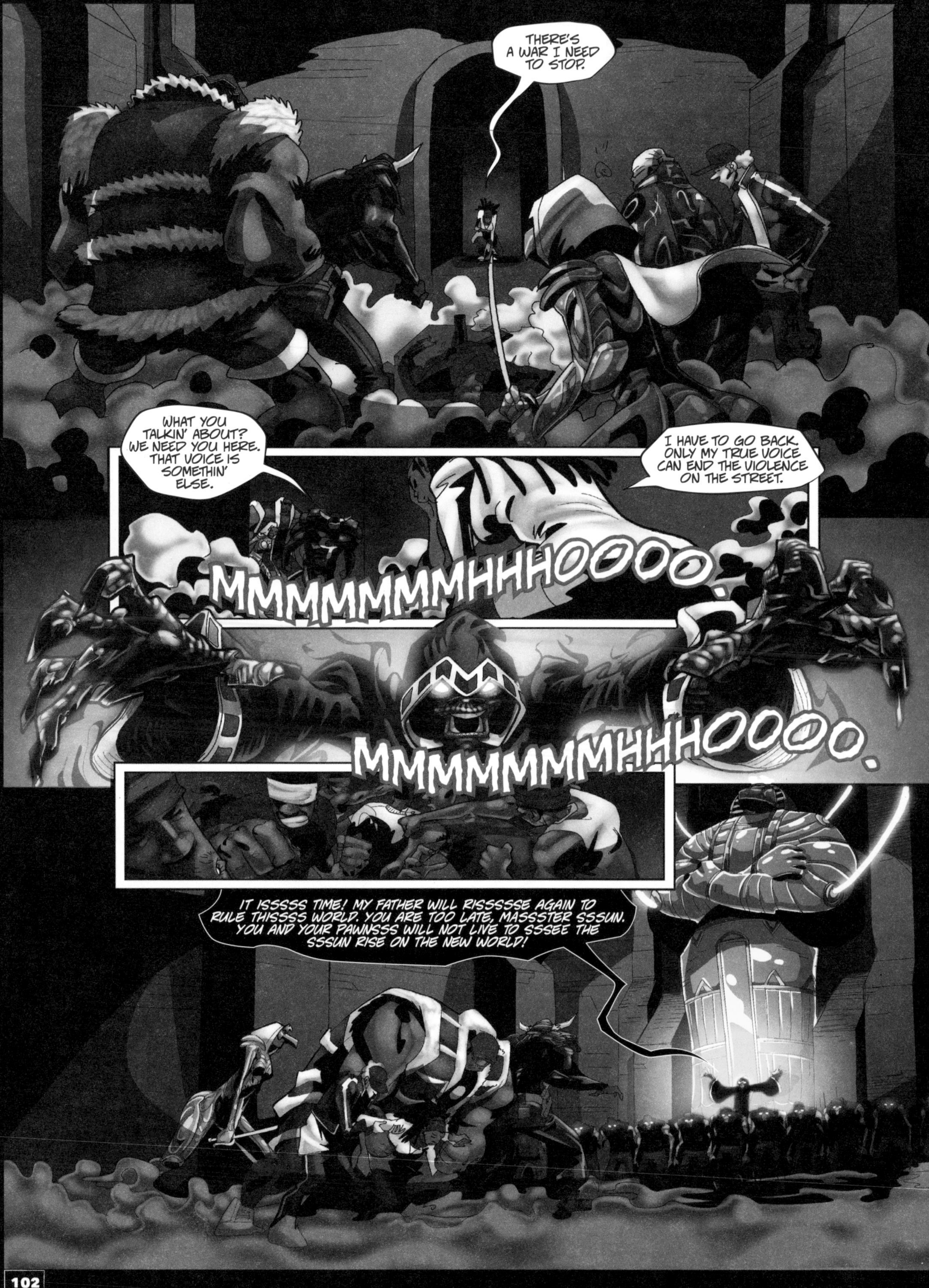

THERE'S A WAR I NEED TO STOP.
WHAT YOU TALKIN' ABOUT? WE NEED YOU HERE. THAT VOICE IS SOMETHIN' ELSE.
I HAVE TO GO BACK. ONLY MY TRUE VOICE CAN END THE VIOLENCE ON THE STREET.
MMMMMMMHHHOOOOO.
MMMMMMMHHHOOOOO.
IT ISSSSS TIME! MY FATHER WILL RISSSSSE AGAIN TO RULE THISSSS WORLD. YOU ARE TOO LATE, MASSSTER SSSUN. YOU AND YOUR PAWNSSS WILL NOT LIVE TO SSSEE THE SSSUN RISE ON THE NEW WORLD!

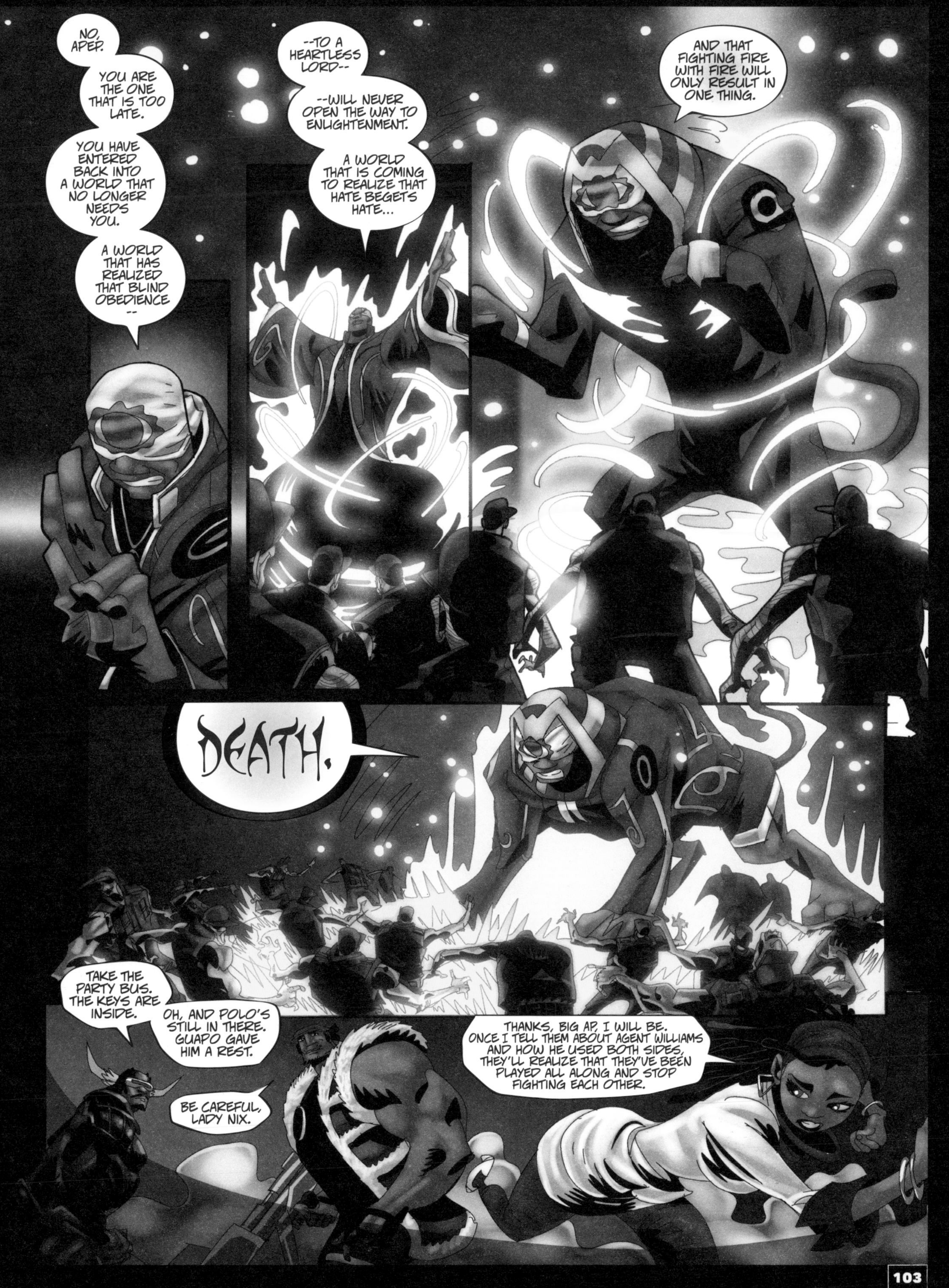
NO, APEP.
YOU ARE THE ONE THAT IS TOO LATE.
YOU HAVE ENTERED BACK INTO A WORLD THAT NO LONGER NEEDS YOU.
A WORLD THAT HAS REALIZED THAT BLIND OBEDIENCE --
--TO A HEARTLESS LORD--
--WILL NEVER OPEN THE WAY TO ENLIGHTENMENT.
A WORLD THAT IS COMING TO REALIZE THAT HATE BEGETS HATE...
AND THAT FIGHTING FIRE WITH FIRE WILL ONLY RESULT IN ONE THING.
DEATH.
TAKE THE PARTY BUS. THE KEYS ARE INSIDE.
OH, AND POLO'S STILL IN THERE. GUAPO GAVE HIM A REST.
BE CAREFUL, LADY NIX.
THANKS, BIG AP, I WILL BE. ONCE I TELL THEM ABOUT AGENT WILLIAMS AND HOW HE USED BOTH SIDES, THEY'LL REALIZE THAT THEY'VE BEEN PLAYED ALL ALONG AND STOP FIGHTING EACH OTHER.

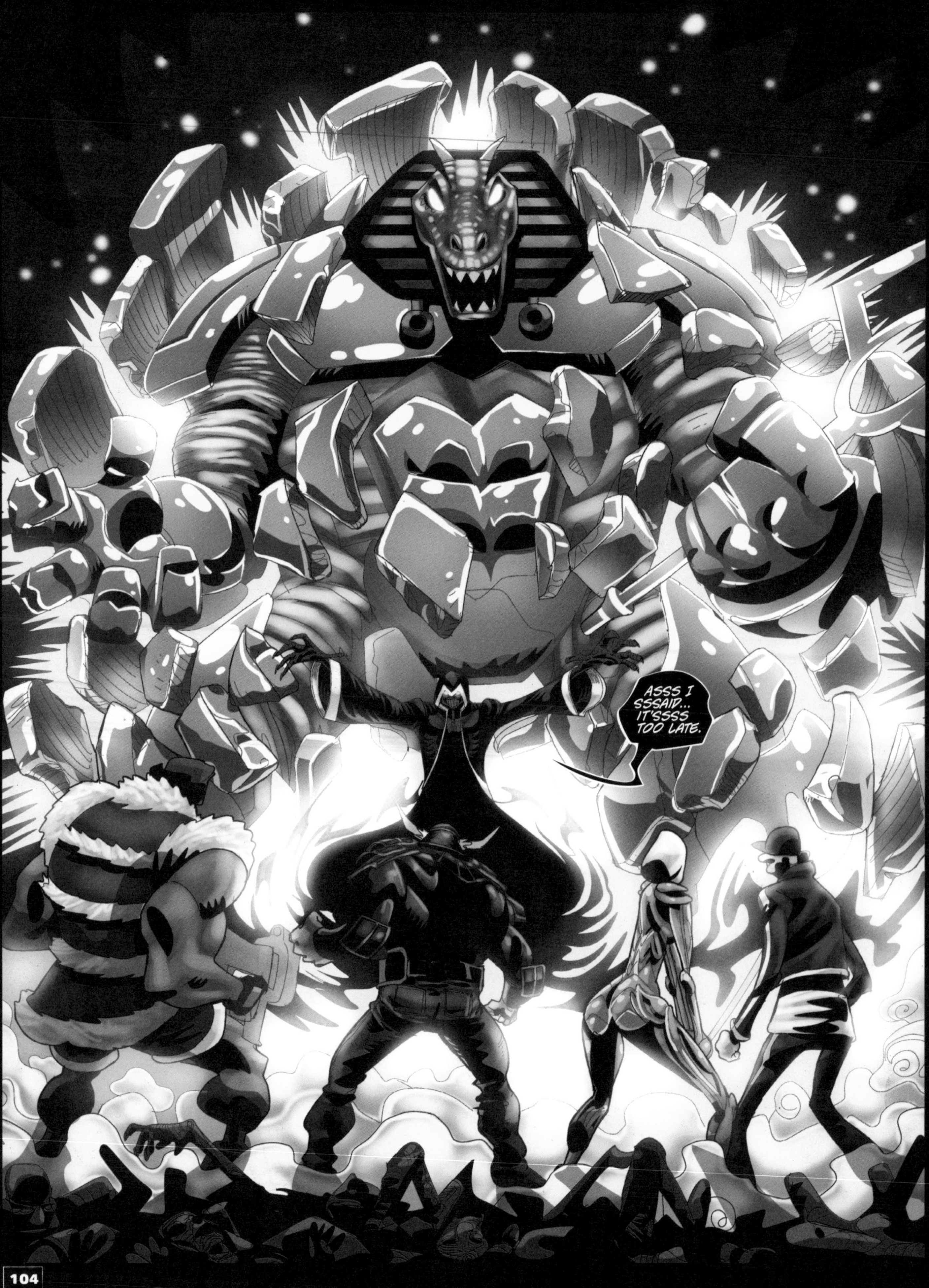
ASSS I SSSAID... IT'SSSS TOO LATE.

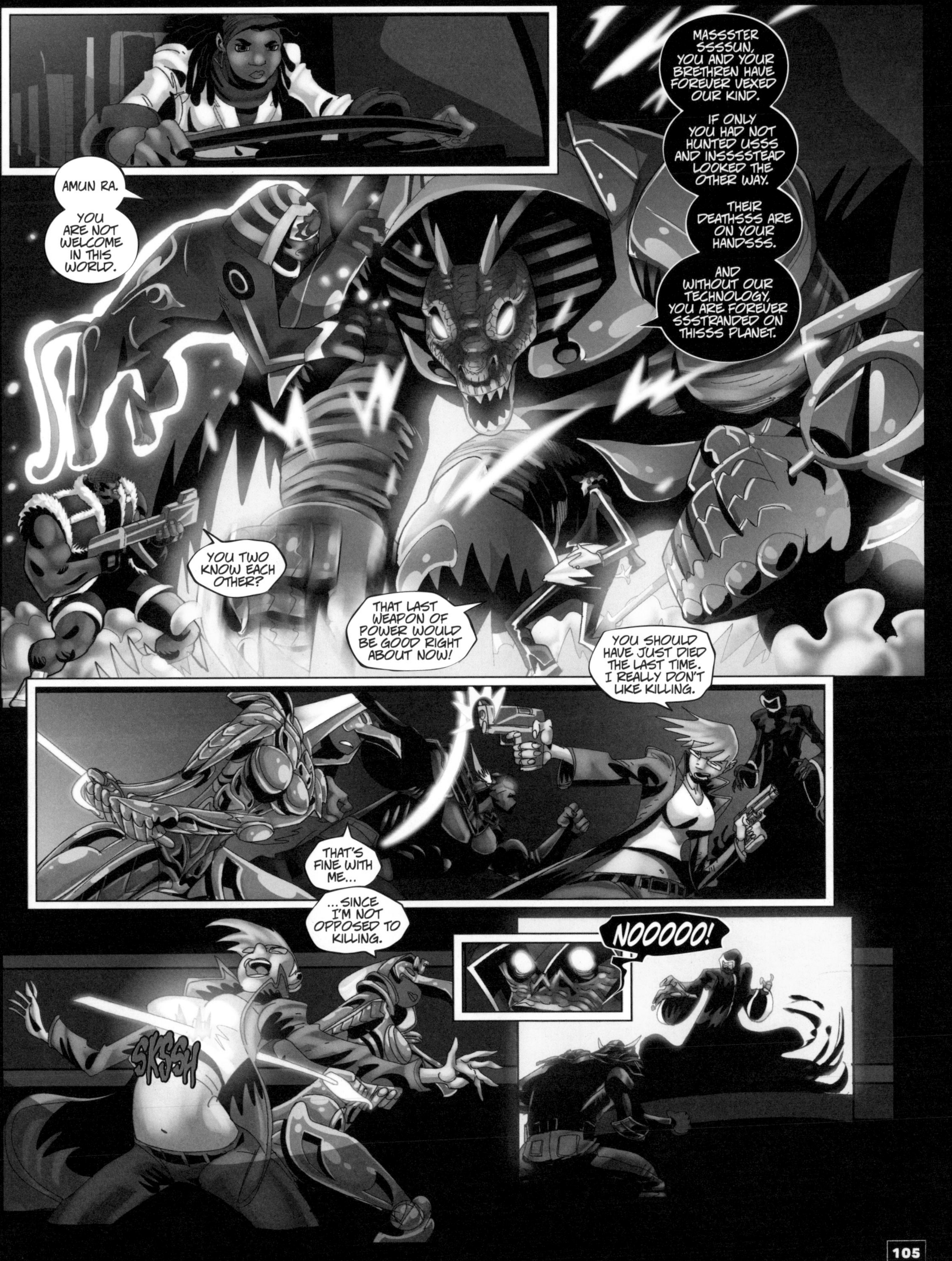
MASSSTER SSSSUN, YOU AND YOUR BRETHREN HAVE FOREVER VEXED OUR KIND.
IF ONLY YOU HAD NOT HUNTED USSS AND INSSSSTEAD LOOKED THE OTHER WAY.
THEIR DEATHSSS ARE ON YOUR HANDSSS.
AND WITHOUT OUR TECHNOLOGY, YOU ARE FOREVER SSSTRANDED ON THISSS PLANET.
AMUN RA.
YOU ARE NOT WELCOME IN THIS WORLD.
YOU TWO KNOW EACH OTHER?
THAT LAST WEAPON OF POWER WOULD BE GOOD RIGHT ABOUT NOW!
YOU SHOULD HAVE JUST DIED THE LAST TIME. I REALLY DON'T LIKE KILLING.
THAT'S FINE WITH ME...
...SINCE I'M NOT OPPOSED TO KILLING.
SKSSH
NOOOOO!

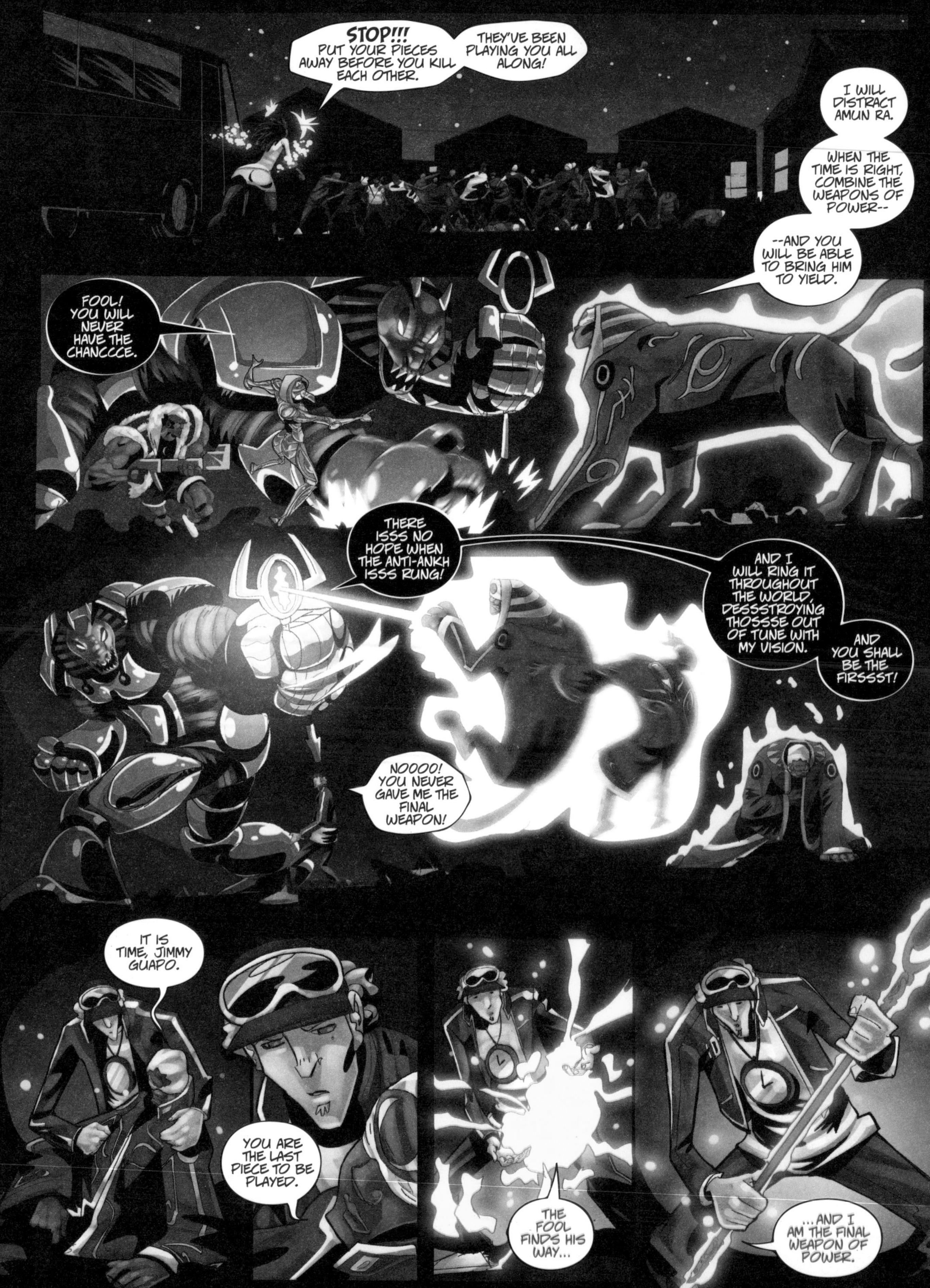
STOP!!! PUT YOUR PIECES AWAY BEFORE YOU KILL EACH OTHER.
THEY'VE BEEN PLAYING YOU ALL ALONG!
I WILL DISTRACT AMUN RA.
WHEN THE TIME IS RIGHT, COMBINE THE WEAPONS OF POWER--
--AND YOU WILL BE ABLE TO BRING HIM TO YIELD.
FOOL! YOU WILL NEVER HAVE THE CHANCCCE.
THERE ISSS NO HOPE WHEN THE ANTI-ANKH ISSS RUNG!
AND I WILL RING IT THROUGHOUT THE WORLD, DESSSTROYING THOSSSE OUT OF TUNE WITH MY VISION.
AND YOU SHALL BE THE FIRSSST!
NOOOO! YOU NEVER GAVE ME THE FINAL WEAPON!
IT IS TIME, JIMMY GUAPO.
YOU ARE THE LAST PIECE TO BE PLAYED.
THE FOOL FINDS HIS WAY...
...AND I AM THE FINAL WEAPON OF POWER.

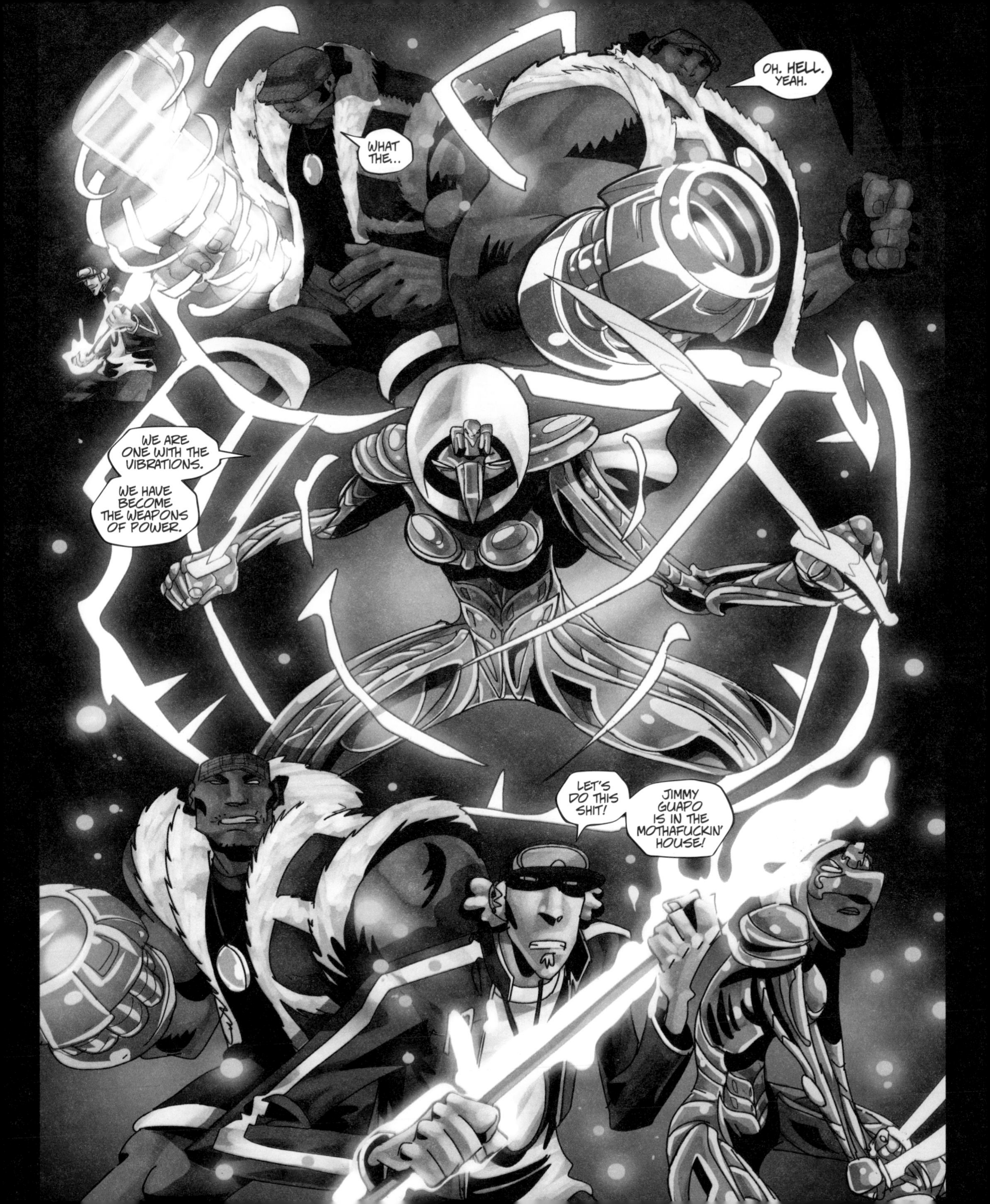

WHAT THE...
OH. HELL. YEAH.
WE ARE ONE WITH THE VIBRATIONS.
WE HAVE BECOME THE WEAPONS OF POWER.
LET'S DO THIS SHIT!
JIMMY GUAPO IS IN THE MOTHAFUCKIN' HOUSE!

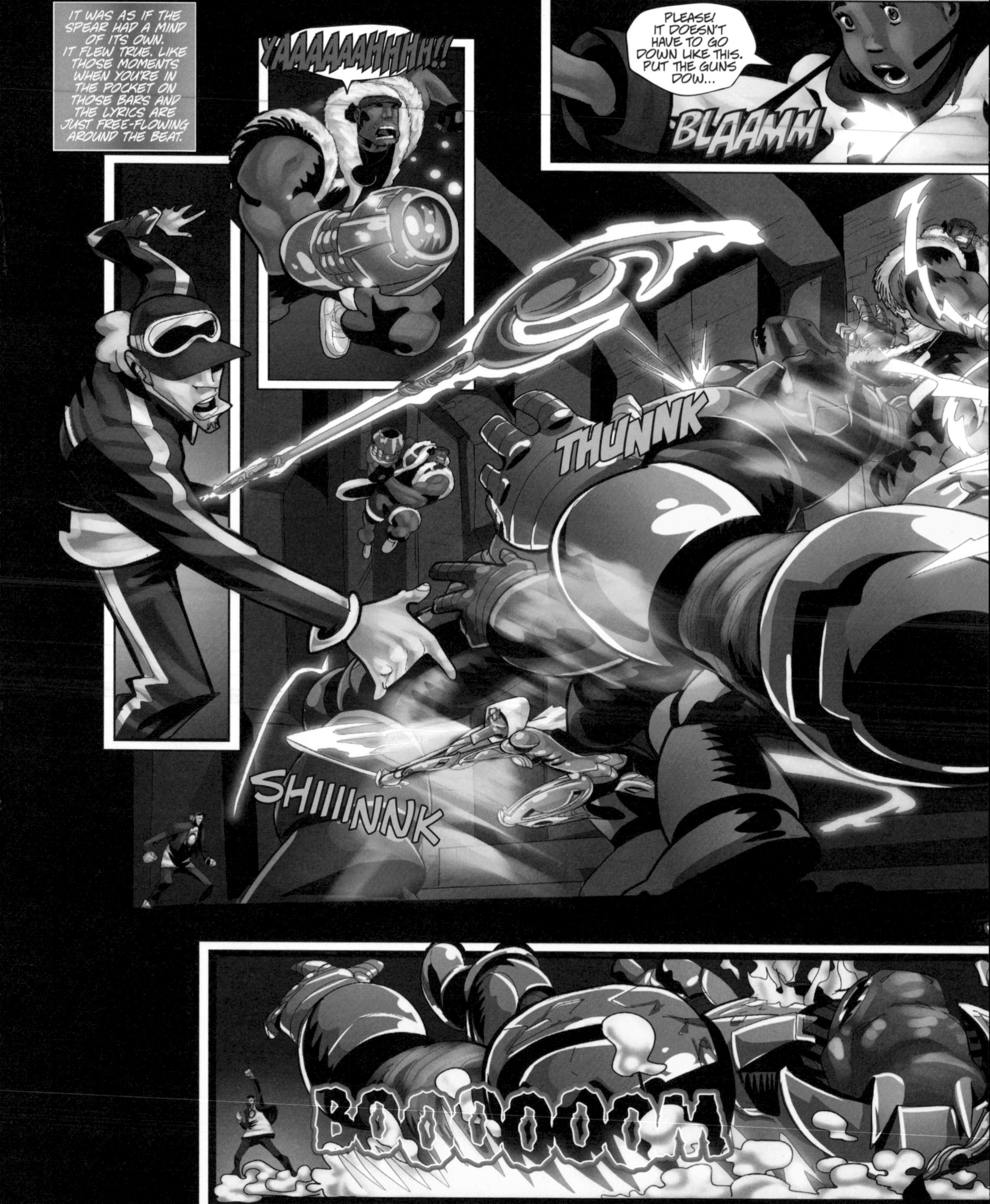
IT WAS AS IF THE SPEAR HAD A MIND OF ITS OWN. IT FLEW TRUE. LIKE THOSE MOMENTS WHEN YOU'RE IN THE POCKET ON THOSE BARS AND THE LYRICS ARE JUST FREE-FLOWING AROUND THE BEAT.
YAAAAAAHHHH!!
PLEASE! IT DOESN'T HAVE TO GO DOWN LIKE THIS. PUT THE GUNS DOW...
BLAAMM
THUNNK
SHIIIINNK
BOOOOOOM

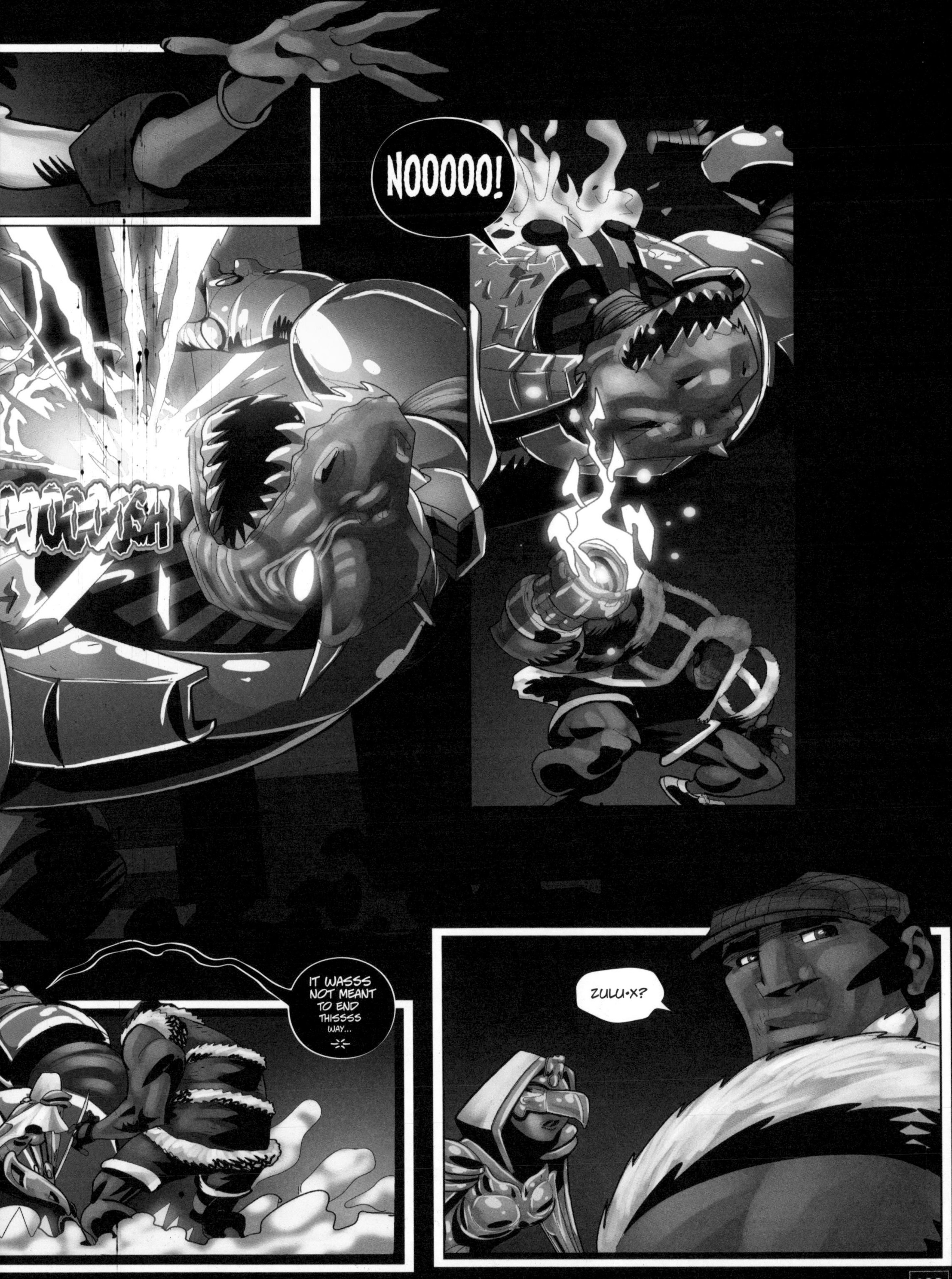
NOOOOO!
WHOOOSH
IT WASSS NOT MEANT TO END THISSSS WAY...
ZULU-X?

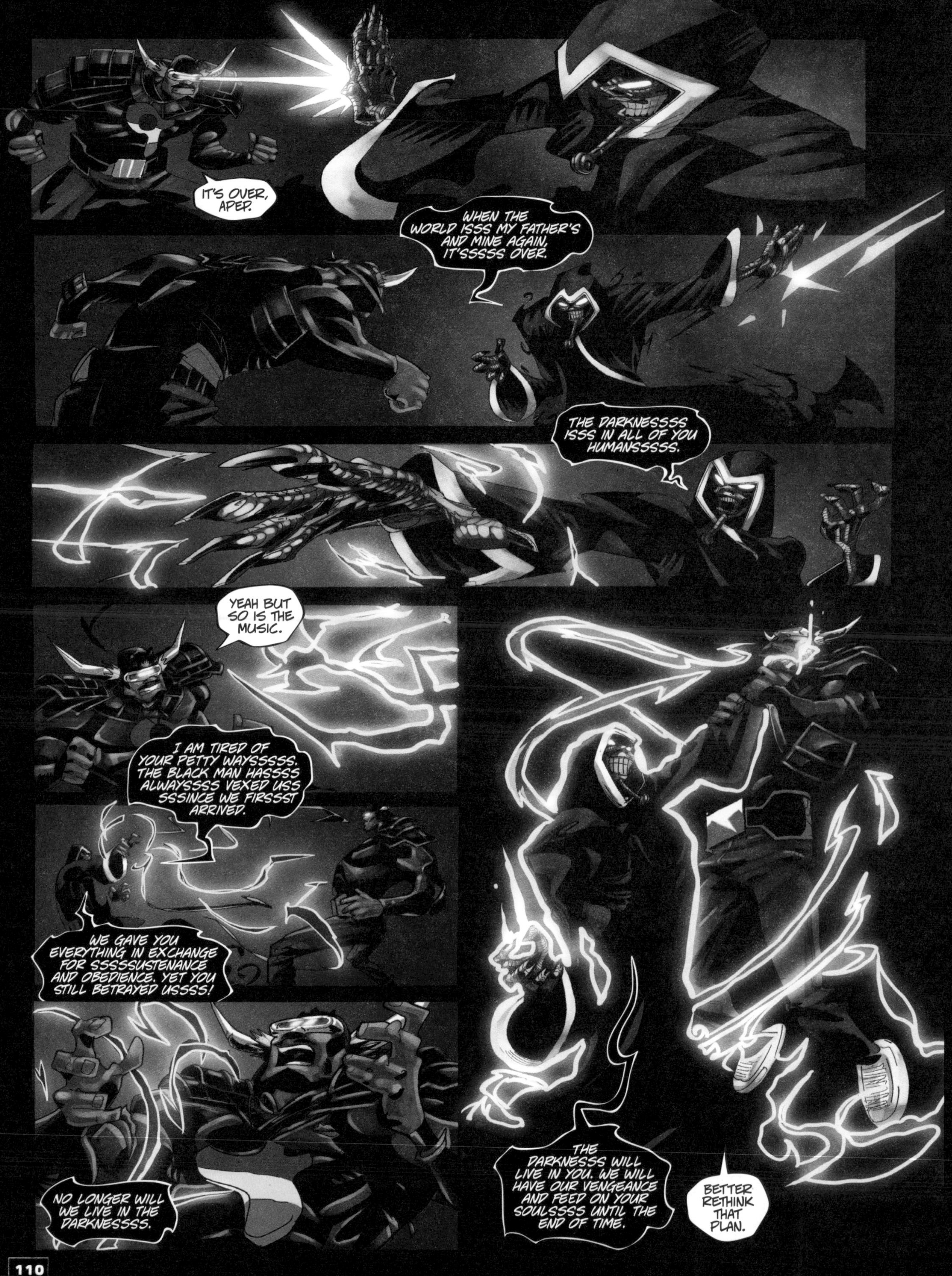
IT'S OVER, APEP.
WHEN THE WORLD ISSS MY FATHER'S AND MINE AGAIN, IT'SSSSS OVER.
THE DARKNESSSS ISSS IN ALL OF YOU HUMANSSSSS.
YEAH BUT SO IS THE MUSIC.
I AM TIRED OF YOUR PETTY WAYSSSSS. THE BLACK MAN HASSSS ALWAYSSSS VEXED USSS SSSINCE WE FIRSSST ARRIVED.
WE GAVE YOU EVERYTHING IN EXCHANGE FOR SSSSSUSTENANCE AND OBEDIENCE. YET YOU STILL BETRAYED USSSS!
NO LONGER WILL WE LIVE IN THE DARKNESSSS.
THE DARKNESSS WILL LIVE IN YOU. WE WILL HAVE OUR VENGEANCE AND FEED ON YOUR SOULSSSS UNTIL THE END OF TIME.
BETTER RETHINK THAT PLAN.

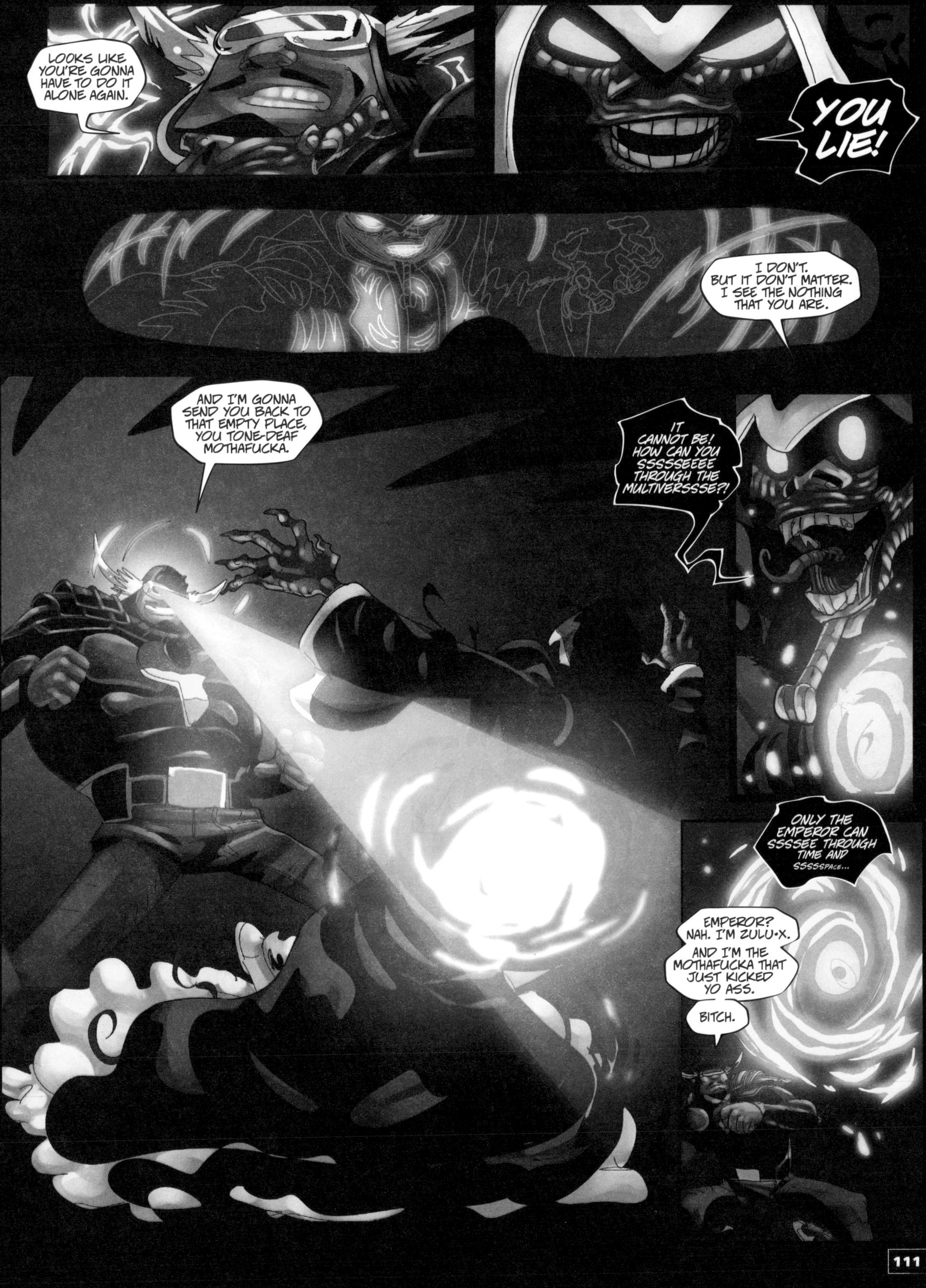

LOOKS LIKE YOU'RE GONNA HAVE TO DO IT ALONE AGAIN.
YOU LIE!
I DON'T. BUT IT DON'T MATTER. I SEE THE NOTHING THAT YOU ARE.
AND I'M GONNA SEND YOU BACK TO THAT EMPTY PLACE, YOU TONE-DEAF MOTHAFUCKA.
IT CANNOT BE! HOW CAN YOU SSSSSEEEE THROUGH THE MULTIVERSSSE?!
ONLY THE EMPEROR CAN SSSSEE THROUGH TIME AND SSSSSPACE...
EMPEROR? NAH. I'M ZULU-X.
AND I'M THE MOTHAFUCKA THAT JUST KICKED YO ASS.
BITCH.

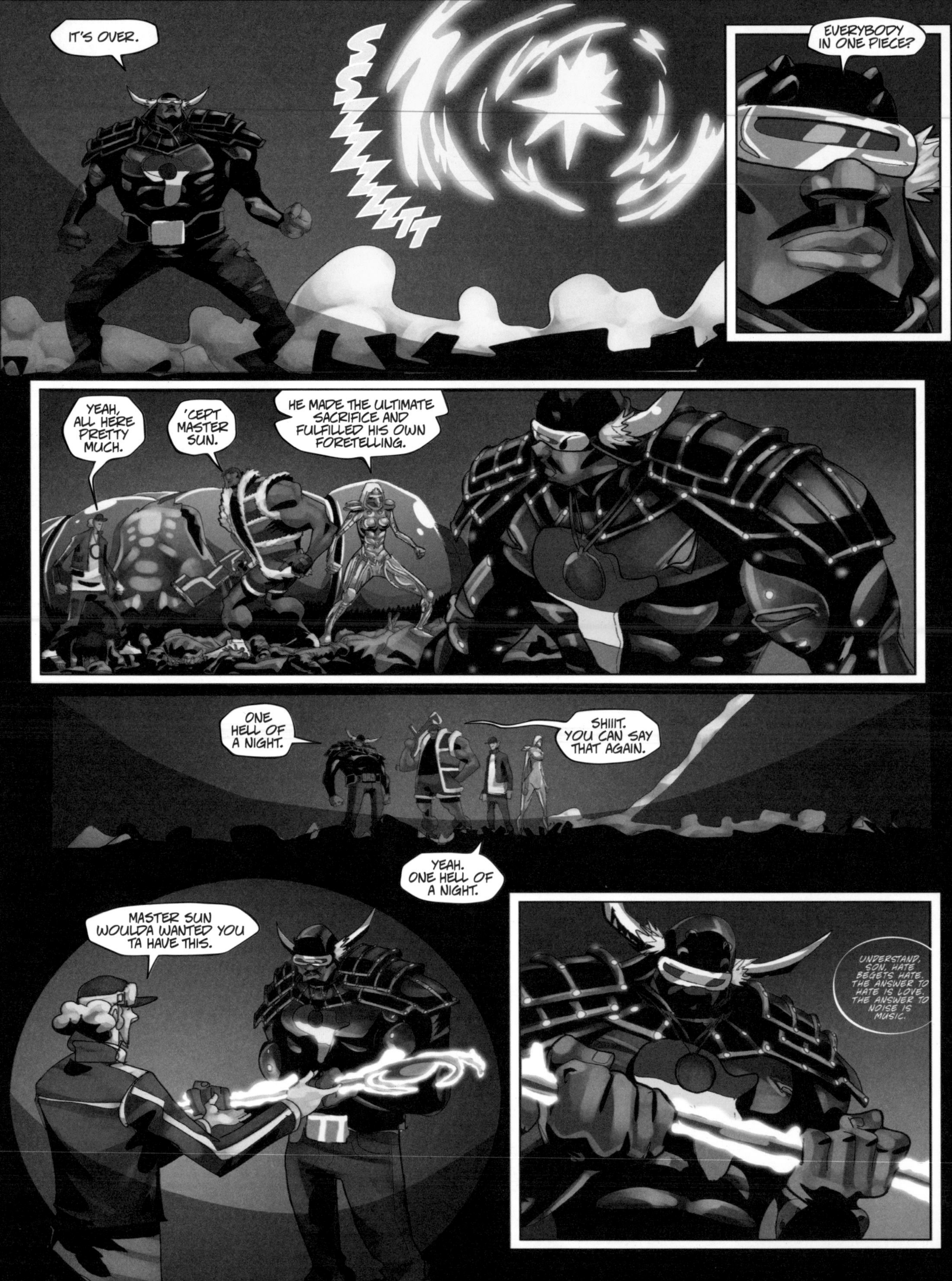
IT'S OVER.
ZZZZZZZZZZTTT
EVERYBODY IN ONE PIECE?
YEAH, ALL HERE PRETTY MUCH.
'CEPT MASTER SUN.
HE MADE THE ULTIMATE SACRIFICE AND FULFILLED HIS OWN FORETELLING.
ONE HELL OF A NIGHT.
SHIIIT. YOU CAN SAY THAT AGAIN.
YEAH. ONE HELL OF A NIGHT.
MASTER SUN WOULDA WANTED YOU TA HAVE THIS.
UNDERSTAND, SON, HATE BEGETS HATE. THE ANSWER TO HATE IS LOVE. THE ANSWER TO NOISE IS MUSIC.

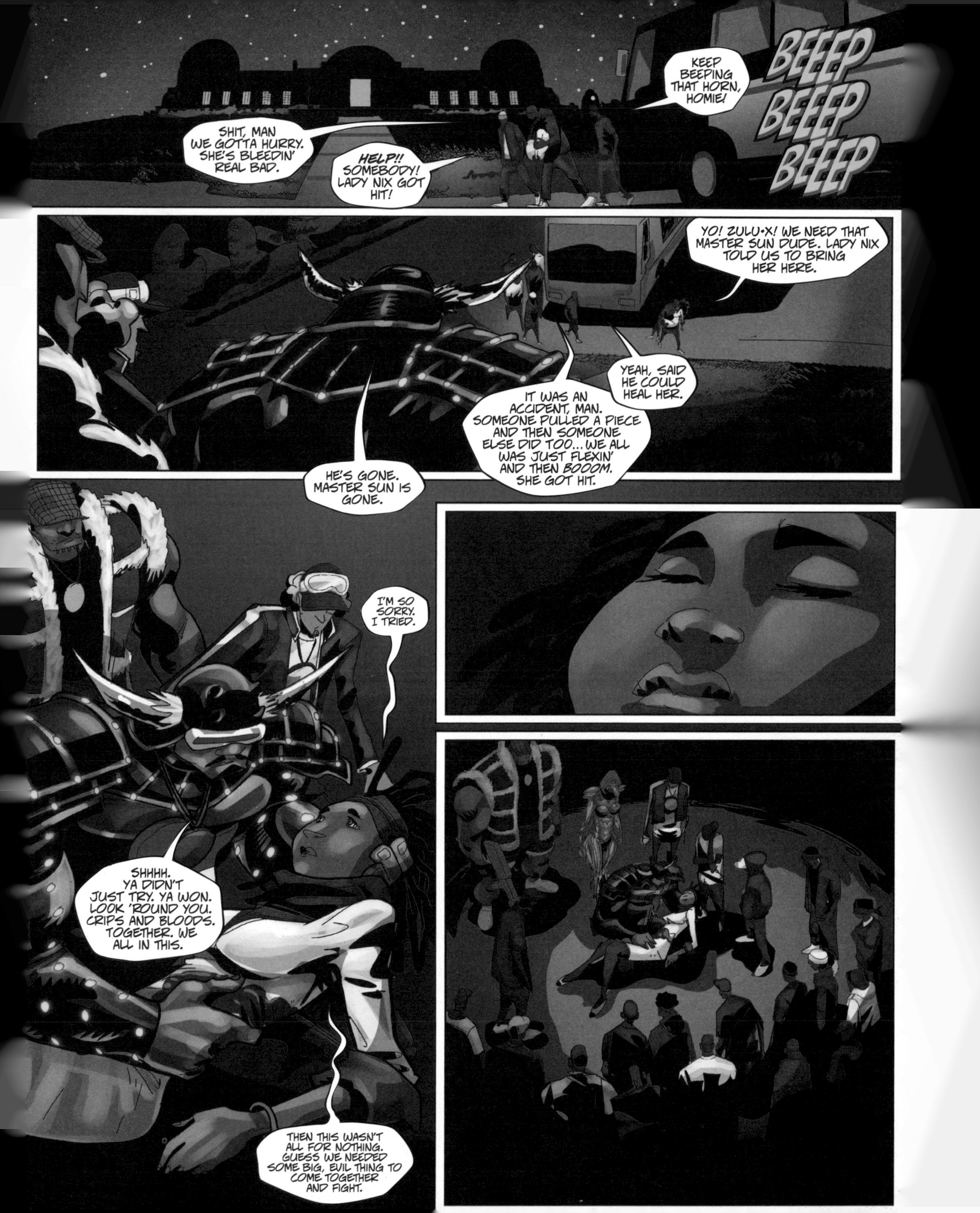
SHIT, MAN WE GOTTA HURRY. SHE'S BLEEDIN' REAL BAD.
HELP!! SOMEBODY! LADY NIX GOT HIT!
KEEP BEEPING THAT HORN, HOMIE!
BEEEP BEEEP BEEEP
YO! ZULU•X! WE NEED THAT MASTER SUN DUDE. LADY NIX TOLD US TO BRING HER HERE.
YEAH, SAID HE COULD HEAL HER.
IT WAS AN ACCIDENT, MAN. SOMEONE PULLED A PIECE AND THEN SOMEONE ELSE DID TOO... WE ALL WAS JUST FLEXIN' AND THEN BOOOM. SHE GOT HIT.
HE'S GONE. MASTER SUN IS GONE.
I'M SO SORRY. I TRIED.
SHHHH. YA DIDN'T JUST TRY. YA WON. LOOK 'ROUND YOU. CRIPS AND BLOODS. TOGETHER. WE ALL IN THIS.
THEN THIS WASN'T ALL FOR NOTHING. GUESS WE NEEDED SOME BIG, EVIL THING TO COME TOGETHER AND FIGHT.

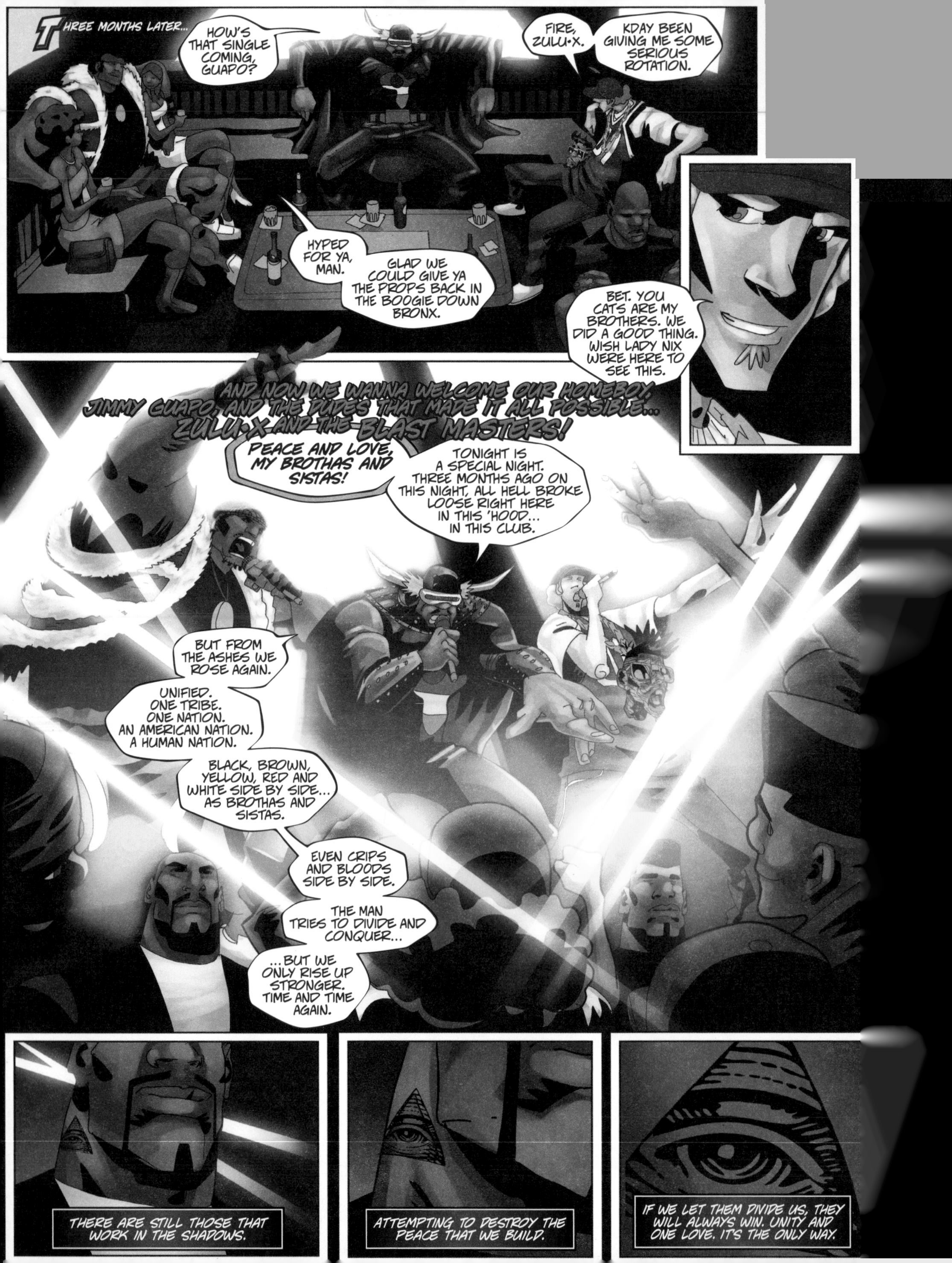
THREE MONTHS LATER...
HOW'S THAT SINGLE COMING, GUAPO?
FIRE, ZULU•X.
KDAY BEEN GIVING ME SOME SERIOUS ROTATION.
HYPED FOR YA, MAN.
GLAD WE COULD GIVE YA THE PROPS BACK IN THE BOOGIE DOWN BRONX.
BET. YOU CATS ARE MY BROTHERS. WE DID A GOOD THING. WISH LADY NIX WERE HERE TO SEE THIS.
AND NOW WE WANNA WELCOME OUR HOMEBOY, JIMMY GUAPO, AND THE DUDES THAT MADE IT ALL POSSIBLE... ZULU•X AND THE BLAST MASTERS!
PEACE AND LOVE, MY BROTHAS AND SISTAS!
TONIGHT IS A SPECIAL NIGHT. THREE MONTHS AGO ON THIS NIGHT, ALL HELL BROKE LOOSE RIGHT HERE IN THIS 'HOOD... IN THIS CLUB.
BUT FROM THE ASHES WE ROSE AGAIN.
UNIFIED. ONE TRIBE. ONE NATION. AN AMERICAN NATION. A HUMAN NATION.
BLACK, BROWN, YELLOW, RED AND WHITE SIDE BY SIDE... AS BROTHAS AND SISTAS.
EVEN CRIPS AND BLOODS SIDE BY SIDE.
THE MAN TRIES TO DIVIDE AND CONQUER...
...BUT WE ONLY RISE UP STRONGER. TIME AND TIME AGAIN.
THERE ARE STILL THOSE THAT WORK IN THE SHADOWS.
ATTEMPTING TO DESTROY THE PEACE THAT WE BUILD.
IF WE LET THEM DIVIDE US, THEY WILL ALWAYS WIN. UNITY AND ONE LOVE. IT'S THE ONLY WAY.

the big book of
casseroles

250 recipes for serious comfort food

by maryana vollstedt

CHRONICLE BOOKS

SAN FRANCISCO

Library of Congress Cataloging-in-Publication Data:
Vollstedt, Maryana.

The big book of casseroles: 250 recipes for serious comfort food/by Maryana Vollstedt.
320 p.   21 x 21 cm.
includes index.
ISBN 0-8118-2260-5 (pbk.)
1. Casserole cookery. I. Titles.
TX693.V65   2000
641.8'21—dc21   99-24508
                                CIP

Printed in the United States.

Designed by Vertigo Design, NYC

Illustrated by Ken Bloomer

Typeset in Bauer Topic and Century Schoolbook

Distributed in Canada by Raincoast Books
8680 Cambie Street
Vancouver, British Columbia V6P 6M9

10 9 8 7 6 5 4 3

Chronicle Books
85 Second Street
San Francisco, California 94105

www.chroniclebooks.com

dedication

Again, with love, to my faithful husband, Reed, chief tester, consultant, and computer person. Throughout the many years of my writing cookbooks, he has encouraged me with support, advice, and assistance. It has been fun cooking together, having testing parties, and giving cooking classes and demonstrations.

This book became a team effort because, without his patience and countless hours on the computer, it could never have been accomplished.

acknowledgements

To Bill LeBlond, senior editor at Chronicle Books, who gave me the opportunity to write a book of this scope and was optimistic that I could complete it in nine months.

To Deborah Kops, for her expert and thorough copyediting and many helpful suggestions and revisions. Thank you.

To Jim Herbold, good friend, computer adviser, and also tester.

And special thanks to friends and family members who contributed to this book and for their willingness to come to impromptu dinner parties to test and critique.

table of contents

A selection of creative fish and shellfish recipes with flavorful toppings.

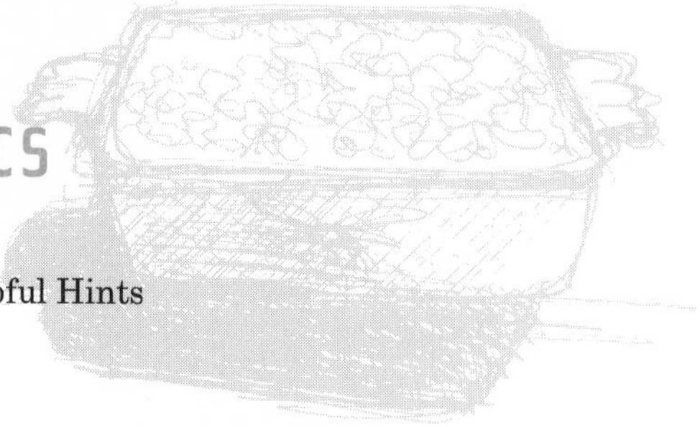

Many favorite classics updated, plus new creative dishes for family and friends.

Still considered the mainstays in many households. Since the meat is combined with vegetables, meat casseroles provide a well-balanced and satisfying meal.

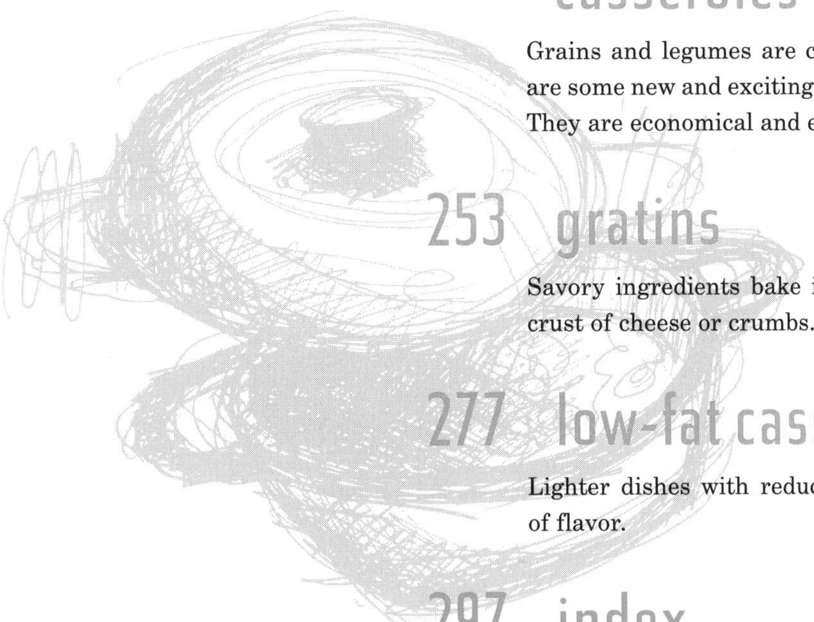

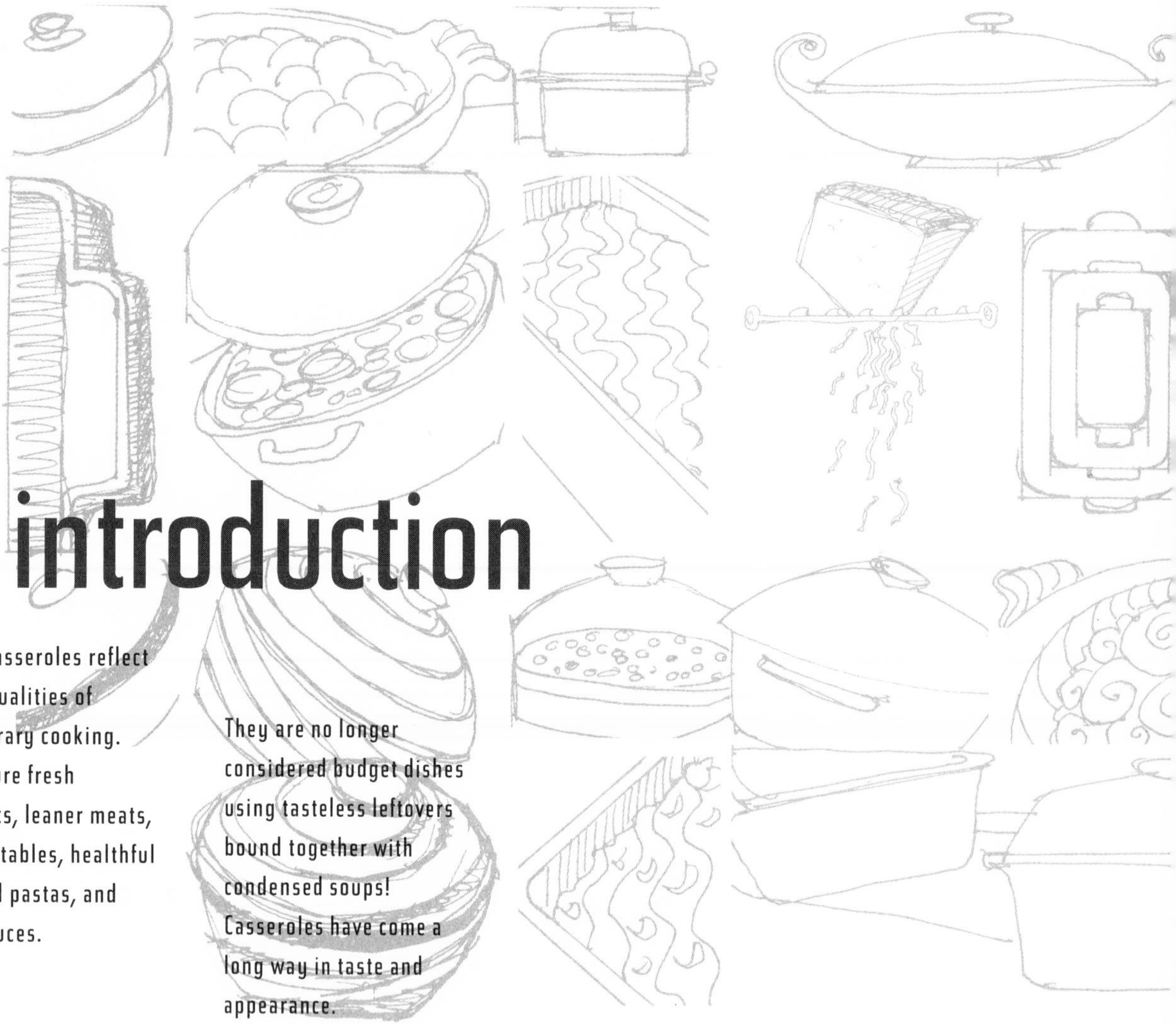

introduction

Today's casseroles reflect the best qualities of contemporary cooking. They feature fresh ingredients, leaner meats, more vegetables, healthful grains and pastas, and lighter sauces.

They are no longer considered budget dishes using tasteless leftovers bound together with condensed soups! Casseroles have come a long way in taste and appearance.

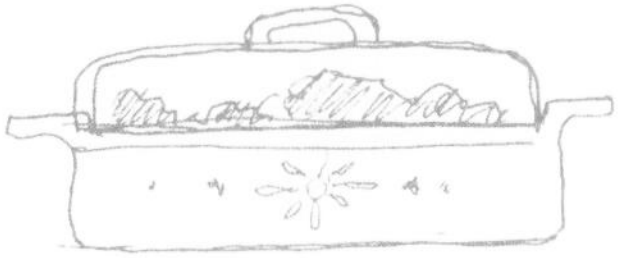

The term *casserole* originated in France in the early 1600s, and derives from the French word *casse,* a deep, round pot or crock for slow cooking. *Casserole* refers to both the preparation and the container in which it is cooked and often served. It may be made from glass (Pyrex), earthenware, stainless steel, enamel-lined cast iron, or some other flame-proof material and come in a variety of sizes, shapes, and colors. It is fun to have an assortment of casserole dishes to fit the contents and occasion.

Casserole ingredients are a combination of complementary foods cooked together in a flavorful sauce or broth. Toppings are often added, including grated cheese, bread or cracker crumbs, parsley, and nuts for added texture and appeal. Casseroles are usually baked in the oven, but they can also be cooked on the stove top or in a microwave oven if proper containers are used. Conventional ovens are preferable because slow baking enhances the flavors of the blended ingredients.

Casseroles have long been known for their convenience. They are popular with busy people, especially dual-employed couples with limited cooking time. Several casseroles can be made on the weekend, then frozen to be used later in the week. These "make ahead, bake later" recipes also appeal to the host or hostess who would like to avoid last-minute kitchen duty before a company dinner.

Casseroles go from oven to table, keeping ingredients hot for a long period of time. Serving is easy, and there is very little clean up. Many casseroles serve as main dishes or "one-pot meals," and others are complementary side dishes. They are perfect for potlucks, picnics, tailgate parties, buffets, or the bedside of a sick friend. A crisp, green salad, and warm crusty bread are all that are needed for a wholesome, satisfying meal.

The Big Book of Casseroles is a collection of over 250 exciting, all-purpose casseroles and oven dishes for every occasion, from family meals to gourmet dinner parties. Well-remembered flavors of the past are made lighter and are updated with fresh ingredients. You will also find new creations that reflect the latest food trends, favorite classics, ethnic-inspired dishes, and specialty casseroles.

Canned soups and dry mixes are not used in *The Big Book of Casseroles*. A simple, easy-to-make white sauce makes a tasteful and healthful substitute. Some canned staples are included for convenience, but fresh alternatives are given.

If you feel your cooking has become boring and dull, these delicious recipes will add interest, variety, and flexibility to your meal planning.

10 Advantages of Casseroles

1. Simplify meal planning.
2. Can be made ahead, refrigerated, or frozen and baked when needed.
3. Cleanup is done at the time of preparation, eliminating last-minute duties.
4. Bake without supervision.
5. Time savers—once the casserole is assembled, most of the work is done.
6. Convenient.
7. Economical, depending on ingredients. Leftovers can often be incorporated into casseroles.
8. Creative and diverse—add variety and interest to the menu.
9. Minimum equipment needed.
10. Can be held in a warm oven after baking to fit today's busy schedules

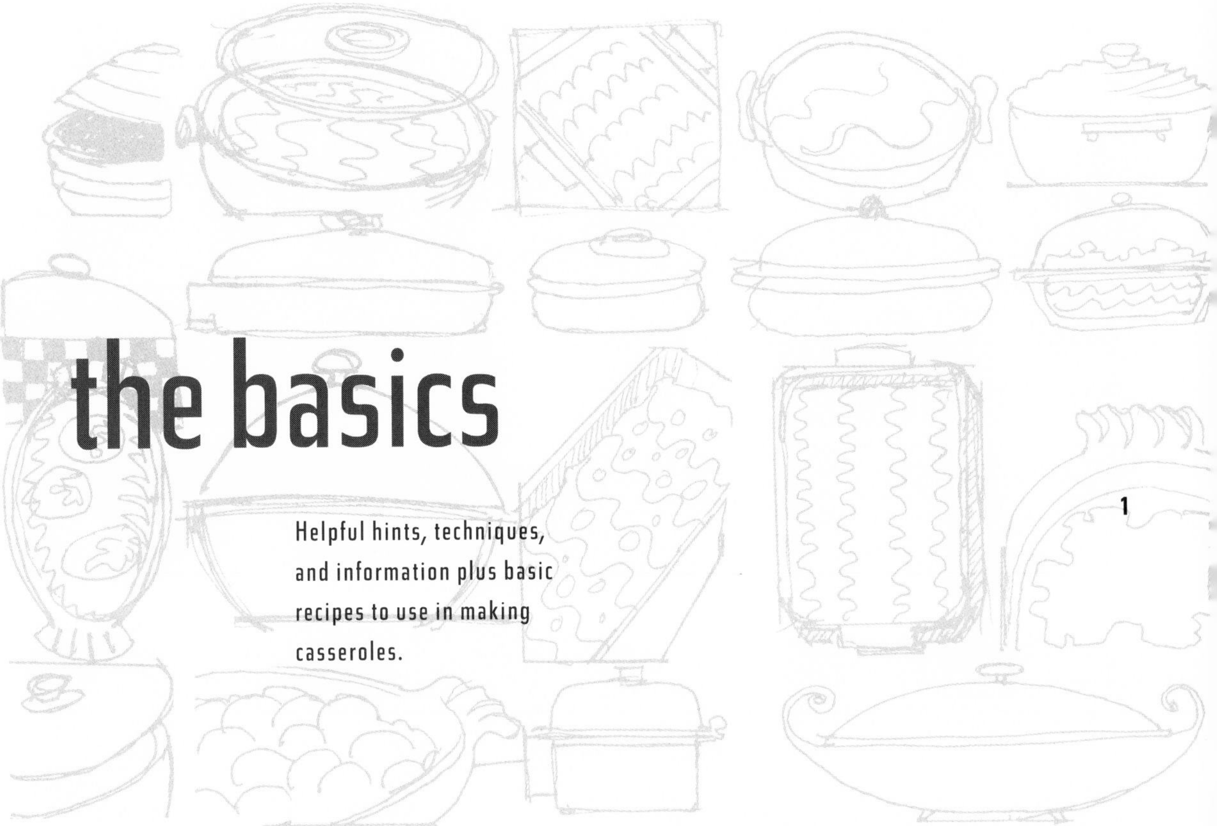

the basics

1

Helpful hints, techniques, and information plus basic recipes to use in making casseroles.

Casserole Tips

Preparing a Casserole

- Stock the pantry, refrigerator, and freezer with basic ingredients that you will need for making casseroles.
- Read the recipe carefully and check on the ingredients you have on hand.
- Make a complete grocery list and shop early (the day before, if making a casserole the next morning).
- Assemble all ingredients, tools, and baking dish.
- Prepare the ingredients.
- Assemble the casserole.

Baking a Casserole

Baking times are approximate and may vary, depending on when the casserole is baked. If baked immediately after preparation and the ingredients are still warm, it will take less time than a casserole that has been made ahead and refrigerated. Ovens may vary, contributing to the difficulty of predicting an exact baking time. Also, if other food is baking in the oven at the same time, the casserole will take slightly longer.

Casseroles are done when heated through and bubbly around the edges. Overbaking will cause a casserole to be dry. Some casseroles improve in flavor and texture if allowed to stand 5 to 10 minutes before serving. Follow the directions in the recipe.

To Assemble Ahead of Time

If the casserole is assembled ahead of time, to be baked later, cool slightly, cover, and store in the refrigerator or freeze as directed below. Bring to room temperature by removing the casserole from the refrigerator 1 hour before baking, but no longer because of the risk of salmonella.

Serving

Most casseroles can go directly from the oven to the table. The exceptions would be if the container is messy or if a more decorative serving dish is desired. Be sure to place a hot casserole on a protective pad or trivet.

Reheating

The microwave is a convenient and quick way to reheat casseroles without overcooking. Transfer leftovers to a smaller microwave-safe baking dish lightly coated with cooking spray or oil. If casserole is dry, add a little liquid called for in the recipe. Lightly cover and heat on high. Check often; it is easy to overcook. To warm in the oven, place in clean container, add more liquid, cover, and bake at 350°F until hot. Leftover casserole ingredients can also be warmed on top of the stove in a pan. Use low heat and stir gently.

Freezing

Before baking: Cover tightly with aluminum foil, label contents, date, and freeze immediately.
After baking: Transfer cooled leftovers to a smaller casserole or a plastic container. Cover tightly, label, and date.

To free up a casserole dish for another use, line bottom and sides of dish with foil before assembling the casserole. Cover and freeze until solid. Lift foil-covered contents out of dish and wrap tightly. To bake, remove wrap and place in original container, thaw, and proceed as directed.

techniques and helpful hints

COOKING PASTAS

The cooking time for pasta will vary according to its size and shape. Follow the directions on the package. Pasta should be cooked in a large pot filled with a generous amount of water—4 to 6 quarts to 1 pound of pasta. The pasta needs to move freely so it will cook evenly and not stick together. Adding salt to the water for flavor is optional.

To Cook Pasta

Bring water to a full boil. Add pasta and salt, if using, and stir. Reduce heat and cook, uncovered, at a gentle, rolling boil, stirring often. To test for doneness, remove a piece and bite into it. It should be *al dente*—firm, yet tender to the bite. Do not overcook. Drain in a large colander immediately, but do not rinse unless using for cold dishes. (Starches clinging to the pasta help thicken sauces.) Then quickly combine with sauce and other ingredients.

COOKING GRAINS

There are some wonderful new grains now available that add variety to casseroles, including barley, corn, millet, oats, quinoa, triticale, buckwheat, and wheat berries. Follow package directions for cooking.

Rice is one of the most commonly used grains. In addition to the standard varieties, many supermarkets stock fragrant rice, such as basmati and texmati, as well as arborio, a short-grain rice used for risotto.

Long-Grain White Rice

In a 2½- to 3-quart saucepan over high heat, bring 2¼ cups water or broth and 1 teaspoon salt (optional) to a boil. Stir in 1 cup rice, reduce heat to low, and simmer, covered, until liquid is absorbed and rice is tender, about 20 minutes. Fluff with a fork. Makes about 3 cups.

Brown Rice

In a 2½- or 3-quart saucepan over high heat, bring 2¼ cups water or broth and 1 teaspoon salt (optional) to a boil. Stir in 1 cup brown rice, reduce heat to low, and simmer, covered, until liquid is absorbed and rice is tender, 45 to 50 minutes. Fluff with a fork. Makes about 3 cups.

Wild Rice

Wild rice is not a true rice, but rather the grain of an aquatic grass. However, it is cooked and eaten like rice.

Place ⅔ cup wild rice in a strainer. Rinse very thoroughly under cold water, lifting rice with fingers to clean and drain. In a 2½ to 3-quart saucepan over high heat, bring 1¾ cups water, ¼ teaspoon salt, and the wild rice to a boil. Reduce heat and simmer, covered, until tender, 40 to 45 minutes. Fluff with a fork and simmer, uncovered, 5 minutes longer. Drain any excess liquid. Makes about 2 cups.

MAKING DRY BREAD CRUMBS

Preheat oven to 250°F. Tear bread into large pieces and process in a food processor until coarse or fine crumbs are formed, or tear into crumbs by hand. Spread crumbs out onto a baking sheet and dry in the oven until light brown,

about 20 minutes. Store in an airtight container in the freezer. Stale bread can be used. One slice of bread makes about 1 cup of bread crumbs. Very fine bread crumbs can be purchased plain or flavored in a carton.

COOKING CHICKEN

Use either skinned and boned chicken breasts or breasts with bone in and skin on. (The bones and skin add extra flavor.)

Poaching Chicken Breasts

Put chicken breasts in a saucepan. Add enough water or chicken stock to cover. For 4 chicken breast halves, add ¼ teaspoon salt, 1 parsley sprig, 1 piece of onion, and several black peppercorns. Bring to a boil over high heat, immediately reduce heat to low, and simmer (liquid should barely bubble), covered, until chicken turns white, about 15 minutes. Remove chicken to a plate to cool until ready to use, or cool in liquid if time allows. Remove any skin and bones, if necessary. Broth may be strained and refrigerated or frozen for other uses.

Poaching a Whole Chicken (fryer)

Remove giblets and set aside. Put chicken in a large pot with enough water to nearly cover. Add 1 unpeeled onion, quartered; 1 carrot, cut into chunks; 1 celery stalk with leaves, cut into chunks; 2 parsley sprigs; 2 or 3 peppercorns; and 1 teaspoon salt. Bring to a boil and skim off and discard any foam. Reduce heat to low and simmer, covered, until tender, about 45 minutes. Lift chicken from pot and cool on a plate. Remove meat and discard skin and bones. Cover and store meat in the refrigerator up to 3 days or divide meat into 2-cup portions and place in containers. Cover tightly and freeze for later use. Strained broth may be used for soups.

Skinning Chicken

With a paper towel, pull skin away from meat. To remove excess fat and remaining skin, trim with stainless steel kitchen scissors.

NOTE: After working with chicken, wash hands, utensils, and cutting boards thoroughly with soapy water to avoid cross-contamination with other foods.

MAKING PERFECT HARD-COOKED EGGS

Put eggs in a saucepan and add enough cold water to cover by at least 1 inch. Bring to a boil over high heat and boil for 15 seconds. Remove from heat, cover, and let stand 20 minutes. Then cool eggs immediately in cold water to prevent further cooking and the formation of a green ring around the yolk. Store in the refrigerator until ready to use.

COOKING FRESH SPINACH

Rinse spinach, drain, and remove stems, if desired. Place spinach in a large pan with ¼ cup water and ¼ teaspoon salt. Bring to a boil over high heat, reduce heat, and cook until wilted, about 2 minutes, tossing with a fork several times while cooking. Drain in a sieve and press with the back of a spoon against the sieve to remove remaining moisture. Blot with a paper towel.

One bag (6 ounces) fresh spinach, cooked, drained, and squeezed dry makes about ½ cup. Alternatively, 1 package (10 ounces) frozen chopped spinach, thawed, drained, and squeezed dry makes about 1¼ cups.

7

ROASTING RED BELL PEPPERS

Preheat the broiler. Cut peppers in half lengthwise and remove seeds and ribs. Make several 1-inch slashes around the edge of each pepper half. Place skin side up on an aluminum foil–lined baking sheet with a rim. Press peppers down with the palm of your hand to flatten. Broil until skin is charred, about 10 minutes. Remove from broiler, fold foil tightly over peppers, and let them steam for 15 minutes. Unwrap peppers and peel off skin.

   Whole peppers can also be roasted over a gas flame by spearing with a long handled fork and turning as they become charred, or placed on a grill and turned with tongs.

COOKING WITH TOMATOES

Removing the Skins

Drop tomatoes into boiling water to cover for 30 seconds. Remove immediately with a slotted spoon and rinse under cold water; then peel. Skins will slip off easily.

Removing the Seeds

Cut tomato in half. Hold tomato half over the sink and gently squeeze, or using a finger lift out seeds along with some of the juice.

Using Canned Tomatoes and other Tomato Products

Canned tomatoes are used often in casseroles. They are available in variety of forms—peeled, whole, crushed, stewed, diced, in a sauce, a paste or a purée, and plain or with herbs. Roma (Italian plum) tomatoes are popular because they are

meatier, have fewer seeds and less juice, and hold up well during canning. Some people prefer organic canned tomatoes. You may have your own preferences.

Sun-dried tomatoes are packed in oil or dry packed. They are intesly flavored and chewy.

Storing Leftover Tomato Paste

Place in a small jar and freeze. Or measure in 1-tablespoon dollops and freeze on a piece of foil. Then seal in a plastic bag and store in freezer.

COOKING WITH HERBS

Use fresh herbs when in season. Dried herbs are available year round and may be more convenient. To substitute dried herbs for fresh herbs, some strengths may vary, but the general rule is to use 1 teaspoon dried for 1 tablespoon fresh. Crumble dried herbs between the fingers to release the flavor before adding to a recipe.

TO SLIVER FRESH BASIL AND OTHER LEAFY HERBS AND VEGETABLES

This procedure is called a chiffonade.

Stack 5 or 6 washed and dried basil leaves on top of each other and tightly roll into a tube. Thinly slice crosswise.

SKINNING PEACHES AND APRICOTS

See instructions for removing tomato skins on previous page.

TO SOFTEN TORTILLAS

There are a number of easy methods for warming tortillas. Fry them one at a time briefly in hot oil and drain. Wrap them in paper towels and microwave for 15 to 20 seconds. Wrap them in aluminum foil and place in a 350°F oven for 6 to 7 minutes. Fry them one at a time over medium heat in a small nonstick skillet or griddle lightly coated with cooking spray or oil. Heat on grill turning once with tongs. Stack tortillas and keep warm until ready to use.

COOKING DRIED BEANS

Presoaking shortens the length of cooking time. Wash beans thoroughly under cold water. Pick over and discard any foreign matter or discolored beans.

Overnight Method

Sort beans for any foreign matter or discolored beans. In a large soup pot, place beans and water to cover. Let stand overnight.

Quick-Soak Method

In a large soup pot, place beans and water to cover. Bring to a boil over high heat and boil 2 minutes. Skim off foam that rises to the surface. Remove from heat, cover, and let stand 1 hour.

NOTE: Do not salt beans until the end of cooking period; salt toughens the beans.

THE BIG BOOK OF CASSEROLES

To Cook Beans

Drain beans and add fresh water to cover by 2 inches. Bring to a boil over high heat, skimming off any foam that rises to the surface. Reduce heat to low, cover, and simmer until beans are tender. Add more liquid if needed.

TOASTING NUTS AND SEEDS

Almonds (whole or slivered), Cashews, Pecans, Peanuts, and Walnuts

Preheat oven to 350°F. Put nuts on a baking sheet and bake, stirring once, 5 to 6 minutes. Cool before using.

Hazelnuts

Preheat oven to 350°F. Spread hazelnuts on a baking sheet and bake until lightly colored and skins are blistered, 12 to 15 minutes. Wrap hot nuts in a clean towel to steam for 1 minute. Then rub the nuts in the towel to remove most of the skins.

Pine Nuts

Place pine nuts in a small nonstick skillet over medium-high heat. Stir with a wooden spoon until toasted, 4 to 5 minutes.

Sesame Seeds

Place seeds in a small nonstick skillet and cook over medium-high heat, stirring until golden, about 2 minutes.

Cooking Terms

Al dente Describes pasta that is firm to the bite, but still chewy. When referring to vegetables, tender-crisp.

Beat To mix vigorously with spoon or mixer.

Blanch To plunge food into boiling water briefly, then into cold water to stop cooking process.

Blend To mix well until smooth.

Boil To heat liquid until bubbles break the surface.

Chop To cut into small irregular pieces.

Cube To cut into ½-inch or larger cubes.

Devein To remove intestine in curved back of a shrimp.

Dice To cut into tiny cubes smaller than a ½ inch.

Flake To separate fish and other foods into sections with a fork.

Flameproof A pan such as a Dutch oven that resists stove top, broiler, and oven temperatures.

Floret The tender blooms or crown of broccoli and cauliflower.

Garnish An edible decoration added to food before serving.

Grate To cut into thin strips using a hand grater or food processor fitted with a grating blade.

Gratin dish A shallow baking dish. Also a term for baked ingredients topped with crumbs, cheese, or both.

Julienne Matchstick strips.

Marinate To soak food in a seasoned liquid to flavor and in some cases tenderize.

Mince To cut into very fine pieces, as in minced garlic.

Pare To remove an outer covering, such as potato or apple skins, with a knife.

Peel To strip off outer covering, such as banana or orange skin, by hand.

Preheat To heat oven to temperature specified in recipe.

Purée To reduce food to a smooth, thick consistency with a food processor or blender.

Sauté To cook food in a small amount of fat on top of stove for a short period of time, stirring often.

Skin To remove skin from poultry or fish.

Slice To cut into flat pieces.

Stir To mix ingredients in a circular motion.

Toss To gently tumble ingredients, such as pasta or salads.

Whisk To stir ingredients together with a wire whip to blend.

Lightening Up

Here are some general hints for trimming fat and calories from your diet:

- Use non-fat or low-fat dairy products such as milk, cottage cheese, yogurt, part-skim cheeses, and buttermilk.
- Coat baking dishes and skillets with nonstick vegetable spray, or use a spray-pump bottle filled with olive oil or canola oil.
- Use fat-free or light mayonnaise, or mix plain nonfat yogurt with mayonnaise.
- Use Nonfat Yogurt Cheese mixed with pasta (page 20).
- Use fewer saturated fats (animal fats) and more unsaturated fats (derived from plants)—especially monounsaturated fats, such as olive, canola, and peanut oils, and polyunsaturated fats, such as saffola, soybean, corn, and sesame oils.
- Remove skin from chicken parts, or use skinned and boned chicken breasts.
- Trim excess fat from meat and poultry.
- Include more white meat—chicken, pork tenderloin, turkey cutlets, and ground turkey—and less red meat in your diet.
- Use fat-free, low-sodium broths.
- Use vegetable purées to thicken and add flavor to sauces and gravies.
- Use more herbs and spices in low-fat recipes to compensate for reduced fat flavor.
- Season vegetables with soy sauce, garlic, or balsamic vinegar to intensify their flavors.

- Substitute 2 egg whites for 1 egg.
- Substitute skim evaporated milk for cream.
- Add broth, wine, or cooking liquid to moisten pasta dishes instead of cream and sour cream.
- Include more pastas, grains, and vegetables in your diet.
- Use nonstick utensils.
- Use cooking methods that require little or no additional fat, such as broiling, baking, grilling, or steaming. Avoid frying.

Basic Recipes

basic white sauce

2 tablespoons butter or margarine

2 tablespoons all-purpose flour

¼ teaspoon salt

⅛ teaspoon white pepper

1 cup milk

NOTE: For a thin white sauce, decrease butter and flour to 1 tablespoon each. For a thick white sauce, increase butter to 4 tablespoons and flour to ¼ cup.

IN a small saucepan over medium heat, melt butter. Add flour, salt, and pepper, stirring constantly, until bubbly. Stir in milk. Heat to boiling, stirring or whisking constantly until thickened, about 1 minute.

MAKES ABOUT 1 CUP

quick tomato sauce

1 can (15 ounces) tomato sauce

½ teaspoon dried oregano

½ teaspoon dried basil

¼ teaspoon dried marjoram, crumbled

2 cloves garlic, minced

Freshly ground pepper to taste

IN a medium saucepan over medium heat, combine all ingredients and simmer, uncovered, 5 to 10 minutes.

MAKES ABOUT 1 CUP

fresh tomato salsa

Serve at room temperature with tortilla chips, in dips, or with grilled fish, chicken, polenta, or as an accompaniment to Mexican casseroles.

4 tomatoes, seeded, chopped, and drained

½ cup diced green bell pepper (optional)

½ cup chopped yellow onion

1 tablespoon seeded and minced jalapeño pepper (see Note), or 1 tablespoon diced canned chiles

2 cloves garlic, minced

Juice of 1 small lime

1 tablespoon olive oil

¼ cup chopped fresh cilantro or parsley

1 tablespoon chopped fresh oregano, or ¾ teaspoon dried oregano

½ teaspoon salt

Freshly ground pepper to taste

IN a medium bowl, stir together all ingredients. Cover and let stand at room temperature at least 1 hour, then store in refrigerator up to 3 days. Drain, if necessary, before using.

MAKES ABOUT 3 CUPS

Note: When handling chiles, wear rubber gloves or hold the chiles under water to protect yourself against oils that may cause burning to the skin. Keep fingers away from face and eyes. Wash hands with soapy water immediately after handling.

basil pesto

2 cups firmly packed fresh basil leaves, washed and dried

2 sprigs fresh parsley

2 cloves garlic, coarsely chopped

3 tablespoons pine nuts

¼ cup freshly grated Parmesan cheese

¼ teaspoon salt

Freshly ground pepper to taste

3 to 4 tablespoons olive oil

NOTE: Pesto will darken on top; this is normal. Stir before using.

PLACE all ingredients except oil in a food processor or blender. Process until minced. With motor running, slowly pour oil through the feed tube and blend until paste forms. Scrape down sides of bowl with spatula. Transfer to a bowl, cover, and refrigerate until ready to use, or freeze an airtight container up to 3 months. Bring to room temperature before mixing with pasta.

MAKES ABOUT ½ CUP

basic polenta

Polenta is a staple of Northern Italy that has recently become popular in the United States. It can be served as a thick, hearty breakfast porridge or combined with other ingredients and served as a main course or side dish. Here are directions for baked, fried, and grilled polenta.

NOTE: For additional flavor, substitute Rich Chicken Stock (page 23) or canned low-sodium chicken broth for water.

1   cup yellow cornmeal
3½ cups cold water
½   teaspoon salt

2   tablespoons freshly grated Parmesan cheese (optional)
1   tablespoon butter or margarine (optional)

IN a small bowl, mix cornmeal with 1 cup water. In a medium saucepan over high heat, combine remaining 2½ cups water and salt and bring to a boil. Slowly pour cornmeal mixture into boiling water, stirring occasionally. Reduce heat to low and simmer, uncovered, stirring constantly, until cornmeal mixture is thick and smooth, about 3 minutes. Remove from heat. If desired, stir in Parmesan cheese and butter. Serve in a bowl as a side dish.

TO BAKE: Preheat oven to 350°F. Turn Basic Polenta into a 7½-by-11¾-inch glass baking dish lightly coated with cooking spray or oil. Sprinkle with grated cheese or top with tomato sauce, if desired. Bake, uncovered, until firm, about 20 minutes. Let stand 5 minutes. Then cut into squares and serve immediately.

TO FRY OR GRILL: Turn Basic Polenta into a 7½-by-11¾-inch glass baking dish lightly coated with cooking spray or oil. Cover and chill several hours until firm. Cut chilled polenta into 2-by-3-inch pieces.

TO FRY: In a large, nonstick skillet over medium heat, cook polenta in 2 to 3 tablespoons butter until golden and crisp, 5 to 6 minutes on each side.

TO GRILL: Brush grill well with vegetable oil and grill until warm and grill marks are visible, 6 to 8 minutes on each side.

MAKES ABOUT 3½ CUPS

nonfat yogurt cheese

For a creamy pasta dish without the calories, try mixing this sauce with your favorite pasta. You'll need to make it ahead.

2   cups nonfat plain yogurt (made without gelatin)

¼   teaspoon dried basil

¼   teaspoon dried oregano

PLACE yogurt in a sieve lined with cheesecloth or a coffee filter. Suspend over a deep bowl, cover tightly with plastic wrap, and refrigerate 12 hours, or overnight. Discard liquid in the bottom of the bowl. Mix in herbs. Use immediately or store in an airtight container up to 1 week.

MAKES ABOUT 2 CUPS

HOMEMADE STOCKS OR BROTH

Homemade stocks provide the richest flavor. They are convenient to have on hand in the freezer.

When making stock, use fresh ingredients, not leftovers. After the stock is made, you can intensify the flavor by boiling it until the desired concentration is achieved. If you're short of time and don't have any stock in storage, use canned fat-free, low-sodium regular strength broth.

fish stock

Bottled clam juice may be substituted for fish stock if you do not want to make your own.

2   pounds fish bones and trimmings
1   celery stalk, sliced
1   yellow onion, sliced
1   clove garlic, unpeeled
8   cups cold water
1   cup dry white wine
1   tablespoon fresh lemon juice
1   teaspoon salt
1   teaspoon peppercorns
½   teaspoon dried thyme
4   sprigs fresh parsley
1   bay leaf

RINSE fish bones and trimmings. In a large Dutch oven over high heat, bring all ingredients to a boil. Skim off foam. Reduce heat to medium-low or low and simmer, covered, about 30 minutes. Strain through a sieve lined with cheesecloth or a very fine sieve. Discard solids. Use immediately or freeze in airtight containers up to 3 months.

MAKES ABOUT 8 CUPS

beef stock

Roasting the bones in the oven makes a richer and browner stock. This step is optional, however.

2½ to 3 pounds meaty beef bones
1 carrot, cut into chunks
1 celery stalk, cut into chunks
1 onion, quartered

2 cloves garlic, halved
6 peppercorns
3 whole cloves
3 sprigs fresh parsley
1 bay leaf
8 cups water

PREHEAT oven to 400°F. Place bones in a roasting pan and brown about 30 minutes. Transfer to a large stockpot, add remaining ingredients, and bring to a boil over high heat. Skim foam from broth, reduce heat to low, and simmer, covered, about 3 hours. Remove bones.

STRAIN broth through a sieve lined with a double thickness of cheesecloth or a very fine sieve. Discard solids. Degrease with a fat separator or cover and refrigerate overnight. Remove layer of fat that forms on the top and discard. Use immediately or freeze in airtight containers for future use. Will keep in refrigerator for 3 or 4 days, and up to 3 months in the freezer.

MAKES ABOUT 8 CUPS

rich chicken stock

To make chicken stock, save up the raw boney parts that you don't cook with and freeze until you have about 3 pounds, or use a whole chicken.

1 yellow onion, quartered

2 celery stalks, cut into chunks

2 carrots, cut into chunks

One 2½ to 3 pound chicken, or 3 pounds chicken parts (backs, wings, necks, and giblets; do not use the liver, which will make the broth cloudy)

8 cups water

4 cloves garlic, unpeeled

1 teaspoon salt

1 bay leaf

10 peppercorns

3 sprigs fresh parsley

½ teaspoon dried thyme

PLACE all the ingredients except thyme in a large stockpot. Bring to a boil over high heat. Skim off foam. Add thyme, reduce heat to low, and simmer, partially covered, about 1 hour. Pour stock through a sieve lined with a double thickness of cheesecloth or a very fine sieve. Discard solids. (Chicken meat may be saved for another use, if desired.) Degrease stock with a fat separator or store, covered, in the refrigerator overnight. Remove layer of fat that forms on the top and discard. Use within 2 to 3 days or freeze in airtight containers up to 3 months.

MAKES ABOUT 8 CUPS

vegetable stock

Vegetable stock is great to have on hand for vegetarian dishes and soups.

3 yellow onions, quartered
6 carrots, cut into chunks
2 parsnips, cut into chunks
2 celery stalks, cut into chunks
3 cabbage leaves, cut up
1 red bell pepper, seeded, and coarsely chopped
2 bay leaves
1 clove garlic, chopped
6 peppercorns
2 whole cloves
8 cups water
1 teaspoon fresh thyme leaves
6 sprigs fresh parsley
Salt to taste

PLACE all ingredients in a large stockpot over high heat. Bring to a boil and skim off gray foam. Reduce heat and simmer, uncovered, about 1 hour. Strain through sieve lined with a double thickness of cheese cloth or a very fine sieve. Discard solids and add salt. Use immediately or freeze in air tight containers for future use. Will keep in refrigerator for 3 or 4 days, and up to 3 months in the freezer.

MAKES ABOUT 8 CUPS

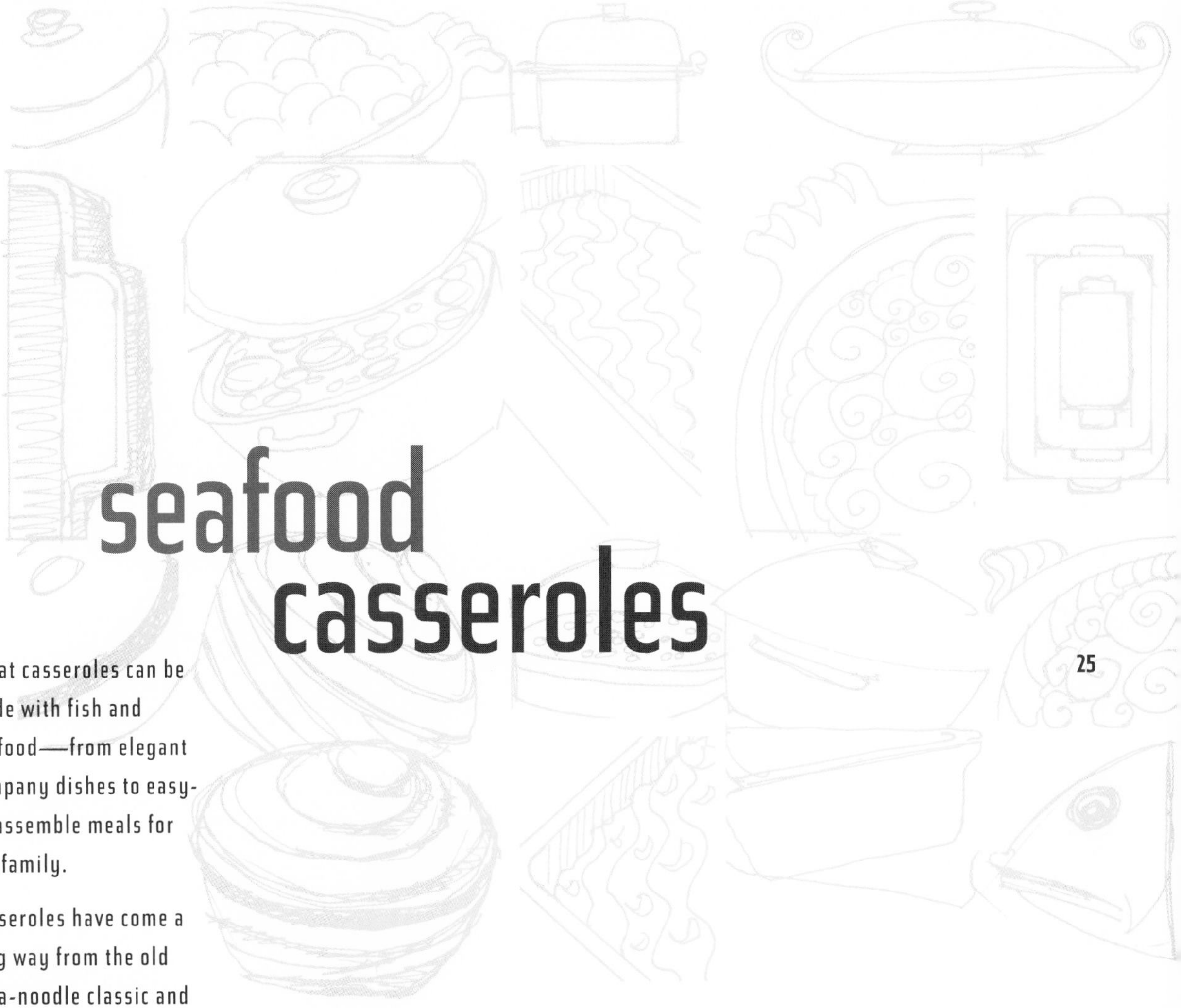

seafood casseroles

Great casseroles can be made with fish and seafood—from elegant company dishes to easy-to-assemble meals for the family.

Casseroles have come a long way from the old tuna-noodle classic and have become popular entrées. They are a way to stretch more expensive seafood by combining it with other ingredients, such as pasta and rice, and still enjoy the taste of the sea.

jambalaya

A tangy New Orleans Creole dish influenced by French and Spanish cuisine, Jambalaya is a combination of seafood, poultry, ham, sausage, tomatoes, seasonings, and rice. Sometimes oysters are included; ingredients vary with the cook.

1 to 1½ tablespoons olive oil

2 chicken breast halves (about 1 pound), cooked (see page 6) and cut into bite-sized pieces

½ pound cooked ham, cubed

½ pound Italian sausage, cooked and cut into ½-inch pieces (see Note)

1 cup chopped yellow onion

4 cloves garlic, minced

1 green bell pepper, seeded and cut into 1-inch pieces

1 cup long-grain white rice

1 can (28 ounces) whole tomatoes, chopped, juice from can included

1 cup Rich Chicken Stock (page 23) or canned low-sodium chicken broth

1 teaspoon Worcestershire sauce

½ teaspoon Tabasco sauce

½ teaspoon dried thyme

1 bay leaf

½ teaspoon salt

Freshly ground pepper to taste

1¼ pounds large shrimp, peeled and deveined

Chopped fresh parsley for garnish

PREHEAT oven to 350°F. In a Dutch oven over medium heat, warm 1 tablespoon oil. Add chicken and meats and cook until they begin to brown, 5 to 10 minutes. Remove to a plate. Add onion, garlic, and green pepper and sauté until tender, about 5 minutes. Add remaining oil, if needed. Stir in rice, tomatoes, stock, Worcestershire sauce, Tabasco sauce, and seasonings. Return meats to pan. Bring to a boil, reduce heat, and simmer, covered, 10 minutes. The dish can be made ahead up to this point and refrigerated (see Note).

COVER the casserole and bake 35 minutes. Tuck in shrimp and bake about 10 minutes, covered, until rice is tender, liquid is absorbed, and shrimp turns pink, stirring once. Remove bay leaf and discard. Sprinkle with parsley and serve immediately in the pan or on a warmed platter for an impressive presentation.

SERVES 6

NOTE: Smoked sausage, which needs no precooking, may be used. To cook fresh sausage, simmer in water 10 to 15 minutes. Drain well.

If the casserole is made ahead, bring to room temperature before baking and allow an extra 15 minutes in the oven.

seafood stew

The focus of this stew is on seafood, which is baked in an herbed tomato sauce. This is a fun supper to share with friends. Serve with warm foccacia, followed by ice cream with toppings for dessert.

3 tablespoons butter or margarine

1 large yellow onion, chopped

2 cloves garlic, minced

3 tablespoons all-purpose flour

2 cans (28 ounces each) whole tomatoes, juice from can included, lightly puréed in food processor

1½ cups chicken stock

½ cup dry white wine

1 bay leaf

1 teaspoon dried basil

½ teaspoon dried oregano

½ teaspoon dried thyme

¾ teaspoon salt

Freshly ground pepper to taste

1 cup chopped fresh parsley

1 pound scallops or white-fleshed fish, such as snapper, flounder, or cod, cut into bite-size pieces

1 pound large shrimp, peeled and deveined

1½ pounds fresh clams in shells, well scrubbed

PREHEAT oven to 400°F. In a Dutch oven over medium heat, melt butter. Add onions and garlic and sauté until tender, about 5 minutes. Add flour and stir until bubbly. Add tomatoes, broth, wine, seasonings, and parsley and simmer, 5 minutes.

BAKE, uncovered, about 30 minutes. Add scallops or fish and bake, covered, 10 minutes. Add clams and shrimp and bake, covered, until shrimp has turned pink and clams have opened, about 10 minutes longer. (Discard any clams that do not open.) Ladle into bowls.

SERVES 6 TO 8

seafood gumbo

Gumbo is a Creole specialty from New Orleans. There are many versions of this zesty, stewlike dish, but the one common ingredient is always okra. Tomatoes, onions, chicken, sausage, and seafood are used as well.

Our first introduction to gumbo was when we were house guests of some friends in Gulf Shores, Alabama. Their traditional Fourth of July dinner was Seafood Gumbo served in bowls over hot rice. We loved it! It can be made on the stove top or baked in the oven, casserole style, as this recipe suggests.

¼ cup all-purpose flour

1½ tablespoons vegetable oil

8 chicken thighs (about 2½ pounds), skinned

2 kielbasa sausages (about 1 pound), cut into ⅜-inch slices

1 cup chopped yellow onion

1 red bell pepper, seeded and diced

1 celery stalk, sliced

2 cups fresh okra, trimmed and sliced into ½-inch slices; or 1 can (14½ ounces) cut okra, rinsed, drained, and sliced

PREHEAT oven to 350°F. In a Dutch oven over medium-low heat, toast flour until golden, 10 to 15 minutes, stirring frequently. Transfer to a small bowl and set aside (see Note).

IN the Dutch oven, over medium-high heat, warm 1 tablespoon oil. Add chicken and brown about 5 minutes on each side. Transfer to a plate. Reduce heat to medium. Add more oil, if needed, and then add the sausages, onions, pepper, celery, okra, and garlic. Sauté until sausage is lightly browned and vegetables are tender, 5 to 10 minutes.

STIR ¼ cup of chicken stock into flour and blend. Add to Dutch oven and stir. Whisk in remaining broth.

3 cloves garlic, minced

2 cups chicken stock

1 can (14½ ounces) crushed
 tomatoes in thick purée

1 teaspoon salt

Freshly ground pepper to taste

1 teaspoon dried thyme

1 bay leaf

3 drops Tabasco sauce

1 pound white-fleshed fish,
 such as red snapper,
 flounder, or lingcod, cut
 into bite-size pieces

1 pound large shrimp, peeled
 and deveined

¼ cup chopped fresh parsley

RETURN chicken to Dutch oven, stir in tomatoes and seasonings, and bring to a boil. Cover and bake 40 minutes. Add seafood and bake until chicken is no longer pink in the center and shrimp has turned pink, 10 to 15 minutes longer. Remove bay leaf and discard. Serve in bowls over rice. Sprinkle with parsley.

SERVES 8

NOTE: Browning the flour adds flavor and color to the sauce, but it may be omitted.

29

seafood lasagna

This got a top rating at one of our casserole tasting parties. Lots of shrimp and crab bake with lasagna noodles in a rich, creamy sauce. It is expensive, but worth it. Serve with a mushroom salad and a tart lemon pie for a special occasion.

4 ounces light cream cheese, at room temperature

1½ cups low-fat cottage cheese

1 cup grated mozzarella cheese

½ cup sliced green onions, including some tender green tops

¼ cup chopped fresh parsley

9 lasagna noodles, cooked and drained

Seafood Sauce (recipe follows)

1 cup freshly grated Parmesan cheese

PREHEAT oven to 350°F. In a medium bowl, blend cream cheese and cottage cheese. Stir in mozzarella, onions, and parsley.

PLACE 3 noodles side by side in a 9-by-13-inch baking dish lightly coated with cooking spray or oil. Add one third of the cheese mixture and cover with one third of the Seafood Sauce (It will not cover completely.) Repeat layers two more times. Top with Parmesan cheese.

BAKE, uncovered, until bubbly, about 45 minutes. Let stand 10 minutes before serving.

SERVES 8

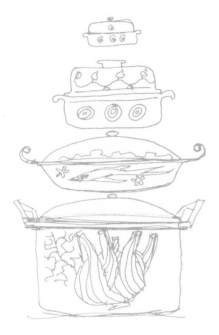

seafood sauce

3	tablespoons all-purpose flour		Freshly ground pepper to taste
¼	cup water	¼	cup dry white wine
1½	cups milk	¾	pound small (bay) shrimp
½	teaspoon dried basil	½	pound crabmeat, picked and flaked
½	teaspoon salt		

IN a small bowl, blend flour with water. In a saucepan over medium heat, warm milk with seasonings. Stir in flour mixture, bring to a boil, and whisk until thickened, 3 to 4 minutes. Add wine and seafood and mix well.

MAKES ABOUT 4 CUPS

spicy bouillabaisse

This wonderful stew is enhanced by the addition of spices. The choice of seafood may vary according to personal preference and availability. Serve with a salad of field greens and a lemon vinaigrette dressing.

3 tablespoons butter or margarine

1 cup chopped yellow onion

3 cloves garlic, minced

3 tablespoons all-purpose flour

½ teaspoon curry powder

½ teaspoon ground cloves

2 tablespoons brown sugar

⅛ teaspoon saffron threads, crumbled

1 teaspoon salt

Freshly ground pepper to taste

1 can (46 ounces) tomato juice

¼ teaspoon Tabasco sauce

1 can (6½ ounces) minced clams, including juice

¼ cup dry white wine

¼ cup chopped fresh parsley

½ pound large shrimp, peeled and deveined

½ pound crabmeat, flaked

½ pound scallops (if large, cut in half)

1½ pounds white-fleshed fish, such as snapper, flounder, or cod, cut into bite-size pieces

PREHEAT oven to 375°F. In a Dutch oven over medium heat, melt butter. Add onion and garlic and sauté until tender, about 5 minutes. Stir in flour and blend. Add curry, cloves, sugar, saffron, salt, and pepper and mix well.

WHISK in tomato juice and Tabasco sauce and bring to a boil, stirring constantly. Reduce heat, add clams and juice, wine, and parsley. Simmer, uncovered, until flavors are blended, about 10 minutes.

ADD seafood and bake, uncovered, until fish flakes, about 20 minutes. Serve in bowls.

SERVES 6 TO 8

cioppino

Originating in San Francisco, this Italian fisherman's stew combines the bounty of the sea with an herbed tomato sauce. The result is one great dish. Serve with a baguette and your favorite salad for a terrific meal.

2 tablespoons vegetable oil

1 large yellow onion, chopped

2 cloves garlic, minced

1 green bell pepper, seeded and chopped

1 can (28 ounces) plum tomatoes, coarsely chopped, juice from can included

1 can (16 ounces) tomato sauce

1 cup dry white wine

1 teaspoon salt

¼ teaspoon dried basil

½ teaspoon dried thyme

¼ teaspoon dried oregano

1 bay leaf

¼ teaspoon freshly ground pepper

1½ pounds white-fleshed fish fillets, such as snapper, flounder, or cod, cut into ½-inch chunks

½ pound large shrimp, peeled and deveined

16 to 20 steamer clams in shells, well scrubbed

¼ cup chopped fresh parsley

PREHEAT oven to 350°F. In a Dutch oven over medium heat, warm oil. Add onion, garlic, and bell pepper and sauté until tender, about 5 minutes. Stir in tomatoes, tomato sauce, wine, and seasonings and simmer to blend flavors, about 5 minutes. Add fish chunks and shrimp.

COVER and bake 20 minutes. Add clams and bake, covered, until clams open, about 10 minutes longer. (Discard any clams that do not open).

REMOVE bay leaf and discard. Stir in parsley. Serve in large bowls.

SERVES 6

33

THE BIG BOOK OF CASSEROLES

classic paella

This Spanish dish is a combination of seafood, meats, vegetables, and saffron rice. Each region in Spain has a different version, and no two are alike. There are several steps involved, but the result is a hearty, one-pot meal with great flavor. *Paella* also refers to the name of the pan in which the dish is baked and served. It is a wide, shallow pan with 2 handles.

½ pound chorizo link sausage, cut into ½-inch-thick slices

2 to 3 tablespoons vegetable oil

2½ pounds chicken legs

1 teaspoon salt, plus more to taste

¼ teaspoon pepper, plus more to taste

2 cups short-grain (arborio) rice

4 cups Rich Chicken Stock (page 23) or canned low-sodium chicken broth

¼ teaspoon dried oregano

⅛ teaspoon powdered saffron

1 large yellow onion, chopped

IN a large nonstick skillet over medium heat, brown chorizo, turning frequently, for 5 minutes. Using a slotted spoon, transfer to a plate. Add 1 to 2 tablespoons of the oil, as needed. Brown chicken legs on all sides, turning frequently, about 10 minutes. Season with salt and pepper to taste. Reduce heat to medium-low, cover, and cook chicken until tender, about 20 minutes. Remove to plate holding chorizo.

MEANWHILE, in a saucepan, combine rice, stock, oregano, 1 teaspoon salt, ¼ teaspoon pepper, and saffron. Bring to a boil, reduce heat to low, cover, and cook until rice is tender, about 20 minutes.

PREHEAT oven to 350°F. Add 1 tablespoon oil to skillet. Add onion, bell pepper, and garlic and sauté over medium heat until tender, about 5 minutes. Add tomatoes, parsley, and pimientos and cook 2 minutes more. Remove vegetable mixture to a bowl.

1   green bell pepper, seeded
    and chopped

1   red bell pepper, seeded and
    chopped

3   cloves garlic, minced

2   large tomatoes, seeded,
    chopped, and drained

¼   cup chopped fresh parsley

1   jar (2 ounces) pimientos,
    drained and chopped

1   cup fresh green peas, or
    frozen green peas, thawed

1   pound large shrimp, peeled
    and deveined

18 to 20 steamer clams in
    shells, well scrubbed

¼   cup chopped fresh parsley
    for garnish

2   limes, cut into wedges, for
    garnish

TRANSFER rice to a paella pan or a 4-quart baking dish lightly coated with cooking spray or oil. Gently mix in chorizo, sautéed vegetables, and peas. Press shrimp into rice mixture and lay chicken legs on top. Arrange clams around them.

BAKE, uncovered, until clams open and paella is heated through, 25 to 30 minutes. (Discard any clams that do not open.) Sprinkle with parsley and garnish with lime wedges. Serve immediately.

SERVES 8

VARIATION: Omit pimientos and add 1 cup pimiento-stuffed green olives with the seafood.

35

baked seafood, orzo, and feta cheese casserole

Of the six casseroles at one of our tasting parties, this was one of the favorites. Halibut and shrimp pair well together with pasta. Serve with a cabbage salad and creamy dill dressing.

1 tablespoon vegetable oil

1 large yellow onion, chopped

3 cloves garlic, minced

1 large can (28 ounces) tomatoes, chopped, juice from can included

¼ cup dry white wine

1 teaspoon sugar

½ teaspoon dried oregano

¾ teaspoon salt

Freshly ground pepper to taste

½ cup orzo

1 pound halibut, cut into bite-size pieces

¾ pound large shrimp, peeled and deveined

3 tablespoons chopped fresh parsley

4 ounces feta cheese, crumbled

PREHEAT oven to 400°F. In a Dutch oven, warm oil over medium heat. Add onion and garlic and sauté until tender, about 5 minutes. Add tomatoes, wine, seasonings, and orzo. Simmer, uncovered, 10 minutes.

FOLD in halibut and shrimp and bake, covered, until halibut is white and shrimp is pink, about 15 minutes. Stir in parsley and cheese and bake, uncovered, until bubbly, about 10 minutes longer.

SERVES 6 TO 8

shrimp, tomatoes, rice, and feta cheese The surprising addition of a feta-cheese topping gives this delicious combination of shrimp, tomatoes, and rice a unique flavor. Serve with a Caesar salad.

1¼ pounds large shrimp, peeled and deveined

Salt and freshly ground pepper to taste

2 tablespoons butter or margarine

1 tablespoon olive oil

3 cloves garlic, minced

½ teaspoon dried oregano

3 tablespoons chopped fresh parsley

2 large tomatoes, seeded, chopped, and drained

¼ cup dry white wine

¼ cup Rich Chicken Stock (page 23) or canned low-sodium chicken broth

2½ cups cooked long-grain white rice

4 ounces crumbled feta cheese

PREHEAT oven to 375°F. Sprinkle shrimp with salt and pepper. In a large skillet over medium-high heat, melt butter with oil. Add garlic and shrimp and sauté until shrimp turns pink, 2 to 3 minutes. Add oregano, parsley, tomatoes, wine, and stock, and simmer 5 minutes.

TRANSFER to a 2½-quart casserole dish lightly coated with cooking spray or oil. Add rice and mix well. Sprinkle with feta cheese.

BAKE, uncovered, until heated through, 20 to 25 minutes.

SERVES 6

shrimp, wild rice, and mushroom bake

The combination of wild rice and white rice complements the succulent shrimp and earthy mushrooms. This makes an elegant company entrée for 8 to 10 guests, but it can easily be halved. Serve with a spinach salad, and chocolate mousse for dessert.

4 cups Rich Chicken Stock (page 23), canned low-sodium chicken broth, or water

¾ teaspoon salt

½ cup wild rice, thoroughly rinsed and drained

1 cup long-grain white rice

3½ tablespoons butter or margarine

1 cup chopped yellow onion

1 pound medium mushrooms, sliced

1 cup chopped celery

2 cloves garlic, minced

1 tablespoon fresh lemon juice

2 tablespoons all-purpose flour

2 teaspoons Worcestershire sauce

3 tablespoons dry white wine

¾ teaspoon dried thyme

Freshly ground pepper to taste

¼ cup freshly grated Parmesan cheese

1¼ pounds large shrimp, shelled and deveined

¼ cup finely chopped fresh parsley

IN a large saucepan over high heat, bring 3 cups stock and ¼ teaspoon salt to a boil. Add wild rice, reduce temperature to medium-low, cover, and cook 25 minutes. Stir in white rice, raise heat, and bring to a boil. Reduce temperature and cook, covered, until liquid is absorbed, about 25 minutes longer. Transfer to a 4-quart casserole dish lightly coated with cooking spray or oil.

PREHEAT oven to 350°F. In a skillet over medium heat, melt 1½ tablespoons butter. Add onion, mushrooms, celery, garlic, and lemon juice and sauté until tender, 6 to 7 minutes. Add to casserole dish.

IN same skillet over medium heat, melt remaining 2 tablespoons butter. Add flour and stir until bubbly. Add remaining 1 cup stock and Worcestershire sauce and stir until thickened, about 2 minutes. Add wine, thyme, remaining ½ teaspoon salt, pepper, and cheese and stir until cheese is melted and sauce is smooth. Add to casserole and mix well.

COVER and bake 25 minutes. Fold in shrimp and bake, covered, until heated through and shrimp turns pink, 15 to 20 minutes longer. Sprinkle with parsley before serving.

SERVES 8 TO 10

spicy shrimp, tomatoes, and rice bake

This recipe calls for small shrimp, sometimes called "salad shrimp" or "bay shrimp." They require no rinsing, peeling, or deveining. The spices add an unusual flavor to this seafood dish.

2 teaspoons vegetable oil

¼ cup chopped green bell pepper

½ cup chopped yellow onion

1 clove garlic, minced

¾ cup long-grain white rice

1 cup canned tomatoes, juice from can included, lightly puréed in food processor

1¼ cups Rich Chicken Stock (page 23), canned low-sodium chicken broth, or water

¼ teaspoon ground cloves

¼ teaspoon chili powder

Dash cayenne pepper

½ teaspoon salt

Freshly ground pepper to taste

½ pound small shrimp

PREHEAT oven to 375°F. Warm oil in a skillet over medium heat. Sauté bell pepper, onion, and garlic until tender, about 5 minutes. Stir in rice. Add tomatoes, stock, and seasonings. Bring to a boil.

TRANSFER to a 2½-quart casserole dish lightly coated with cooking spray or oil. Stir in shrimp, cover, and bake until liquid is absorbed, about 1 hour.

SERVES 4

shrimp and crab spaghetti

The two most popular shellfish are combined with spaghetti and baked in an herbed cheese sauce. This makes a delicious casserole to serve at a party, along with a salad bar and assorted toppings.

3 tablespoons butter or margarine

8 ounces mushrooms, sliced

1 cup sliced green onions, including some tender green tops

2 cloves garlic, minced

3 tablespoons all-purpose flour

1 cup Rich Chicken Stock (page 23), or canned low-sodium chicken broth

1 cup light cream or milk

2 tablespoons dry white wine

¼ teaspoon dried oregano

¼ teaspoon dried marjoram

½ teaspoon salt

Freshly ground pepper to taste

¼ cup freshly grated Parmesan cheese, plus extra for topping

¾ pound small cooked shrimp

½ pound crabmeat, flaked

8 ounces spaghetti, broken up, cooked, and drained

PREHEAT oven to 375°F. In a saucepan over medium heat, melt butter. Add mushrooms, onions, and garlic and sauté until tender, about 5 minutes. Stir in flour and blend. Add stock, cream, wine, and seasonings and stir until thickened, about 2 minutes. Stir in ¼ cup cheese, shrimp, and crabmeat.

IN a 4-quart casserole dish lightly coated with cooking spray or oil, combine spaghetti and seafood sauce and mix well. Sprinkle with remaining cheese. Bake, uncovered, until bubbly, about 45 minutes.

SERVES 6

tangy baked shrimp

Here is an easy way to prepare shrimp. The shrimp is baked in a beer marinade and served on rice. Sugar snap peas go well with this dish.

- ½ cup beer, allowed to go flat
- 1 tablespoon vegetable oil
- 2 cloves garlic, minced
- 2 teaspoons chili powder
- 1 teaspoon ground cumin
- 2 drops Tabasco sauce
- ¼ teaspoon salt
- Freshly ground pepper to taste
- 1¼ pounds large shrimp, peeled and deveined
- ¼ cup chopped fresh parsley

- 1 cup long-grain white rice, cooked (see page 5)

IN a 9-by-13-inch baking dish, mix all ingredients except shrimp and parsley. Add shrimp and mix again. Marinate 1 hour, at room temperature, turning occasionally. Meanwhile, preheat oven to 425°F.

IN the same dish, bake shrimp uncovered with marinade until shrimp turns pink, about 10 minutes.

SPOON shrimp and some of sauce over rice. Sprinkle with parsley.

SERVES 4

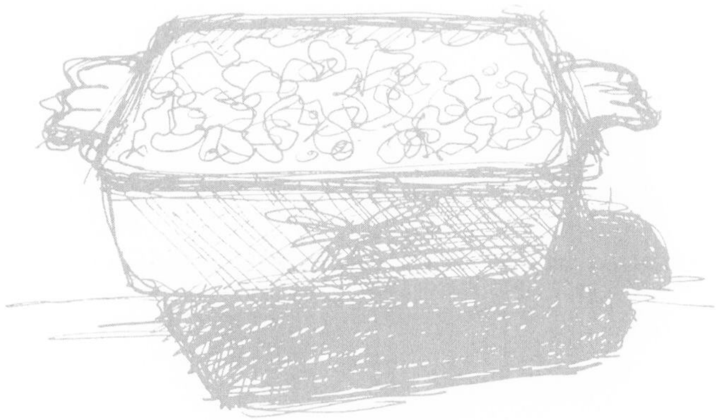

crab and shrimp casserole

There are many ways to combine crab and shrimp, but this is one of the best. The distinct blend of flavors makes this a terrific company dinner. Serve with your favorite tossed green salad and offer a strawberry pie for dessert.

4 tablespoons butter or margarine

1 cup chopped celery

1 cup chopped yellow onion

½ red bell pepper, seeded and chopped

3 tablespoons all-purpose flour

2 cups milk

½ teaspoon salt

1 teaspoon Worcestershire sauce

2 tablespoons dry white wine

½ cup light sour cream

1½ pounds small cooked shrimp

½ pound crabmeat, flaked

3 cups cooked long-grain rice

¼ cup toasted slivered almonds (see page 11)

1½ cups grated cheddar cheese

PREHEAT oven to 350°F. In a medium saucepan over medium heat, melt 1 tablespoon of the butter. Add celery, onion, and bell pepper and sauté until tender, about 5 minutes. Transfer vegetables to a 4-quart casserole dish lightly coated with cooking spray or oil.

ADD remaining butter to pan and then add flour, stirring constantly until bubbly. Add milk and stir until thickened, 2 to 3 minutes. Add salt, Worcestershire sauce, and wine. Fold in sour cream.

ADD the cream sauce to the casserole dish along with shrimp, crabmeat, rice, and almonds and mix gently. Top with cheese. Bake, uncovered, until bubbly, 45 to 55 minutes. Let stand 5 to 10 minutes before serving.

SERVES 8 TO 10

crab and mushroom stroganoff

Sweet, luscious crabmeat and mushrooms are blended with a rich cream sauce and spinach noodles for an elegant dinner entrée. A mixed green salad with avocado and red onion complements this dish.

2   tablespoons vegetable oil

½   cup finely diced yellow onion

½   cup finely diced red bell pepper

1   clove garlic, minced

8   ounces mushrooms, sliced

2   tablespoons butter or margarine

2   tablespoons all-purpose flour

1   cup Rich Chicken Stock (page 23) or canned low-sodium chicken broth

3   tablespoons dry white wine

¼   teaspoon dried dill weed

¼   teaspoon salt

⅛   teaspoon white pepper

2   drops Tabasco sauce

1   cup light sour cream

¾   pound crabmeat, flaked

8   ounces (about 3 cups) spinach or plain noodles, cooked and drained

PREHEAT oven to 350°F. In a medium saucepan over medium heat, warm oil. Add onion, bell pepper, garlic, and mushrooms and sauté until tender, about 5 minutes. Transfer to a 2½-quart casserole dish lightly coated with cooking spray or oil.

IN the same pan, melt butter. Stir in flour and continue stirring until bubbly. Add stock, wine, and seasonings and bring to a boil, stirring constantly, until thickened, 2 to 3 minutes. Remove from heat. Stir in sour cream and crabmeat. Add mixture to casserole dish along with noodles and mix well.

BAKE, uncovered, until bubbly, stirring once, 30 minutes.

SERVES 6 TO 8

crab and spinach manicotti with parmesan cheese

sauce
This is a great casserole to make ahead and have ready for out-of-town company. Serve with a salad of mixed greens, mushrooms, red onion, and a basil vinaigrette dressing, and some cookies for dessert.

½   pound crabmeat, flaked

1   package (10 ounces) frozen chopped spinach, thawed and squeezed dry

1½ cups ricotta cheese

¼   cup freshly grated Parmesan cheese

½   cup chopped green onions, including some tender green tops

1   large egg, beaten

1   teaspoon salt

12 manicotti shells, cooked and drained

Parmesan Cheese Sauce (recipe follows)

PREHEAT oven to 400°F. In a medium bowl, combine crabmeat, spinach, cheeses, onions, egg, and salt and mix well.

WITH a spoon or with your fingers, fill shells and place in a 9-by-13-inch glass baking dish lightly coated with cooking spray or oil. Top with Parmesan Cheese Sauce.

BAKE, uncovered, until bubbly, about 25 minutes.

SERVES 8

parmesan cheese sauce

4   tablespoons butter or margarine

4   tablespoons all-purpose flour

2½ cups milk

1   cup freshly grated Parmesan cheese

¼   teaspoon salt

⅛   teaspoon white pepper

IN a saucepan over medium heat, melt butter. Add flour and stir until bubbly. Add milk and stir until thickened, 2 to 3 minutes. Add cheese, salt, and pepper and stir until cheese melts, about 5 minutes.

MAKES ABOUT 2½ CUPS

crab florentine

Crabmeat is usually expensive, so make this dish for a special-occasion dinner. Whole crab is less expensive if you don't mind extracting the meat yourself. (You will probably need two crabs.) Layered with spinach, this is an impressive entrée.

2 packages (10 ounces each) frozen chopped spinach, thawed and squeezed dry

1 cup sliced green onions, including some tender green tops

1 pound crabmeat, flaked

1½ cups grated Monterey Jack cheese

Salt and freshly ground pepper to taste

1 cup light sour cream

PREHEAT oven to 350°F. In a 7-by-11¾-inch baking dish lightly coated with cooking spray or oil, layer half the spinach, half the onions, half the crabmeat, and half the cheese. Season with salt and pepper. Repeat the layers. Spread sour cream evenly on top and bake, uncovered, until bubbly, 35 to 40 minutes.

SERVES 6

seafood-broccoli strata

This is a great dish to serve to company because it should be made a day in advance. Serve for a luncheon along with a fresh fruit salad and homemade rolls.

6 slices sourdough bread ½ inch thick, crusts removed, and cubed (about 8 cups)

⅓ cup butter, melted

3 cups grated cheddar cheese

1 cup cooked and flaked white-fleshed fish, such as snapper, flounder, or cod

1 cup crabmeat, flaked, or small shrimp, or combination of the two

2 cups cooked chopped broccoli

3 large eggs

2 cups 2 percent milk

¾ teaspoon salt

½ teaspoon dry mustard

Freshly ground pepper to taste

IN a bowl toss bread cubes with butter. In a 9-by-13-inch baking dish lightly coated with cooking spray or oil, layer half the bread cubes, half the cheese, all the seafood, broccoli, and remaining bread cubes.

IN a bowl beat eggs, milk, and seasonings. Pour over casserole. Top with remaining cheese. Cover and refrigerate about 12 hours or overnight.

PREHEAT oven to 325°F. Bring casserole to room temperature. Uncover and bake until knife inserted in the middle comes out clean, about 50 minutes. Let stand 10 minutes before serving. Cut into squares.

SERVES 8

salmon and spinach noodle casserole

Freshly cooked salmon is the key to this delightful casserole of salmon, spinach noodles, and a creamy sauce. Other firm fish, such as halibut or tuna, can be substituted for salmon.

8	ounces light cream cheese, cut into cubes
1	cup milk
½	teaspoon salt
¼	cup freshly grated Parmesan cheese, plus extra cheese for sprinkling on top
6	ounces (about 3½ cups) spinach noodles, cooked and drained
2	cups poached fresh salmon (1 large salmon steak), flaked and bones removed (see Note)

PREHEAT oven to 375°F. In a small saucepan over medium heat, melt cream cheese in milk. Add salt and whisk in ¼ cup Parmesan cheese until cheese is melted and sauce is smooth.

PLACE sauce, noodles, and salmon in a 2½-quart casserole dish lightly coated with cooking spray or oil. With 2 forks, toss until blended. Sprinkle with Parmesan cheese. Cover and bake until heated through, about 25 minutes.

SERVES 6 TO 8

NOTE: To poach salmon, in a skillet over high heat, add 1½ cups water, 2 tablespoons dry white wine (optional), 1 bay leaf, a small piece of onion, 4 peppercorns, ¼ teaspoon salt, and 2 parsley sprigs. Bring to a boil. Add salmon. Reduce heat to low and simmer, covered, until fish flakes, about 10 minutes. Carefully lift fish out of poaching liquid and remove skin.

salmon and peas

As the salmon bakes, a coating of mayonnaise keeps it moist and flavorful. A border of fresh peas adds color and eye appeal. This is a simple way to prepare a premier fish.

¼ cup light mayonnaise

½ teaspoon dried tarragon, crumbled

1 tablespoon chopped fresh parsley

2 teaspoons fresh lemon juice

½ teaspoon salt

Freshly ground pepper

3 salmon steaks (1½ to 2 pounds combined weight)

1½ cups fresh peas, or frozen peas, thawed

Lemon wedges for garnish

PREHEAT oven to 425°F. In a small bowl, mix mayonnaise, tarragon, parsley, lemon juice, salt, and pepper.

SPREAD a thin layer of the mayonnaise mixture on the bottom of a 6-by-10-inch baking dish. Add salmon. Spread remaining mayonnaise on top of salmon.

BAKE, uncovered, 8 minutes. Sprinkle peas around the edge of the dish. Bake until fish flakes and peas are tender, 5 to 6 minutes longer. Garnish with lemon wedges.

SERVES 4 TO 6

salmon loaf

Here is a way to use leftover salmon (should you be lucky enough to have any). You can also use a good quality canned salmon. Serve with Dijon Mayonnaise and New Potatoes and Fresh Spinach Bake (page 189).

2 cups cooked salmon, flaked and bones removed (see Note, page 47); or 1 can (15½ ounces) canned salmon, drained, flaked, skin removed, and bones mashed

⅔ cup dry bread crumbs (see page 5)

¼ cup finely chopped yellow onion

3 tablespoons chopped fresh parsley

1 large egg, beaten

1 teaspoon Worcestershire sauce

½ cup light mayonnaise

1 tablespoon fresh lemon juice

¼ teaspoon salt

¼ teaspoon dried dill weed

¼ teaspoon dried tarragon

Freshly ground pepper to taste

Lemon wedges for garnish

PREHEAT oven to 350°F. In a large bowl, mix all of the ingredients except lemon wedges. Place in a 4-by-8-inch loaf pan with 2½-inch sides, lightly coated with cooking spray or oil.

BAKE until flavors are blended and loaf is crisp around the edges, about 1 hour. Let stand 10 minutes, then remove from pan and place on a plate. Garnish with lemon wedges and serve with Dijon mayonnaise.

SERVES 4 TO 6

49

dijon mayonnaise

½ cup light mayonnaise

¼ nonfat plain yogurt

1 tablespoon Dijon mustard

1 teaspoon fresh lemon juice

BLEND all ingredients in a small bowl. Refrigerate until needed.

MAKES ABOUT 1 CUP

ahi and papaya in citrus sauce

Ahi is the Hawaiian name for yellowfin tuna. It has a stronger flavor than albacore tuna and is darker in color. Here it is baked in a spicy citrus sauce and topped with papaya, for a tropical accent. Serve with hot fluffy rice.

4   ahi (tuna) steaks (about 2 pounds)
1   ripe papaya, peeled, seeded, and cubed
¼   cup toasted slivered almonds (see page 11)
2   kiwis, peeled and sliced

PREHEAT oven to 425°F.

ARRANGE ahi in a 9-by-13-inch baking dish lightly coated with cooking spray or oil. Top with papaya and half of the citrus sauce. Bake, uncovered, until fish flakes, about 10 minutes. Sprinkle with almonds.

PLACE ahi on a platter and garnish with kiwi slices. Pass remaining sauce in a pitcher.

SERVES 4 TO 6

citrus sauce

2   cups orange juice
1   tablespoon fresh lemon juice
¼   teaspoon ground ginger
⅓   cup brown sugar
3   tablespoons soy sauce
¼   teaspoon Worcestershire sauce
2½ tablespoons cornstarch

PLACE all ingredients for the sauce in a saucepan over medium heat and whisk until thickened, about 5 minutes. Keep warm over low heat.

MAKES ABOUT 2¼ CUPS

baked tuna and peppers

Eat healthy and include more fish and vegetables in your diet with this colorful and delicious combination. Other seafood may be used, such as snapper.

1   tablespoon vegetable oil

1   cup chopped yellow onion

½   red bell pepper, seeded and chopped

½   green bell pepper, seeded and chopped

½   yellow bell pepper, seeded and chopped

2   cloves garlic, chopped

¾   cup long-grain white rice

¼   cup dry white wine

1½ cups Fish Stock (page 21), clam juice, or water

½   teaspoon salt

Freshly ground pepper to taste

1¼ pounds fresh tuna steaks, cut into 1½-inch pieces

¼   cup chopped fresh parsley or chives

PREHEAT oven to 375°F. In a Dutch oven over medium heat, warm oil. Add onion, peppers, and garlic and sauté until tender, about 5 minutes. Stir in rice. Add wine, stock, salt, and pepper and bring to a boil.

BAKE, covered, 20 to 25 minutes. Gently stir in tuna. Cover and bake until liquid is absorbed and fish flakes, about 10 minutes longer. Sprinkle with parsley before serving.

SERVES 6

tuna-noodle casserole

This is the mother of all casseroles, and no casserole book is complete without it. A light white sauce is used in place of condensed soup, and hard-cooked eggs are added.

3   cups egg noodles, cooked
    and drained

2   cans (6 ounces each) light
    tuna in water, drained

2   hard-cooked eggs, chopped

1   cup Basic White Sauce
    (page 16)

¾   cup grated cheddar cheese

PREHEAT oven to 375°F. In 2½-quart casserole dish, mix all ingredients together except cheese. Sprinkle cheese on top.

BAKE, uncovered, until hot and bubbly, about 25 minutes.

SERVES 4

VARIATION: Omit eggs and add 1 large tomato, seeded, chopped, and drained.

cod with peppers, tomatoes, and white beans   The contrasting ingredients in this dish make it colorful as well as flavorful. Any white fish may be used, depending on availability and your preference.

1½ pounds cod or other white-fleshed fish, such as red snapper

1 tablespoon vegetable oil

1 green bell pepper, seeded and cut lengthwise into ⅜-inch strips

1 yellow onion, sliced into rings

2 cloves garlic, chopped

1 can (14½ ounces) Italian-style stewed tomatoes, including juice from can

1 can (15 ounces) white beans, rinsed and drained

¼ cup dry white wine

1 tablespoon chopped fresh basil, or ¾ teaspoon dried basil

½ teaspoon salt

Freshly ground pepper to taste

2 teaspoons capers, drained

¼ cup chopped fresh parsley

PREHEAT oven to 425°F. Place fish in a 7½-by-11¾-inch baking dish lightly coated with cooking spray or oil.

IN a medium skillet over medium heat, warm oil. Add bell pepper, onion, and garlic and sauté until tender, about 5 minutes. Add tomatoes, beans, wine, seasonings, and capers and simmer 5 minutes. Pour over fish.

BAKE, uncovered, until fish flakes, about 20 minutes. Sprinkle with parsley before serving.

SERVES 4

halibut with yogurt-cucumber topping

This is a "no-fuss" dish that can be made ahead and served for company. Include a green vegetable on the menu for taste and eye appeal.

2   pounds halibut or other white-fleshed fish fillets, such as sole or cod

Salt to taste

½   cup plain nonfat yogurt or light sour cream

1   teaspoon fresh lemon juice

1   tablespoon light mayonnaise

¼   teaspoon dried dill weed

½   cup seeded and chopped cucumber

¼   cup pitted and sliced green olives

2   tablespoons chopped fresh parsley

PREHEAT oven to 425°F. Place fish in a 7½-by-11¾-inch baking dish lightly coated with cooking spray or oil. Season with salt. In a medium bowl, stir together all remaining ingredients. Spread evenly over fish.

BAKE until fish flakes, about 12 to 15 minutes. Transfer to warmed individual plates and serve immediately.

SERVES 4

red snapper stew

Here is a Friday night dinner special. Fresh vegetables and fish simmer in a savory sauce for a satisfying one-bowl meal. Serve with cheese bread and follow with a refreshing lemon sorbet.

½ small head green cabbage, cut into wedges

3 carrots, peeled and cut into 1-inch diagonal slices

1 yellow onion, cut into wedges

3 new potatoes, quartered, or 8 whole baby new potatoes

8 ounces mushrooms

2 cups Rich Chicken Stock (page 23) or canned low-sodium chicken broth

½ teaspoon salt

¼ teaspoon dried thyme

½ teaspoon dried dill weed

Freshly ground pepper to taste

1 pound red snapper, or any white-fleshed fish, cut into bite-size pieces

Chopped fresh parsley for sprinkling on top

PREHEAT oven to 350°F. In a Dutch oven over medium heat, add vegetables, stock, and seasonings. Bring to a boil.

COVER and bake until vegetables are tender, about 35 minutes. Add fish and bake, uncovered, until fish flakes, about 10 minutes longer. Serve in bowls and sprinkle with parsley.

SERVES 4

cod or snapper and fresh vegetables

In this dish, vegetables are sautéed briefly to retain their fresh flavor and character and are then added to the fish and baked in the oven.

4   cod or snapper fillets
    (about 1½ pounds)

2   tablespoons vegetable oil

1   cup chopped yellow onion

½   cup chopped green bell
    pepper

½   cup chopped red bell
    pepper

4   ounces mushrooms, sliced

2   cloves garlic, chopped

1   tablespoon chopped fresh
    basil, or 1 teaspoon dried
    basil

½   teaspoon salt

Freshly ground pepper to taste

1   large tomato, seeded,
    chopped, and drained

2   tablespoons fresh lemon
    juice

PREHEAT oven to 425°F. Place fish in a 7½-by-11¾-inch baking dish lightly coated with cooking spray or oil. In a medium skillet over medium heat, warm oil. Add onion, bell pepper, mushrooms, and garlic and sauté until tender, about 7 minutes. Stir in seasonings, tomato, and lemon juice. Sauté until well blended, about 2 minutes longer.

POUR vegetable mixture over fish. Bake, uncovered, until fish flakes, about 20 minutes.

SERVES 4 TO 6

halibut, broccoli, and cherry tomato casserole

In this colorful dish, the gleaming white halibut contrasts with broccoli and cherry tomatoes, and a flavorful cheese sauce caps the inviting presentation. A fresh fruit salad is a complementary addition.

3 cups broccoli florets

½ cup water

1½ pounds halibut fillets or other white-fleshed fish, such as snapper, flounder, or cod

Salt to taste

1 tablespoon fresh lemon juice

4 tablespoons butter or margarine

3 tablespoons all-purpose flour

2 cups milk

3 tablespoons dry white wine

1 cup grated Swiss cheese

½ teaspoon salt

⅛ teaspoon white pepper

Paprika for sprinkling on top

2 tablespoons toasted slivered almonds (see page 11)

1 cup cherry tomatoes

PREHEAT oven to 375°F. Put broccoli and water in a medium saucepan over medium heat. Bring to a boil and cook, covered, 4 minutes. Drain under cold water.

PLACE halibut in the center of a 9-by-13-inch baking dish lightly coated with cooking spray or oil. Season with salt and sprinkle with lemon juice. Arrange broccoli around the outside. Set aside.

IN a saucepan over medium heat, melt butter and add flour, stirring until bubbly. Add milk and stir until thickened, about 2 minutes. Add wine, cheese, salt, and pepper and stir until blended. Pour sauce over fish and broccoli. Sprinkle with paprika and almonds. Bake, uncovered, until fish begins to flake, about 20 minutes, but baking time will vary depending on thickness of fillet. Add cherry tomatoes, alternating with broccoli florets. Bake until heated through, 5 to 10 minutes longer.

SERVES 4 TO 6

THE BIG BOOK OF CASSEROLES

halibut and fresh spinach

Halibut is known for its firm flesh and mild flavor. Here it is prepared simply with fresh spinach and baked with Parmesan cheese on top. Serve with a potato dish.

1 tablespoon butter or margarine

½ cup chopped yellow onion

2 bags (6 ounces each) fresh spinach, lightly rinsed and stems removed, if desired

3 or 4 halibut steaks (1½ to 2 pounds)

3 teaspoons fresh lime or lemon juice

Salt and freshly ground pepper to taste

¼ cup freshly grated Parmesan cheese

Lime wedges for garnish

PREHEAT oven to 425°F. In a large saucepan over medium heat, melt butter. Add onion and sauté 2 minutes. Add spinach and cook, covered, until spinach wilts, tossing once with a fork, 2 to 3 minutes longer.

SPREAD spinach in the bottom of a 7½-by-11¾-inch baking dish lightly coated with cooking spray or oil. Place halibut on top, sprinkle with lime juice, and season with salt and pepper. Sprinkle with Parmesan cheese.

BAKE, uncovered, until fish flakes, 12 to 15 minutes. Serve garnished with lime wedges.

SERVES 4 TO 6

halibut topped with sautéed vegetables

Prepare the sautéed vegetables first. Mild, tender halibut is fried and then smothered with the vegetables and finished in the oven. Complete the dinner with a green salad and warm French bread.

2 tablespoons butter or margarine

Juice of 1 lemon

1½ to 2 pounds halibut fillet, cut into serving-size pieces

Salt and freshly ground pepper to taste

Sautéed Vegetables (recipe follows)

Freshly grated Parmesan cheese for topping

PREHEAT oven to 375°F. In a skillet over medium heat, melt butter with lemon juice. Cook halibut until lightly browned, 4 to 5 minutes on each side. Season with salt and pepper.

PLACE fish in a 7½-by-11¾-inch glass baking dish lightly coated with cooking spray or oil and top with Sautéed Vegetables. Sprinkle with Parmesan cheese and bake, uncovered, until flavors are blended, about 15 minutes.

SERVES 4

59

sautéed vegetables

1 tablespoon butter or margarine

1 tablespoon vegetable oil

2 carrots, peeled and grated

4 green onions, including some tender green tops, chopped

8 mushrooms, sliced

1 tomato, seeded, chopped, and drained

½ teaspoon salt

Freshly ground pepper to taste

2 tablespoons chopped fresh parsley

IN a medium skillet over medium heat, melt butter with oil. Add carrots, onions, and mushrooms and sauté until tender, about 5 minutes. Add tomato, salt, pepper, and parsley, stir, and remove from heat.

baked pesto scallops

Scallops are a popular bivalve mollusk with two beautiful fan-shaped shells that are often used as containers. Because they are sweet and mild in flavor, scallops appeal to almost everyone. Here they are coated with pesto crumbs and quickly baked.

3   cups dry bread crumbs (see page 5)

¼   cup Basil Pesto (see page 18) or commercially prepared pesto

¼   cup plain nonfat yogurt

1   pound large scallops

PREHEAT oven to 425°F. In a large bowl, mix bread crumbs with pesto and yogurt. Add scallops and toss to coat. Arrange scallops in single layer in a 7½-by-11¾-inch baking dish lightly coated with cooking spray or oil.

BAKE, uncovered, until scallops are cooked through and crumbs are lightly browned, 10 to 12 minutes.

SERVES 4

scallops, mushrooms, and rice in cream sauce   This is a

delicious combination of sweet scallops, mushrooms, and rice blended with a rich sauce.

Serve with a spinach salad and warm French bread.

4   tablespoons butter or
    margarine
1   pound large scallops,
    rinsed and drained
8   ounces fresh mushrooms,
    sliced
¼   cup finely chopped yellow
    onion
1   clove garlic, minced
½   cup dry white wine
½   cup half-and-half or milk
1   tablespoon Dijon mustard
1   teaspoon fresh lemon juice
¼   teaspoon salt
Freshly ground pepper to taste
1½ cups cooked long-grain
    white rice
¼   cup chopped fresh parsley

PREHEAT oven to 350°F. In a medium skillet over medium heat, melt 2 tablespoons of the butter. Add scallops and sauté, stirring constantly, until lightly browned and cooked through, about 5 minutes. Transfer to a 2½-quart casserole dish lightly coated with cooking spray or oil.

RETURN pan to medium heat and melt remaining 2 tablespoons butter. Add mushrooms, onions, and garlic and sauté 3 minutes. Add wine and boil until liquid is reduced to about 2 tablespoons, about 2 minutes. Add half-and-half, mustard, lemon juice, salt, and pepper and stir until blended.

POUR sauce over scallops. Add rice and mix well. Cover and bake until bubbly, about 30 minutes. Sprinkle with parsley before serving.

SERVES 4

scallop and chicken bake

This elegant dish takes time to prepare, but it is bound to please your guests. Serve with a fruit salad with a mint dressing.

2 tablespoons olive oil

4 skinned and boned chicken breast halves (about 2 pounds), cut into large pieces

½ pound large scallops, halved

½ cup dry white wine

¾ cup light cream

¼ teaspoon dried thyme

Salt and freshly ground pepper to taste

2 bags (6 ounces each) fresh spinach, cooked (see page 7)

Chopped fresh parsley for garnish

PREHEAT oven to 375°F. In a medium skillet over medium heat, warm 1 tablespoon oil. Add chicken and cook until lightly browned, about 5 to 10 minutes. Remove to a plate. Add remaining oil and sauté scallops until lightly browned and cooked through, about 4 minutes. Remove to plate holding chicken. Deglaze pan with wine, stirring to loosen brown bits. Add cream and seasonings and stir until reduced and slightly thickened, about 5 minutes.

PLACE spinach in a 7½-by-11¾-inch baking dish lightly coated with cooking spray or oil. Lay chicken and scallops on top and cover with sauce. Bake, uncovered, until bubbly, about 15 minutes. Sprinkle with parsley.

SERVES 4 TO 6

sole and scallops

Mild, tender sole is baked with a savory topping of scallops, tomatoes, and herbs for a fresh seafood taste.

1 to 2 tablespoons butter or margarine

¼ cup chopped yellow onion

½ pound small scallops

2 tomatoes, seeded, chopped, and drained

2 tablespoons dry white wine

Salt and freshly ground pepper to taste

¼ teaspoon dried thyme

¼ teaspoon dried tarragon, crumbled

4 large sole fillets (about 1½ pounds combined weight)

3 tablespoons chopped fresh parsley

¼ cup freshly grated Parmesan cheese

PREHEAT oven to 375°F. In a medium skillet over medium heat, melt butter. Add onion and sauté 2 minutes. Add more butter if needed. Add scallops and tomatoes and sauté until vegetables are tender and scallops are heated through, about 3 minutes longer. Add wine and seasonings and mix well.

PLACE fillets in an 8-by-8-inch baking dish lightly coated with cooking spray or oil. Spoon scallop mixture over sole. Sprinkle with parsley and cheese. Bake, uncovered, until bubbly, about 25 minutes.

SERVES 4

sea rolls with almond-rice filling

Delicate, mild-tasting sole fillets are rolled around an almond-nut filling and topped with a creamy white sauce. Simple to prepare, but elegant enough for a guest dinner. Serve with a spinach and mushroom salad.

1 cup cooked long-grain white rice

¼ cup chopped toasted almonds (see page 11)

1 cup Basic White Sauce (page 16)

½ teaspoon dried dill weed

1½ pounds sole fillets

½ cup light sour cream

¼ cup dry white wine

3 tablespoons chopped fresh parsley

PREHEAT oven to 425°F. In a medium bowl, combine rice, almonds, ¼ cup white sauce, and dill. Lay fillets on a sheet of wax paper. Place about 2 tablespoons rice mixture on each fillet. Roll up and place seam side down in a 7½-by-11¾-inch baking dish lightly coated with cooking spray or oil.

COMBINE remaining sauce with sour cream and wine and pour over fish. Bake, uncovered, until fish flakes, 12 to 15 minutes. Sprinkle with parsley before serving.

SERVES 4

sole florentine
This casserole has style and flavor, but is still easy to make. Serve with a salad of fresh seasonal fruit and grapes.

2   packages (10 ounces each) frozen chopped spinach, thawed and squeezed dry

1½ cups light sour cream

2   tablespoons all-purpose flour

¼   cup chopped green onions, including some tender green tops

Juice of 1 lemon

¼   teaspoon dried thyme

1   teaspoon salt

Freshly ground pepper to taste

1½ pounds sole fillets

Paprika for sprinkling on top

¼   cup toasted slivered almonds (see page 11)

Chopped fresh parsley for garnish

PREHEAT oven to 375°F. Place spinach in a medium bowl. In a small bowl, blend 1 cup sour cream, flour, onions, lemon juice, and seasonings. Combine half this mixture with the spinach. Spread spinach mixture evenly on the bottom of a 9-by-13-inch baking dish lightly coated with cooking spray or oil. Arrange sole on top. Spread remaining sour cream mixture on top of sole. Sprinkle with paprika and almonds.

BAKE, uncovered, until fish flakes, about 25 minutes. Sprinkle with parsley before serving.

SERVES 4 TO 6

fillet of sole in hazelnut sauce

This classy baked sole is enhanced with a lemon butter—hazelnut sauce. Serve on rice or noodles.

- 3 tablespoons all-purpose flour
- 1 teaspoon paprika
- ½ teaspoon salt
- Freshly ground pepper to taste
- 1½ pounds sole fillets
- 4 tablespoons butter or margarine
- ½ cup chopped toasted hazelnuts (see page 11)
- ¼ cup fresh lemon juice
- ¼ cup chopped fresh parsley

PREHEAT oven to 375°F. On a sheet of wax paper, combine flour, paprika, salt, and pepper. Toss fish in mixture to coat.

IN a large skillet over medium heat, melt 2 tablespoons butter. Brown fillets about 5 minutes on each side. Transfer to a 2½-quart casserole dish lightly coated with cooking spray or oil.

IN same skillet, melt remaining butter. Add nuts and stir until lightly browned, about 2 minutes. Add lemon juice and parsley. Pour over fish and bake, uncovered, until fish flakes, about 10 minutes.

SERVES 4 TO 6

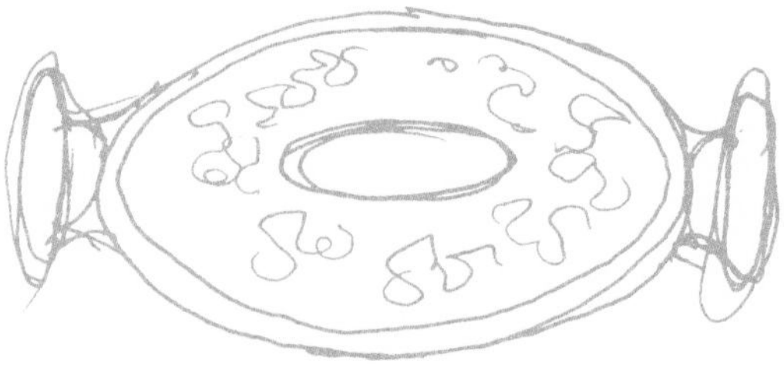

filled sole roll-ups

Sole works well for this recipe because it is thin and can be rolled easily. Its mild flavor goes well with the rice filling and lemon-butter sauce.

6   tablespoons butter or margarine, melted

3   tablespoons fresh lemon juice

1   package (10 ounces) frozen chopped spinach, thawed and squeezed dry

1   cup cooked brown rice (see page 5)

1   cup grated Swiss cheese

¼   teaspoon salt

Freshly ground pepper to taste

2   drops Tabasco sauce

6 to 8 sole fillets (about 1½ pounds)

Paprika for sprinkling on top

PREHEAT oven to 400°F. Mix butter and lemon juice in a cup. In a medium bowl, combine remaining ingredients except sole and paprika. Stir in half of butter-lemon mixture.

LAY fillets flat on an a sheet of wax paper and divide spinach-rice mixture among them. Roll up and secure with toothpicks. Place in an 8-by-8-inch baking dish lightly coated with cooking spray or oil. Pour remaining butter-lemon mixture over fish. Sprinkle with paprika.

BAKE, uncovered, until bubbly and fish flakes, about 20 minutes.

67

SERVES 4

northwest oysters

Fresh oysters are available in the shell or shucked. If they are truly fresh they will smell like the ocean. Here they are dressed up with seasonings and a buttery sauce. Serve as an appetizer or first course with sliced French bread.

1   cup dry bread crumbs (see page 5)
½   cup freshly grated Parmesan cheese
2   tablespoons chopped fresh parsley
½   teaspoon dried thyme
1   teaspoon salt
¼   teaspoon freshly ground pepper
2   cloves garlic, minced
1   pint small fresh oysters, rinsed, drained, and dried
4   tablespoons butter or margarine, melted
2   tablespoons dry white wine
1   teaspoon Worcestershire sauce
2   drops Tabasco sauce
1   tablespoon fresh lemon juice

PREHEAT oven to 400°F. In a small bowl, mix crumbs, cheese, parsley, seasonings, and garlic. Sprinkle one-third of crumb mixture in the bottom of an 8-by-8-inch baking dish lightly coated with cooking spray or oil. Place oysters in a single layer on top of crumbs. Sprinkle remaining crumb mixture on top.

IN a cup, combine butter, wine, Worcestershire sauce, Tabasco sauce, and lemon juice and pour over mixture.

BAKE, uncovered, until bubbly, about 20 minutes. Serve immediately in individual shell-shaped dishes.

SERVES 4

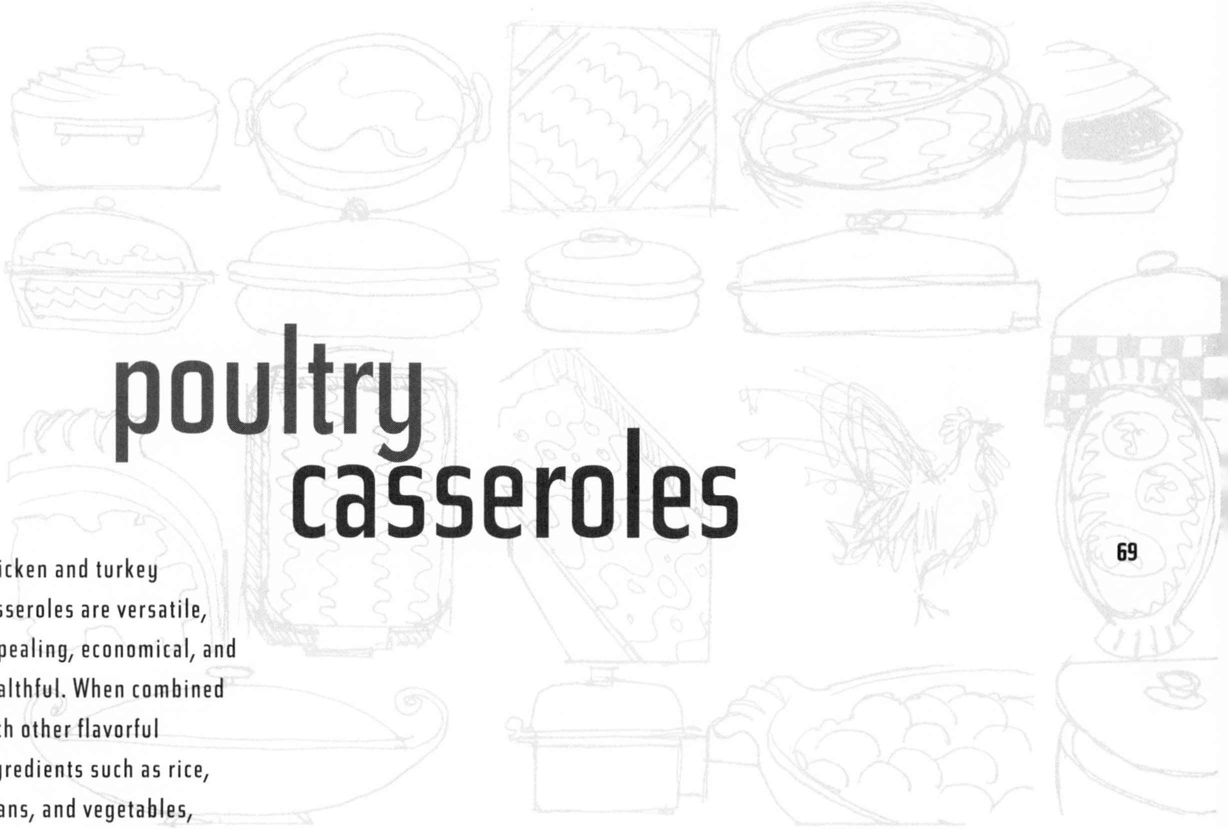

poultry casseroles

Chicken and turkey casseroles are versatile, appealing, economical, and healthful. When combined with other flavorful ingredients such as rice, beans, and vegetables, they become exciting entrées. The possibilities are endless.

This section features a variety of casseroles, from variations on ethnic dishes to family favorites and real home cooking.

chicken cacciatore sauce on polenta

Here is a combination of two of my favorite recipes: chicken cacciatore and polenta. *Cacciatore* means "hunter's style"—chicken simmered in tomatoes, wine, onions, garlic, and herbs. This sauce is also good on pasta.

CHICKEN CACCIATORE SAUCE

2 tablespoons vegetable oil

½ yellow onion, chopped

½ green bell pepper, seeded and chopped

1 clove garlic, minced

4 ounces mushrooms, sliced

3 skinned and boned chicken breast halves (about 1 pound; see page 7), cut into bite-size pieces

1 can (14½ ounces) crushed tomatoes in thick purée

3 tablespoons dry white wine

½ teaspoon salt

¼ teaspoon dried oregano

½ teaspoon dried basil

Freshly ground pepper to taste

Basic Polenta (see page 19), at room temperature

¼ cup freshly grated Parmesan cheese

THE BIG BOOK OF CASSEROLES

PREHEAT oven to 350°F.

MAKE THE CHICKEN CACCIATORE SAUCE: In a large skillet, warm 1 tablespoon oil over medium heat. Sauté onion, green pepper, garlic, and mushrooms until vegetables are tender, about 10 minutes. Remove to a plate.

IN the skillet used for the vegetables, warm remaining oil over medium-high heat. Sauté chicken until lightly browned, about 5 minutes on each side. Add tomatoes, wine, seasonings, and reserved vegetables. Reduce heat to low and simmer, uncovered, 10 minutes. Set aside.

SPREAD polenta in a 7½-by-11¾-inch glass baking dish lightly coated with cooking spray or oil. Pour Chicken Cacciatore Sauce over polenta, cover, and bake 30 minutes. Remove cover and sprinkle with Parmesan cheese.

BAKE, uncovered, until bubbly, 10 minutes longer. Let stand 5 to 10 minutes. Cut into squares to serve.

SERVES 6

chicken, ham, and fresh tomatoes

Here is a colorful combination of chicken, ham, and tomatoes in a flavorful wine sauce—a dish that has lots of eye and taste appeal. The ham adds a salty counterpoint to the chicken. Serve with a crisp green salad.

¼ cup all-purpose flour

½ teaspoon salt

Freshly ground pepper to taste

1 chicken (3 to 3½ pounds), cut into serving pieces (use meaty pieces and save bony parts for Rich Chicken Stock, page 23)

2 to 3 tablespoons vegetable oil

4 ounces cooked ham, cubed

2 large tomatoes (about 1¼ pounds), seeded, chopped, and drained

½ cup long-grain white rice

½ cup Rich Chicken Stock or canned low-sodium chicken broth

¼ cup dry white wine

¼ teaspoon dried thyme

½ teaspoon dried basil

2 tablespoons chopped fresh parsley

PREHEAT oven to 350°F. On a sheet of wax paper, combine flour, salt, and pepper. Toss chicken in mixture to coat. Shake off excess flour.

IN a Dutch oven over medium-high heat, warm 2 tablespoons oil. Brown chicken about 5 minutes on each side, adding more oil if needed. Transfer to a plate.

REDUCE temperature to medium and stir ham, tomatoes, and rice into Dutch oven. Add stock, wine, seasonings, and parsley and cook, 2 to 3 minutes. Remove from heat and place chicken on top of ham-tomato mixture.

COVER and bake until rice is tender and chicken is no longer showing pink in the center, about 1 hour. Taste for seasoning, and add salt and pepper if needed.

SERVES 4

chicken, ham, and rice casserole

A convenient "make-ahead casserole" that puts leftovers to good use. The addition of ham and cheese adds flavor to this savory dish.

3 cups cooked long-grain white rice

2 tablespoons butter or margarine

4 ounces mushrooms, sliced

4 green onions, including some tender green tops, sliced

1¼ cups 2 percent milk

2 large eggs, beaten

¼ teaspoon salt

½ teaspoon dried dill weed

¼ teaspoon dried marjoram

2 cups cubed cooked chicken

1 cup cubed cooked ham

2 cups grated Swiss cheese

PREHEAT oven to 350°F. Place rice in a 2½-quart casserole dish lightly coated with cooking spray or oil.

IN a saucepan over medium heat, melt butter. Sauté mushrooms and onions until soft, about 5 minutes. Remove from heat, whisk in milk, eggs, and seasonings. Add to casserole along with chicken, ham, and cheese and mix well. Cover and bake until bubbly, 50 to 60 minutes.

SERVES 6 TO 8

roasted chicken thighs and peppers

Here is a full meal in one dish that goes together in minutes—perfect for casual dining. Roasting intensifies the flavor of the chicken and vegetables and adds interest and color to the dish.

8 chicken thighs (about 2½ pounds)

4 to 6 cloves garlic, halved

3 new potatoes, quartered

1 red bell pepper, seeded and cut lengthwise into ½-inch strips

1 green bell pepper, seeded and cut lengthwise into ½-inch strips

1 yellow onion, quartered and cut into 1-inch wedges

1 tablespoon olive oil

½ teaspoon dried thyme

½ teaspoon salt

Freshly ground pepper to taste

PREHEAT oven to 425°F. Toss all ingredients in a 9-by-13-inch baking dish lightly coated with cooking spray or oil. Spread out ingredients in a single layer.

ROAST uncovered until vegetables are tender-crisp, about 30 minutes. Turn chicken and vegetables and cook until chicken is no longer pink in the center, 15 to 20 minutes longer. Arrange on a heated platter and serve immediately.

SERVES 4

chicken italian

Influenced by Italian cuisine, this home-style, robust dish goes from stove top to oven to table. Serve with a tossed green salad and lots of garlic bread.

2   tablespoons olive oil

1   large yellow onion, sliced

1   red bell pepper, seeded and sliced lengthwise

4   cloves garlic, chopped

8   chicken thighs (about 2½ pounds), or other meaty parts, extra fat and skin removed, if desired (see page 7)

1   can (14½ ounces) crushed tomatoes in thick purée, or 1 can (15 ounces) tomato sauce

¼   cup red wine

½   teaspoon dried thyme

½   teaspoon dried basil

½   teaspoon dried oregano

1   teaspoon salt

Freshly ground pepper to taste

2   cans (15 ounces each) cannellini (white kidney beans), rinsed and drained

3   tablespoons chopped fresh parsley

1   cup pitted kalamata or canned black olives

Freshly grated Parmesan cheese for sprinkling on top

PREHEAT oven to 350°F. In a Dutch oven over medium heat, warm 1 tablespoon oil. Add onion, bell pepper, and garlic and sauté until vegetables are slightly tender, about 7 minutes. Remove to a plate.

ADD remaining oil and brown chicken about 5 minutes on each side. Drain on paper towels and remove excess grease from pan. Return chicken, vegetables, and remaining ingredients to Dutch oven and mix gently.

COVER and bake until chicken is no longer pink in the center, about 1 hour, stirring once.

SERVES 6

herbed chicken and vegetables on brown rice

Preparation time is quick and easy for this flavorful, healthy dish. Choice chicken pieces are marinated in a lemon-herb marinade, then baked on a bed of brown rice and fresh vegetables.

Juice of 1 lemon

1 tablespoon olive oil

½ teaspoon salt

½ teaspoon dried oregano

½ teaspoon dried thyme

Freshly ground pepper to taste

1 chicken (3 to 3½ pounds), cut into serving pieces, skin removed if desired (see page 7)

1 cup brown rice

2 cups Rich Chicken Stock (page 23) or canned low-sodium chicken broth

½ cup sliced green onions, including some tender green tops

1 zucchini, unpeeled, halved crosswise then halved lengthwise and cut into ½-inch slices

1 cup sliced celery

PREHEAT oven to 350°F.

IN a large bowl, mix lemon juice, olive oil, and seasonings. Add chicken and turn to coat. Cover and marinate 15 to 30 minutes.

PLACE rice in a 9-by-13-inch baking dish lightly coated with cooking spray or oil. In a saucepan over high heat, bring stock to a boil. Pour over rice and stir. Place onions, zucchini, and celery on top of rice. Add chicken and marinade on top of vegetables.

COVER and bake about 1 hour. Then uncover, and bake until chicken is no longer pink in the center and vegetables and rice are tender, about 15 minutes longer.

SERVES 4

classic chicken and dumplings
For a good old-fashioned dinner on a cold winter night, try this satisfying chicken and dumpling dish. It takes a while to prepare, but it is well worth it. Serve with a mixed fruit salad.

½ cup all-purpose flour

¾ teaspoon salt

Freshly ground pepper to taste

1 chicken (3 to 3½ pounds), cut into serving pieces

1 tablespoon butter or margarine

2 tablespoons vegetable oil

1 cup chopped yellow onion

½ cup chopped red bell pepper

4 ounces mushrooms, sliced

1 clove garlic, minced

3 carrots, peeled and cut diagonally into 1-inch slices

2 celery stalks, cut diagonally into 1-inch slices

4 cups Rich Chicken Stock (page 23) or canned low-sodium chicken broth

1 bay leaf

½ teaspoon dried thyme

Parslied Buttermilk Dumplings (recipe follows)

PREHEAT oven to 350°F. On a sheet of wax paper, combine flour, ¼ teaspoon of the salt, and pepper. Toss chicken in mixture to coat and reserve the excess (about ¼ cup).

IN a large Dutch oven over medium-high heat, melt butter with 1 tablespoon oil. Brown chicken in two batches, cooking pieces about 5 minutes on each side. Add more oil if needed. Remove chicken to a plate.

ADD remaining oil to Dutch oven and add vegetables. Sauté until tender, about 5 minutes. Stir in remaining flour. Add stock, bring to a boil, and whisk until smooth. Add bay leaf, thyme, and remaining ½ teaspoon salt. Return chicken to Dutch oven.

COVER and bake until chicken is no longer pink in the center, about 1 hour. In the meantime, make the dumplings.

REMOVE lid from chicken, remove bay leaf and discard. Place dumplings on top. Bake, uncovered, 10 minutes. Cover, and bake until toothpick inserted into center of a dumpling comes out clean, 10 minutes longer. Serve immediately.

SERVES 6

parslied buttermilk dumplings

- 2 cups all-purpose flour
- 1 tablespoon baking powder
- ½ teaspoon salt
- ¼ cup chopped fresh parsley
- 1 cup buttermilk

IN a medium bowl, mix flour, baking powder, salt, and parsley. With a fork, stir in buttermilk until dough is just blended. With a large soup spoon, scoop out 12 dumplings and place them on top of the chicken as directed.

MAKES ABOUT 12 DUMPLINGS

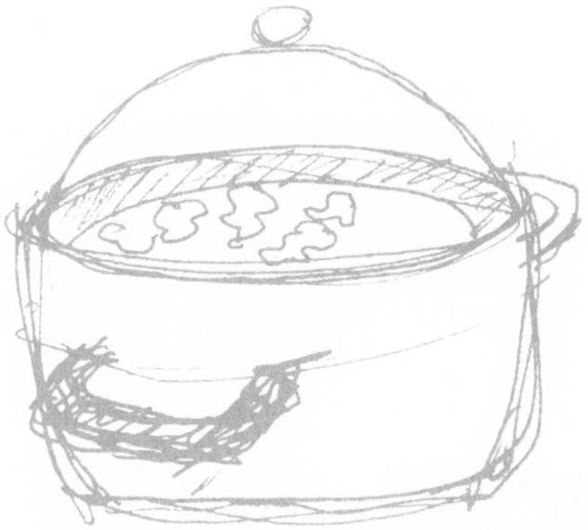

baked chicken and fruit

This wonderful dish includes a variety of fruits and exotic spices that give it a Middle Eastern flavor. Fragrant basmati rice is a good choice for an accompaniment.

1 chicken (3 to 3½ pounds), cut into serving pieces

Salt and freshly ground pepper to taste

Paprika for sprinkling on chicken

1 to 2 tablespoons vegetable oil

½ cup toasted slivered almonds (see page 11)

¼ cup golden raisins (optional)

1 cup pineapple chunks (fresh or canned), drained

4 peach halves (fresh, peeled; or canned and drained)

8 dried prunes

½ teaspoon ground cinnamon

⅛ teaspoon ground cloves

2 cups orange juice

PREHEAT oven to 350°F. Sprinkle chicken with salt, pepper, and paprika.

IN a Dutch oven over medium-high heat, warm 1 tablespoon oil. Brown chicken until golden, about 5 minutes on each side. Add more oil if needed. Add almonds, fruits, seasonings, and orange juice.

COVER and bake until chicken is no longer pink in the center, about 50 minutes. Baste with sauce several times while cooking. Remove lid and cook 10 minutes longer.

TRANSFER to a platter and arrange fruit around chicken. Spoon juices on top.

SERVES 4

THE BIG BOOK OF CASSEROLES

chicken and black beans
The addition of black beans gives this dish a Mexican twist. Serve with warm flour tortillas.

¼ cup all-purpose flour

1 teaspoon salt

1 chicken (3 to 3½ pounds), cut into serving pieces, skin removed if desired (see page 7)

1½ tablespoons vegetable oil

1 cup chopped yellow onion

2 celery stalks, cut into 1-inch slices

1 clove garlic, minced

1 can (14½ ounces) whole tomatoes, chopped, juice from can included

1 cup Rich Chicken Stock (page 23) or canned low-sodium chicken broth

1 tablespoon tomato paste

¼ teaspoon dried thyme

¼ teaspoon chili powder

½ teaspoon salt

Freshly ground pepper to taste

1 can (15 ounces) black beans, rinsed and drained

2 tablespoons cornstarch mixed with 3 tablespoons water (optional)

½ cup sliced green onions, including some tender green tops

PREHEAT oven to 400°F. On a sheet of wax paper, combine flour and ½ teaspoon salt. Toss chicken in mixture to coat. In a Dutch oven over medium-high heat, warm 1 tablespoon oil. Brown chicken about 5 minutes on each side. Remove to a plate.

ADD onion, celery, and garlic and remaining ½ tablespoon oil if needed. Sauté vegetables over medium heat until tender, about 5 minutes. Return chicken to Dutch oven. Add tomatoes, stock, tomato paste, thyme, chili powder, salt, and pepper. Bring to a boil and cook 5 minutes.

ADD beans, cover, and bake 45 minutes. Remove lid and bake until chicken is no longer pink in the center, about 15 minutes longer. Stir in cornstarch mixture, if desired, to thicken the sauce.

SKIM off fat from juices in pan if necessary. Serve in the Dutch oven or in a warmed decorative bowl. Sprinkle onions on top.

SERVES 6

greek chicken and rice

This simple Greek-inspired dish of chicken, vegetables, and rice with a subtle lemon flavor is hard to beat. Serve with warm pita bread and a zesty salad of tomatoes, cucumbers, and feta cheese.

2   tablespoons olive oil

1½ pounds skinned and boned chicken breasts (see page 7), cut into large bite-size pieces

1   cup chopped yellow onion

1   cup chopped green bell pepper

1   cup long-grain white rice

2¼ cups Rich Chicken Stock (page 23) or canned low-sodium chicken broth

Juice of 1 lemon

½   cup kalamata olives, pitted

¾   teaspoon dried oregano

½   teaspoon salt

Freshly ground pepper to taste

PREHEAT oven to 350°F. In a large Dutch oven over medium heat, warm 1 tablespoon oil. Add chicken and brown, about 5 minutes on each side. Remove to a plate.

ADD remaining 1 tablespoon oil and sauté onion and green pepper until tender, about 5 minutes. Stir in rice. Add remaining ingredients.

RETURN chicken to pan, cover, and bake until rice is tender and liquid is absorbed, about 50 minutes.

SERVES 4 TO 6

soy chicken with papaya and kiwi

If you're looking for a quick, full-flavored casserole requiring a minimum amount of effort, try this chicken and soy sauce dish with exotic fruit. Serve with plain rice.

5 or 6 skinned and boned chicken breast halves (1½ to 2 pounds; see page 7)

2 teaspoons cornstarch

½ cup orange juice

¼ cup soy sauce

¼ cup water

¼ teaspoon sugar

¼ cup chopped green onions, including some tender green tops

¼ cup cashews

Papaya slices for garnish

Kiwi slices for garnish

PREHEAT oven to 350°F. Arrange chicken in a 7½-by-11¾-inch baking dish lightly coated with cooking spray or oil.

IN a small pan over medium heat, stir together cornstarch, orange juice, soy sauce, water, and sugar and cook until mixture bubbles and thickens, about 5 minutes. Pour over chicken. Sprinkle onions and nuts along the center.

BAKE, uncovered, basting with sauce several times, until chicken is no longer pink in the center, about 45 minutes. Transfer to a platter and arrange fruit around chicken.

SERVES 4 TO 6

chicken florentine

Thin chicken breast cutlets are lightly browned, topped with spinach and mozzarella cheese, and baked in a tomato-wine sauce. This makes a colorful company dish. Serve with fettucini and a salad of roasted beets, walnuts, and orange segments with a raspberry vinaigrette.

3 tablespoons all-purpose flour

Salt and freshly ground pepper to taste

6 skinned and boned chicken breast halves (about 3 pounds; see page 7), pounded very thin between sheets of plastic wrap

1½ tablespoons olive oil

1 cup chopped yellow onion

2 cloves garlic, minced

1 can (15 ounces) tomato sauce

¼ cup dry white wine

½ teaspoon dried basil

2 packages (6 ounces each) fresh spinach, cooked, drained, and chopped (see page 7); or 1 package (10 ounces) frozen chopped spinach, thawed and squeezed dry

1 cup grated mozzarella cheese

PREHEAT oven to 375°F. On a sheet of wax paper, combine flour, salt, and pepper. Toss cutlets in mixture to coat.

IN a medium skillet over medium heat, warm 1 tablespoon oil. Brown chicken about 5 minutes on each side. Remove to a 2½-quart casserole dish lightly coated with cooking spray or oil.

ADD remaining ½ tablespoon oil to the skillet. Add onion and garlic and sauté until tender, about 5 minutes. Add tomato sauce, wine, and basil. Simmer 2 minutes. Taste for seasonings and add more salt if necessary.

SPREAD spinach on top of chicken. Pour tomato sauce mixture around chicken, lifting the edges to allow the sauce to flow underneath. Sprinkle with cheese. Bake, uncovered, until chicken is no longer pink in the center, about 35 minutes.

SERVES 4 TO 6

chicken with olives and tangy beer-tomato sauce

Here is a great recipe that can be made in just minutes. Serve with plain rice or noodles to absorb the delicious sauce and a plate of sliced red onions, oranges, and cucumbers alongside.

TANGY BEER-TOMATO SAUCE

1   can (6 ounces) tomato paste

1   cup beer, allowed to go flat

¼   teaspoon salt

2   cloves garlic, minced

1   can (4 ounces) diced green chiles, drained

1   chicken (3 to 3½ pounds), cut into serving pieces

Salt and freshly ground pepper to taste

1   cup pitted black olives, drained

TO MAKE THE BEER-TOMATO SAUCE: In a medium bowl, whisk together all ingredients. Set aside.

PREHEAT oven to 350°F. Season chicken with salt and pepper. Place in a 4-quart casserole dish lightly coated with cooking spray or oil. Pour sauce over chicken. Cover and bake until chicken is no longer pink in the center, about 1 hour. Add olives and cook, uncovered, 5 minutes longer.

SERVES 6

83

chicken breasts and mushrooms in lemon sauce

Chicken breasts are moist and juicy when baked in this delicious lemon sauce; the earthy flavor of mushrooms enhances this dish. Serve with a rice dish and fruit salad for a company dinner.

4 to 5 tablespoons butter or margarine

8 ounces mushrooms, thickly sliced

6 green onions, including some tender green tops, sliced

2 cloves garlic, minced

¼ cup all-purpose flour

1 tablespoon chopped fresh rosemary, or ¼ teaspoon dried rosemary

½ teaspoon salt

⅛ teaspoon white pepper

¼ teaspoon paprika

4 to 6 skinned and boned chicken breast halves (1½ to 2 pounds; see page 7)

½ cup Rich Chicken Stock (page 23) or canned low-sodium chicken broth

¼ cup dry white wine

¼ cup fresh lemon juice

¼ cup toasted slivered almonds (see page 11)

IN a large skillet over medium heat, melt 2 tablespoons butter. Add mushrooms, onions, and garlic and sauté until tender, about 5 minutes. Transfer to a 2½-quart casserole dish lightly coated with cooking spray or oil.

ON a sheet of wax paper, mix flour, rosemary, salt, pepper, and paprika. Toss chicken in mixture to coat and reserve the excess.

IN the skillet over medium-high heat, add 2 tablespoons butter and brown chicken, about 5 minutes on each side. Transfer chicken to casserole dish with slotted spoon.

PREHEAT oven to 350°F. Add 1 tablespoon butter to skillet if needed. Stir in reserved flour mixture and blend. Add stock, wine, and lemon juice and whisk until slightly thickened and smooth. Pour over chicken and mix well.

COVER and bake until chicken is no longer pink in the center, about 30 minutes. Uncover and sprinkle with almonds. Bake until bubbly, 10 minutes longer.

SERVES 4 TO 6

chicken paprika

In this classic Hungarian dish, the flavors mingle as the chicken bakes with onion, bell pepper, and broth. Sour cream is added at the end of the cooking time, creating a pretty, creamy-pink sauce. Serve with spaetzle or rice.

¼ cup all-purpose flour

1 teaspoon salt

1 chicken (3 to 3½ pounds), cut into serving pieces

2 tablespoons butter or margarine

2 tablespoons vegetable oil

1 cup chopped yellow onion

½ cup chopped green bell pepper

1 tablespoon paprika (preferably Hungarian)

Freshly ground pepper to taste

1½ cups Rich Chicken Stock (page 23) or canned low-sodium chicken broth

1 cup light sour cream

PREHEAT oven to 350°F. On a sheet of wax paper, combine flour and salt. Toss chicken pieces in mixture to coat and reserve the excess flour.

IN a Dutch oven over medium-high heat, melt butter with oil. Brown chicken, 5 to 10 minutes on each side. Remove to a plate.

REDUCE temperature to medium. Add onions and bell pepper and sauté until tender, about 5 minutes. Add paprika, pepper, and remaining flour and stir until bubbly. Add stock and stir until thickened.

RETURN chicken to Dutch oven; cover and bake until chicken is no longer pink in the center, about 50 minutes. Blend in sour cream and bake, uncovered, 10 minutes longer.

SERVES 4

mediterranean chicken

The five basic Mediterranean food items are simple and readily available—olive oil, garlic, fresh basil, tomatoes, and lemons. This recipe incorporates them all along with onion and red bell pepper for a delicious chicken entrée.

1   chicken (3 to 3 ½ pounds), quartered or cut into serving pieces

MEDITERRANEAN MARINADE

Juice of 1 lemon

2   tablespoons olive oil

2   cloves garlic, minced

2   tablespoons chopped fresh basil, or 1 teaspoon dried basil

¼   teaspoon dried oregano

¾   teaspoon salt

Freshly ground pepper to taste

1   onion, cut into wedges

1   red bell pepper, seeded and cut lengthwise into eighths

3   plum tomatoes, seeded and cut into wedges

10 pitted kalamata or canned black olives

Chopped fresh parsley for sprinkling on top

Fresh basil leaves for garnish

PLACE chicken in a 9-by-13-inch baking dish lightly coated with cooking spray or oil.

MAKE THE MARINADE: In a small bowl, mix all of the marinade ingredients together.

POUR marinade over chicken. Turn to coat, cover, and place in refrigerator for 2 or 3 hours, turning once. Bring to room temperature ½ hour before baking. In the meantime, preheat oven to 350°F.

ARRANGE onion, red pepper, and tomatoes around chicken. Spoon marinade over vegetables. Bake, uncovered, basting several times, until chicken is no longer pink in the center and vegetables are very tender, about 1 hour. Add olives and bake 10 minutes longer. Transfer chicken and vegetables to a platter. Sprinkle with parsley and garnish with basil leaves.

SERVES 4

NOTE: The marinade is also good on lamb.

chicken with mushrooms and swiss cheese

Just reading this recipe will make you hungry, and it tastes just as good as it sounds. The paprika gives the chicken a pretty golden color. A crisp green vegetable, such as broccoli or chard, will complement this entrée.

3   tablespoons all-purpose flour

½   teaspoon salt

¼   teaspoon dried oregano

¼   teaspoon freshly ground pepper

1   teaspoon paprika

6   skinned and boned chicken breast halves (about 2 pounds; see page 7)

2   tablespoons vegetable oil

2   tablespoon butter or margarine

10 green onions, including some tender green tops, sliced

8   ounces large mushrooms, sliced

2   cloves garlic, minced

½   cup Rich Chicken Stock (page 23) or canned low-sodium chicken broth

½   cup dry white wine

½   cup light sour cream

1   cup grated Swiss cheese

PREHEAT oven to 350°F. On a sheet of wax paper, combine flour, salt, oregano, pepper, and paprika. Toss chicken in mixture to coat.

IN a large skillet over medium-high heat, warm oil. Brown chicken about 5 minutes on each side. Transfer to a 2½-quart casserole dish lightly coated with cooking spray or oil.

IN the same skillet over medium heat, melt butter. Add onions, mushrooms, and garlic and sauté until tender, about 5 minutes. Add stock and wine and bring to a boil. Pour over chicken and bake, covered, 30 minutes.

IN a small bowl, mix sour cream and cheese. Stir into the juices in the casserole. Bake, uncovered, until chicken is no longer pink in the center and sauce is bubbly, 15 minutes longer.

SERVES 4

baked tandoori chicken on lentils

This is an adaptation of a classic Indian dish—chicken marinated in a spicy yogurt sauce and baked on a bed of lentils. Serve with pita bread and sliced cucumbers.

2 tablespoons white wine vinegar

Juice of ½ lemon

½ teaspoon ground cumin

1 teaspoon paprika

¾ teaspoon ground coriander

¼ teaspoon ground ginger

½ to 1 teaspoon curry powder (depending on taste)

½ teaspoon salt

2 cloves garlic, minced

¼ cup chopped fresh parsley

1 cup plain nonfat yogurt

1 teaspoon cornstarch

1 chicken (3 to 3½ pounds), cut into serving pieces

Cooked Lentils (recipe follows)

IN a large bowl, stir together all ingredients except chicken and lentils. Add chicken pieces and turn to coat evenly. Cover and marinate in the refrigerator several hours. Bring to room temperature before baking.

PREHEAT oven to 350°F. Spread Cooked Lentils in the bottom of a 7½-by-11¾-inch baking dish lightly coated with cooking spray or oil. Place chicken on top. Pour remaining marinade over the chicken. Cover and bake until chicken is no longer pink in the center, about 1 hour.

SERVES 4

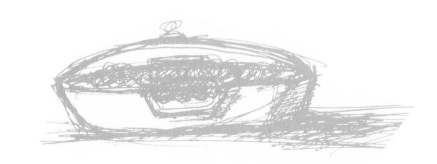

cooked lentils

Lentils do not require presoaking, but they need to be rinsed and picked over to remove any foreign matter.

1 cup dried brown lentils, rinsed and picked over
1 clove garlic, minced
1 bay leaf
3 cups Rich Chicken Stock (page 23) or canned low-sodium chicken broth or water

¼ teaspoon salt
1 tomato, seeded, chopped, and drained

IN a medium saucepan, combine lentils, garlic, bay leaf, stock, and salt. Bring to a boil, reduce heat to medium-low, cover, and simmer until tender and liquid is absorbed, about 55 to 60 minutes.

REMOVE bay leaf and discard. Stir in tomatoes.

MAKES ABOUT 2 CUPS

chicken and bell peppers
Baked chicken topped with a mixture of red, green, and yellow bell peppers makes a colorful presentation. Serve with Sesame Rice (page 238).

2 to 3 tablespoons vegetable oil

2 cloves garlic, chopped

1 red bell pepper, seeded and sliced lengthwise into ½-inch strips

1 green bell pepper, seeded and sliced lengthwise into ½-inch strips

1 yellow bell pepper, seeded and sliced lengthwise into ½-inch strips

1 yellow onion, sliced crosswise into rings

1 tablespoon chopped fresh basil, or 1 teaspoon dried basil

1 chicken (3 to 3½ pounds), cut into serving pieces

½ teaspoon salt

Freshly ground pepper to taste

PREHEAT oven to 350°F. In a large skillet over medium heat, warm 2 tablespoons of oil. Add garlic, peppers, and onion and sauté until tender-crisp, about 8 minutes.

ADD seasonings and sauté until flavors are blended, 2 to 3 minutes longer. Remove to a plate and set aside.

IN same skillet over medium-high heat, warm remaining 1 tablespoon oil. Brown chicken about 5 minutes on each side. Season with salt and pepper.

PLACE chicken in a 7½-by-11¾-inch baking dish lightly coated with cooking spray or oil. Cover and bake 45 minutes. Uncover and top chicken with pepper mixture. Bake, uncovered, until chicken is no longer pink in the center, 15 to 20 minutes longer.

SERVES 4

tarragon chicken breasts and mushrooms

Here is an elegant dish for your next dinner party. It can easily be doubled. Serve with rice and Herbed Baked Tomatoes (page 195).

2 tablespoons vegetable oil

6 skinned and boned chicken breast halves (about 2½ pounds; see page 7)

Salt and freshly ground pepper to taste

½ cup chopped green onions, including some tender green tops

1 clove garlic, minced

8 ounces mushrooms, sliced

½ cup Rich Chicken Stock (page 23) or canned low-sodium chicken broth

¼ cup dry white wine

2 tablespoons chopped fresh tarragon, or ½ teaspoon dried tarragon

¼ teaspoon dried chervil, crumbled

⅛ teaspoon white pepper

2 tablespoons all-purpose flour

½ cup light sour cream

Fresh tarragon sprigs for garnish

PREHEAT oven to 350°F. In a large skillet over medium-high heat, warm 1 tablespoon oil. Brown chicken about 5 minutes on each side. Season with salt and pepper. Place in a 2½-quart casserole dish lightly coated with cooking spray or oil.

ADD remaining 1 tablespoon oil to skillet and over medium heat, sauté onions, garlic, and mushrooms until tender, about 5 minutes. Add to chicken in casserole. To the skillet add stock, wine, tarragon, chervil, pepper and stir. Remove from heat.

IN a small bowl, mix flour and sour cream. Whisk into broth mixture until smooth. Pour over chicken.

COVER and bake until chicken is no longer pink in the center, about 35 minutes. Arrange breasts on a platter and top with mushrooms and sauce. Garnish with tarragon sprigs.

SERVES 4 TO 6

coq au vin (chicken with wine)

This classic French dish is composed of selected chicken pieces, sauced with mushroom, onions, bacon, herbs, and wine. Although red wine is often used, white wine gives a more appealing color and is just as flavorful.

3 thick bacon slices, cubed

3 pounds meaty chicken parts

3 tablespoons all-purpose flour

½ teaspoon dried thyme

½ teaspoon dried marjoram

½ teaspoon salt

Freshly ground pepper to taste

1 bay leaf

1 cup dry white wine

1 cup Rich Chicken Stock (page 23) or canned low-sodium chicken broth

8 ounces mushrooms (halved or quartered if large)

1½ cups baby carrots

1 cup frozen small whole onions, thawed

3 tablespoons chopped fresh parsley

IN a Dutch oven over medium-high heat, cook bacon until crisp, 4 to 5 minutes. With a slotted spoon, remove bacon to a large plate. Add chicken to Dutch oven and brown in bacon drippings 5 minutes on each side. Transfer chicken to the plate holding bacon, leaving 2 tablespoons drippings in pan.

PREHEAT oven to 350°F. Over medium heat, add flour to Dutch oven and stir until bubbly. Add seasonings, wine, and stock. Stir until thickened, 1 to 2 minutes. Add mushrooms, carrots, and onions. Return bacon and chicken and any accumulated juices to Dutch oven.

COVER and bake until chicken is no longer pink in the center and vegetables are tender, about 1 hour. Remove bay leaf and discard. Sprinkle dish with parsley before serving.

SERVES 6 TO 8

chicken bundles with dijon-wine sauce

For a company dish, serve these chicken breasts filled with prosciutto (Italian ham) and Swiss cheese and baked in wine sauce.

8   skinned and boned chicken breast halves (3 to 3½ pounds; see page 7)

Salt and freshly ground pepper to taste

8   thin slices Swiss cheese

8   thin slices prosciutto

Dijon-Wine Sauce (recipe follows)

PREHEAT oven to 350°F. Place chicken breasts between 2 sheets of plastic wrap and pound with meat mallet until ¼ inch thick. Season with salt and pepper. On each breast, place 1 cheese slice and top with 1 prosciutto slice. Roll up, beginning with narrow end of chicken breast, and secure in place with a toothpick. Place the 8 rolls in a 7½-by-11¾-inch baking dish lightly coated with cooking spray or oil. Pour sauce over the chicken.

BAKE, uncovered, basting with sauce several times, until chicken is no longer pink in the center, about 40 minutes. Transfer to a warmed platter and serve immediately.

SERVES 4 TO 6

dijon-wine sauce

½   cup dry white wine

1   tablespoon Dijon mustard

1   tablespoon firmly packed brown sugar

2   tablespoon butter or margarine

½   teaspoon salt

IN a small pan over low heat, combine all ingredients. Stir until sugar dissolves, butter melts, and ingredients are blended, 1 to 2 minutes.

MAKES ABOUT ½ CUP

country chicken stew

Settle in by a cozy fire in the fireplace while this savory stew bubbles away in the oven. It will cheer you up on a cold rainy night. Serve with mashed potatoes.

¼ cup all-purpose flour

1 teaspoon salt

1 teaspoon paprika

¼ teaspoon freshly ground pepper

1 chicken (3 to 3½ pounds), cut into serving pieces

1 tablespoon butter

1 tablespoon vegetable oil

1 cup frozen small whole onions, thawed

3 carrots, peeled and cut diagonally into 1-inch pieces

1 can (14½ ounces) whole tomatoes, including juice, lightly puréed in food processor

½ cup dry white wine

½ teaspoon dried thyme

1 bay leaf

6 to 8 mushrooms, quartered

¼ cup water

Salt to taste

PREHEAT oven to 350°F. On a sheet of wax paper, combine flour, salt, paprika, and pepper. Toss chicken in mixture to coat and reserve the excess.

IN a Dutch oven over medium-high heat, melt butter with oil. Brown chicken, 5 minutes on each side. Add onions, carrots, tomatoes, wine, thyme, and bay leaf and stir to loosen any browned bits.

COVER and bake 45 to 50 minutes. Add mushrooms and continue baking, covered, until chicken is no longer pink in the center, about 15 minutes longer.

TO thicken juices, mix leftover flour mixture with water and stir into juices. Bake, uncovered, 5 minutes longer. Check seasonings and add more salt if needed. Remove bay leaf and discard.

SERVES 4 TO 6

orange-hazelnut chicken

Chicken breasts are dipped in fresh orange juice and then tossed in a delicious nut-crumb coating. Assemble this oven dish ahead of time and bake just before serving. Add orange slices and parsley for extra color.

1 cup dry bread crumbs (see page 5)

¼ cup finely chopped toasted hazelnuts or almonds (see page 11)

½ teaspoon salt

½ teaspoon dried thyme

⅛ teaspoon freshly ground pepper

3 tablespoons chopped fresh parsley

2 tablespoons butter or margarine

¼ cup freshly squeezed orange juice

4 to 6 skinned and boned chicken breast halves (about 2½ pounds; see page 7)

Orange slices for garnish

Fresh parsley sprigs for garnish

PREHEAT oven to 350°F. On a sheet of wax paper, combine bread crumbs, nuts, seasonings, and parsley.

IN a small skillet over medium heat, melt butter and add orange juice. Remove from heat.

DIP chicken, one piece at a time, in butter and juice mixture and then toss in crumb-nut mixture. Place in a 7½-by-11¾-inch baking dish lightly coated with cooking spray or oil. Pour any leftover butter and juice mixture over chicken.

BAKE, uncovered, until chicken is golden and crisp and is no longer pink in the center, about 35 minutes. Transfer to a plate and garnish with orange slices and parsley.

SERVES 4

spicy chicken, peaches, and sugar snap peas

This dish features an unusual combination of chicken, spices, peaches, and fresh sugar snap peas—a triple taste treat. Fresh peaches are best, but if they are not available, canned peaches may be used.

- 1 cup water
- 1 cup orange juice
- 1 cup long-grain white rice
- ¼ teaspoon salt
- ¼ teaspoon ground cinnamon
- ¼ teaspoon ground ginger
- ⅛ teaspoon ground cloves
- 2 cups cubed cooked chicken breast (see page 6)
- 3 peaches, peeled (see page 9), and sliced
- 1½ cups sugar snap peas, trimmed
- ¼ cup toasted slivered almonds (see page 11)

PREHEAT oven to 350°F. In a Dutch oven over medium heat, bring water and orange juice to a boil. Stir in rice and seasonings.

COVER and bake 45 minutes. Add remaining ingredients and gently mix. Cover and bake until heated through, liquid is absorbed, and vegetables are tender-crisp, about 15 minutes longer.

SERVES 4

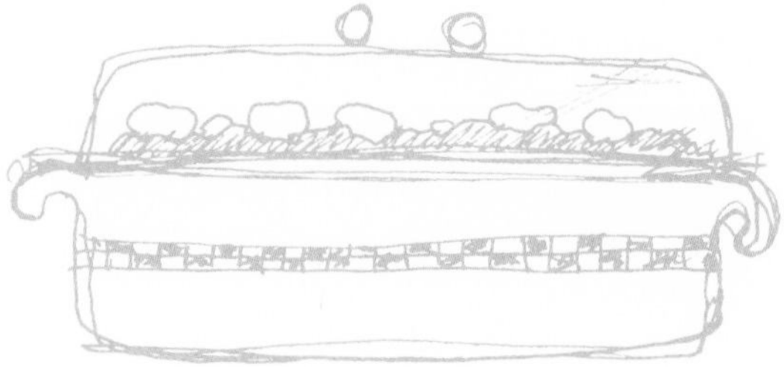

chicken, artichoke, and broccoli casserole

Layers of tender chicken breasts, artichokes, and crisp broccoli meld together in a flavorful cheese sauce. This casserole takes time to prepare, but once the casserole is made, your dinner party will be a success.

4   cups broccoli florets

4   tablespoons butter or margarine

12 ounces mushrooms, sliced

4   tablespoons all-purpose flour

2½ cups Rich Chicken Stock (page 23) or canned low-sodium chicken broth

1   teaspoon Dijon mustard

½   teaspoon dried thyme

½   teaspoon salt

Freshly ground pepper to taste

1   cup grated cheddar cheese

4   cooked chicken breast halves (about 2 pounds; see page 6), cut into bite-size pieces

1   can (14 ounces) quartered artichoke hearts, drained

Freshly grated Parmesan cheese for sprinkling on top

ADD some water to a pan fitted with a steamer rack over medium heat. Place broccoli on rack and steam, covered, over gently boiling water until tender-crisp, about 6 minutes. Drain under cold water and set aside on a large plate.

IN a medium skillet over medium heat, melt 1 tablespoon butter. Add mushrooms and sauté until slightly tender, about 5 minutes. With a slotted spoon, remove to plate holding the broccoli.

MELT remaining 3 tablespoons butter in the skillet over medium heat. Add flour and blend. Add stock, mustard, and seasonings and whisk until sauce thickens, about 2 minutes. Add cheese and stir until smooth.

PREHEAT oven to 350°F. In a 4-quart casserole dish place half the chicken, top with half the vegetables, and repeat layers once more. Pour sauce over all. Cover and bake until bubbly, about 40 minutes. Stir and top with Parmesan cheese. Bake, uncovered, until cheese melts, 5 to 10 minutes longer.

SERVES 8

roasted chicken and vegetables
Chicken and vegetables are seasoned with butter and herbs and baked with vegetables in one pan for an easy oven dinner. Real comfort food!

2½ tablespoons butter or margarine

2 tablespoons vegetable oil

2 large cloves garlic, minced

1 teaspoon dried thyme

1 teaspoon dried basil

½ teaspoon paprika

1 teaspoon salt

¼ teaspoon freshly ground pepper

2 drops Tabasco sauce

1 chicken (3 to 3½ pounds), quartered

3 large new potatoes (about 1½ pounds), quartered

1 large yellow onion, quartered

3 large carrots, peeled and sliced

1 small zucchini, unpeeled, halved lengthwise

1 cup fresh peas, or frozen peas, thawed

Chopped fresh parsley for garnish

PREHEAT oven to 375°F. Put butter, oil, garlic, thyme, basil, paprika, salt, pepper, and Tabasco in a large roasting pan. Place in oven. When butter melts, stir ingredients together and spread evenly over bottom of pan.

ADD chicken to pan and turn to coat all sides evenly with butter-herb mixture. Remove chicken to a plate. Add potatoes, onion, carrots, and zucchini and roll in butter-herb mixture. Place chicken on top of vegetables.

BAKE, uncovered, about 50 minutes. Add peas and cook until chicken is no longer pink in the center and vegetables are tender, about 10 minutes longer.

TRANSFER chicken to center of a warmed platter and place vegetables attractively around chicken. Sprinkle with parsley and serve immediately.

SERVES 4 TO 6

mexican chicken with vegetables
Colorful peppers, tomatoes, and corn bake along with chicken pieces in this zesty, Mexican-inspired dish. Serve flan for dessert.

1 to 2 tablespoons vegetable oil

3 pounds chicken drumsticks and thighs, combined

Salt and freshly ground pepper to taste

1 red bell pepper, seeded and sliced lengthwise into ½-inch strips

1 green bell pepper, seeded and sliced lengthwise into ½-inch strips

1 yellow onion, sliced crosswise into rings

2 cloves garlic, minced

3 tomatoes, seeded, chopped, and drained

1 cup cooked fresh corn kernels (about 2 ears) or 1 cup canned and drained corn, or frozen corn, thawed

½ teaspoon dried oregano

¼ teaspoon ground cumin

¼ teaspoon chili powder (or more to taste)

2 to 3 tablespoons canned diced chiles, drained

¾ cup pitted black olives

½ lemon, thinly sliced

PREHEAT oven to 350°F. In a large skillet over medium-high heat, warm 1 tablespoon oil. Add chicken and brown about 5 minutes on each side. Season with salt and pepper. Transfer to a 2½-quart casserole dish lightly coated with cooking spray or oil.

ADD remaining oil to skillet, if needed, and over medium heat, sauté peppers, onion, and garlic until tender, about 5 minutes. Stir in tomatoes, corn, seasonings, and chiles. Simmer 1 minute. Pour over chicken.

COVER and bake 45 minutes. Uncover and stir in olives. Lay lemon slices on top and continue to bake, uncovered, until chicken is no longer pink in the center, about 15 minutes longer.

SERVES 4 TO 6

festive chicken casserole

This is a good casserole to make for a party because it should be assembled several hours ahead or even the night before baking. Layers of tortillas, chicken, chiles, and cheese in a creamy sauce will get you "raves" on this casserole dish. Serve with a salad of orange and jicama slices.

2   cups light sour cream

1   can (7 ounces) diced green chiles, drained

½   teaspoon paprika

¼   teaspoon ground cumin

¼   teaspoon salt

½   cup chopped green onions, including some tender green tops

2   cloves garlic, minced

9   corn tortillas, softened (see page 10)

4   cups cubed cooked chicken breasts (about 2 pounds; see page 6)

4   cups (about 1 pound) grated Monterey Jack cheese

Salsa (fresh, see page 17, or commercially prepared) for topping

IN a medium bowl, mix sour cream, chiles, paprika, cumin, salt, onions, and garlic. In a 9-by-13-inch baking dish lightly coated with cooking spray or oil, place 3 tortillas so that they overlap slightly. In layers, add one third of the chicken, one-third of the sour cream mixture (it will not cover chicken completely), and one third of the cheese. Repeat layers 2 more times, beginning with tortillas. Cover and refrigerate several hours, or overnight.

PREHEAT oven to 350°F. Bring casserole to room temperature and then bake, covered, until bubbly, about 30 minutes. Let stand 5 to 10 minutes before serving. Serve with salsa as an accompaniment.

SERVES 6

creamy chicken enchiladas

These chicken-filled tortillas topped with a creamy white sauce and cheese will melt in your mouth! Serve with avocado slices and red onion rings on bibb lettuce.

1 tablespoon vegetable oil

1 cup chopped yellow onion

1 clove garlic, minced

3 cups cubed cooked chicken breast (see page 6)

1 can (7 ounces) diced green chiles, drained

¼ cup light sour cream

½ teaspoon salt

9 corn tortillas, softened (see page 10)

2 tablespoons butter or margarine

2 tablespoons all-purpose flour

2 cups milk

⅛ teaspoon white pepper

4 ounces cream cheese, diced

Freshly grated Parmesan cheese for sprinkling on top

PREHEAT oven to 350°F. In a medium skillet over medium heat, warm oil. Add onion and garlic and sauté until tender, about 5 minutes. Transfer to a medium bowl and add chicken, chiles, sour cream, and ¼ teaspoon salt.

LAY a tortilla on a flat surface. Place about ¼ cup chicken mixture down the center of each tortilla. Roll and place seam side down in a 9-by-13-inch baking dish lightly coated with cooking spray or oil.

IN the same medium skillet over medium heat, melt butter. Add flour and stir until bubbly. Add milk, remaining salt, and pepper and whisk until thickened, about 2 minutes. Add cream cheese and whisk until blended, about 1 minute. Pour over tortillas. Sprinkle with Parmesan cheese.

BAKE, uncovered, until heated through and bubbly, about 40 minutes.

SERVES 6

chicken, black bean, and tortilla casserole   This

combination of beans, chicken, tortillas, and cheese makes a great crowd pleaser.

1   tablespoon vegetable oil

1   large yellow onion, chopped

½   green bell pepper, seeded and chopped

2   cloves garlic, minced

1   can (14½ ounces) tomatoes, including juices, lightly puréed in a food processor

½   cup Fresh Tomato Salsa (page 17), or commercially prepared salsa

1   teaspoon ground cumin

½   teaspoon dried oregano

¾   teaspoon salt

Freshly ground pepper to taste

2   cans (15 ounces) black beans, rinsed and drained

3   cups cubed cooked chicken breasts (see page 6)

8   corn tortillas

4   cups (about 1 pound) grated Monterey Jack cheese

OPTIONAL TOPPINGS

Plain nonfat yogurt

Sour cream

Avocado slices

Sliced green onions

Chopped olives

Salsa

IN a large skillet over medium heat, warm oil. Add yellow onion, green pepper, and garlic and sauté until vegetables are tender, about 5 minutes. Add tomatoes, salsa, cumin, oregano, salt, and pepper and mix well. Stir in beans and chicken.

PREHEAT oven to 350°F. In a 4-quart casserole dish or large oval baking dish lightly coated with cooking spray or oil, spread one third of the bean and chicken mixture over the bottom. Top with 4 tortillas and sprinkle with 1 cup cheese. Add another third of the bean and chicken mixture, 4 more tortillas, and 1 cup cheese. Finish with remaining bean and chicken mixture. Cover and bake, 40 minutes. Remove lid, add remaining cheese, and bake until bubbly, about 10 minutes longer.

LET stand 5 to 10 minutes. Serve with toppings.

SERVES 8

chicken tortilla casserole

This is a great recipe for a party. It can be assembled ahead and baked just before guests arrive. Serve with guacamole and chips, black beans, and a tossed green salad.

1 tablespoon vegetable oil

2 cups chopped yellow onion

3 cloves garlic, minced

2 cans (15 ounces each) tomato sauce

1¾ cups Rich Chicken Stock (page 23) or canned low-sodium chicken broth

1 can (4 ounces) diced green chiles, drained

2 teaspoons chili powder

2 teaspoons dried basil

¾ teaspoon dried oregano

¼ teaspoon ground cumin

½ teaspoon salt

1 teaspoon sugar

12 corn tortillas

4 cups cooked cubed chicken breasts (see page 6)

4 cups (about 1 pound) grated cheddar cheese

1 cup pitted black olives

Light sour cream, for passing in a bowl

IN a large saucepan over medium heat, warm oil. Add onions and garlic and sauté until tender, about 5 minutes. Add tomato sauce, stock, chiles, seasonings, and sugar. Bring to a boil, reduce temperature, and simmer, uncovered, 10 minutes.

IN a 9-by-13-inch baking dish lightly coated with cooking spray or oil, place 6 tortillas so that they overlap slightly. Add half the chicken, half the sauce, half the cheese, and all the olives. Repeat the first 3 layers. Cover and refrigerate several hours or overnight. Bring to room temperature before baking.

PREHEAT oven to 375°F. Bake, loosely covered with aluminum foil, until heated through and bubbly, 45 to 50 minutes. Remove foil during last 10 minutes of baking time. Let stand 10 minutes before serving. Pass the sour cream.

SERVES 10 TO 12

chicken enchiladas

Enjoy the flavors from South of the Border with these chicken enchiladas. Serve with other typical companion dishes: Spicy Baked Black Beans (page 247), guacamole and chips, and jicama slaw.

Homemade Enchilada Sauce (recipe follows), or 3 cans (10 ounces each) enchilada sauce, 2 mild and 1 hot

1 package (12) corn tortillas, at room temperature

4 skinned and boned chicken breast halves (about 2 pounds), cooked (see page 6) and cut into ½-inch strips

2 cups grated Monterey Jack cheese

½ cup light sour cream

8 green onions, including some tender green tops, sliced

2 cups grated cheddar cheese

½ cup pitted canned black olives (optional)

Light sour cream or plain nonfat yogurt as an accompaniment

MAKE Homemade Enchilada Sauce or mix canned enchilada sauces in a medium saucepan and keep warm over medium-low heat.

PREHEAT oven to 350°F. Spread ¼ cup of the enchilada sauce in the bottom of a 9-by-13-inch baking dish or large decorative casserole dish lightly coated with cooking spray or oil.

DIP a tortilla in the sauce in the pan for a few seconds to soften. Remove with tongs and lay flat on a plate. Immediately add another tortilla to sauce.

PLACE several chicken strips in the center of the tortilla on the plate. Top with a row of Monterey Jack cheese, 2 teaspoons sour cream, and a few chopped onions. Roll up and place seam side down in baking dish. Repeat procedure with remaining tortillas. Pour remaining sauce evenly over tortillas. Sprinkle with cheddar cheese and dot with olives. Bake, uncovered, until hot and bubbly, 30 to 35 minutes. Serve immediately with sour cream or yogurt.

SERVES 6

homemade enchilada sauce

1 can (15 ounces) tomato
  sauce
1 can (6 ounces) tomato
  paste
¾ cup water
1 can (10½ ounces) beef
  broth, undiluted
¼ teaspoon ground cumin
¼ teaspoon garlic powder

2 teaspoons chili powder
  (or more to taste)
¼ teaspoon paprika
½ teaspoon dried oregano
¼ teaspoon salt
2 to 3 drops Tabasco sauce
Freshly ground pepper to
  taste

BLEND all ingredients in a saucepan. Simmer over low heat, uncovered, 5 to 10 minutes.

MAKES ABOUT 4 CUPS

chicken enchilada bake with salsa cream sauce   Almost

everyone seems to like Mexican food, and this casserole is a winner. For variety, a light

creamy sauce replaces the usual tomato sauce. Serve with more warm tortillas and an

avocado salad.

3   tablespoons butter or
    margarine
3   tablespoons all-purpose
    flour
1½ cups Rich Chicken Stock
    (page 23) or canned low-
    sodium chicken broth
¼   teaspoon salt
Freshly ground pepper to taste
1   cup light sour cream
½   cup Fresh Tomato Salsa
    (page 17), or commercially
    prepared salsa
10 corn tortillas, cut into ¾-
    inch strips
2½ cups cubed cooked chicken
    breast
6   green onions, including
    some tender green tops,
    sliced
1   cup pitted canned black
    olives
2½ cups grated Monterey Jack
    cheese
Lime wedges for garnish
Papaya slices for garnish

IN a medium saucepan over medium heat, melt butter. Add flour and blend. Whisk in stock, salt, and pepper and stir until mixture boils and is thickened, about 2 minutes. Remove from heat. Stir in sour cream and salsa and mix well.

COVER the bottom of a 9-by-13-inch baking dish with one third of the sauce. Scatter half of the tortilla strips on top. Next scatter the chicken, onions, olives, and half the cheese, and pour one third of the sauce over all. Top with remaining tortillas, sauce, and cheese.

PREHEAT oven to 375°F. Bake, covered, 30 minutes. Remove cover and bake until bubbly, about 15 minutes longer. Let stand 10 minutes before serving. Garnish with lime wedges and papaya slices.

SERVES 6 TO 8

arroz con pollo (chicken with rice)

A popular dish, arroz con pollo is served often in Spain and Mexico. This version includes the typical ingredients plus salsa for extra flavor. Pass around sour cream and more salsa in bowls.

1 tablespoon vegetable oil

½ cup chopped yellow onion

½ cup chopped green bell pepper

1 clove garlic, minced

1 teaspoon dried oregano

1 teaspoon ground cumin

1 teaspoon salt

Freshly ground pepper to taste

1 cup long-grain rice

2 cups Rich Chicken Stock (page 23) or canned low-sodium chicken broth

1 cup commercially prepared chunky salsa

3 skinned and boned chicken breast halves (about 1½ pounds), cooked and cut into bite-size pieces (see page 6)

1 cup fresh peas, or frozen peas, thawed

2 tablespoons chopped fresh cilantro or parsley

PREHEAT oven to 350°F. In a large skillet over medium heat, warm oil. Add onion, bell pepper, and garlic and sauté until tender, about 5 minutes. Add seasonings and stir in rice. Add stock and salsa and bring to a boil. Transfer to a 2½-quart casserole dish lightly coated with cooking spray or oil.

BAKE, covered, 40 minutes. Stir in chicken and peas and continue baking, covered, until liquid is absorbed and heated through, about 10 minutes longer. Sprinkle with cilantro or parsley before serving.

SERVES 6

chicken pot pie with fresh vegetables

A fresh look and taste are given to an old favorite. Preparing the vegetables takes a little extra time, but the improved flavor is worth it.

2   carrots, peeled and thinly sliced

1   celery stalk, cut into ½-inch slices

½   cup chopped yellow onion

1½   cups Rich Chicken Stock (page 23) or canned low-sodium chicken broth

1   cup frozen corn kernels thawed or 1 ear corn on the cob, cooked and kernels cut off

1   cup fresh peas or frozen peas, thawed

2   cups cooked cubed chicken breast (see page 6)

3   tablespoons butter or margarine

3   tablespoons all-purpose flour

¾   teaspoon salt

Freshly ground pepper to taste

½   cup 2 percent milk

¼   cup chopped fresh parsley

Flaky Pie Crust (recipe follows)

IN a medium saucepan over medium heat, cook carrots, celery, and onion in ½ cup of the broth, covered, until tender, about 10 minutes. Drain vegetables, reserving broth.

PREHEAT oven to 350°F. Place vegetable mixture, corn, peas, and chicken in a 10-inch pie plate, 2 inches deep.

IN the saucepan over medium heat, melt butter. Add flour and seasonings and stir until bubbly. Add remaining stock, reserved broth, and milk and bring to a boil, stirring constantly, until thickened, about 2 minutes. Add parsley, pour over vegetables, and mix well.

PLACE pie crust over vegetables, fold edges under, and flute. Make slits in crust to prevent puffing. Bake until vegetables are bubbly and pastry is golden on top, about 35 minutes.

SERVES 6

flaky pie crust

1¼ cups all-purpose flour

½ teaspoon salt

6 tablespoons chilled butter, cut into small pieces

3 tablespoons chilled vegetable shortening

2 to 3 tablespoons ice water

PLACE all ingredients in a food processor except water. With on-off pulses, process until mixture resembles coarse meal, about 30 pulses. With the motor running, slowly add water, one tablespoon at a time, until dough sticks together and before a ball forms (you may not need all the water). Turn dough onto a sheet of wax paper and flatten into a 6-inch disk. Wrap with wax paper and chill 30 minutes.

ON a lightly floured surface and with a floured rolling pin, roll dough from the center to the edges until pastry is 2 inches larger than pie plate.

MAKES ONE 10-INCH PIE CRUST

chicken saltimbocca
Veal is usually called for in this Italian dish, but chicken breast can also be used. Serve with a Caesar salad and baked polenta (page 19) or Tuscan Beans (page 252).

¼ cup all-purpose flour
¼ teaspoon salt
Freshly ground pepper to taste
8 skinned and boned chicken breast halves (about 3 pounds)
8 thin slices mozzarella cheese
8 thin slices prosciutto (Italian ham)
8 to 10 fresh sage leaves, slivered (see page 9), or 1 teaspoon dried sage
6 tablespoons butter
½ cup dry white wine
Juice of 1 lemon
3 tablespoons chopped fresh parsley

PREHEAT oven to 400°F. On a large sheet of wax paper, combine flour, salt, and pepper and set aside.

PLACE chicken breasts between 2 sheets of plastic wrap and pound with a meat mallet until chicken is about ¼ inch thick.

LAY a slice of cheese on each chicken breast half. Top with a slice of prosciutto and a few fresh sage slivers (or if using dried sage, sprinkle lightly on top of prosciutto). Roll up each chicken breast half from narrow end and secure with a toothpick. Toss in flour mixture to coat evenly.

IN a large skillet over medium heat, melt 3 tablespoons of the butter. Add chicken and brown lightly on all sides, about 10 minutes. Transfer to a 9-by-13-inch baking dish lightly coated with cooking spray or oil. Bake, uncovered, about 10 minutes.

MEANWHILE, add wine and lemon juice to the same skillet over medium heat. Deglaze, stirring to loosen browned bits, about 3 minutes. Gradually whisk in remaining 3 tablespoons butter in small pieces.

REDUCE oven temperature to 350°F and pour sauce from skillet over chicken. Continue baking, uncovered, until chicken is no longer pink in the center, about 20 minutes longer.

TRANSFER chicken rolls to a warmed platter, remove toothpicks, and pour sauce over top. Sprinkle with parsley and serve immediately.

SERVES 8

THE BIG BOOK OF CASSEROLES

cassoulet

An authentic French cassoulet is a complex dish that usually includes a variety of meats—sausage and duck or goose, vegetables, and always, white beans. In this version, chicken legs are substituted for duck, and the directions have been simplified.

2 cloves garlic, minced

1 large yellow onion, chopped

2 carrots, peeled and thinly sliced

½ red bell pepper, seeded and coarsely chopped

1 cup water

1 can (14½ ounces) whole tomatoes, chopped, juice from can included

1¾ cups Rich Chicken Stock (page 23) or canned low-sodium chicken broth

½ cup dry red wine

½ teaspoon salt

Freshly ground pepper to taste

½ teaspoon dried thyme

¼ teaspoon ground allspice

1 bay leaf

2 drops Tabasco sauce

6 chicken drumsticks (about 1½ pounds)

1 pound kielbasa sausage, cut into ½-inch slices

2 cans (15 ounces each) white beans, rinsed and drained

Chopped fresh parsley for sprinkling on top

PREHEAT oven to 350°F. In a Dutch oven over medium-high heat, cook garlic and vegetables in water, stirring often, until water evaporates and vegetables begin to brown and stick to the pan, about 15 minutes. Add tomatoes, stock, wine, and seasonings.

ADD chicken and sausage and bake, covered, 45 minutes. Add beans and continue to bake, uncovered, until chicken is no longer pink in the center and flavors are blended, about 15 minutes longer. Remove bay leaf and discard. Serve in large bowls and sprinkle with parsley.

SERVES 4 TO 6

chicken with vegetables and rice

Prepare this main-course dish when you need a casserole you can assemble ahead of time and bake later. Leftover chicken or turkey may be used. Serve with a fruit platter of cantaloupe spears, watermelon pieces, and green grapes, and follow with ginger cookies, to complete the menu.

4 skinned and boned chicken breast halves (about 2 pounds; see page 7)

1 cup Rich Chicken Stock (page 23) or canned low-sodium chicken broth

1 sprig fresh parsley

2 tablespoons vegetable oil

1 cup chopped yellow onion

½ red bell pepper, seeded and chopped

1 celery stalk, sliced

8 ounces mushrooms, sliced

½ cup long-grain white rice

1 can (14½ ounces) tomatoes, chopped, juice from can included

½ teaspoon dried thyme

¼ teaspoon dried marjoram

½ teaspoon salt

Freshly ground pepper to taste

1 cup grated Swiss cheese

IN a medium saucepan over medium heat, simmer chicken in stock with parsley, covered, until no longer pink, about 15 minutes. Reserve stock. Cut chicken into 1-inch pieces and transfer to a 4-quart casserole dish lightly coated with cooking spray or oil.

PREHEAT oven to 350°F. In a large skillet over medium heat, warm oil. Add onion, bell pepper, celery, and mushrooms and sauté until tender, 6 to 7 minutes. Stir in rice. Add tomatoes, reserved stock, and seasonings and simmer, uncovered, 5 minutes. Pour over chicken.

COVER and bake until liquid is absorbed and rice is tender, about 55 minutes. Add cheese and bake, uncovered, until cheese melts, 5 minutes longer.

SERVES 6

turkey or chicken tetrazzine

This combination of poultry and spaghetti baked in a cheese sauce has long been a popular American favorite. Although the dish is named after the Italian opera singer Luisa Tetrazzine (1871–1940), it is thought to have originated in San Francisco. This is another way to use leftover turkey after the holidays.

4 tablespoons butter or margarine

½ cup chopped yellow onion

2 cloves garlic, minced

8 ounces mushrooms, sliced

¼ cup all-purpose flour

1 cup Rich Chicken Stock (page 23) or canned low-sodium chicken broth

1½ cups half-and-half or milk

3 tablespoons dry white wine

¾ teaspoon salt

⅛ teaspoon white pepper

½ cup freshly grated Parmesan cheese, plus extra for topping

3 to 4 cups cooked turkey or chicken, cut into bite-size pieces (see page 6)

8 ounces spaghetti, broken into thirds, cooked, and drained

PREHEAT oven to 350°F. In a medium saucepan over medium heat, melt 2 tablespoons butter. Sauté onion, garlic, and mushrooms until tender, about 5 minutes. With a slotted spoon, remove vegetables to a plate. Add remaining 2 tablespoons butter to saucepan and blend in flour. Add stock, cream, wine, salt, pepper, and cheese. Stir until smooth and thickened, about 2 minutes. Return vegetables to pan and mix thoroughly.

IN a 9-by-13-inch baking dish lightly coated with cooking spray or oil, combine sauce with turkey or chicken, add spaghetti, and toss lightly.

COVER and bake 30 minutes. Sprinkle with remaining cheese. Bake, uncovered, until bubbly and top is golden, 10 to 15 minutes longer.

SERVES 6 TO 8

113

turkey or chicken casserole with cheese sauce   This

makes a festive luncheon dish when served with a seasonal fruit salad.

2   cups Rich Chicken Stock
    (page 23), canned low-
    sodium chicken broth, or
    water

1   cup long-grain white rice

2 to 3 tablespoons butter or
    margarine

8   ounces mushrooms, sliced

½   red bell pepper, seeded and
    chopped

2   tablespoons chopped
    yellow onion

¼   cup sliced almonds

¼   cup chopped fresh parsley

1   tablespoon chopped fresh
    basil, or ¾ teaspoon dried
    basil

3 to 4 cups cubed cooked
    chicken or turkey breast
    (see page 6)

Parmesan Cheese Sauce
    (recipe follows)

Salt and freshly ground pepper
    to taste

IN a medium saucepan, bring stock or water to a boil. Add rice, reduce heat to low, and cook, covered, until liquid is absorbed, about 20 minutes. Place in a 4-quart casserole dish lightly coated with cooking spray or oil.

PREHEAT oven to 350°F. In a medium skillet over medium heat, melt butter. Add mushrooms, bell pepper, onion, and almonds. Sauté until vegetables are soft, about 5 minutes. Stir in parsley and basil. Add to rice in casserole and stir in chicken or turkey and Parmesan Cheese Sauce. Mix well and season with salt and pepper.

BAKE, covered, until bubbly, about 45 minutes.

SERVES 6

parmesan cheese sauce

3   tablespoons butter or
    margarine

3   tablespoons flour

¼   teaspoon salt

¾   cup Rich Chicken Stock
    (page 23) or canned low-
    sodium chicken broth

1   cup milk

2   tablespoons dry white
    wine

3   tablespoons freshly
    grated Parmesan cheese

½   cup light sour cream

IN a small saucepan over medium heat, melt butter. Add flour and salt and stir until bubbly. Add stock and stir until slightly thickened. Add milk, wine, and Parmesan cheese, and stir until smooth and flavors are blended, about 2 minutes. Remove from heat and whisk in sour cream.

MAKES ABOUT 2 CUPS

turkey or chicken and spaghetti

This spaghetti and turkey casserole is made with a light tomato sauce, a nice change from the usual thick and meaty sauce. Leftover turkey or chicken may be used. A tossed green salad with an oil and vinegar dressing is a good accompaniment. Follow with vanilla frozen yogurt and caramel sauce for dessert.

1   tablespoon vegetable oil

1   cup chopped yellow onion

2   cloves garlic, minced

½   cup chopped green or red bell pepper, or a combination of the two

2   tablespoons butter or margarine

2   tablespoons all-purpose flour

1   can (8 ounces) tomato sauce

2   cups Rich Chicken Stock (page 23) or canned low-sodium chicken broth

¾   teaspoon salt

Freshly ground pepper to taste

4   cups cubed cooked turkey or chicken (see page 6)

¾   cup pimiento-stuffed green olives, sliced

10 ounces spaghetti, cooked and drained

1   cup grated cheddar cheese

¼   cup freshly grated Parmesan cheese

PREHEAT oven to 350°F. In a large skillet over medium heat, warm oil. Add onion, garlic, and bell pepper and sauté until tender, about 5 minutes. Remove to a 4-quart casserole dish coated with cooking spray or oil.

IN same skillet over medium heat, melt butter, add flour and stir until bubbly. Add tomato sauce, stock, salt, and pepper and stir until thickened, about 2 minutes. Stir in turkey and olives.

TRANSFER mixture to the casserole dish, add spaghetti, and gently mix all the ingredients in the dish. Top with cheeses, cover, and bake until hot and bubbly, 30 to 40 minutes.

SERVES 6

turkey loaf and baked sweet potatoes

Fresh ground turkey is readily available in most supermarkets. There are several grades, so look for the leanest and best quality. Since ground turkey is bland, extra seasonings are needed for flavor. Serve this loaf as a main course with sweet potatoes, or as a pâté on small slices of toasted French bread with tiny pickles.

1 slice white bread, crust removed, torn into small pieces (about 1 cup)

¼ cup Rich Chicken Stock (page 23) or canned low-sodium chicken broth

1¼ pounds lean ground turkey

1 large egg

¼ cup finely chopped yellow onion

¼ cup finely chopped red or green bell pepper, or combination of the two

¼ cup chopped fresh parsley

1 teaspoon commercially prepared horseradish

1 teaspoon Dijon mustard

1 teaspoon Worcestershire sauce

½ teaspoon salt

¼ teaspoon freshly ground pepper

4 to 6 medium sweet potatoes

Light sour cream or nonfat yogurt, for topping

2 tablespoons snipped fresh chives

PREHEAT oven to 350°F. In a large bowl, add all ingredients except sweet potatoes and chives and mix thoroughly. Place in a 4½-by-8½-by-2-inch loaf pan lightly coated with cooking spray or oil. Bake, uncovered, for about 1 hour.

WHILE the turkey loaf is baking, place potatoes in a 7½-by-11¾-inch baking dish lightly coated with cooking spray or oil and bake for about 1 hour, piercing skins with a fork halfway through the cooking time.

WHEN the turkey loaf is done, remove from oven and let it stand 10 minutes. Run a knife around the sides of the pan and invert loaf onto a platter. Cut potatoes in half and arrange around turkey loaf. Add a dollop of sour cream or yogurt and sprinkle with chives.

SERVES 6 TO 8

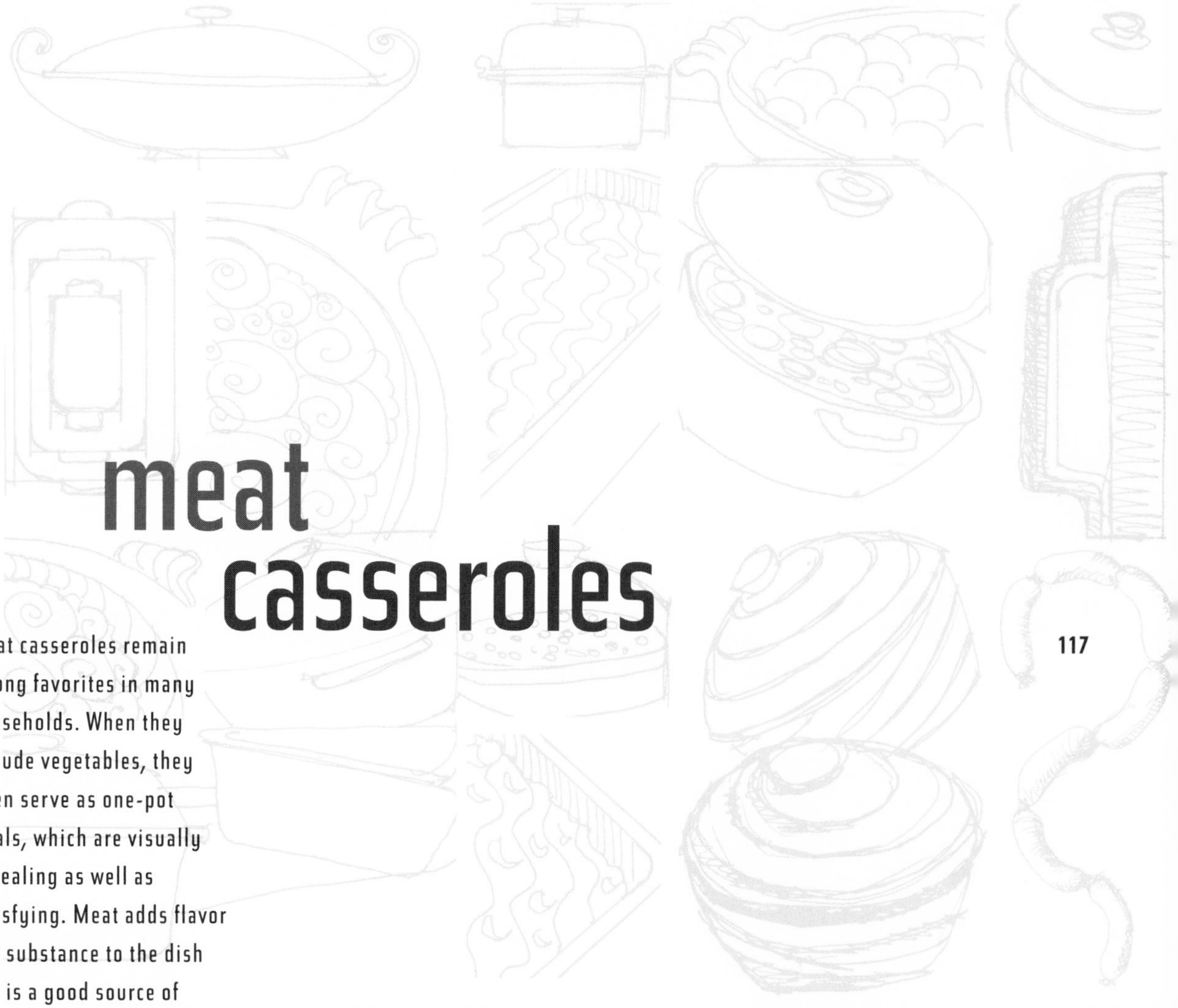

meat casseroles

Meat casseroles remain strong favorites in many households. When they include vegetables, they often serve as one-pot meals, which are visually appealing as well as satisfying. Meat adds flavor and substance to the dish and is a good source of protein. Some of the less expensive cuts of meat work well in casserole dishes because long cooking tenderizes the meat.

In this chapter, some old favorite meat casseroles are included along with new and inventive combinations. There are fun dishes for the hungry family as well as sophisticated company fare.

osso bucco

This popular Italian dish is often a featured special in fine restaurants. The recipe has been streamlined so you can easily make this impressive dish at home. Serve with *gremolata*—a classic garnish for osso bucco—and a side dish of baked polenta.

3 to 3½ pounds veal or lamb shanks, cut into 3-inch pieces by your butcher

⅓ cup all-purpose flour

1 teaspoon paprika

1 teaspoon salt

Freshly ground pepper to taste

3 tablespoons vegetable oil

1 yellow onion, chopped

3 celery stalks, sliced into 1-inch pieces

2 cups baby carrots

4 or 5 cloves garlic, chopped

1 tablespoon chopped fresh basil, or ¾ teaspoon dried basil

½ teaspoon dried oregano

½ teaspoon dried thyme

1 cup dry red wine

1 teaspoon grated lemon zest

1 bay leaf

1 can (14½ ounces) crushed tomatoes in thick puree

1 cup Rich Chicken Stock (page 23) or canned low-sodium chicken broth

RINSE meat and pat dry with a paper towel. On a sheet of wax paper or a plate, combine flour, paprika, salt, and pepper. Coat meat on all sides in seasoned flour, shaking off the excess.

PREHEAT oven to 350°F. In a Dutch oven over medium-high heat, warm 2 tablespoons oil. Add meat and brown on all sides, about 8 to 10 minutes. Transfer to a plate. Reduce heat to medium. Add remaining oil to Dutch oven along with onion, celery, carrots, garlic, basil, oregano, and thyme. Cook, stirring occasionally, until vegetables begin to brown, about 10 minutes. Add wine, lemon zest, and bay leaf. Increase heat to medium-high and boil to reduce liquid, about 5 minutes. Return meat to Dutch oven. Stir in tomatoes and broth and cook until ingredients are warm throughout.

COVER and bake for 1½ hours. Remove lid and stir. Continue baking until meat is very tender and falling off the bones, about 30 minutes longer.

GREMOLATA

¼ cup dry bread crumbs (see page 5)

¼ cup chopped fresh parsley

1 teaspoon chopped fresh rosemary, or ½ teaspoon dried rosemary

1 tablespoon grated lemon zest

1 clove garlic, minced

Salt and freshly ground pepper to taste

IN the meantime, make the gremolata: In a small bowl, mix all ingredients. Set aside.

WHEN the osso bucco is done, skim off fat, if necessary. Remove bay leaf and discard. Taste for seasoning and add salt and pepper, if needed.

TRANSFER to a warm serving dish and sprinkle with Gremolata. Serve immediately.

SERVES 4 TO 6

NOTE: If a thicker sauce is desired, mix 2 tablespoons flour with ¼ cup water and stir until blended. Stir into hot sauce and blend.

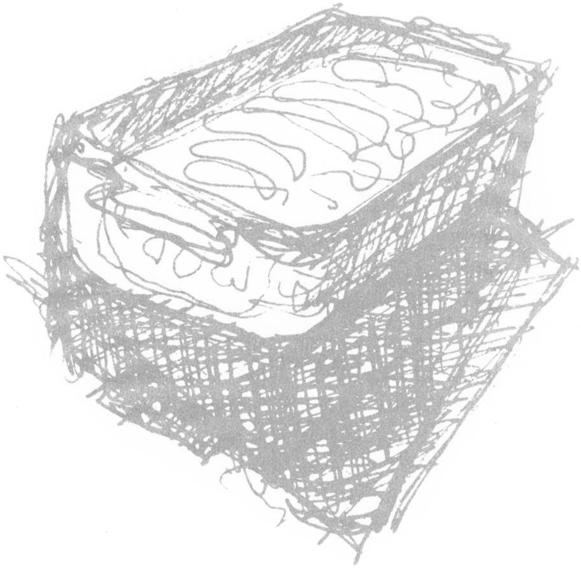

tailgate casserole

At our first tailgate party (Oregon State versus University of Oregon) in an Airstream trailer over thirty years ago, we were served this dish. It is a combination of beef, tomato sauce, cheeses, and noodles, and it's perfect for a pregame party. Serve with French bread and crudités.

1½ pounds lean ground beef

1 teaspoon vegetable oil (optional)

1 can (15 ounces) tomato sauce

¾ teaspoon salt

Freshly ground pepper to taste

½ cup sour cream

1 package (3 ounces) cream cheese, at room temperature

1 cup low-fat cottage cheese

6 green onions, including some tender green tops, sliced

½ green or red bell pepper, seeded and chopped (optional)

6 ounces egg noodles, cooked and drained

2 cups grated cheddar cheese

PREHEAT oven to 350°F. In a large skillet over medium-high heat, brown beef until meat is no longer pink, about 5 minutes. Add oil if needed. Add tomato sauce, salt, and pepper and simmer 5 minutes.

WITH an electric mixer, beat together sour cream, cream cheese, and cottage cheese in a medium bowl. Fold in onions and bell pepper and mix well.

IN a 9-by-13-inch baking dish lightly coated with cooking spray or oil, add half of the noodles, half the cheese mixture, and half the meat mixture in layers. Repeat the layers, ending with meat mixture. Top with cheddar cheese.

COVER and bake 30 minutes. Uncover and bake until bubbly, about 15 minutes longer. Let stand 5 to 10 minutes before serving.

SERVES 6 TO 8

beef tamale bake

This is a simplified variation on a Mexican tamale. Meat, beans, corn, and tomatoes are layered and capped with a cornmeal topping, which takes the place of a corn husk wrapper. It makes a great dish to serve a crowd. Serve with fresh salsa and an avocado salad.

CORNMEAL TOPPING

1   cup yellow cornmeal
½   teaspoon salt
4   cups water

1   pound lean ground beef
1   cup chopped yellow onion
½   cup chopped green bell pepper
1   clove garlic, minced
1   tablespoon chili powder
½   teaspoon dried oregano
¾   teaspoon salt
Freshly ground pepper to taste
1   can (14½ ounces) crushed tomatoes in thick purée
1   can (16 ounces) kidney beans, rinsed and drained
2   cups corn kernels, (fresh, frozen and thawed, or canned and drained)
2   cups grated cheddar cheese

PREHEAT oven to 350°F. Make the cornmeal topping: In a saucepan over medium heat, mix all ingredients. Bring to a boil, reduce heat, and cook, stirring, until thickened, about 5 minutes.

IN a large skillet over medium heat, cook beef, onion, bell pepper, and garlic, breaking up the meat with a spoon, until meat is no longer pink and vegetables are tender, about 5 minutes. Stir in seasonings, tomatoes, beans, and corn and simmer about 5 minutes.

IN a 9-by-13-inch baking dish lightly coated with cooking spray or oil, place meat and vegetable mixture. Spread cornmeal topping over the mixture and sprinkle with cheese.

BAKE, uncovered, until bubbly and cheese is melted, about 30 minutes. Let stand 10 minutes before serving.

SERVES 8 TO 10

121

THE BIG BOOK OF CASSEROLES

lasagna with meat sauce
Here is a great dish to take to a potluck dinner or a casual gathering. Noodles are layered with a meaty tomato sauce and a creamy cheese filling, and the dish is baked until golden brown. Serve with a tossed green salad and garlic bread.

1 pound lean ground beef

1 cup chopped yellow onion

3 cloves garlic, minced

1 can (14½ ounces) crushed tomatoes in thick purée

1 can (15 ounces) tomato sauce

1 tablespoon chopped fresh basil, or ¾ teaspoon dried basil

1 tablespoon chopped fresh oregano, or ¾ teaspoon dried oregano

¼ teaspoon sugar

½ teaspoon salt

Freshly ground pepper to taste

1 container (16 ounces) low-fat cottage cheese or ricotta cheese

2 cups grated mozzarella cheese

¼ cup low-fat sour cream

½ cup freshly grated Parmesan cheese

3 tablespoons chopped fresh parsley

9 large lasagna noodles, cooked and drained

PREHEAT oven to 350°F. In a large skillet over medium heat, cook beef, onion, and garlic, stirring to break up meat, until meat is no longer pink and vegetables are tender, about 5 minutes. Stir in tomatoes, tomato sauce, basil, oregano, sugar, salt, and pepper. Bring to a boil, reduce temperature to low, and simmer, uncovered, 10 minutes.

IN a medium bowl, mix cottage cheese, 1 cup of the mozzarella cheese, sour cream, ¼ cup of the Parmesan cheese, and parsley.

IN a 9-by-13-inch baking dish lightly coated with cooking spray or oil, spread 1 cup meat sauce. In layers add 3 noodles, then one third of cheese mixture (will not completely cover), and one third of remaining meat sauce. Repeat layers two more times, ending with meat sauce. Sprinkle remaining 1 cup mozzarella and ¼ cup Parmesan on top.

COVER and bake 45 minutes. Remove cover and bake until hot and bubbly, 15 minutes longer. Let stand 10 minutes before serving.

SERVES 8

spicy beef enchilada casserole

This Mexican-inspired dish combines everyone's favorite ingredients. It makes a large quantity and is a great entrée to serve at a postgame party or potluck. I like to make it in an oval, decorative Mexican pottery dish.

1¼ pounds ground chuck
1 cup chopped yellow onion
½ teaspoon salt
Freshly ground pepper to taste
2 cans (10 ounces each) enchilada sauce
1 can (8 ounces) tomato sauce
¼ teaspoon chili powder, or to taste
1 large egg, beaten
1 cup low-fat cottage cheese
9 corn tortillas
2 cups grated Monterey Jack cheese
2 cups grated cheddar cheese
Light sour cream as an accompaniment

PREHEAT oven to 375°F. In a large skillet over medium heat, brown meat with onions until meat is no longer pink and onions are tender, about 5 minutes. Season with salt and pepper. Add sauces and chili powder and stir until blended. Remove from heat.

IN a small bowl, mix egg and cottage cheese. Set aside.

IN a 9-by-13-inch baking dish lightly coated with cooking spray or oil, spread a little of the meat sauce. Add three tortillas (they will overlap), one third of the Monterey Jack cheese, all the egg–cottage cheese mixture, and one third of the remaining meat sauce. Repeat the layers of tortillas, Monterey Jack cheese, and meat sauce two more times. Sprinkle cheddar cheese on top.

BAKE, uncovered, until bubbly, about 45 minutes. Let stand 10 minutes before serving. Pass around sour cream in a bowl.

SERVES 8 TO 10

tortillas with meat, beans, and chili sauce

This is an old standby casserole of tortillas filled with savory meat and beans and topped with a peppy chili sauce, lots of cheese, and olives. Your guests will love it. Team with a cooling jicama slaw and serve beer or iced tea.

2 cans (10¾ ounces each) tomato purée

1¾ cups Beef Stock (page 22) or canned beef broth

1 tablespoon cider vinegar

2 tablespoons chili powder

2 tablespoons chopped fresh parsley

2 cloves garlic, minced

1 pound lean ground beef

1 cup chopped yellow onion

1 to 2 teaspoons vegetable oil (optional)

1 can (15 ounces) pinto or kidney beans, drained and rinsed

½ teaspoon salt

Freshly ground pepper to taste

8 flour tortillas, softened (see page 10)

4 cups (about 1 pound) grated cheddar cheese

1 cup pitted ripe black olives, sliced

Light sour cream or plain nonfat yogurt as an accompaniment

PREHEAT oven to 350°F. In a medium saucepan over medium heat, combine purée, stock, vinegar, chili powder, parsley, and garlic and simmer, uncovered, 10 minutes. Set aside.

IN a medium skillet over medium heat, add beef and onion. Stir, breaking up meat with a spoon, and cook until beef is no longer pink and onions are tender, about 10 minutes. Add oil, if needed.

PUT beans in a small bowl and mash briefly with a potato or bean masher. Add to beef and mix well. Season with salt and pepper.

ADD ½ cup of the tomato sauce to a 9-by-13-inch baking dish lightly coated with cooking spray or oil. On a clean work surface, lay out a tortilla. Spread a strip (about ¼ cup) of meat and bean mixture in the center. Roll and place seam side down in the baking dish. Continue to fill the remaining tortillas and arrange in baking dish in one layer. Pour the remaining sauce evenly over all the tortillas. Scatter olives and sprinkle cheese on top.

COVER and bake until bubbly, about 35 minutes. Uncover and bake about 10 minutes longer. Let stand 10 minutes before serving. Pass around sour cream in a bowl.

SERVES 8 TO 10

THE BIG BOOK OF CASSEROLES

spaghetti bake with meat sauce and three cheeses

No more watery spaghetti! The spaghetti absorbs the seasoned sauce as it bakes with vegetables and a mixed cheese topping. Serve with garlic bread.

1   pound lean ground beef

1   small yellow onion, chopped

6 to 8 mushrooms, sliced

2   cloves garlic, minced

1 to 2 teaspoons vegetable oil (optional)

1   can (14½ ounces) crushed tomatoes in rich purée

1   can (8 ounces) tomato sauce

3   tablespoons chopped fresh parsley

½   teaspoon salt

¼   teaspoon dried marjoram

¼   teaspoon dried basil

¼   teaspoon dried oregano

Freshly ground pepper to taste

8   ounces spaghetti, cooked and drained

½   cup grated cheddar cheese

½   cup grated mozzarella cheese

¼   cup freshly grated Parmesan cheese

PREHEAT oven to 350°F. In a large skillet over medium heat, sauté meat, onion, mushrooms, and garlic until meat is no longer pink and vegetables are tender, 6 to 7 minutes. Add oil if needed. Stir in tomatoes, tomato sauce, parsley, and seasonings. Simmer, uncovered, until slightly thickened, about 15 minutes.

COMBINE meat sauce and spaghetti in a 4-quart casserole dish lightly coated with cooking spray or oil and mix thoroughly. Top with cheeses.

BAKE, uncovered, until bubbly, 50 to 55 minutes. Let stand 10 minutes before serving.

SERVES 6

jamoke casserole

Fill the kids up with this satisfying casserole of sausage, macaroni, and vegetables. Most kids love it. Add a lettuce wedge with ranch dressing and follow with lots of chocolate chip cookies for a family meal.

1 pound bulk sausage meat or lean ground beef

1 small yellow onion, chopped

½ cup chopped green bell pepper

1 stalk celery, chopped

1 can (14½ ounces) whole tomatoes, coarsely chopped, juice from can included

1 can (8 ounces) tomato sauce

½ teaspoon sugar

¾ teaspoon salt

1 teaspoon chili powder

Freshly ground pepper to taste

1½ cups elbow macaroni, cooked and drained

PREHEAT oven to 350°F. In a large skillet over medium heat, cook sausage, breaking up with a spoon, about 5 minutes. Stir in onion, bell pepper, and celery and cook until meat is no longer pink and vegetables are tender, about 5 minutes longer. Add tomatoes, tomato sauce, and seasonings and mix well.

PLACE macaroni in a 2½- quart casserole dish lightly coated with cooking spray or oil, add sauce, and mix well.

COVER and bake until bubbly, about 45 minutes. Let stand 10 minutes and stir before serving.

SERVES 4 TO 6

victory casserole

This beef, spinach, and rice casserole got its name when it was served to us at a winning post-game party. To accompany the dish, our hostess served a large green salad with a creamy Caesar-style dressing and a garlic and onion bread.

1   pound lean ground beef

1   cup chopped yellow onion

2   cloves garlic, minced

1   package (10 ounces) frozen spinach, thawed and squeezed dry

3   cups cooked long-grain white rice

2   cups grated cheddar cheese

3   large eggs

¾   cup milk

1   teaspoon salt

Freshly ground pepper to taste

1   cup Quick Tomato Sauce (page 16)

PREHEAT oven to 350°F. In a medium skillet over medium heat, sauté beef, onion, and garlic until meat is no longer pink and vegetables are tender, about 5 to 10 minutes. Transfer to a 4-quart casserole dish lightly coated with cooking spray or oil. Add spinach, rice, and 1 cup of the cheese.

IN a small bowl, combine eggs, milk, salt, and pepper. Stir into meat and rice mixture and mix well.

BAKE, covered, 30 minutes. Top with Quick Tomato Sauce and remaining cheese and bake, uncovered, until bubbly, about 15 minutes longer.

SERVES 6

127

dutch oven dinner combo

Simmered meat and vegetables are a perfect choice for a rainy winter night. Just watch your timing for best results. Serve with an apple, celery, and walnut salad, and frosted brownies for dessert.

2 tablespoons vegetable oil

1 boneless beef rump roast (3½ to 4 pounds)

½ cup tomato juice

¼ cup dry red wine

1 tablespoon Worcestershire sauce

1 teaspoon dried basil

1½ teaspoons salt

Freshly ground pepper to taste

3 to 4 carrots, peeled and cut diagonally into 1-inch pieces

1 large yellow onion, quartered

2 potatoes, peeled and quartered

2 cloves garlic, chopped

1 large zucchini, unpeeled, cut into 1-inch slices

8 ounces mushrooms, halved if large

3 tablespoons all-purpose flour

¼ cup water

PREHEAT oven to 350°F. In a Dutch oven over medium heat, warm oil. Brown roast on all sides for about 10 minutes.

IN a small bowl mix tomato juice, wine, Worcestershire sauce, basil, salt, and pepper and pour over meat.

COVER and bake 1½ hours. Stir in carrots, onion, potatoes, and garlic and bake, covered, 15 minutes longer. Add zucchini and mushrooms and bake, covered, until meat and vegetables are tender, about 30 minutes longer.

IN a cup, blend flour and water and stir into pan. Bake until juices are thickened, about 5 minutes longer.

SERVES 6

beef, sausage, and rigatoni
This hearty casserole combines the flavors of three meats, which are baked in an assertive tomato sauce, and then combined with pasta for the finishing touch. Men love this dish. The meat and sauce bake for two hours, so you may want to cook them a day ahead.

4   tablespoons olive oil
2   yellow onions, chopped
4   cloves garlic, minced
1   pound cubed boneless beef
8   beef short ribs (about 3 pounds)
4   Italian sausages (1 pound), cut into 1-inch pieces
2   cans (15 ounces each) tomato sauce
1   can (6 ounces) tomato paste
3   cups Beef Stock (page 22) or canned beef broth
2   cups dry red wine
1   tablespoon dried basil
2   teaspoons dried oregano
1   teaspoon salt
Freshly ground pepper to taste
1   pound rigatoni (or other tubular pasta), cooked and drained
¼   cup chopped fresh parsley

PREHEAT oven to 325°F. In a Dutch oven (see Note) over medium heat, warm 1 tablespoon oil. Add onions and garlic and sauté until tender, about 5 minutes. Remove to a large plate.

INCREASE heat to medium-high, add remaining oil, and brown beef cubes and ribs in two batches, about 10 minutes each. Remove to plate holding vegetables. Reduce heat to medium. Add sausages and brown about 5 minutes. Return vegetables and meats to pan. Stir in remaining ingredients, except rigatoni and parsley, and simmer 10 minutes.

COVER and bake until meats are very tender, about 2 hours. Add rigatoni and mix well. Bake, uncovered, until flavors are blended, 20 minutes longer. Sprinkle with parsley.

SERVES 10 TO 12

NOTE: This recipe makes a large quantity. If your Dutch oven isn't big enough, brown the onions and the beef in a skillet and bake in a roasting pan. This recipe may be halved.

super stroganoff

There is something warming about a beef dish simmering in the oven on a cold winter night. The addition of mushrooms and sour cream makes this dish special. Serve with plain rice or noodles to absorb the delicious sauce.

6   tablespoons all-purpose
     flour

½   teaspoon salt

Freshly ground pepper to taste

2   pounds cubed lean beef
     stew meat

3   tablespoons butter or
     margarine

1   can (10½ ounces) double-
     strength beef broth,
     undiluted

1   teaspoon Worcestershire
     sauce

1   teaspoon Dijon mustard

¼   cup dry white wine

6 to 8 green onions, including
     some tender green tops,
     sliced

3   cloves garlic, minced

8   mushrooms, halved or
     quartered (depending on
     size)

½   cup light sour cream

PREHEAT oven to 350°F. On a sheet of wax paper, combine flour, salt, and pepper. Toss meat in the mixture to coat.

IN a large skillet over medium heat, melt 2 tablespoons butter. Add beef and brown on all sides, about 10 minutes. Add broth, Worcestershire sauce, and mustard and bring to a boil, stirring until blended. Stir in wine and transfer to a 2½-quart casserole dish lightly coated with cooking spray or oil.

COVER and bake 1 hour. Add onions, garlic, and mushrooms and bake, covered, 30 minutes longer. Blend in sour cream. Bake, uncovered, until meat is tender and sauce is warmed through, about 10 minutes.

SERVES 6

oven beef and vegetables

It's hard to believe this casserole has such great flavor when all you have to do is toss the ingredients together and slow-bake, unattended, for over an hour. Serve with garlic mashed potatoes.

¼ cup soy sauce

1 teaspoon Worcestershire sauce

¼ cup all-purpose flour

½ teaspoon salt

Freshly ground pepper to taste

2 pounds cubed lean beef stew meat

2 cups baby carrots, or 4 carrots, peeled and cut into 1-inch pieces

1 yellow onion, sliced

1 cup sliced celery

3 cloves garlic

¼ teaspoon dried thyme

¼ teaspoon dried marjoram

1 cup dry red wine

1 cup Beef Stock (page 22) or canned beef broth

8 ounces mushrooms, whole or halved (depending on size)

PREHEAT oven to 325°F. In a Dutch oven, blend soy sauce, Worcestershire sauce, salt, flour, and pepper. Toss beef in mixture to coat. Stir in remaining ingredients.

COVER and bake until meat is very tender, about 1½ hours.

SERVES 6 TO 8

131

THE BIG BOOK OF CASSEROLES

round steak and onions with sour cream

This hearty dish was served to us by friends we visited in Montana. We enjoyed it, and I think you will, too. Our kids called it "cowboy steak."

¼   cup all-purpose flour

½   teaspoon salt

1   tablespoon butter or margarine

2   tablespoons vegetable oil

2   pounds round steak, cut into serving pieces

Freshly ground pepper to taste

2   large yellow onions, sliced into rings

2   cloves garlic, minced

1   cup Beef Stock (page 22) or canned beef broth

½   cup dry white wine

1   teaspoon Worcestershire sauce

1   teaspoon soy sauce

½   cup light sour cream

PREHEAT oven to 350°F. On a sheet of wax paper, combine flour and salt. Toss meat in mixture to coat.

IN a large skillet over medium heat, melt butter and 1 tablespoon of oil. Brown meat on both sides, 5 to 10 minutes. Season with pepper. Remove to a 2½-quart casserole dish lightly coated with cooking spray or oil.

IN the skillet, warm remaining tablespoon oil. Add onions and garlic and sauté until vegetables are slightly tender, about 5 minutes. Stir in stock, wine, Worcestershire sauce, and soy sauce and bring to a boil. Pour over meat in casserole.

COVER and bake 1½ hours. Stir in sour cream and bake, uncovered, until heated through, 15 minutes longer.

SERVES 6

baked beef brisket with vegetables

Brisket is the flat cut from the breast section of beef. It has a minimal amount of fat and requires a long, slow cooking period for tender and flavorful results. The beef makes great sandwiches the next day.

1   beef brisket (4 to 5 pounds)

1   bottle (12 ounces) beer, allowed to go flat, or Beef Stock (page 22) or canned beef broth

1   tablespoon pickling spices

1   teaspoon dry mustard

¼   teaspoon salt

Freshly ground pepper to taste

2   cloves whole garlic, halved

6   fresh parsley sprigs

2   cups baby carrots

1   medium parsnip, peeled and sliced

2   yellow onions, cut into wedges

1   small head green cabbage, cut into wedges

Assorted flavored mustards

TRIM fat from brisket and place in a large nonreactive baking pan. Add beer, seasonings, garlic, parsley, and enough water, if needed, to cover meat. Stir gently. Cover and marinate several hours in refrigerator, turning once. Bring to room temperature for 1 hour before baking. In the meantime, preheat oven to 350°F.

COVER and bake (in the same pan) with the marinade 2 hours. Add carrots, parsnip, and onions and bake, covered, 30 minutes longer. Spoon liquid over meat and vegetables. Tuck in cabbage wedges and bake, covered, until meat and vegetables are tender, about 30 minutes longer.

TRANSFER meat to a warm platter and let stand 5 to 10 minutes. Slice beef at an angle and arrange vegetables around meat. Strain liquid and spoon several tablespoons over meat. Pass remaining liquid in a pitcher, if desired. Serve with mustards.

SERVES 8 TO 10

beef burgundy

Beef, wine, onions, and mushrooms are the essence of this rustic French stew. It starts on the stove top, then slow-bakes in the oven while tempting aromas fill the air. Accompany with mashed potatoes or noodles and a salad to round out the meal.

6   slices bacon, cut into
    ½-inch pieces

1½ to 2 pounds beef round
    steak, cut into 1-inch cubes

1   cup Burgundy wine

2   cups Beef Stock (page 22)
    or canned beef broth

1   tablespoon red wine
    vinegar

1   tablespoon tomato paste

2 or 3 cloves garlic, minced

1   teaspoon salt

½   teaspoon dried thyme

¼   teaspoon dried bouquet
    garni (see Note)

Freshly ground pepper to taste

1   bay leaf

1   ½-inch-by-2-inch strip of
    orange zest

¼   cup chopped fresh parsley

1½ cups baby carrots

12 ounces mushrooms, halved
    or quartered if large

1   cup frozen small whole
    onions, thawed; or canned
    pearl onions, drained

¼   cup water

2   tablespoons all-purpose
    flour

PREHEAT oven to 325°F. In a large Dutch oven over medium heat, cook bacon until brown and crisp, about 5 minutes. Remove with a slotted spoon to a plate. Add beef and brown on all sides, 5 to 10 minutes. Add wine, stock, vinegar, tomato paste, garlic, salt, thyme, garni, pepper, bay leaf, orange peel, parsley, and carrots. Bring to a boil.

COVER and bake in oven until beef is tender, about 2 hours. Stir in mushrooms and onions and cook, covered, 15 minutes longer. Remove bay leaf and orange zest and discard. Mix water and flour and add to casserole, stirring until thickened. Bake 5 minutes longer.

SERVES 6

NOTE: Dried bouquet garni—a mixture of parsley, thyme, and bay leaf—is available in the herbs and spices section of most supermarkets.

beef, barley, and mushroom stew

Few dishes compare to this slowly simmered beef stew with vegetables and herbs. Barley, a hearty grain that is chewy and nutlike, adds an earthy flavor and thickens the stew. This makes a complete meal when served with a tossed green salad and country-style bread.

2 tablespoons vegetable oil

2½ pounds round steak, cut into bite-size pieces

2 yellow onions, chopped

3 cloves garlic, minced

2 cups baby carrots

2 cups chopped celery

½ teaspoon salt

½ teaspoon dried thyme

½ teaspoon dried rosemary

1 bay leaf

Freshly ground pepper to taste

¼ cup chopped fresh parsley

½ cup barley, rinsed well and drained

2 cups Beef Stock (page 22) or canned beef broth

½ cup dry red wine

16 ounces mushrooms, quartered or halved (depending on size)

PREHEAT oven to 350°F. In a Dutch oven over medium-high heat, warm oil. Add steak and brown 5 minutes. Add onions and garlic and sauté until tender, 5 minutes longer. Add remaining ingredients, except mushrooms, and blend well.

COVER and bake 1 hour. Stir in mushrooms and bake, covered, until meat and mushrooms are tender, about 30 minutes longer. Remove bay leaf and discard.

SERVES 6

135

country stew

This big pot of stew is the centerpiece of our kitchen table for a family dinner or an informal supper with friends. Everything is combined and baked, unattended, for 4 hours with no peeking. Serve with plain noodles or rice.

2 pounds lean beef stew meat, well trimmed and cut into ¾-to 1-inch cubes

1 yellow onion, quartered

4 carrots, peeled and cut into 1-inch pieces

4 celery stalks, cut into 1-inch pieces

1 green bell pepper, seeded and cut into 1-inch pieces

¼ cup quick-cooking tapioca

½ cup dry bread crumbs (see page 5)

1 pound whole mushrooms

1¼ teaspoons salt

¼ teaspoon pepper

1 can (14½ ounces) whole tomatoes, coarsely chopped, juice from can included

1 cup dry red wine

PREHEAT oven to 300°F. Combine all ingredients in a Dutch oven or 4-quart casserole dish lightly coated with cooking spray or oil, stirring to mix well.

COVER and bake 4 hours.

SERVES 6

beer beef stew with parslied buttermilk dumplings

This beef stew with old-fashioned dumplings is a family favorite. Serve with a tossed green salad with blue-cheese dressing and warm crusty bread.

¼ to ⅓ cup all-purpose flour

¼ teaspoon salt

¼ teaspoon freshly ground pepper

3 pounds lean beef stew meat, cut into 1-inch cubes

4 tablespoons vegetable oil

2 yellow onions, sliced and rings separated

6 cloves garlic, minced

2 cups Beef Stock (page 22) or canned beef broth

1 cup beer, allowed to go flat

1 bay leaf

1 tablespoon brown sugar

2 tablespoons red wine vinegar

1 tablespoon Dijon mustard

2 teaspoons dried thyme

½ cup fresh chopped parsley

2 teaspoons salt

¼ teaspoon freshly ground pepper

Parslied Buttermilk Dumplings (page 77)

PREHEAT oven to 350°F. On a sheet of wax paper, combine flour, salt, and pepper. Toss meat in mixture to coat.

IN a Dutch oven over medium-high heat, warm 2 tablespoons oil. Brown meat in batches, adding more oil if needed, about 10 minutes. With a slotted spoon remove meat to a plate. Add 1 tablespoon oil to Dutch oven and sauté onion and garlic until soft, about 5 minutes. Add stock and beer and deglaze pan, stirring with a wooden spoon to loosen browned bits. Add remaining ingredients, return meat to broth, and bring to a boil.

BAKE, covered, until meat is tender, 1½ to 2 hours. In the meantime, make dumplings.

REMOVE bay leaf from stew and discard. Drop dumpling batter by heaping tablespoonfuls on top of juices. Return to oven and bake, uncovered, 10 minutes. Cover, and bake until toothpick inserted into center of dumpling comes out clean, 10 minutes longer. Serve meat and dumplings in the Dutch oven.

SERVES 6 TO 8

classic hungarian goulash

Hungarians know how to make a stew! This variation calls for beef, but veal or pork can be used. Just before serving, sour cream is added to make a rich, flavorful sauce to ladle on noodles.

2 tablespoons vegetable oil

1½ to 2 pounds round steak, cut into 1-inch cubes

2 large yellow onions, chopped

2 cloves garlic, minced

Salt and freshly ground pepper to taste

1 tablespoon paprika (preferably Hungarian)

1 teaspoon caraway seeds

½ teaspoon dried marjoram

1 cup Beef Stock (page 22) or canned beef broth

1 cup dry red wine

1 teaspoon red wine vinegar

2 tablespoons tomato paste

1 cup baby carrots or peeled and sliced carrots

1 cup fresh peas or frozen peas, thawed

1 tablespoon all-purpose flour

½ cup light sour cream

PREHEAT oven to 350°F. In a Dutch oven over medium-high heat, warm 1 tablespoon oil. Add beef and brown, 5 to 10 minutes. Transfer to a plate. Reduce heat to medium, add remaining oil and sauté onions and garlic until tender, about 5 minutes. Stir in seasonings. Stir in stock, wine, vinegar, tomato paste, and carrots. Bring to a boil.

COVER and bake until meat is tender, about 1½ hours. Stir in peas. Mix flour with sour cream and stir into juices. Bake, uncovered, until bubbly and sauce is slightly thickened, 10 to 15 minutes longer. Taste for seasoning and add more salt, if needed.

SERVES 4 TO 6

beef strips with mushrooms and artichokes

This casserole has a real beef flavor that is enhanced by a robust red wine. It is a good make-ahead casserole for a company dinner. Serve with Rice Verde (page 234) and marinated tomatoes.

1 tablespoon butter or margarine

1½ tablespoons vegetable oil

1½ pounds top sirloin steak, cut into 1-inch strips

6 green onions, including some tender green tops, sliced

8 ounces mushrooms, sliced

1 can (14 ounces) artichoke hearts, drained and halved

¼ cup dry red wine

1 teaspoon salt

Freshly ground pepper to taste

PREHEAT oven to 350°F. In a medium skillet over medium-high heat, melt 1 tablespoon butter with 1 tablespoon oil. Add meat and brown on all sides, 5 to 10 minutes. Remove meat to a 2½-quart casserole dish lightly coated with cooking spray or oil.

REDUCE heat to medium. Stir in remaining oil and sauté onions and mushrooms until tender, about 5 minutes. Add artichokes, wine, salt, and pepper. Pour over meat.

BAKE, uncovered, until heated through, about 35 minutes, stirring once.

SERVES 4

thick oven-baked chili

Offer this flavorful chili with assorted toppings for a casual get-together after a football game or for Super Bowl Sunday. Serve in big bowls with assorted toppings along with snacks—chips, pretzels, crudités, and cheese bread.

1 teaspoon vegetable oil

1½ pounds lean ground beef

1 pound kielbasa sausage, cut into ½-inch slices

1 yellow onion, chopped

½ green or red bell pepper, seeded and chopped

2 cloves garlic, minced

2 cans (15 ounces each) kidney beans, drained and rinsed

1 can (14½ ounces) whole tomatoes, coarsely chopped, juice from can included

1 can (15 ounces) tomato sauce

2 bay leaves

1 teaspoon salt

1 tablespoon chili powder (or more to taste)

1 teaspoon dried oregano

¼ teaspoon cayenne pepper

Freshly ground pepper to taste

TOPPINGS:

Sour cream

Sliced green onions

Grated cheddar cheese

PREHEAT oven to 325°F. In a Dutch oven over medium heat, warm oil. Sauté beef, sausage, onion, bell pepper, and garlic until meat is no longer pink and vegetables are tender, about 10 minutes. Add remaining ingredients and blend well.

COVER and bake about 1 hour, stirring occasionally. Uncover and bake 30 minutes longer. Remove bay leaves and discard.

SERVES 6 TO 8

swedish meatballs

A blend of traditional spices give these meatballs an authentic taste. Serve as a main course with noodles, or make smaller meatballs and serve as hors d'oeuvres.

1½   pounds lean ground beef
½   pound bulk sausage or ground veal
½   cup finely chopped yellow onion
2   eggs, beaten
1   cup dry bread crumbs (see page 5)
½   cup milk
1   teaspoon salt
Freshly ground pepper to taste
¼   teaspoon ground nutmeg
½   teaspoon ground ginger
¼   teaspoon dried dill weed
½   teaspoon ground allspice
¼   teaspoon ground cardamom
¼   cup Beef Stock (page 22) or canned beef broth
½   cup light sour cream

IN a large bowl, mix meats and onion. Add eggs, bread crumbs, milk, and seasonings. Mix well with a large spoon or your hands. Cover and refrigerate for 1 hour for easier handling. In the meantime, preheat oven to 400°F.

SHAPE meat mixture into 1-inch balls and arrange on a baking sheet with a rim. Bake until lightly browned, about 10 minutes. Transfer meatballs along with juices and beef stock to a 2½-quart casserole dish lightly coated with cooking spray or oil.

REDUCE oven temperature to 350°F. Cover and bake meatballs until heated through, about 30 minutes. Stir in sour cream and bake, uncovered, until heated through once again, 10 minutes longer.

SERVES 6

NOTE: For an hors d'oeuvre, transfer meatballs to a chafing dish and serve with toothpicks.

gourmet meatballs

This deluxe variation of meatballs incorporates ham with the usual ground beef. Browning is done in the oven and then transferred to a casserole for the final baking. A flavorful Sour Cream—Horseradish Sauce is added just before serving. Accompany with noodles or rice.

1¼ pounds lean ground beef

¼ pound ground ham

¼ cup finely chopped yellow onion

2 large eggs, lightly beaten

1½ cups dry bread crumbs (see page 5)

⅓ cup 2 percent milk

½ teaspoon salt

¼ teaspoon ground allspice

Freshly ground pepper to taste

½ cup Beef Stock (page 22) or canned beef broth

IN a large bowl, combine beef, ham, onion, eggs, bread crumbs, milk, and seasonings and mix well. Cover and refrigerate 1 hour for easier handling.

IN the meantime, preheat oven to 400°F.

SHAPE meat mixture into 1-inch balls. Place on a baking sheet with a rim and bake until browned, about 10 minutes. Transfer to a 2½-quart casserole dish along with any drippings that may have accumulated. Gently stir in beef stock.

REDUCE oven temperature to 350°F. Bake meatballs covered, 40 minutes. Remove lid and stir in sour cream–horseradish sauce. Bake, uncovered, until bubbly, 10 minutes longer.

SERVES 4

sour cream—horseradish sauce

½ cup light sour cream

1 tablespoon catsup

1 tablespoon prepared horseradish

IN a small bowl, stir together all ingredients.

MAKES ABOUT ½ CUP

meatballs with barbecue sauce
These spicy meatballs are always a hit with all ages. Serve as a main course or as an hors d'oeuvre for a cocktail party (see Note.)

1½ pounds lean ground beef

2 tablespoons finely chopped yellow onion

1 large egg, beaten

¼ cup dry bread crumbs (see page 5)

¼ cup freshly grated Parmesan cheese

½ cup 2 percent milk

¼ teaspoon salt

Freshly ground pepper

Barbecue Sauce (recipe follows)

IN a medium bowl, mix all ingredients except Barbecue Sauce thoroughly. Cover and refrigerate for 1 hour for easier handling. In the meantime, preheat oven to 400°F. Form meat into 1-inch balls.

PLACE meatballs on a baking sheet with a rim and bake until lightly browned, 10 to 12 minutes. Transfer to a 2½-quart casserole dish lightly coated with cooking spray or oil.

REDUCE heat to 350°F. Pour sauce over meatballs. Cover and bake until heated through, 35 to 40 minutes.

SERVES 4 TO 6

NOTE: Make ½-inch balls if serving as hors d'oeuvres, and make a double batch. They disappear fast.

barbecue sauce

1 cup chili sauce

1 cup catsup

¼ cup cider vinegar

1 cup water

1 clove garlic, minced

2 tablespoons Worcestershire sauce

¼ cup granulated sugar

½ teaspoon chili powder

¼ teaspoon cayenne pepper

IN a saucepan over medium heat, combine all ingredients and simmer 5 minutes.

MAKES ABOUT 4 CUPS

hawaiian pork

Serve this Hawaiian-inspired dish of pork, vegetables, and pineapple with a sweet-and-sour sauce over fluffy rice or thin noodles. A tropical fruit plate is a perfect companion dish.

2   tablespoons vegetable oil

1½ pounds pork steak, cut into
    1-inch cubes, fat trimmed

Salt and freshly ground pepper
    to taste

2   stalks celery, cut diagonally
    into 1-inch pieces

½   cup chopped yellow onion

½   green bell pepper, seeded
    and cut into 1-inch pieces

2   tablespoons cornstarch

⅓   cup water

2½ tablespoons soy sauce

2   tablespoons cider vinegar

1   can (8 ounces) pineapple
    chunks, including juice

PREHEAT oven to 350°F. In a large skillet over medium-high heat, warm 1 tablespoon oil. Brown pork on all sides, about 10 minutes. Season with salt and pepper. Transfer to a 2½-quart casserole dish lightly coated with cooking spray or oil.

ADD remaining oil to the skillet if needed. Add vegetables and sauté over medium heat until tender, about 5 minutes. Transfer to casserole dish.

IN a small bowl, blend cornstarch and water. Add remaining ingredients to the skillet. Add cornstarch mixture and stir until thickened, about 2 minutes. Pour over meat and vegetables in casserole and mix well.

BAKE, uncovered, until bubbly, about 45 minutes. Taste for seasoning and add more salt and pepper, if needed.

SERVES 6

pork chops mozzarella

Pork chops and zucchini pair well in this Italian-inspired casserole. Serve with a tossed green salad with Italian dressing.

2   zucchini, unpeeled, sliced

1   tablespoon vegetable oil

6   bone-in pork chops, ½ inch thick (about 3 pounds)

Salt and freshly ground pepper to taste

6   thin slices mozzarella cheese, trimmed to dimensions of chops

1   can (8 ounces) tomato sauce

¼   cup dry white wine

½   teaspoon dried oregano

¼   teaspoon dried basil

3   tablespoons chopped fresh parsley

¼   cup freshly grated Parmesan cheese, for topping

PREHEAT oven to 350°F. Place zucchini slices, slightly overlapping, on the bottom of a 9-by-13-inch glass baking dish lightly coated with cooking spray or oil.

IN a medium skillet over medium-high heat, warm oil. Brown chops about 5 minutes on each side. Season with salt and pepper. Place on top of zucchini. Place a cheese slice on top of each chop.

IN the skillet over medium heat, stir together tomato sauce, wine, seasonings, and parsley and heat thoroughly. Pour over chops.

COVER and bake 30 minutes. Sprinkle with Parmesan cheese and bake, uncovered, until chops are no longer pink in the center and zucchini is tender, about 30 minutes.

SERVES 4 TO 6

145

pork chops with lemon-caper sauce

For easy cooking, try this oven dish of pork, fresh green beans, and onions. The lemony sauce adds a sprightly flavor.

1   pound green beans, trimmed

½   teaspoon salt

1½ tablespoons vegetable oil

6   bone-in pork chops, ½ inch thick (about 2 pounds)

1   yellow onion, sliced and rings separated

Juice of 1 lemon

½   cup dry white wine

1   tablespoon capers, drained

½   teaspoon grated lemon zest

Freshly ground pepper to taste

PREHEAT oven to 350°F. In a medium saucepan over high heat, put beans with water to cover. Add salt, and bring water to a boil. Reduce heat to medium and cook, uncovered, until tender-crisp, about 5 minutes. Drain and transfer beans to a 4-quart casserole dish lightly coated with cooking spray or oil.

IN a large skillet over medium-high heat, warm 1 tablespoon oil. Brown chops about 5 minutes on each side. Place on top of beans. Add remaining oil and cook onion until lightly browned, about 4 minutes. Place on top of chops.

IN a small bowl, mix remaining ingredients. Pour over contents of casserole dish.

COVER and bake until chops are tender, about 30 minutes.

SERVES 4 TO 6

pork chops and red cabbage dinner

Tender pork chops and sweet-and-sour cabbage with apples are a great combination to serve for an Autumn dinner. Add a platter of thickly sliced beefsteak tomatoes, drizzled lightly with olive oil and balsamic vinegar and sprinkled with chopped fresh basil.

½ teaspoon salt plus more to taste

Freshly ground pepper to taste

1½ tablespoons vegetable oil

6 bone-in pork chops, ½ inch thick (about 2 pounds)

1 cup chopped yellow onion

1 small head red cabbage (1½ pounds), cored, and shredded

2 red delicious apples, unpeeled, cored, and sliced

¼ cup dry red wine or water

¼ cup red wine vinegar

3 tablespoons firmly packed brown sugar

PREHEAT oven to 350°F. Season both sides of pork chops with salt and pepper to taste. In a large skillet over medium-high heat, warm oil and brown pork chops about 5 minutes on each side. Remove to a plate.

ADD remaining ingredients to the skillet, including ¼ teaspoon salt. Stir and toss until cabbage begins to wilt, about 2 minutes. Transfer to a 9-by-13-inch baking dish lightly coated with cooking spray or oil. Place chops on top.

COVER and bake until chops and cabbage are tender, about 40 minutes.

SERVES 6

147

sweet-and-sour pork chops

Looking for a new way to prepare pork chops? In this recipe, thick, juicy pork chops bake along with pineapple and green pepper in a tasty sauce. Serve with a plate of kiwi and papaya slices.

2 tablespoons vegetable oil

4 boneless pork chops, 1 inch thick (about 2 pounds)

Salt and freshly ground pepper to taste

1 can (8 ounces) pineapple chunks, drained, and ½ cup juice reserved

1 small green bell pepper, seeded and cut into 1-inch pieces

⅓ cup firmly packed brown sugar

¼ cup white vinegar

1 teaspoon soy sauce

¼ teaspoon salt

1 clove garlic, minced

2 tablespoons cornstarch

¼ cup water

PREHEAT oven to 350°F. In a medium skillet over medium-high heat, warm oil. Add pork chops and brown, about 5 minutes on each side. Season with salt and pepper.

TRANSFER pork chops to a 2½-quart casserole dish lightly coated with cooking spray or oil. Add pineapple and green bell pepper.

IN a small bowl mix sugar, reserved pineapple juice, vinegar, soy sauce, salt, and garlic. Pour over chops.

COVER and bake until pork chops are tender, about 50 minutes.

IN another small bowl, blend cornstarch and water. Stir into casserole juices. Bake, uncovered, until thickened, 10 minutes longer.

SERVES 4

148

pork chops in mustard sauce

Pork chops are baked in a superb mustardy sauce with dill pickle for a flavor surprise. Serve with Barley-Rice Pilaf (page 243).

2 tablespoons butter or margarine

1 tablespoon vegetable oil

8 bone-in pork chops, ½ inch thick (about 2½ pounds)

Salt and freshly ground pepper to taste

6 green onions, including some tender green tops, sliced

1 clove garlic, minced

1 large dill pickle, chopped

¼ cup all-purpose flour

2 cups Rich Chicken Stock (page 23) or canned low-sodium chicken broth

1 tablespoon Dijon mustard

¼ cup dry white wine

⅛ teaspoon salt

PREHEAT oven to 350°F. In a large skillet over medium-high heat, melt butter with oil. Add chops and brown about 5 minutes on each side. Season with salt and pepper while browning. Transfer to a 9-by-13-inch baking dish lightly coated with cooking spray or oil.

ADD onions and garlic to drippings in skillet and sauté over medium heat until tender, about 2 minutes. Add pickle, stir in flour, and blend. Add remaining ingredients and bring to a boil, stirring constantly, until thickened. Pour over chops.

COVER and bake until chops are tender, about 40 minutes.

149

SERVES 4

pork chops and onions in sour cream sauce

For a creative entrée, try this easy-to-prepare pork chop dish baked in a creamy sauce flavored with sage. Serve with Sweet Onion and Rice Bake (page 184) and fresh asparagus.

4	boneless pork chops, 1 inch thick (about 2 pounds)
1	teaspoon dried sage
	Salt and freshly ground pepper to taste
1	tablespoon vegetable oil
½	yellow onion, sliced and rings separated
½	cup light sour cream
1	teaspoon Dijon mustard
1	tablespoon all-purpose flour
½	cup Rich Chicken Stock (page 23) or canned low-sodium chicken broth
¼	cup dry white wine
¼	cup chopped fresh parsley

PREHEAT oven to 350°F. Season chops generously with sage, salt, and pepper. In a large skillet over medium-high heat, warm oil. Add pork chops and brown about 5 minutes on each side. Transfer to an 8-by-8-inch baking dish lightly coated with cooking spray or oil. Lay onion rings on top.

IN a small bowl, blend sour cream, mustard, and flour and set aside.

ADD stock and wine to the skillet and boil 1 minute, stirring occasionally. Remove from heat. Whisk in sour cream mixture and parsley. Pour over pork chops.

BAKE, uncovered, until bubbly, about 40 minutes.

SERVES 4

pork chops stuffed with spinach, feta, and pine nuts

Preparation for this dish takes time, but once it is assembled, an elegant company entrée is ready to bake in the oven. Serve with Parmesan Cheese—Mashed Potato Gratin (page 268).

2 tablespoons vegetable oil

1 cup finely chopped yellow onion

2 cloves garlic, minced

2 tablespoons pine nuts

1 cup cooked fresh spinach, drained and chopped, or 1 cup chopped frozen spinach, thawed and squeezed dry

¼ cup crumbled feta cheese

½ teaspoon salt plus more to taste

Freshly ground pepper to taste

4 boneless pork chops, 1 inch thick (about 2 pounds), with a pocket (see Note)

½ cup Rich Chicken Stock (page 23) or canned low-sodium chicken broth

2 tablespoons white wine vinegar

IN a medium skillet over medium heat, warm 1 teaspoon oil. Add onion, garlic, and pine nuts and sauté until vegetables are tender, about 5 minutes. Remove to a medium bowl. Add spinach, cheese, salt, and pepper to the bowl and mix well.

PREHEAT oven to 350°F. Stuff each pork chop with one fourth of the spinach mixture. Secure with a toothpick.

SPRINKLE pork chops with salt and pepper. In the skillet, over medium-high heat, warm remaining oil. Brown pork chops about 5 minutes on each side. Stir in stock and vinegar. Transfer chops and broth to a 2½-quart casserole dish lightly coated with cooking spray or oil.

COVER casserole and bake until chops are tender, about 35 minutes.

SERVES 4

NOTE: With a sharp knife, cut a pocket in the thickest part of the chop or have your butcher do it for you.

151

burgundy ribs

These delicious pork ribs are baked in a bold, red wine sauce, offering a change from the usual barbecue sauce. Serve with coleslaw and Easy Baked Beans (page 248) for a traditional ribs dinner.

4 pounds spareribs
½ cup Burgundy or any full-bodied red wine
1 tablespoon red wine vinegar
1 cup catsup
½ cup water
1 clove garlic, minced
2 tablespoons honey
1 tablespoon Worcestershire sauce
1 tablespoon Dijon mustard
1 teaspoon chili powder
1 yellow onion, sliced and rings separated

PREHEAT oven to 375°F. Cut ribs into large pieces (3 to 4 ribs) and place in a large, shallow, nonreactive roasting pan. Bake, uncovered, 1 hour, turning once. Pour off excess grease.

MEANWHILE, in a small saucepan over medium heat, stir together remaining ingredients except onion rings. Bring to a boil, reduce heat to a simmer, and cook, uncovered, 10 minutes.

LAY onion rings on top of ribs. Pour sauce over both.

REDUCE oven temperature to 350°F and continue baking ribs, uncovered, until flavors are blended, 30 to 35 minutes longer.

SERVES 4

posole

This dish originated in Jalisco, Mexico, and is traditionally served at Christmas time. It is a thick, hearty soup that is served in a bowl with salad toppings and a squeeze of lime juice. Accompany with warm tortillas.

1   tablespoon vegetable oil

1   cup chopped yellow onion

1   cup chopped red bell pepper

2   cloves garlic, minced

2   pork steaks (about 1½ pounds), cut into cubes

1   can (15 ounces) hominy, rinsed and drained

1   can (8 ounces) tomato sauce

1   cup Rich Chicken Stock (page 23) or canned low-sodium chicken broth

1   tablespoon chili powder

½   teaspoon dried oregano

½   teaspoon ground cumin

¼   teaspoon salt

Freshly ground pepper

½   cup chopped fresh cilantro or parsley

Lime wedges for garnish

Flour tortillas, warmed (see page 10)

TOPPINGS

Shredded iceberg lettuce

Sliced radishes

Grated cheddar cheese

Chopped green onions

Diced avocado

PREHEAT oven to 350°F. In a Dutch oven over medium-high heat, warm oil. Add onion, bell pepper, garlic, and pork and sauté until vegetables are tender and pork is browned, 6 to 7 minutes. Stir in hominy, tomato sauce, stock, seasonings, and cilantro.

BAKE, uncovered, until meat is tender and flavors are blended, about 40 minutes. Garnish with lime and serve with tortillas. Pass around toppings in small bowls.

SERVES 4

pork chili and beans with rice

Tender pork cubes are seasoned with a spicy blend of herbs and spices and baked with beans and rice for a wonderful flavor. Serve with warm tortillas.

1 to 1½ tablespoons chili powder

1 teaspoon dried oregano

¾ teaspoon salt

½ teaspoon ground cumin

¼ teaspoon ground coriander

Freshly ground pepper to taste

2 tablespoons vegetable oil

2 pounds boneless pork loin, cut into bite-size pieces

1 cup chopped yellow onion

2 cloves garlic, minced

½ cup long-grain white rice

¾ cup Rich Chicken Stock (page 23) or canned low-sodium chicken broth

1 can (4 ounces) diced green chiles, drained

2 large tomatoes, seeded, chopped, and drained

1 can (16 ounces) kidney beans, rinsed and drained

PREHEAT oven to 350°F. In a large bowl, combine chili powder, oregano, ½ teaspoon salt, cumin, coriander, and pepper. Add meat and toss to coat.

IN a Dutch oven over medium heat, warm 1 tablespoon oil. Add meat and brown on all sides, 5 to 10 minutes. Transfer to a plate. Add remaining oil to Dutch oven, if needed, and sauté onion and garlic until soft, about 5 minutes. Stir in rice. Add stock, chiles, tomatoes, beans, and remaining ¼ teaspoon salt. Return meat to Dutch oven, and mix well.

COVER, and bake until bubbly, and rice is tender, about 45 minutes, stirring once.

SERVES 6 TO 8

asian pork, peas, and mushrooms with rice

Pork cubes cook with rice in a delicious soy-orange sauce for a one-dish meal. Serve with cucumber slices marinated in rice vinegar.

2½ tablespoons vegetable oil

2 pounds boneless pork shoulder, cut into bite-size pieces

¾ cup chopped green onions, including some tender green tops

2 cups sliced mushrooms

1 cup long-grain white rice

2 cups Rich Chicken Stock (page 23) or canned low-sodium chicken broth

¼ cup orange juice

3 tablespoons soy sauce

¼ teaspoon ground ginger

1 teaspoon grated orange zest

1 cup fresh peas or frozen peas, thawed

PREHEAT oven to 350°F. In a large skillet over medium-high heat, warm 1½ tablespoons oil. Add pork and brown 5 to 10 minutes. Transfer to a 2½-quart casserole dish lightly coated with cooking spray or oil.

TO same skillet over medium heat, add remaining 1 tablespoon oil. Sauté onions and mushrooms until tender, about 5 minutes. Stir in rice, stock, orange juice, soy sauce, ginger, and orange zest. Bring to a boil and pour over pork in casserole.

COVER and bake until rice is tender and liquid is absorbed, about 45 minutes. Stir in peas and cook, uncovered, 10 minutes longer.

SERVES 4 TO 6

VARIATION: Chicken breasts may be substituted for pork.

german sausage and sauerkraut

Sausage is tucked into this seasoned sauerkraut and baked until the flavors are blended. Serve with pumpernickel bread and spicy applesauce, followed by ginger snaps for dessert.

1   jar (16 ounces) sauerkraut, rinsed and drained

½   red bell pepper, seeded and chopped

½   cup chopped red onion

2   tablespoons white wine vinegar

1   teaspoon caraway seeds

1   tablespoon firmly packed brown sugar

1   pound smoked German sausage of your choice, sliced

PREHEAT oven to 350°F. Place all ingredients in a 2½-quart casserole dish lightly coated with cooking spray or oil and mix well. Cover the sausage with sauerkraut.

COVER the dish and bake until heated through, 35 to 40 minutes.

SERVES 4

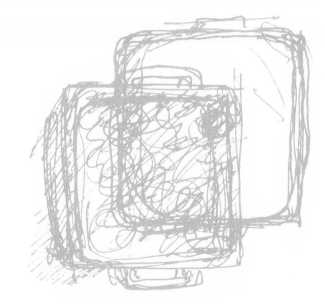

sausage, broccoli, and rice casserole

As already noted, Dutch ovens are wonderful to have because they are flameproof and go from stove top, to oven, to table. This casserole shows off their advantages: The meats are browned in the Dutch oven on top of the stove, then all ingredients are added and baked in the oven for a no-fuss, one-dish meal.

6   thick bacon slices, cubed

1   pound bulk Italian sausage meat

1   cup long-grain white rice

2½ cups Rich Chicken Stock (page 23) or canned low-sodium chicken broth

1   teaspoon salt

Freshly ground pepper to taste

4   cups broccoli florets

PREHEAT oven to 375°F. In a Dutch oven over medium heat, cook bacon 2 minutes. Add sausage, breaking it up with a wooden spoon, and cook until sausage is no longer pink and bacon is crisp, about 10 minutes. Drain off excess fat. Stir in rice. Stir in stock, salt, and pepper and bring to a boil.

COVER and bake 30 minutes. Add broccoli, stir, and bake, covered, until liquid is absorbed and broccoli is tender-crisp, about 20 minutes longer.

SERVES 6

sausage, peppers, and pasta

Two kinds of sausage and peppers highlight this savory dish with a tomato sauce and pasta. Serve with a green salad and warm, crusty bread.

½ pound bulk Italian sausage meat

2 smoked Italian sausages (about ½ pound), cut into ½-inch slices

½ red bell pepper, seeded and cut lengthwise into ½-inch strips

½ green bell pepper, seeded and cut lengthwise into ½-inch strips

2 cloves garlic, minced

1 can (14½ ounces) whole tomatoes, cut up, juice from can included

1 tablespoon tomato paste

1 tablespoon red wine vinegar

½ teaspoon salt

Freshly ground pepper to taste

4 ounces (about 1½ cups) corkscrew pasta, cooked and drained

Parmesan cheese for sprinkling on top

PREHEAT oven to 350°F. In a Dutch oven over medium heat, cook bulk sausage, breaking up with a wooden spoon, 5 minutes. Add sliced sausage, peppers, and garlic and stir. Cook until sausage is no longer pink and vegetables are tender, about 8 minutes longer. Stir in tomatoes, tomato paste, vinegar, salt, and pepper. Bring to a boil. Add pasta and mix well.

COVER and bake until heated through and bubbly, about 40 minutes. Stir and sprinkle with Parmesan cheese. Bake, uncovered, 5 to 10 minutes longer.

SERVES 6

ham and lima bean bake

Ham and lima beans complement each other in this easy supper dish. Though lima beans are often overlooked by home cooks, they are very nutritious and are available fresh, frozen, canned, or dried.

2   tablespoons butter or margarine
½   cup chopped yellow onion
2   tablespoons all-purpose flour
1   cup 2 percent milk
¼   teaspoon salt
Freshly ground pepper to taste
3   cups cooked long-grain rice
1½ cups cubed cooked ham
1½ cups frozen baby lima beans, thawed
1   cup grated Monterey Jack cheese

PREHEAT oven to 375°F. In a small saucepan over medium heat, melt butter. Add onion and sauté until tender, about 5 minutes. Add flour and stir until bubbly. Add milk, salt, and pepper and stir until thickened, about 5 minutes. Set aside.

IN a 2½-quart casserole dish lightly coated with cooking spray or oil, place rice, ham, beans, and onion mixture. Mix well. Sprinkle with cheese.

BAKE, uncovered, until bubbly and cheese is melted, about 30 minutes.

SERVES 4

159

ham and potato casserole

Ham and potatoes are mixed with a cheese sauce and topped with tomato and egg slices for an appealing one-dish entrée. Serve with a mixed green salad.

2 tablespoons butter or margarine

1 cup chopped yellow onion

2 tablespoons all-purpose flour

1½ cups 2 percent milk

½ cup light sour cream

2 cups grated Monterey Jack cheese

1 tablespoon chopped fresh parsley

½ teaspoon salt

½ teaspoon paprika

2 or 3 drops Tabasco sauce

Freshly ground pepper to taste

5 cups sliced cooked potatoes (3 medium potatoes, about 1 pound)

1 cup cubed cooked ham

2 hard-cooked eggs, sliced

2 tomatoes, seeded, thinly sliced, and drained

PREHEAT oven to 350°F. In a saucepan over medium heat, melt butter. Add onion and sauté until tender, about 5 minutes. Add flour and stir until bubbly. Add milk and stir until thickened, about 2 minutes. Add sour cream, 1 cup cheese, parsley, salt, paprika, Tabasco, and pepper and mix well.

IN a 2½-quart casserole dish lightly coated with cooking spray or oil, place potatoes and ham. Add cheese sauce and mix. Top with egg and tomato slices. Sprinkle with remaining cheese.

BAKE, uncovered, until bubbly, about 40 minutes.

SERVES 6

ham, peppers, sugar snap peas, and pineapple in sweet and sour sauce

Here is a recipe that may bring back memories of Hawaii. Serve with plain rice or noodles and a plate of exotic fruit.

1 tablespoon vegetable oil

1 yellow onion, sliced and rings separated

1 green bell pepper, seeded and cut lengthwise into 1-inch strips

2 cloves garlic, minced

2 cups cubed cooked ham

1 tablespoon cornstarch

½ teaspoon salt

⅓ cup cider vinegar

1⅓ cup catsup

1 can (8 ounces) pineapple chunks, drained, and juice reserved

1 cup sugar snap peas, trimmed

PREHEAT oven to 350°F. In a large skillet over medium heat, warm oil. Add onion, bell pepper, and garlic and sauté until tender, about 5 minutes. Stir in ham. Transfer to a 2½-quart casserole dish lightly coated with cooking spray or oil.

IN a small saucepan over medium heat, blend cornstarch, salt, vinegar, catsup, and reserved juice. Stir until thickened, about 5 minutes. Add pineapple chunks and peas. Pour over vegetables and ham.

COVER and bake until flavors are blended, about 30 minutes.

SERVES 4 TO 6

161

lamb-vegetable casserole

This "all-in-one" aromatic dish is a convenient casserole to make for an informal dinner. Serve with a chopped salad of cucumbers, green onions, and fresh mint.

2 tomatoes, seeded, sliced, and drained

2 small zucchini, cut into ¼-inch slices

1 cup chopped yellow onion

1 pound ground lamb, cooked and crumbled

½ teaspoon salt

¼ teaspoon oregano

Freshly ground pepper to taste

½ cup long-grain white rice

1 tablespoon golden raisins (optional)

1 tablespoon olive oil

1 cup Rich Chicken Stock (page 23) or canned low-sodium chicken broth

2 tablespoons tomato paste

⅓ cup crumbled feta cheese

Fresh mint leaves for garnish

PREHEAT oven to 375°F. Lay half of the tomato slices on bottom of a 2½-quart casserole dish lightly coated with cooking spray or oil. Top with half of the zucchini slices and sprinkle with half of the onions. Add lamb and sprinkle with seasonings. Add rice, raisins, and remaining onions. Overlap the remaining tomato slices and zucchini slices on top. Drizzle with oil.

IN a small pan over high heat, bring stock and tomato paste to a boil. Pour over casserole. Cover casserole tightly and bake until bubbly and rice is tender, about 1 hour. Sprinkle with feta cheese and garnish with mint leaves.

SERVES 6

lamb stew

Since our niece raises champion Southdown sheep, we get the freshest and best quality lamb available. When good lamb is used in a stew, it is company fare.

2   tablespoons olive oil

2   pounds lamb shoulder, fat trimmed and cut into 1-inch cubes

1   yellow onion, quartered

2   cloves garlic, chopped

2½ cups Rich Chicken Stock (page 23) or canned low-sodium chicken broth

1   cup dry white wine

2   tablespoons tomato paste

1   tablespoon chopped fresh rosemary, or 1 teaspoon dried rosemary

1   tablespoon chopped fresh thyme, or 1 teaspoon dried thyme

1   bay leaf

½   teaspoon salt

¼   teaspoon freshly ground pepper

3   carrots, peeled and cut into 1½-inch pieces

4   red new potatoes, unpeeled, quartered

1   green, red, or yellow bell pepper, seeded and cut into wedges

¼   cup cold water (optional)

2   tablespoons all-purpose flour (optional)

¼   cup chopped fresh parsley

Fresh rosemary sprigs for garnish

PREHEAT oven to 350°F. In a Dutch oven over medium-high heat, warm oil. Add lamb and brown 5 to 10 minutes. Reduce heat to medium, add onion and garlic, and sauté until tender, about 5 minutes longer. Add stock and wine, stirring to loosen browned bits. Stir in tomato paste, seasonings, and carrots and bring to a boil.

COVER and bake until lamb is almost done, about 40 minutes. Add potatoes and bell pepper and bake, covered, until meat and vegetables are tender, about 25 minutes longer. Remove bay leaf and discard.

FOR a thicker sauce, blend water and flour in a small bowl and stir into juices. Cook 5 minutes longer. Sprinkle with parsley and garnish with rosemary sprigs before serving.

SERVES 6

lamb meatballs and orzo

Dilled lamb meatballs are browned in the oven and then combined with orzo and a lemon sauce for a Mediterranean-style casserole. Serve with a Greek salad and olive bread.

1   large egg

1   pound ground lamb

2   large cloves garlic, minced

¼   cup finely chopped onion

½   cup dry bread crumbs (see page 5)

¼   cup milk

2   teaspoons chopped fresh dill, or ½ teaspoon dried dill weed

½   teaspoon salt

Freshly ground pepper to taste

1¾   cups Rich Chicken Stock (page 23) or canned low-sodium chicken broth

2   tablespoons fresh lemon juice

½   teaspoon grated lemon zest

1   cup orzo

Dill sprigs for garnish

IN a medium bowl, beat egg. Add lamb, garlic, onion, bread crumbs, milk, and seasonings and mix well. Cover and refrigerate 1 hour for easier handling.

PREHEAT oven to 400°F. Form lamb mixture into 1-inch balls and place on a baking sheet with a rim. Bake until browned, about 10 minutes. Remove from oven and set aside.

IN a medium saucepan over high heat, bring stock, lemon juice, and lemon zest to a boil. Stir in orzo and boil 1 minute. Transfer to a 2½-quart casserole dish lightly coated with cooking spray or oil. Place meatballs on top.

REDUCE oven temperature to 350°F and bake, covered, until liquid is absorbed, 40 to 50 minutes. Let stand 5 minutes before serving. Garnish with dill sprigs.

SERVES 4 TO 6

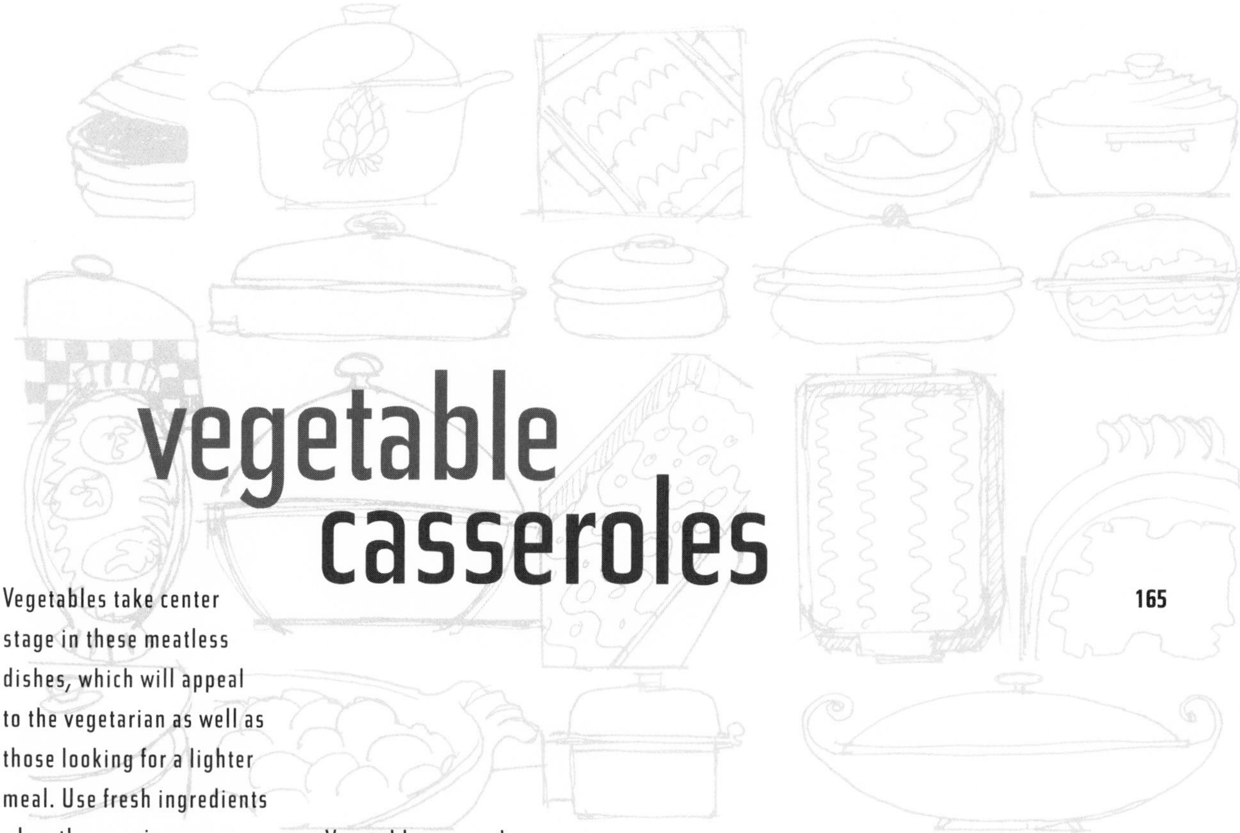

vegetable casseroles

Vegetables take center stage in these meatless dishes, which will appeal to the vegetarian as well as those looking for a lighter meal. Use fresh ingredients when they are in season, but for convenience and availability, frozen vegetables may be substituted.

Vegetable casseroles are nutritious as well as tasty. They can serve as main courses or as accompaniments to other dishes. You will be surprised at the flavor and appeal of a well-prepared vegetable casserole.

moussaka

Originating in Greece, this dish is popular throughout the Near East as well as in this country. It basically consists of layered eggplant and other vegetables and ground lamb or beef, but the variations are endless. In this version, rice replaces the meat. Before the moussaka is assembled, the eggplant bakes in the oven instead of frying in oil.

2   cups Rich Chicken Stock (page 23), canned low-sodium chicken broth, or water

¾   cup long-grain white rice

2 medium eggplants (1¼ pounds each), unpeeled, cut into ½-inch slices

3   tablespoons olive oil

¼   cup pine nuts

1   large yellow onion, diced

4   cloves garlic, minced

1   teaspoon salt

¼   teaspoon ground allspice

½   teaspoon ground cumin

¼   teaspoon ground cardamom

Freshly ground pepper to taste

2   teaspoons fresh lemon juice

1   can (14½ ounces) crushed tomatoes in rich purée

2   large tomatoes, seeded, sliced, and drained

1   cup crumbled feta cheese

THE BIG BOOK OF CASSEROLES

PREHEAT oven to 375°F. In a small saucepan over high heat, bring stock or water to a boil. Stir in rice, reduce heat to medium-low, and cook, covered, until liquid is absorbed, about 20 minutes.

PLACE eggplant slices on a baking sheet lightly coated with cooking spray or oil, and brush tops with 2 tablespoons olive oil. Bake until softened and lightly browned, about 20 minutes.

IN a medium skillet, add remaining 1 tablespoon olive oil. Add pine nuts and sauté until golden, about 2 minutes. Add onion, garlic, and seasonings and sauté until tender, about 5 minutes. Stir in lemon juice and canned tomatoes and cook until blended, about 2 minutes.

REDUCE oven temperature to 350°F. In a 9-by-13-inch baking dish lightly coated with cooking spray or oil, arrange in layers half of the eggplant slices, half of the rice, all of the tomato slices, and half of the tomato sauce. Repeat the layers.

COVER and bake 25 minutes. Uncover and sprinkle with feta cheese. Bake, uncovered, until bubbly, about 20 minutes longer.

SERVES 8 TO 10

greek pie

This variation of the Greek dish spanakopita includes cottage cheese along with traditional ingredients, such as spinach, feta cheese, and phyllo dough. It can be served as a main course or as a side dish alongside Lamb Meatballs (page 164).

1 tablespoon olive oil

½ cup chopped yellow onion

3 packages (10 ounces each) frozen chopped spinach, thawed and squeezed dry

3 large eggs, beaten

1 cup crumbled feta cheese

1 cup cottage cheese

¼ cup chopped fresh parsley

1 tablespoon dried dill weed

1 teaspoon salt

Freshly ground pepper to taste

½ cup (1 stick) butter or margarine, melted

16 sheets (about ½ pound) frozen phyllo dough, thawed

PREHEAT oven to 350°F. In a large skillet over medium heat, warm oil. Add onion and sauté until tender, about 5 minutes. Mix in spinach and set aside.

IN a large bowl, mix eggs, cheeses, parsley, and seasonings. Add onion-spinach mixture and blend well.

BRUSH a 9-by-13-inch baking dish with butter. Layer 8 phyllo sheets in the dish, one by one, brushing each sheet with butter. Work quickly so phyllo won't dry out (see Note). Spread spinach mixture over phyllo. Cover with remaining sheets, brushing each layer, including the top one, with remaining butter.

WITH a sharp knife, cut partially through top 8 sheets diagonally in 3 inch intervals. Cut in the opposite direction to form nine 3-inch diamonds.

BAKE, uncovered, until top is puffed and lightly browned, 35 to 40 minutes. Let stand 5 minutes before serving.

SERVES 8

NOTE: If possible, have another person help with the process. Phyllo sheets will not fit perfectly in baking dish. Fold ends over; it is not necessary to trim the sheets except the top one, for a neat appearance. A damp towel may be laid over phyllo dough to keep it from drying out.

oven ratatouille

This popular dish is from the French region of Provence. The focus is on herbs, olive oil, and fresh vegetables slowly simmered in the oven in their natural juices. Serve hot or at room temperature. Ratatouille is also good mixed with pasta.

½ cup chopped fresh parsley

¼ cup chopped fresh basil, or 1 teaspoon dried basil

1 tablespoon chopped fresh oregano, or 1 teaspoon dried oregano

1 teaspoon chopped fresh thyme, or ½ teaspoon dried thyme

2 teaspoons salt

Freshly ground pepper to taste

1 large yellow onion, sliced

3 cloves garlic, minced

1 small eggplant, unpeeled, cut into ½-inch cubes

1 green bell pepper, seeded and cut into 1-inch pieces

1 zucchini, unpeeled, cut into ¾-inch slices

4 tomatoes, seeded, sliced, and drained

2 tablespoons olive oil

PREHEAT oven to 350°F. In a small bowl, combine herbs, salt, and pepper. In a 4-quart casserole dish lightly coated with cooking spray or oil, layer vegetables alternately with herb mixture. Drizzle oil over the top.

COVER and bake until vegetables are tender, about 1 hour. Gently stir and bake, uncovered, 10 to 15 minutes longer to reduce liquid.

SERVES 6

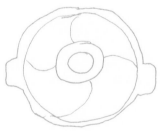

succotash

This popular southern dish of corn and lima beans was first introduced to early European settlers by the Indians. Red bell pepper has been added for flavor and color. For a richer dish, use half-and-half instead of milk. Serve with grilled sausage.

1 cup water

1½ cups fresh lima beans, or 1 package (10 ounces) frozen lima beans, thawed

1½ cups fresh corn kernels, or 1 package (10 ounces) frozen corn, thawed

¼ cup chopped red bell pepper

1 tablespoon butter or margarine

½ cup chopped yellow onion

½ cup milk or half-and-half

¼ teaspoon salt

Freshly ground pepper to taste

½ teaspoon sugar

2 tablespoons snipped chives

PREHEAT oven to 350°F. In a medium saucepan over medium heat, bring water to a boil. Add beans and cook, uncovered, about 5 minutes. Stir in corn and bell pepper and cook until vegetables are tender-crisp, about 3 minutes longer. Drain and place in a 2½-quart casserole dish lightly coated with cooking spray or oil.

IN the saucepan over medium heat, melt butter. Add onion and sauté until tender, about 5 minutes. Stir in milk, seasonings, and sugar and simmer for 2 minutes. Pour over vegetables.

BAKE, uncovered, stirring once, until slightly thickened, about 40 minutes. Sprinkle with chives before serving.

SERVES 6

artichoke and broccoli casserole with mushroom

sauce   This elegant vegetable dish originally called for cream of mushroom soup. Instead, I have used a white sauce with mushrooms that just takes minutes to make and is more flavorful and healthful.

3   cups broccoli florets

1   can (14 ounces) artichoke hearts, drained and halved

Mushroom Sauce (recipe follows)

⅓   cup freshly grated Parmesan cheese

¼   cup slivered almonds

PREHEAT oven to 350°F. Add some water to a pan fitted with a steamer rack over medium heat. Place broccoli on rack and steam, covered, over gently boiling water, until tender-crisp, 6 to 8 minutes. Drain under cold water.

TRANSFER to a 2½-quart casserole dish or decorative baking dish lightly coated with cooking spray or oil. Add artichokes and Mushroom Sauce and gently mix. Sprinkle with Parmesan cheese.

BAKE, uncovered, until heated through and bubbly, about 30 minutes. Sprinkle the top with nuts and bake 10 minutes longer.

SERVES 4 TO 6

mushroom sauce

2	tablespoons butter or margarine	1	cup Rich Chicken Stock (page 23) or canned low-sodium chicken broth
4	ounces mushrooms, sliced		
2	tablespoons all-purpose flour	2	tablespoons dry white wine
¼	teaspoon salt	½	cup light sour cream
Freshly ground pepper to taste			

IN a medium saucepan over medium heat, melt butter. Add mushrooms and sauté until tender, about 5 minutes. Stir in flour, salt, and pepper. Add stock and stir until thickened, about 2 minutes. Stir in wine. Remove from heat and blend in sour cream.

MAKES ABOUT 1½ CUPS

broccoli-mushroom casserole

This is a year-round casserole because broccoli and mushrooms are always available. Assemble this ahead of time for a company dinner.

5   cups broccoli florets

3   tablespoons butter or margarine

1   cup sliced mushrooms

3   tablespoons all-purpose flour

1¾ cups whole or 2 percent milk

2   tablespoons dry white wine (optional)

½   teaspoon Dijon mustard

½   teaspoon salt

⅛   teaspoon white pepper

1   cup grated cheddar cheese

2   tablespoons freshly grated Parmesan cheese

¼   cup slivered almonds

3   tablespoons dry bread crumbs

PREHEAT oven to 375°F. In a large pot over high heat, cover broccoli with water and bring to a boil. Reduce heat to medium and cook until tender-crisp, about 4 minutes. Drain and rinse under cold water. Place in a 2½-quart casserole dish lightly coated with cooking spray or oil.

IN a medium saucepan over medium heat, melt 1 tablespoon butter. Add mushrooms and sauté until slightly tender, about 5 minutes. Add to casserole. Melt remaining butter and stir in flour until blended. Add milk and wine, whisking constantly until thickened, about 2 minutes. Stir in mustard, salt, pepper, and cheeses. Whisk until cheese melts and sauce is smooth. Pour over broccoli and mushrooms and mix gently. Sprinkle with almonds and bread crumbs.

BAKE, uncovered, until bubbly, about 35 minutes.

SERVES 4 TO 6

broccoli-noodle casserole

This is a great accompaniment for roast turkey or ham. It also makes a satisfying main course when served with a crisp salad of mixed greens.

1 tablespoon vegetable oil

½ cup chopped yellow onion

1 clove garlic, minced

1 tablespoon butter or margarine

2 tablespoons all-purpose flour

1 cup milk

½ teaspoon dried marjoram

½ teaspoon salt

Freshly ground pepper to taste

1 cup low-fat cottage cheese

6 ounces (about 2½ cups) egg noodles, cooked and drained

1 package (10 ounces) frozen chopped broccoli, thawed

1 cup grated cheddar cheese

3 tablespoons freshly grated Parmesan cheese

PREHEAT oven to 350°F. In a medium saucepan over medium heat, warm oil. Add onion and garlic and sauté until tender, about 5 minutes. Add butter and flour and stir until bubbly. Pour in milk and seasonings and whisk until thickened, about 3 minutes. Remove from heat and stir in cottage cheese.

IN a 2½-quart casserole dish lightly coated with cooking spray or oil, place noodles, white sauce, and broccoli and mix well. Top with cheeses.

BAKE, uncovered, until bubbly, about 35 minutes.

SERVES 6

brussels sprouts and baby onions with mustard

Often called "little cabbages," Brussels sprouts rate high on the list of healthful foods to include in your diet. Combined with onions and mustard, they make an assertive vegetable dish.

1 pound Brussels sprouts

1 cup Rich Chicken Stock (page 23) or canned low-sodium chicken broth

1 cup frozen small whole onions, thawed

1 tablespoon Dijon mustard

Salt and freshly ground pepper to taste

PREHEAT oven to 375°F. Cut off stem ends of Brussels sprouts and any discolored outer leaves. In a medium saucepan over high heat, bring stock to a boil. Add Brussels sprouts, reduce temperature to low, and cook, covered, until tender, about 8 minutes. Add onions, stir, and cook 1 minute. Stir in mustard. Season with salt and pepper.

PLACE vegetables and stock in a 2½-quart casserole dish lightly coated with cooking spray or oil. Cover and bake until flavors are blended, about 25 minutes.

SERVES 4

minted carrot and zucchini strips
Prepare this carrot and zucchini dish when fresh mint is available. If it is not available, parsley may be used. The flavor will be pleasing, but not the same.

4   carrots (about 1 pound), peeled, halved lengthwise, then quartered crosswise

½   cup Rich Chicken Stock (page 23) or canned low-sodium chicken broth, or water

½   teaspoon salt

Freshly ground pepper to taste

2   tablespoons chopped fresh mint or parsley

1   zucchini (about 1 pound), unpeeled, halved crosswise, and each half cut lengthwise into quarters

2   tablespoons butter or margarine, cut up

PREHEAT oven to 350°F. Place carrots in a 2½-quart casserole dish lightly coated with cooking spray or oil. Stir in stock, salt, pepper, and mint.

COVER and bake 30 minutes. Add zucchini and dot with butter. Cover and bake until vegetables are tender, about 30 minutes longer.

SERVES 4

175

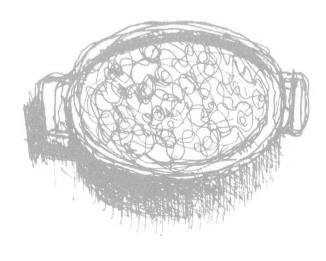

corn-chili polenta

Although polenta is an Italian staple, the addition of corn, cheese, and chiles makes it a complementary dish to serve with Mexican-style foods such as Spicy Baked Black Beans (page 247) and tomato salsa.

4   tablespoons butter or margarine, melted

2   large eggs, beaten

¼   cup Rich Chicken Stock (page 23) or canned low-sodium chicken broth

1   cup grated cheddar cheese

2   cups (about 3 ears) fresh corn kernels, or 1 can (16 ounces) corn, drained; or 1 package (10 ounces) frozen corn, thawed and well drained

½   cup yellow cornmeal

1   cup light sour cream

1   teaspoon sugar

½   teaspoon salt

1   can (4 ounces) diced green chilies, drained

¼   cup freshly grated Parmesan cheese

PREHEAT oven to 350°F. In a large bowl mix together all ingredients except Parmesan cheese. Put in an 8-by-8-inch baking dish lightly coated with cooking spray or oil.

BAKE, uncovered, until firm, about 40 minutes. Sprinkle with Parmesan cheese and bake 5 minutes longer.

SERVES 6

corn and black bean polenta

Fresh corn, spicy black beans, and red bell pepper team together in a tempting casserole for a side dish or main course.

1 can (15 ounces) black beans, rinsed, drained, and patted dry with a paper towel

¼ teaspoon ground cumin

¼ teaspoon dried oregano

Basic Polenta (page 19)

1 cup (about 2 ears) cooked fresh corn kernels, or 1 cup frozen corn, thawed

1 cup chopped red bell pepper

1 can (8 ounces) tomato sauce

2 cups firmly packed grated Monterey Jack cheese

Light sour cream as an accompaniment

IN a small bowl, season beans with cumin and oregano.

PREHEAT oven to 350°F. Make polenta and turn it into a 7½-by-11¾-inch baking dish lightly coated with cooking spray or oil. Add corn in a layer on top of the polenta, then add the beans in one layer and then the pepper. Pour tomato sauce over all and sprinkle with cheese.

BAKE, uncovered, until bubbly, about 30 minutes. Let stand 5 to 10 minutes. Cut into squares and serve immediately. Pass sour cream in a bowl.

SERVES 6

hominy, chiles, and cheese casserole

Hominy is dried white or yellow corn kernels with the hull and germ removed. When combined with chiles and cheese, it's a tasty complement to chicken or steak.

2 cans (14 ounces each) white hominy, rinsed and drained

1 cup chopped yellow onion

1 tomato, seeded, chopped, and drained

1 cup grated Monterey Jack cheese

1 can (7 ounces) diced green chiles, drained

½ cup grated cheddar cheese for topping

½ cup sliced pitted black olives for topping (optional)

PREHEAT oven to 350°F. Place half of the hominy in a 2½-quart casserole dish lightly coated with cooking spray or oil. In layers, add half of the onion, half of the tomatoes, half of the Monterey Jack cheese, and half of the chiles. Repeat the layers and top with cheddar cheese.

SPRINKLE with olives, cover, and bake until flavors are blended, about 30 minutes.

SERVES 4 TO 6

178

chiles rellenos casserole

This casserole has been a long-time favorite side dish to serve with a Mexican dinner. It calls for milk instead of half-and-half, with just as good results. Serve with warm flour tortillas.

1   large (7 ounces) and 1 small (4 ounces) can whole green chiles, drained, seeded, and cut lengthwise into quarters

3   cups grated cheddar cheese

2   tomatoes, seeded, sliced, and drained

8   green onions, including some tender green tops, sliced

2   large eggs

2   cups milk

½   cup all-purpose flour

½   teaspoon salt

PREHEAT oven to 350°F. Arrange chiles in a 7½-by-11¾-inch glass baking dish lightly coated with cooking spray or oil. Layer with half the cheese and in another layer, place tomato slices and onions.

IN a medium bowl, beat eggs, milk, flour, and salt. Pour batter over chile mixture. Top with remaining cheese.

BAKE, uncovered, until puffed and set, about 40 minutes. Let stand 10 minutes before serving.

SERVES 6

VARIATION: Omit tomato slices. Bake, uncovered, 30 minutes. Add 1 can (8 ounces) tomato sauce on top. Do not stir. Bake, uncovered, until bubbly, about 10 minutes longer.

179

eggplant parmigiana

Eggplant is considered a vegetable, but it is actually a fruit. Of the many varieties, the one most commonly used in the United States is the large, purple, pear-shaped variety. In an updated version of this popular Italian dish, red bell pepper and mushrooms are added.

1   large eggplant (about 1 pound) peeled or unpeeled, cut into ⅜-inch slices

Olive oil or cooking spray for coating eggplant slices

Salt and freshly ground pepper to taste

2   tablespoons vegetable oil

½   cup chopped yellow onion

½   red bell pepper, seeded and chopped

9   ounces mushrooms, chopped

2   cloves garlic, minced

1   can (14½ ounces) ready-cut peeled tomatoes, including juice from can

2   tablespoons dry red wine (optional)

½   teaspoon dried basil

¼   teaspoon dried oregano

½   teaspoon salt

Freshly ground pepper to taste

2   tablespoons chopped fresh parsley

⅓   cup freshly grated Parmesan cheese

1   cup grated mozzarella cheese

PREHEAT oven to 375°F. Place eggplant on a baking sheet. Spray or brush both sides lightly with oil. Sprinkle top side with salt and pepper. Bake until slightly soft, about 15 minutes. In a single layer, place eggplant slices in a 7½-by-11¾-inch baking dish lightly coated with cooking spray or oil.

IN a large skillet over medium heat, warm vegetable oil. Add onion, bell pepper, mushrooms, and garlic and sauté until tender, about 5 minutes. Stir in tomatoes, wine, seasonings, and parsley and simmer, uncovered, 10 minutes.

SPRINKLE Parmesan cheese on eggplant. Pour sauce on top and sprinkle with mozzarella cheese.

BAKE, uncovered, until bubbly, about 30 minutes. Let stand 10 minutes before serving.

SERVES 6

THE BIG BOOK OF CASSEROLES

mushroom casserole
Serve this traditional dish of creamy mushrooms with prime rib and mashed potatoes. This recipe can easily be halved.

1 cup (2 sticks) butter or margarine

2 pounds medium mushrooms, sliced

1 tablespoon fresh lemon juice

8 green onions, including some tender green tops, sliced

1 clove garlic, minced

2 tablespoons all-purpose flour

1 teaspoon salt

½ teaspoon dried marjoram

1 cup light sour cream

¼ cup chopped fresh parsley

2 cups fresh bread crumbs (see Note)

PREHEAT oven to 350°F. In a large skillet over medium heat, melt ¾ cup (1½ sticks) butter. Add mushrooms, lemon juice, onions, and garlic and sauté until tender, 6 to 7 minutes. Add flour and seasonings and stir until bubbly. Remove from heat. Add sour cream and parsley and mix well.

TRANSFER mushroom mixture to a 2½-quart casserole dish lightly coated with cooking spray or oil.

MELT remaining butter and mix with crumbs. Cover mushrooms with crumb mixture.

BAKE mushrooms, uncovered, until bubbly and crumbs are crisp, 35 to 40 minutes. Let stand 5 to 10 minutes before serving.

SERVES 6

NOTE: To make fresh bread crumbs, cut off the crusts and process slices briefly in the food processor. (Do not toast.)

181

mushroom-spinach casserole
Quickly prepared, this combination goes great with seafood, especially salmon.

2 tablespoons butter or margarine

8 ounces mushrooms, sliced

1 clove garlic, minced

1 tablespoon fresh lemon juice

3 bags (6 ounces each) fresh spinach, cooked (see page 7), chopped, and drained; or 2 packages (10 ounces each) frozen spinach, thawed and squeezed dry

1 cup cottage cheese

¼ teaspoon dried thyme

½ teaspoon salt

Freshly ground pepper to taste

Dash of ground nutmeg

2 tomatoes, seeded, sliced, and drained

1 cup grated mozzarella cheese

2 tablespoons freshly grated Parmesan cheese

PREHEAT oven to 350°F. In a medium skillet over medium heat, melt butter. Add mushrooms and garlic and sauté until tender, about 5 minutes. Stir in lemon juice and set aside.

IN a large bowl, mix spinach, cottage cheese, seasonings, and mushroom mixture. Place in a 7½-by-11¾-inch baking dish lightly coated with cooking spray or oil. Lay tomato slices on top and sprinkle with cheeses.

BAKE, uncovered, until heated through and cheeses are melted, about 30 minutes.

SERVES 4

stuffed green bell peppers

Orzo is used instead of rice for a different twist to an old favorite. For those who don't like green bell peppers, red peppers are a good substitute.

4 green bell peppers, ½ inch sliced off the tops, ribs and seeds removed

¾ pound lean ground beef

½ yellow onion, chopped

2 cloves garlic, minced

½ teaspoon dried basil

½ teaspoon dried oregano

¾ teaspoon salt

Freshly ground pepper to taste

2 teaspoons Worcestershire sauce

1 cup cooked orzo

1½ cups canned tomato sauce

Parmesan cheese for sprinkling on top

PREHEAT oven to 325°F. Blanch peppers in boiling water to cover, 2 minutes. Remove and drain. Place cut sides up in a pie plate lightly coated with cooking spray or oil.

IN a medium skillet over medium heat, cook beef, onion, and garlic until onions are soft and meat is no longer showing pink, about 7 minutes. Add seasonings, Worcestershire sauce, and orzo. Stir until well blended.

SPOON mixture into pepper shells. Add 2 tablespoons tomato sauce on top of each pepper. Sprinkle with Parmesan cheese. Pour remaining sauce in baking dish around peppers.

BAKE until peppers are tender, about 30 minutes.

SERVES 4

sweet onion and rice bake

In this creamy dish, onions and rice are combined with cheese. Use sweet onions—Vidalia, Walla Walla, or Texas Sweet—if available, but yellow onions will work just as well.

½ cup long-grain white rice

4 cups water

¾ teaspoon salt

3 or 4 large sweet onions, sliced and rings separated (about 8 cups)

½ cup Rich Chicken Stock (page 23) or canned low-sodium chicken broth

1½ cups grated Swiss cheese

¼ cup milk

⅛ teaspoon white pepper

¼ cup chopped fresh parsley

PREHEAT oven to 350°F. In a large pot over high heat, boil rice in water with ½ teaspoon salt, 5 minutes. Drain and place rice in a 4-quart casserole dish lightly coated with cooking spray or oil. Add onions, stock, cheese, milk, ¼ teaspoon salt, and pepper and mix well.

COVER and bake until rice and onions are tender, about 1 hour. Stir in parsley.

SERVES 6

baked potato strips with cheese
Bake this potato dish in the oven along with a main-dish casserole for an easy oven meal. Baking potatoes or new potatoes can be used.

4   new potatoes (about 1½ pound), unpeeled, or 4 small baking potatoes, peeled; cut into strips shaped like French fries
¼   cup 2 percent milk
½   teaspoon Tabasco sauce
½   teaspoon salt
Freshly ground pepper to taste
1   cup grated cheddar cheese

PREHEAT oven to 350°F. Place cut-up potatoes in a bowl of water during preparation to keep them from discoloring. Drain and dry with paper towels. Place in a 7½-by-11¾-inch baking dish lightly coated with cooking spray or oil.

IN a small bowl, mix milk, Tabasco sauce, salt, and pepper. Pour over potatoes and mix well.

BAKE, uncovered, until potatoes are tender-crisp, stirring once, about 45 minutes. Sprinkle with cheese and bake until cheese is melted, about 5 minutes longer.

SERVES 4

new potato and swiss cheese casserole

This is a great springtime casserole that is easy to make. Serve with baked chicken and fresh asparagus.

6   new potatoes (about 2 pounds), unpeeled, halved lengthwise
½   teaspoon salt
1   cup light sour cream
1   teaspoon Dijon mustard
3   tablespoons chopped fresh parsley
½   cup sliced green onions, including some tender green tops
1½ cups grated Swiss cheese
Parmesan cheese for sprinkling on top

PREHEAT oven to 350°F. In a medium saucepan over medium heat, put potatoes, water to cover, and ¼ teaspoon salt. Cook until tender, about 20 minutes. Drain and slice.

IN a small bowl, mix sour cream, mustard, remaining ¼ teaspoon salt, and parsley.

IN a 2½-quart casserole dish lightly coated with cooking spray or oil, layer half of the potatoes, half of the sour cream mixture, half of the onions, and half of the Swiss cheese. Repeat the layers once more. Sprinkle Parmesan cheese on top.

BAKE, uncovered, until bubbly and potatoes are tender, about 45 minutes.

SERVES 4 TO 6

186

lemon potatoes

Crisp, lemony potatoes with a Greek accent are easy to make and different. (Yes, they bake at 450°F!) Use the food processor for quick slicing.

4   large baking potatoes
    (about 2½ pounds), peeled
    and sliced
¼   cup fresh lemon juice
2   tablespoons olive oil
1   teaspoon dried oregano
¾   teaspoon salt
Freshly ground pepper to taste
3   cloves garlic, minced
1½ cups boiling water

PREHEAT oven to 450°F. Mix all ingredients except water in a 2½-quart casserole dish lightly coated with cooking spray or oil. Add water.

BAKE, uncovered, until potatoes are tender, about 1 hour. Stir and bake until crispy on top and water is absorbed, about 15 minutes longer.

SERVES 4 TO 6

scalloped potatoes with red pepper   Red pepper and parsley add

color and a new flavor to an old-fashioned dish. Serve with a beef or pork roast.

4   large baking potatoes
    (about 2½ pounds), peeled
    and sliced

1   small yellow onion, thinly
    sliced

1   red bell pepper, seeded and
    chopped

⅓   cup chopped fresh parsley

1   cup milk

2   tablespoons all-purpose
    flour

1   teaspoon salt

Freshly ground pepper to taste

1   teaspoon paprika

½   teaspoon dry mustard

2   cups firmly packed grated
    Swiss cheese (preferably
    Gruyére)

PREHEAT oven to 350°F. In a 2½-quart casserole dish lightly coated with cooking spray or oil, layer half the potatoes, then all the onion, bell pepper, parsley, and 1 cup cheese. Top with remaining potatoes.

IN a small bowl, whisk together milk, flour, salt, pepper, paprika, and mustard. Pour over potatoes. Do not stir.

COVER and bake about 45 minutes. Sprinkle with remaining cheese and bake, uncovered, until potatoes are tender and cheese is melted, about 15 minutes longer.

SERVES 4 TO 6

new potatoes and fresh spinach bake

In this updated version of potatoes, red pepper, and spinach, chicken broth is used instead of the usual cream for a lighter dish.

6 new potatoes (about 2½ pounds) unpeeled, thinly sliced

1 red bell pepper, seeded and cut into ½-inch squares

2½ cups grated Swiss cheese

Salt and freshly ground pepper to taste

4 ounces fresh spinach leaves, washed and dried

1 tablespoon butter, cut into bits

¾ cup Rich Chicken Stock (page 23) or canned low-sodium chicken broth

Chopped fresh parsley for sprinkling on top

PREHEAT oven to 350°F. In a 9-by-13-inch baking dish lightly coated with cooking spray or oil, layer half of the potatoes, half of the bell pepper, and half of the cheese. Season lightly with salt and pepper. Layer all the spinach on top. Repeat potato, bell pepper, and cheese layers. Season with salt and pepper. Dot top with butter. Pour stock evenly over potato mixture.

BAKE, uncovered, until potatoes are tender and top is golden, about 1 hour. Sprinkle with parsley before serving.

SERVES 6 TO 8

new potato and blue-cheese pie

For the blue-cheese fan, this combination of new potatoes and blue cheese makes a complementary side dish for beef. As the cheese melts into the broth, it forms a delicious sauce, coating the potato slices.

6   new potatoes (about 2
    pounds), unpeeled, sliced

Salt and freshly ground pepper
    to taste

½   cup crumbled blue cheese

½   cup Rich Chicken Stock
    (page 23) or canned low-
    sodium chicken broth

PREHEAT oven to 350°F. In a 10-inch pie plate 2 inches deep, lightly coated with cooking spray or oil, arrange half of the potato slices. Season with salt and pepper. Sprinkle blue cheese evenly over potatoes. Add remaining potato slices and season with salt and pepper again. Pour stock around the edge.

COVER tightly with aluminum foil and bake until potatoes are tender, about 35 minutes. Remove foil and bake until potatoes are lightly browned, about 10 minutes longer.

SERVES 4 TO 6

190

italian potato casserole
Italian seasonings, mozzarella cheese, and tomatoes add a new dimension to this potato casserole. It goes well with a pork or veal roast. Add a chocolate fudge cake for a company dinner.

6   large baking potatoes (about 2½ pounds), peeled and cut into slices ¼ inch thick

1   yellow onion, sliced

3   tomatoes, seeded, sliced, and drained

¼   teaspoon dried oregano

¼   teaspoon dried basil

1   teaspoon salt

¼   teaspoon pepper

2   cups grated mozzarella cheese

⅓   cup freshly grated Parmesan cheese

3   tablespoons butter or margarine, cut into bits

PREHEAT oven to 350°F. In a 2½-quart baking dish lightly coated with cooking spray or oil, add in layers half of the potatoes, half of the onions, and half of the tomato slices. Season with oregano, basil, salt, and pepper. Sprinkle half of each of the cheeses on top. Repeat layers. Dot with butter.

COVER and bake 30 minutes. Uncover and bake until potatoes are tender and top is golden, about 30 minutes longer.

SERVES 6

new potato, tomato, and onion casserole with fresh herbs

Potatoes are so versatile, they can be prepared in many ways. Here is an easy summertime dish to serve at a patio supper.

4   new potatoes (about 1½ pounds, unpeeled, thinly sliced (see Note)

Salt and freshly ground pepper to taste

3   tomatoes, peeled (see page 8), sliced, seeded, and drained

1   yellow onion, sliced and rings separated

2   cloves garlic, minced

1   teaspoon snipped fresh thyme, or ½ teaspoon dried thyme

1   tablespoon chopped fresh basil, or ¾ teaspoon dried basil

2   tablespoons chopped fresh parsley

½   cup Rich Chicken Stock (page 23) or canned low-sodium chicken broth

1   tablespoon butter or margarine, cut up

1   cup grated cheddar cheese

PREHEAT oven to 350°F. In a 7½-by-11¾-inch baking dish lightly coated with cooking spray or oil, arrange half of the potatoes. Season with salt and pepper. In layers, add half of the tomatoes, half of the onion rings, and in combination, half of the garlic and herbs. Repeat layers. Pour stock evenly over vegetables. Dot with butter.

COVER and bake 50 minutes. Sprinkle cheese over the top and bake, uncovered, until the vegetables are tender-crisp and the cheese is melted, about 10 minutes longer.

SERVES 6

NOTE: Cover potatoes with water and a dash of salt to prevent discoloration while slicing, then drain thoroughly.

cheesy mashed potatoes with garlic and onions

Avoid the last-minute rush of mashing potatoes by making this dish ahead and baking in the oven just before serving time.

4 large baking potatoes (about 2 pounds), peeled and quartered

3 or 4 cloves garlic, peeled

½ teaspoon salt

½ cup 2 percent milk

Freshly ground pepper to taste

1 cup grated cheddar cheese

2 drops Tabasco sauce

1 to 2 tablespoons butter

6 green onions, including some tender green tops, sliced

PREHEAT oven to 350°F. In a medium saucepan over high heat, place potatoes, garlic, salt, and water to cover. Bring to a boil. Reduce heat to low and cook, covered, until potatoes are tender, about 15 minutes. Drain well.

ADD milk and with a hand-held electric mixer, beat in the saucepan until smooth. Add pepper, cheese, Tabasco sauce, and butter and beat until cheese and butter are blended.

TURN into a 2½-quart casserole dish lightly coated with cooking spray or oil. Sprinkle onions on top.

COVER and bake until warmed through, about 30 minutes.

SERVES 4

mashed garlic potatoes and rosemary

Mashed potatoes are welcome at a holiday dinner. These potatoes have a hint of garlic and a touch of rosemary to make them special. Double this recipe for a crowd.

6   baking potatoes (about 2½ pounds), peeled and quartered

4   cloves garlic, peeled

2   cups water

1   teaspoon salt

⅔   cup milk or buttermilk

2   tablespoons butter or margarine

¼   cup freshly grated Parmesan cheese

1   tablespoon chopped fresh rosemary, or ¾ tablespoon dried rosemary

Freshly ground pepper to taste

Paprika for sprinkling on top

PREHEAT oven to 350°F. In a medium saucepan over high heat, place potatoes, garlic, water, and ½ teaspoon of the salt. Bring to a boil. Reduce heat to low and cook, covered, until tender, about 15 minutes. Drain well. Add milk and butter and beat with a hand-held electric mixer until smooth. Add cheese and rosemary and beat until fluffy. Season with remaining ½ teaspoon salt and pepper to taste.

TURN potatoes into a 2½-quart casserole dish lightly coated with cooking spray or oil. Sprinkle with paprika.

COVER and bake until heated through, about 20 minutes.

SERVES 4 TO 6

194

THE BIG BOOK OF CASSEROLES

herbed baked tomatoes

Garden fresh tomatoes are best for this casserole, which makes a colorful side dish. To retain fresh flavor and firm texture, do not overbake.

4   large vine-ripened
      tomatoes, halved and
      seeded
¼   cup dry bread crumbs (see
      page 5)
¼   teaspoon garlic powder
1   teaspoon mixed dried
      herbs of your choice
4   tablespoons olive oil
Salt and freshly ground pepper
      to taste
3   tablespoons finely chopped
      fresh parsley
Freshly grated Parmesan
      cheese for sprinkling
      on top
2   teaspoons pine nuts

TURN tomatoes cut side down on paper towels to drain for 10 minutes.

PREHEAT oven to 350°F. In a small bowl, mix bread crumbs, garlic powder, and herbs.

ARRANGE tomato halves, cut sides up, in a 6-by-10-inch baking dish lightly coated with cooking spray or oil. Brush tops with oil and season with salt and pepper. Place crumb mixture evenly on top of each half. Sprinkle with parsley, cheese, and pine nuts.

BAKE, uncovered, until heated through, 12 to 15 minutes, depending on size.

SERVES 6

195

baked pesto tomatoes

Here is another creative way to prepare tomatoes with an unusual flavor. They add variety and interest to the menu.

2   tomatoes, halved and seeded

Salt and freshly ground pepper to taste

2   tablespoons Basil Pesto (page 18) or commercially prepared pesto

⅓   cup grated Monterey Jack cheese

2   green onions, including some tender green tops, sliced

2   tablespoons chopped fresh parsley

PREHEAT oven to 375°F. Drain tomatoes, cut side down, on paper towels for 10 minutes. Place cut sides up in an 8-by-8-inch baking dish lightly coated with cooking spray or oil. Season with salt and pepper.

IN a small bowl, mix pesto, cheese, onions, and parsley. Spread each tomato half equally with the pesto-cheese mixture.

BAKE, uncovered, until tomatoes are warmed through and cheese is melted, 8 to 10 minutes. Do not overcook, as tomatoes will get mushy.

SERVES 4

golden squash and mushroom bake

Bring the garden to the table with a late summer vegetable dish when there is a surplus of squash. Serve with Lamb Meatballs (page 164).

3 yellow crookneck squash (1½ pounds), unpeeled, cut into ⅜-inch slices

1 yellow onion, sliced and rings separated

1 red or green bell pepper, seeded and cut lengthwise into ⅜-inch strips

8 ounces mushrooms, sliced

2 cloves garlic, minced

½ teaspoon salt

Freshly ground pepper to taste

1 tablespoon snipped fresh dill, or ¾ teaspoon dried dill weed

1 tablespoon butter or margarine, cut up

2 cups grated cheddar or Monterey Jack cheese

2 tablespoons freshly grated Parmesan cheese

PREHEAT oven to 350°F. In a large bowl, combine squash, onion, bell pepper, mushrooms, and garlic. Layer half of the vegetables in a 4-quart casserole dish lightly coated with cooking spray or oil. Sprinkle with salt, pepper, and dill. Add the remaining vegetables in a second layer. Dot with butter.

BAKE, covered, about 30 minutes. Sprinkle cheeses on top and bake, uncovered, until squash is tender and cheese is melted, 10 to 15 minutes longer.

197

SERVES 6 TO 8

savory fruit-filled squash

Make this fall vegetable dish to serve with a harvest dinner. A fruit filling of grapes and pears enhances the flavor of the squash and makes it special.

3 acorn squash, halved and seeded

2 tablespoons butter or margarine

2 tablespoons light brown sugar

2 cups seedless green grapes

2 pears, peeled, cored, and chopped

½ teaspoon grated lemon zest

2 tablespoons chopped walnuts

PREHEAT oven to 350°F. Place squash, cut sides down, in a baking pan lightly coated with cooking spray or oil, and bake until tender, about 1 hour.

MEANWHILE, in a small saucepan, melt butter over medium heat. Stir in sugar. Add fruit, lemon zest, and nuts and stir until blended.

FILL each squash equally with filling. Bake until filling is warm, 10 to 15 minutes longer.

SERVES 6

great grated zucchini
Grating gives a new taste and a different texture to zucchini. Baked in the oven and mixed with sour cream, this innovative dish is crisp and appealing.

2   large zucchini (about 1¼ pounds combined weight), unpeeled, grated, and blotted dry with a paper towel

1½ tablespoons butter or margarine, cut into small pieces

¼ to ⅓ cup light sour cream

¼   teaspoon salt

Freshly ground pepper to taste

Freshly grated Parmesan cheese for topping

PREHEAT oven to 350°F. Place grated zucchini in an 8-by-8-inch baking dish lightly coated with cooking spray or oil. Dot with butter.

BAKE, uncovered, for 15 minutes. Stir in sour cream, salt, and pepper. Sprinkle with Parmesan cheese and bake until zucchini is tender-crisp and cheese melts, about 10 minutes longer.

SERVES 4 TO 6

cheese-stuffed zucchini

When zucchini comes into season, be ready with a variety of ways to prepare it. For a change, try this special cheese-laced version.

3   large zucchini, unpeeled, cut in half crosswise

1½ cups grated Monterey Jack cheese

¾   cup low-fat cottage cheese or ricotta cheese

2   tablespoons freshly grated Parmesan cheese

1   tablespoon chopped fresh parsley

2   tablespoons dry bread crumbs (see page 5)

Paprika for sprinkling on top

IN a medium saucepan over high heat, place zucchini with salted water to cover. Bring to a boil, reduce heat to low, cover, and simmer until partially cooked, about 7 minutes. Drain and immerse in cold water to stop the cooking process. Drain again.

CUT zucchini halves in half lengthwise. Using a small spoon, scoop out seeds and a small amount of pulp and discard. Place zucchini, cut sides down, on paper towels to drain for a few minutes.

PREHEAT oven to 350°F. In a small bowl, combine cheeses, parsley, and bread crumbs and stir to mix well. Arrange zucchini halves, hollow sides up, in a 9-by-13-inch baking dish lightly coated with cooking spray or oil. Fill each half with an equal amount of cheese mixture. Sprinkle with paprika.

BAKE until zucchini is tender and cheese is melted, about 15 minutes.

SERVES 4 TO 6

zucchini and crookneck squash casserole

For a fresh-tasting vegetable dish, combine two kinds of squash with light sour cream and top with cheese. Serve with Turkey Loaf (page 116) for an oven dinner.

1½ pounds of a combination of zucchini and crookneck squash, unpeeled, and cut into ¾-inch slices

4 green onions, including some tender green tops, sliced

½ cup light sour cream

¼ teaspoon dried thyme

¼ teaspoon salt

⅛ teaspoon white pepper

½ cup dry sourdough bread crumbs (see page 5)

1 cup grated cheddar cheese

PREHEAT oven to 375°F. Add some water to a pan fitted with a steamer rack over medium heat. Place squash in rack and steam over gently boiling water until slightly tender, about 5 minutes.

IN a medium bowl, mix squash, onions, sour cream, thyme, salt, and pepper. Place in an 8-by-8-inch baking dish lightly coated with cooking spray or oil. Sprinkle with crumbs and top with cheese.

BAKE until heated through and cheese is melted, about 20 minutes.

SERVES 4 TO 6

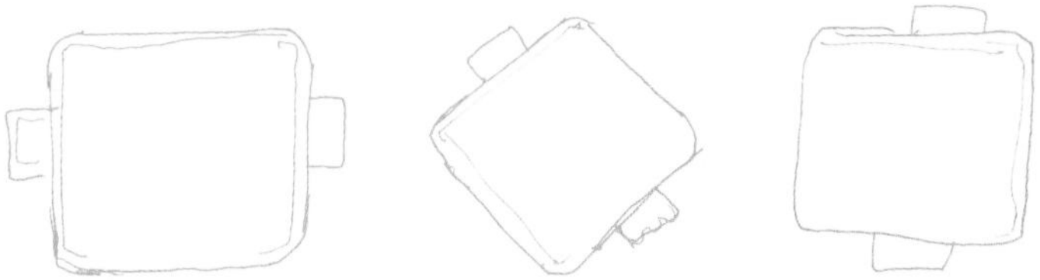

zucchini and cheese bake

This dish can be made any time of the year, but it is best made in the summer, when zucchini is abundant. The feta cheese and lemon juice add a Greek accent. Serve with grilled lamb chops.

2   tablespoons olive oil

4   zucchini, unpeeled, thinly sliced (about 6 cups; see Note)

1   cup (2 bunches) sliced green onions, including some tender green tops

1   clove garlic, minced

1   teaspoon dried oregano

½   teaspoon salt

Freshly ground pepper to taste

2   large eggs

1   cup grated Monterey Jack cheese

½   cup crumbled feta cheese

¼   cup chopped fresh parsley

2   tablespoons fresh lemon juice

2   tablespoons freshly grated Parmesan cheese

PREHEAT oven to 350°F. In a large skillet over medium heat, warm oil. Add zucchini, green onions, and garlic and sprinkle with oregano, salt, and pepper. Sauté until tender-crisp, 5 to 6 minutes. Transfer to a 2½-quart casserole dish lightly coated with cooking spray or oil.

IN a medium bowl, beat eggs. Stir in cheeses, parsley, and lemon juice. Mix with zucchini and onion. Sprinkle with Parmesan cheese.

BAKE, uncovered, until bubbly, 35 to 40 minutes.

SERVES 6

NOTE: Use a food processor to make quick work of slicing zucchini.

root vegetable purée

Root vegetables grow underground. They include celery root, beets, carrots, turnips, parsnips, rutabagas, and sweet potatoes. They are inexpensive, healthful, and add variety to a winter menu. In this recipe, four root vegetables are combined and puréed to make an imaginative dish to serve with lamb or turkey.

2 sweet potatoes, peeled and quartered (see Note)

2 carrots, peeled and cut into 3-inch pieces

2 parsnips, peeled and sliced into large chunks

2 turnips, peeled and quartered

1 large rutabaga, peeled and quartered

3 tablespoons butter

1 tablespoon red wine vinegar

¼ cup light sour cream

1 tablespoon chopped fresh dill, or 1 teaspoon dried dill weed

1 teaspoon salt

Fresh dill sprigs for garnish

ADD water to a pan fitted with a steamer rack over medium heat. Place vegetables in rack and steam over gently boiling water until they are tender, 15 to 20 minutes.

PREHEAT oven to 375°F. In two batches, transfer vegetables to food processor or blender. Add remaining ingredients, except dill sprigs, and process until smooth. Transfer to a 2½-quart casserole dish lightly coated with cooking spray or oil.

COVER and bake until flavors are blended, 25 to 30 minutes.

SERVES 6 TO 8

NOTE: In case you get confused, rutabagas are round with orange flesh, turnips are smoother with some light purple coloring and white flesh, and parsnips are shaped like carrots, only white. When cutting vegetables, make their sizes as uniform as possible. Use a potato peeler for easy peeling.

casserole of mixed garden vegetables
Put this healthful casserole in the oven, and in about one hour you will have a delicious blend of contrasting flavors and colors.

1   small green bell pepper, seeded and cut into ½-inch strips

2   large carrots, peeled and cut into strips

1   yellow onion, sliced

2   cloves garlic, minced

6   large mushrooms, quartered

¼   cup Rich Chicken Stock (page 23) or canned low-sodium chicken broth

1   tablespoon olive oil

3   tablespoons chopped fresh parsley

¼   teaspoon dried dill weed

½   teaspoon salt

Freshly ground pepper to taste

2   celery stalks, sliced into 2-inch lengths

1   zucchini, unpeeled, halved and then sliced lengthwise into strips like French fries

PREHEAT oven to 350°F. In a 2½-quart casserole dish, add all vegetables except celery and zucchini. Add stock, olive oil, parsley, and seasonings and mix.

COVER and bake 30 minutes. Add celery and zucchini and bake, covered, until vegetables are tender, about 30 minutes longer.

SERVES 4 TO 6

vegetable pie

This crustless pie is a savory combination of vegetables, eggs, and cheese similar to a quiche. Serve for a luncheon dish with a fruit salad and yogurt-honey dressing.

2 tablespoons butter or margarine

2 cups sliced mushrooms

2 cups chopped zucchini

1 cup chopped yellow onion

½ cup chopped green bell pepper

1 clove garlic, minced

2 tablespoons chopped fresh parsley

4 large eggs

2 cups cottage cheese

2 cups grated Monterey Jack cheese

2 bags (6 ounces each) fresh spinach, cooked (see page 7), drained, and chopped; or 1 package (10 ounces) frozen spinach, thawed and squeezed dry

¼ teaspoon dried dill weed

½ teaspoon salt

Freshly ground pepper to taste

Freshly grated Parmesan cheese for topping

PREHEAT oven to 350°F.

IN a large skillet over medium heat, melt butter. Add the vegetables and parsley and sauté until slightly tender, about 5 minutes. Place in a 10-inch quiche dish or deep-dish pie plate lightly coated with cooking spray or oil.

IN a medium bowl, mix eggs, cottage cheese, Monterey Jack cheese, spinach, dill, salt, and pepper. Spread mixture over vegetables. Sprinkle with Parmesan cheese.

BAKE until firm and bubbly, about 40 minutes. Cut into wedges to serve.

SERVES 6

205

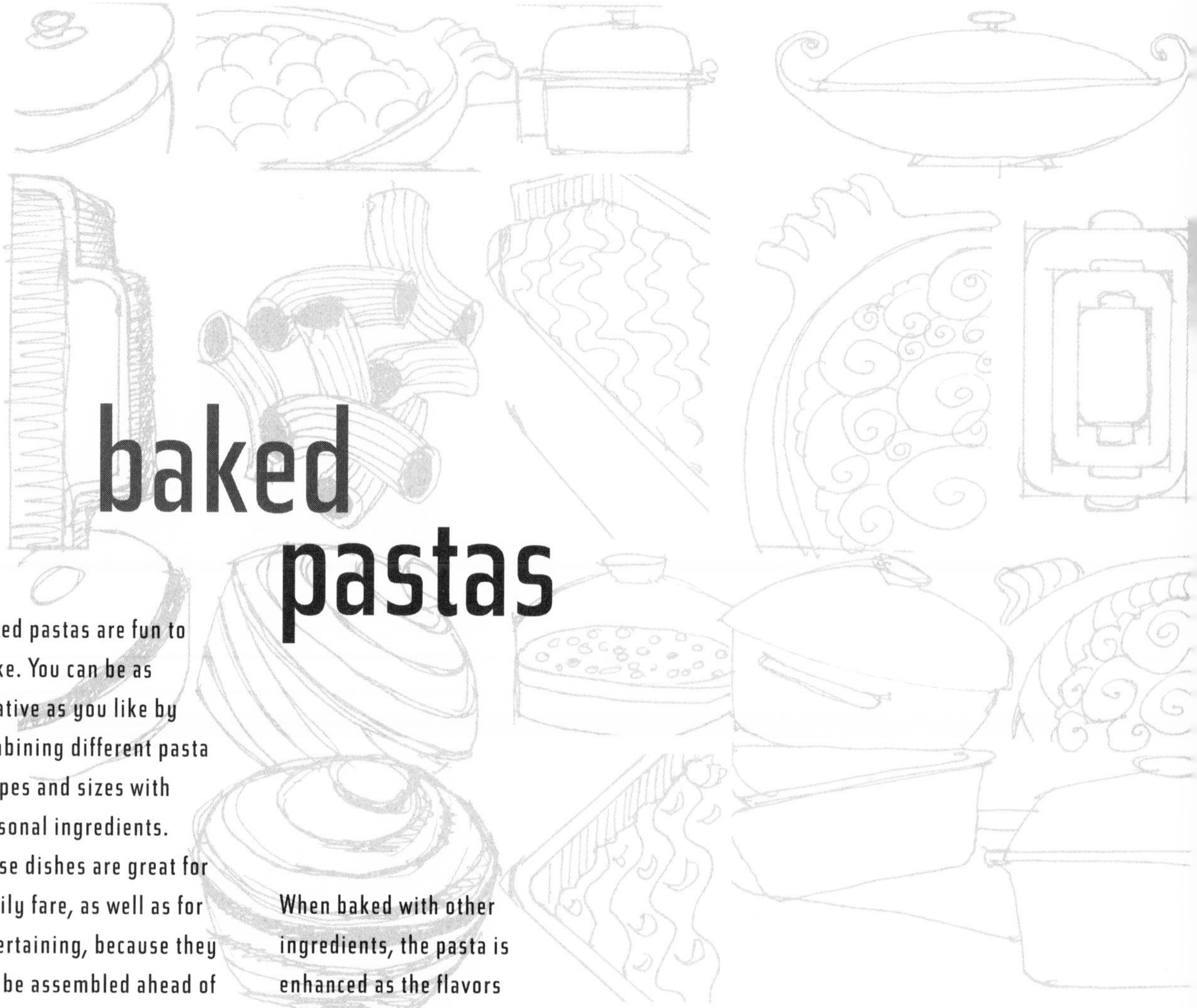

baked pastas

Baked pastas are fun to make. You can be as creative as you like by combining different pasta shapes and sizes with seasonal ingredients. These dishes are great for family fare, as well as for entertaining, because they can be assembled ahead of time and baked later.

When baked with other ingredients, the pasta is enhanced as the flavors meld together. Baked pastas are convenient, often economical, and tasty.

pesto-spinach lasagna

Here is an updated version of lasagna with a pesto cream sauce. It is a perfect dish for a buffet or casual supper. Include an introductory antipasto on the menu and lots of garlic bread.

2 tablespoons butter or margarine

2 tablespoons all-purpose flour

1¾ cups skim milk

½ teaspoon salt

Freshly ground pepper to taste

½ cup Basil Pesto (page 18), or commercially prepared pesto

1 large egg

2 bags (6 ounces each) fresh spinach, cooked (see page 7), drained, and chopped; or 1 package (10 ounces) frozen chopped spinach, thawed and squeezed dry

¼ cup chopped green onions, including some tender green tops

2 cups low-fat cottage cheese or ricotta cheese

2 cups grated mozzarella cheese

½ cup freshly grated Parmesan cheese

9 lasagna noodles, cooked and drained

PREHEAT oven to 350°F. In a medium saucepan over medium heat, melt butter. Add flour and stir until bubbly. Whisk in milk and stir until mixture boils and is thickened, about 2 minutes. Add salt and pepper. Remove from heat and stir in pesto.

TO make filling, in a medium bowl, beat egg. Add spinach, onions, cottage cheese, mozzarella, and ¼ cup of the Parmesan and mix well.

IN a 9-by-13-inch baking dish lightly coated with cooking spray or oil, place 3 noodles. Add one third of filling mixture, spreading it evenly over noodles. Spoon one third of pesto sauce on top. Repeat layers 2 more times, making sure all noodles are covered with sauce.

BAKE, loosely covered, until bubbly, 45 to 50 minutes. Remove cover and sprinkle with remaining Parmesan cheese. Bake, uncovered, until cheese is melted, 5 minutes longer. Let stand 10 minutes before serving. Cut into squares.

SERVES 8

three-cheese manicotti

This classic cheese manicotti is an all-time favorite for a family dinner or an informal gathering. Serve with a salad of mixed greens and garlic bread.

SAUCE

1 tablespoon olive oil
1 cup chopped yellow onion
2 cloves garlic, minced
1 can (14½ ounces) whole tomatoes, including juice, lightly puréed in food processor
1 can (8 ounces) tomato sauce
1 bay leaf
1 teaspoon dried oregano
1 teaspoon dried basil
½ teaspoon sugar
½ teaspoon salt
Freshly ground pepper to taste

FILLING

1 large egg, beaten
2½ cups grated mozzarella cheese
2 cups ricotta or cottage cheese
½ cup freshly grated Parmesan cheese
⅓ cup chopped fresh parsley

9 manicotti shells, cooked and drained
Parmesan cheese for sprinkling on top

PREHEAT oven to 350°F.

MAKE THE SAUCE: In a large saucepan over medium heat, warm oil. Add onion and garlic and sauté until tender, about 5 minutes. Add remaining ingredients. Bring to a boil, reduce heat and simmer, uncovered, until slightly thickened, about 20 minutes. Remove bay leaf and discard.

MEANWHILE, make the filling: In a large bowl, mix egg, cheeses, and parsley. Set aside.

PLACE one third of the sauce into a 9-by-13-inch baking dish lightly coated with cooking spray or oil. Spoon filling mixture into cooked shells and arrange in a single layer on top of sauce. Pour remaining sauce over shells. Sprinkle lightly with Parmesan cheese.

COVER and bake until bubbly, 35 to 40 minutes. Remove cover last 5 minutes of cooking time. Let stand 10 minutes before serving.

SERVES 6 TO 8

pasta primavera
This beautiful combination of pasta, assorted vegetables, and a light cream sauce is baked in the oven to blend all the delicious flavors.

8 slender asparagus spears, cut into 1½-inch pieces

½ red bell pepper, seeded and cut into ⅜-by-2-inch strips

1 zucchini (about 8 ounces), unpeeled, cut into ⅜-by-2-inch strips

1 yellow squash (about 8 ounces), unpeeled, cut into ⅜-by-2-inch strips

4 green onions, sliced

2 cloves garlic, chopped

8 ounces mushrooms, quartered

1 cup sugar snap peas, trimmed

1 large tomato, seeded, coarsely chopped, and drained

3 fresh basil leaves, chopped, or 1 teaspoon dried basil

¼ cup chopped fresh parsley

1 cup Rich Chicken Stock (page 23) or canned low-sodium chicken broth

1 cup light sour cream

½ cup freshly grated Parmesan cheese

1 teaspoon salt

Freshly ground pepper to taste

10 ounces (about 3 cups) penne, cooked and drained

PREHEAT oven to 350°F. Add some water to a pan fitted with a steamer rack over medium heat. Remove and discard tough ends of asparagus. Place asparagus and red pepper on rack and steam, covered, over gently boiling water, 2 minutes. Add zucchini, yellow squash, onions (including some tender green tops), garlic, mushrooms, and peas. Cover and steam until vegetables are tender-crisp, about 6 minutes longer. Remove vegetables to a medium bowl. Add tomato, basil, and parsley and mix. Set aside.

IN a small bowl, whisk together chicken stock and sour cream. Add ¼ cup of the Parmesan cheese, salt, and pepper.

TO assemble, mix pasta, vegetables, and cheese sauce in a 4-quart casserole dish lightly coated with cooking spray or oil. Top with remaining ¼ cup Parmesan cheese.

COVER and bake 30 minutes. Uncover and bake until heated through, 10 to 15 minutes longer.

SERVES 6 TO 8

baked pasta with chicken and puttanesca sauce

This spicy tomato sauce gets its name from the Italian word *puttana,* or "ladies of the night." Combined with penne and chicken, this makes a great dish for a crowd. Serve with a mixed green salad and crusty bread.

2   tablespoons olive oil

1   cup chopped yellow onion

2   cloves garlic, chopped

4   ounces mushrooms, chopped

2   cans (14½ ounces each) crushed tomatoes in thick purée

¾   teaspoon dried oregano

¾   teaspoon dried basil

½   teaspoon red pepper flakes, crushed

½   teaspoon salt

Freshly ground pepper to taste

2   teaspoons anchovy paste (optional)

2   tablespoons drained capers

1   small red bell pepper, roasted (see page 8) and chopped, or ½ cup chopped commercially prepared roasted red pepper

3   cups cubed cooked chicken

¼   cup chopped fresh parsley

1   cup pitted kalamata or canned black olives

6   ounces (about 2 cups) penne, cooked and drained

1   cup grated Asiago cheese

IN a large saucepan over medium heat, warm oil. Add onion, garlic, and mushrooms and sauté until tender, about 5 minutes. Add tomatoes, seasonings, anchovy paste, capers, and roasted pepper. Reduce heat and simmer, uncovered, until thickened, about 20 minutes. In the meantime, preheat oven to 350°F.

ADD chicken, parsley, and olives to sauce. Transfer to a 3- or 4-quart casserole dish lightly coated with cooking spray or oil. Add penne and mix well.

SPRINKLE with cheese and bake, uncovered, until bubbly, 40 to 45 minutes. Let stand 5 to 10 minutes before serving.

SERVES 8

NOTE: Asiago cheese is a semifirm Italian cheese with a rich, nutty flavor.

THE BIG BOOK OF CASSEROLES

penne with chicken, crookneck squash, mushrooms, and tomato sauce

Make this main dish of chicken, vegetables, and pasta in the morning to enjoy at mealtime after a busy day at work. It is nutritious as well as delicious. Serve with a crisp wedge of iceberg lettuce with blue-cheese dressing.

1 large crookneck squash, unpeeled, cut into ½-inch slices

4 ounces mushrooms, quartered

2 cups Quick Tomato Sauce (page 16)

2 cups cubed cooked chicken breasts (see page 6)

8 ounces (about 2½ cups) penne, cooked and drained

Salt and freshly ground pepper to taste

Freshly grated Parmesan cheese for topping

PREHEAT oven to 350°F. Add some water to a pan fitted with a steamer rack over medium heat. Place squash and mushrooms on the rack. Cover and steam over gently boiling water until tender-crisp, about 6 minutes. Transfer to a 2½-quart casserole dish lightly coated with cooking spray or oil. Add tomato sauce, chicken, penne, salt, and pepper and mix well. Sprinkle with Parmesan cheese.

COVER and bake until bubbly, about 40 minutes.

SERVES 4

211

baked noodle and cheese casserole

Easy to make and to serve, this casserole is perfect as a side dish for a summer barbecue. Assemble it early in the cool of the morning, and bake later. The recipe can be doubled for a crowd.

6   ounces (about 2 cups) egg noodles, cooked and drained

1   cup low-fat cottage cheese

1   cup light sour cream

¼   cup sliced green onions, including some tender green tops

2   cloves garlic, minced

1   teaspoon Worcestershire sauce

2   drops Tabasco sauce

2   tablespoons freshly grated Parmesan cheese

3   tablespoons chopped fresh parsley

¼   teaspoon salt

Freshly ground pepper to taste

1   cup grated cheddar cheese

PREHEAT oven to 350°F. In a 2½ quart casserole dish lightly coated with cooking spray or oil, combine all ingredients except cheddar cheese.

COVER and bake 30 minutes. Sprinkle with cheddar cheese and bake, uncovered, until bubbly and cheese is melted, about 15 minutes longer.

SERVES 6

212

baked orzo and chili casserole

Orzo is a small oval pasta with a creamy texture. Chiles add zip to this casserole, making it a complementary dish to serve with Mexican food.

2 cups Rich Chicken Stock (page 23), canned low-sodium chicken broth, or water

1 cup orzo

1 cup grated Monterey Jack cheese

½ cup chopped red bell pepper

1 can (4 ounces) diced green chiles, drained

½ cup light sour cream

½ cup freshly grated Parmesan cheese

PREHEAT oven to 375°F. In a medium saucepan over high heat, bring stock or water to a boil. Add orzo, reduce heat to low, and cook, covered, until tender and liquid is absorbed, about 15 minutes.

TRANSFER to a 1½-quart casserole dish lightly coated with cooking spray or oil. Stir in Monterey Jack cheese, bell pepper, and chiles. Spread sour cream over top and sprinkle with Parmesan cheese.

BAKE, uncovered, until golden and bubbly, about 20 minutes.

SERVES 6

baked macaroni and cheese

Macaroni and cheese has been a favorite with children for many years. Here is an easy way to make this popular dish in the oven without a white sauce. The bread crumbs give a crunchy topping.

12 ounces (about 3 cups) elbow macaroni, cooked and drained
2 tablespoons flour
1 teaspoon salt
Freshly ground pepper to taste
3 tablespoons butter or margarine
3 cups grated cheddar cheese
1 cup whole milk
1 teaspoon Worcestershire sauce
1 cup fresh bread crumbs (see Note on page 181)

PREHEAT oven to 350°F. Place half of the macaroni in a 9-by-13-inch baking dish lightly coated with cooking spray or oil. Sprinkle with flour, salt, and pepper. Dot with 1 tablespoon of the butter, cut into bits. In layers add half of the cheese, the remaining macaroni, and then the remaining cheese.

IN a cup, mix milk and Worcestershire sauce and pour over casserole. Melt remaining butter and mix with bread crumbs. Sprinkle over top.

COVER and bake 40 minutes. Remove cover and bake until bubbly, 10 minutes longer. Let stand 5 minutes before serving.

SERVES 6 TO 8

noodles and spinach casserole
These noodles buried in a creamy mixture of sour cream, cottage cheese, and fresh spinach make an ideal accompaniment for meat or fish.

8   ounces (about 2½ cups) egg noodles, cooked, drained, and cooled slightly

1   cup low-fat cottage cheese

1   cup light sour cream

2   cloves garlic, minced

¼   cup chopped green onion, including some tender green tops

2   packages (6 ounces each) fresh spinach, cooked (see page 7), drained, and chopped; or 1 package (10 ounces) frozen chopped spinach, thawed and squeezed dry

3   drops Tabasco sauce

1   teaspoon Worcestershire sauce

Dash of ground nutmeg

½   teaspoon salt

Freshly ground pepper to taste

1   tomato, seeded, sliced, and drained

¾   cup grated Monterey Jack cheese

PREHEAT oven to 350°F. In a large bowl, mix together all ingredients except tomato slices and Monterey Jack cheese. Transfer to a 2½-quart casserole dish lightly coated with cooking spray or oil.

COVER and bake 15 minutes. Remove lid and layer tomatoes followed by cheese on top. Bake, uncovered, until bubbly and cheese melts, about 20 minutes longer.

SERVES 6

ziti, spinach, and mushroom casserole

Ziti is a straight-cut, narrow, tubular macaroni. It has many uses in salads, soups, and pasta dishes. This is a good side dish to serve with seafood.

2 tablespoons butter or margarine

4 ounces mushrooms, sliced

1 package (10 ounces) frozen spinach, thawed and squeezed dry

2 cups low-fat cottage cheese

1 cup grated Monterey Jack cheese

¼ teaspoon dried thyme

¼ teaspoon salt

Freshly ground pepper to taste

8 ounces ziti (about 2¼ cups), cooked and drained

2 tomatoes, seeded, thinly sliced, and drained

2 tablespoons freshly grated Parmesan cheese

PREHEAT oven to 350°F. In a medium skillet over medium heat, melt butter. Sauté mushrooms until tender, about 5 minutes. Stir in spinach and remove from heat.

IN a 2½-quart casserole dish lightly coated with cooking spray or oil, mix mushroom-spinach mixture with cottage cheese, Monterey Jack cheese, seasonings, and ziti. Place tomato slices on top and sprinkle with Parmesan cheese.

BAKE, uncovered, until heated through, about 40 minutes.

SERVES 4

penne, vegetables, and two cheeses
In this recipe, crunchy
vegetables bake along with pasta in a wine-flavored cheese sauce.

1 tablespoon vegetable oil

1 yellow onion, chopped

1 clove garlic, minced

8 ounces mushrooms, sliced

1 large zucchini, unpeeled,
cut into ⅜-by-2-inch strips

2 tomatoes, seeded, chopped,
and drained

¼ cup chopped fresh basil, or
1 teaspoon dried basil

¼ teaspoon salt

Freshly ground pepper to taste

¼ cup chopped fresh parsley

½ cup dry white wine

½ cup crumbled blue cheese

⅓ cup freshly grated
Parmesan cheese

6 ounces (about 2 cups)
penne, cooked and drained

PREHEAT oven to 350°F. In a large skillet over medium heat, warm oil. Add onion, garlic, mushrooms, and zucchini and cook until tender-crisp, about 5 minutes. Add tomatoes, basil, salt, pepper, parsley, wine, and cheeses and stir until blended, about 1 minute. Add penne and toss. Transfer to a 2½-quart casserole dish lightly coated with cooking spray or oil.

COVER and bake until bubbly, about 35 minutes, stirring once during cooking.

SERVES 6

217

rotini, fresh basil, pinenuts, and cheese casserole

When served with a crisp green salad and warm bread, this filling pasta dish can be the centerpiece of the meal. Fresh basil adds a distinctive flavor.

8 ounces (about 2½ cups) rotini, cooked and drained

2 cans (14½ ounces each) crushed tomatoes in thick purée

2 tablespoons toasted pine nuts (see page 11)

¼ cup slivered fresh basil (see page 9), or 1 teaspoon dried basil

¾ teaspoon salt

Freshly ground pepper to taste

¼ cup chopped fresh parsley

1 cup grated Havarti cheese

Freshly grated Parmesan cheese for sprinkling on top

PREHEAT oven to 375°F. Place rotini in a 2½-quart casserole dish lightly coated with cooking spray or oil.

IN a medium saucepan over medium heat, stir together tomatoes, pine nuts, seasonings, and parsley. Simmer 2 to 3 minutes. Add to casserole and mix with pasta. Add Havariti cheese and mix again. Sprinkle Parmesan cheese on top.

BAKE, uncovered, until bubbly, 35 to 40 minutes. Let stand 10 minutes before serving.

SERVES 6

NOTE: Havarti cheese is a semisoft Danish cheese, mild, but tangy.

ziti with tomatoes, basil, cheese, and olives

Tomatoes and seasonings are slow-simmered to make a savory sauce, then baked with pasta and cheese. This was served to us before a choir concert along with a salad of baby greens and a plate of homemade cookies for dessert. Our hostess was in the choir and had to leave early, and this made a nice, easy supper for her to serve.

1   tablespoon olive oil

1   cup chopped yellow onion

2   cloves garlic, minced

1   can (28 ounces) whole tomatoes, including juices, lightly puréed in food processor

¼   cup Rich Chicken Stock (page 23) or canned low-sodium chicken broth

1   tablespoon chopped fresh basil, or ¾ teaspoon dried basil

¼   teaspoon dried oregano

2   drops Tabasco sauce

½   teaspoon salt

Freshly ground pepper to taste

10   ounces (about 3 cups) ziti, cooked and drained

1   cup grated Monterey Jack cheese

¾   cup pitted kalamata or canned black olives, halved

½   cup freshly grated Parmesan cheese plus extra to pass around in a bowl

Fresh basil leaves for garnish

PREHEAT oven to 375°F. In a large saucepan over medium heat, warm oil. Add onion and garlic and sauté until tender, about 5 minutes. Add tomatoes, broth, and seasonings. Bring to a boil. Reduce heat to medium-low and simmer, uncovered, until slightly thickened, about 30 minutes, stirring occasionally. Add pasta, Monterey Jack cheese, and olives to sauce and mix well.

TRANSFER to a 7½-by-11¾-inch baking dish lightly coated with cooking spray or oil.

COVER and bake 20 minutes. Uncover, stir, and sprinkle with Parmesan cheese. Bake until bubbly, about 25 minutes longer. Let stand 5 to 10 minutes before serving. Pass extra Parmesan cheese.

SERVES 6

rotelle with zucchini, italian style

Serve this meatless dish for a light supper with a green salad and garlic bread, or as a side dish with grilled meats.

1 tablespoon vegetable oil

2 zucchini, unpeeled, cut into ½-inch slices, and slices quartered

1 yellow onion, chopped

2 cloves garlic, minced

1 can (14½ ounces) whole tomatoes, chopped, juice from can included

4 tablespoons tomato paste

½ teaspoon dried basil

¼ teaspoon dried oregano

¼ teaspoon salt

Freshly ground pepper to taste

3 tablespoons chopped fresh parsley

4 ounces (about 1½ cups) rotelle, cooked and drained

1 container (15 ounces) ricotta cheese

1 cup grated mozzarella cheese

½ cup freshly grated Parmesan cheese

PREHEAT oven to 350°F. In a large nonstick skillet over medium heat, warm oil. Add zucchini, onion, and garlic and sauté until tender, about 5 minutes. Stir in tomatoes, tomato paste, seasonings, and parsley. Reduce heat and simmer, uncovered, 10 minutes. Stir in pasta and set aside.

IN a medium bowl, mix ricotta, mozzarella, and ¼ cup of the Parmesan.

TO assemble, spread half of the zucchini and pasta mixture in an 7¾-by-11¾-inch baking dish lightly coated with cooking spray or oil. Spread cheese mixture on top. Layer remaining zucchini mixture over the cheese. Sprinkle remaining Parmesan cheese on top.

COVER and bake 40 minutes. Remove cover and bake until bubbly, about 10 minutes longer. Let stand 5 to 10 minutes before serving.

SERVES 6

fettucini with basil pesto

Pesto adds a fresh taste to this simple and easily prepared pasta dish. It goes well with seafood.

- ½ cup Basil Pesto (page 18), or commercially prepared pesto
- ½ cup light sour cream or nonfat yogurt
- 8 ounces fettucini, cooked and drained

PREHEAT oven to 350°F. In a small bowl, stir together pesto and sour cream. Toss with fettucini. Transfer to a 2½-quart casserole dish lightly coated with cooking spray or oil. Cover and bake until heated through and flavors are blended, about 20 minutes.

SERVES 6

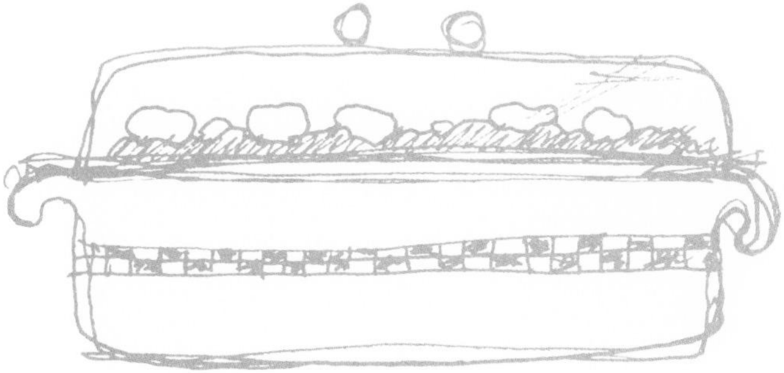

fettucini with spinach, ricotta cheese, and pancetta

This versatile pasta dish is full of flavor. It serves as a hearty main course along with a green salad and frosted brownies for dessert.

4   ounces pancetta (Italian bacon) or bacon, chopped

½   cup chopped yellow onion

1   cup ricotta cheese or cottage cheese

¾   cup milk

3   tablespoons freshly grated Parmesan cheese, plus extra for topping

¼   teaspoon salt

Freshly ground pepper to taste

¼   teaspoon dried thyme

8   ounces fettucini, cooked and drained

1   package (10 ounces) frozen chopped spinach, thawed and squeezed dry

PREHEAT oven to 375°F. In a medium skillet over medium heat, sauté pancetta for 5 minutes. Add onions and sauté until onions are tender and pancetta is crisp, about 5 minutes longer. Pour off excess grease and set aside.

IN food processor or blender, blend ricotta, milk, 3 tablespoons Parmesan cheese, salt, pepper, and thyme. Place cheese sauce, fettucini, spinach, and pancetta-onion mixture in a 4-quart casserole dish lightly coated with cooking spray or oil. With 2 forks, toss until thoroughly mixed. Top with Parmesan cheese.

BAKE, uncovered, until heated through, about 30 minutes. Stir before serving.

SERVES 6

angel-hair pasta with oysters and bacon

This is a pasta for oyster lovers. Plump oysters are sautéed briefly and mixed with bacon and pasta. The bacon adds a salty flavor that compliments the oysters.

4 pounds bacon, chopped

½ cup chopped red onion

2 cloves garlic, minced

4 tablespoons butter or margarine

1 pound shucked oysters, rinsed and drained, halved if large

¼ teaspoon red pepper flakes, crushed

¼ teaspoon salt

½ cup dry white wine

8 ounces angel-hair pasta, cooked and drained

¼ cup chopped fresh parsley

PREHEAT oven to 375°F. In a medium skillet over medium heat, cook bacon, onion, and garlic. Pour off excess grease and transfer mixture to a 2½-quart casserole dish lightly coated with cooking spray or oil.

IN the same skillet over medium-high heat, melt butter. Add oysters and sauté until lightly browned, about 5 minutes. Sprinkle with seasonings. Stir in wine and bring to a boil.

ADD oysters and wine to casserole, add pasta, and gently mix. Bake until heated through, about 20 minutes. Sprinkle with parsley.

SERVES 6

223

mediterranean linguini with scallops

The contrasting colors and flavors of this pasta dish make it an appealing and delicious main course combination. A topping of feta cheese adds a tangy flavor.

4   ounces pancetta or bacon, chopped

2   cloves garlic, minced

3   plum tomatoes, chopped, seeded, and drained

1   cup sugar snap peas

1   cup sliced mushrooms

½   cup dry white wine

½   teaspoon salt

Freshly ground pepper to taste

1   pound large scallops, halved

8   ounces linguini, cooked and drained

¾   cup crumbled feta cheese

PREHEAT oven to 350°F. In a medium skillet over medium heat, sauté pancetta until almost cooked, about 3 minutes. Add garlic, tomatoes, peas, and mushrooms and sauté 2 to 3 minutes longer. Stir in wine, salt, and pepper and bring to a boil. Add scallops and stir until scallops are heated through, about 2 minutes.

TRANSFER to a 2½-quart casserole dish lightly coated with cooking spray or oil, add linguini, and stir. Sprinkle with feta cheese.

BAKE, uncovered, until heated through and flavors are blended, about 30 minutes.

SERVES 6

sea shell casserole

Shell pasta is a natural choice for pasta cooked in a seafood casserole. The shape captures the creamy sauce and blends with the other ingredients. Include a crisp green salad with a vinaigrette dressing.

8 ounces light cream cheese, cut into cubes

½ cup light sour cream

½ cup low-fat cottage cheese

1 tablespoon vegetable oil

½ cup green onions, including some tender green tops, sliced

8 ounces mushrooms, sliced

¼ teaspoon salt

Freshly ground pepper to taste

4 ounces small shrimp

4 ounces crabmeat, flaked

8 ounces (about 2 cups) large shell pasta, cooked and drained

1 large tomato, seeded, sliced, and drained

2 tablespoons chopped fresh parsley

PREHEAT oven to 375°F. In food processor or blender, blend cream cheese, sour cream, and cottage cheese. Set aside.

IN a medium skillet over medium heat, warm oil. Add onions and mushrooms and sauté until tender, about 5 minutes. Season with salt and pepper.

TRANSFER to a 2½-quart casserole dish lightly coated with cooking spray or oil. Add cheese mixture, seafood, and pasta and mix well. Arrange tomato slices on top.

BAKE, uncovered, until bubbly, 35 to 40 minutes. Sprinkle with parsley before serving.

SERVES 4 TO 6

226

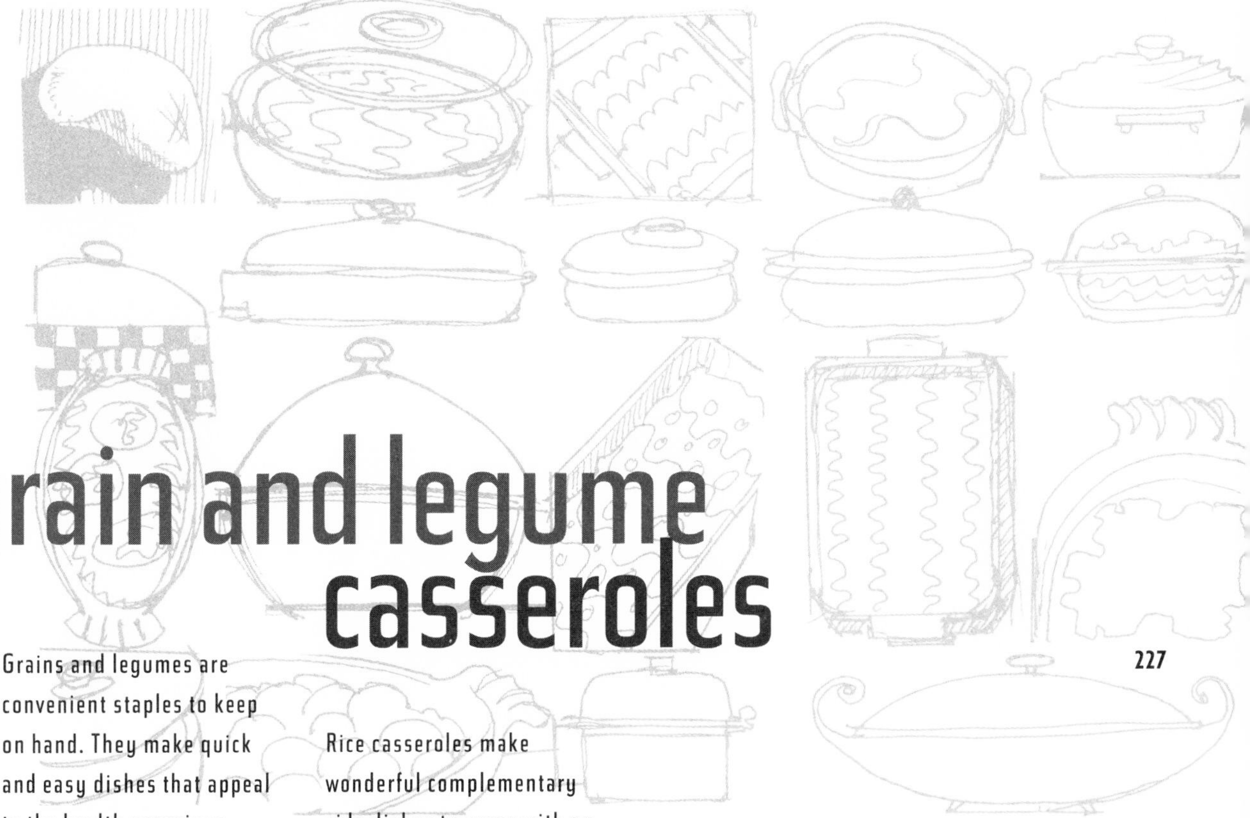

grain and legume casseroles

Grains and legumes are convenient staples to keep on hand. They make quick and easy dishes that appeal to the health conscious. With the introduction of some new grains and a renewed interest in some of the old standbys, grains are returning to the spotlight.

Rice is classified as short grain, long grain, and fragrant grain. White rice is milled to remove the husk and bran. Brown rice has the husk removed but not the bran. Converted rice has been boiled in its husk and is more nutritious.

Rice casseroles make wonderful complementary side dishes to serve with an entrée. The neutral flavor of rice makes a base for other ingredients and adds stability to the dish.

Legumes are dried beans, peas, lentils, and soybeans. They are rich in nutrients, especially protein, and are often served as a meat substitute. They are filling, satisfying, and economical.

polenta lasagna

Lasagna doesn't always have to be made with noodles. Here, homemade polenta slices are arranged in layers with a tomato-mushroom sauce, spinach, pesto, and ricotta cheese, and the dish is topped with mozzarella. Make the polenta several hours or a day ahead to allow it to firm up before assembling.

Basic Polenta (page 19), turned into a rectangular dish and chilled

2 teaspoons vegetable oil

½ cup chopped yellow onion

2 cloves garlic, minced

4 ounces small mushrooms, sliced

1 can (15 ounces) crushed tomatoes in thick purée

1 teaspoon salt

Freshly ground pepper to taste

1 package (10 ounces) frozen spinach, thawed and squeezed dry

¼ cup Basil Pesto (page 18) or commercially prepared pesto

1 cup ricotta or cottage cheese

1 cup grated mozzarella cheese

3 tablespoons freshly grated Parmesan cheese

MAKE Basic Polenta.

IN a saucepan over medium heat, warm oil. Add onion, garlic, and mushrooms and sauté until tender, about 5 minutes. Stir in tomatoes, ½ teaspoon of the salt, and pepper and simmer, uncovered, 5 minutes. Set aside.

IN a small bowl, mix spinach, pesto, ricotta cheese, and remaining salt.

PREHEAT oven to 350°F. When polenta is firm, remove from dish, place on a smooth surface, and cut into ½-inch slices. Arrange a layer of polenta slices in a 7½-by-11¾-inch baking dish lightly coated with cooking spray or oil. (Trim slices to fit; there may be some left over.) With a spoon, spread half of the spinach mixture over polenta slices. In layers, cover with half of the sauce, and then half of the mozzarella cheese. Repeat the layers, beginning with polenta slices. Sprinkle with Parmesan cheese.

BAKE, uncovered, until bubbly, about 45 minutes. Let stand 10 minutes before serving. Cut into squares to serve.

SERVES 6

creamy polenta with sautéed vegetables

Here, Basic Polenta (page 19) is made creamier by adding ricotta cheese then topping it with cooked vegetables and herbs.

VEGETABLE SAUTÉ

1	tablespoon vegetable oil
½	cup chopped yellow onion
½	cup chopped red bell pepper
1	small zucchini, unpeeled, cut into ⅜-inch slices
1	clove garlic, minced
8	ounces (8 to 10) mushrooms, quartered
2	tablespoons dry white wine
½	cup chopped tomatoes, drained
2	tablespoons chopped fresh parsley
3	fresh basil leaves, slivered (see page 9), or ¾ teaspoon dried basil
¼	teaspoon salt

Freshly ground pepper to taste

Basic Polenta (page 19), freshly made

½	cup ricotta cheese
3	tablespoons freshly grated Parmesan cheese

PREHEAT oven to 350°F. Make the vegetable sauté: In a medium skillet over medium heat, warm oil. Sauté onion and bell pepper, 2 minutes. Add remaining vegetables, except tomatoes, and sauté until vegetables are tender-crisp, about 10 minutes longer. Add wine, tomatoes, parsley, and basil. Season with salt and pepper and simmer several minutes to reduce wine and blend flavors. Set aside.

IN a large bowl, mix Basic Polenta and ricotta cheese. Turn into a 10-inch deep-dish pie plate lightly coated with cooking spray or oil. Pour Vegetable Sauté over polenta and sprinkle with Parmesan cheese.

BAKE, uncovered, until bubbly, about 30 minutes.

SERVES 6

229

california casserole

Serve this delicious side dish of rice, chiles, vegetables, and cheese to accompany a marinated pork roast and corn on the cob for your next backyard gathering (or any time of the year). Prepare in advance for relaxed entertaining.

2 cups Rich Chicken Stock (page 23), canned low-sodium chicken broth, or water

¾ cup long-grain white rice

2 cups light sour cream

2 cans (4 ounces each) diced green chiles, drained

½ cup sliced green onions, including some tender green tops

1 teaspoon dried oregano

½ teaspoon salt

Freshly ground pepper to taste

2 tablespoons chopped fresh parsley

2 large zucchini, unpeeled, cut into ¼-inch slices

3 tomatoes, seeded, sliced, and drained

4 cups (about 1 pound) grated Monterey Jack cheese

PREHEAT oven to 350°F. In a medium saucepan over high heat, bring stock to a boil. Add rice, reduce heat to low, and cook, covered, until liquid is absorbed, about 20 minutes. Set aside.

IN a medium bowl, mix sour cream, chiles, onions, oregano, salt, pepper, and parsley.

IN a 4-quart casserole dish lightly coated with cooking spray or oil, add half of each of the following in layers: rice, sour cream mixture, zucchini, tomatoes, and cheese. Repeat the layers, ending with cheese.

BAKE, uncovered, until bubbly, 45 to 50 minutes. Let stand 5 minutes before serving.

SERVES 6

famous spinach-rice casserole

I am repeating this special recipe from one of my other cookbooks because it is so good and definitely belongs in a casserole book. It is a family favorite to serve with whole salmon or turkey.

Famous Spinach-Rice Casserole was adapted from a dish served at Lupos, an old San Francisco restaurant no longer in operation. I think it will become one of your favorites, too.

3   large eggs

⅔   cup milk

2   tablespoons butter or margarine, melted

½   cup finely chopped yellow onion

2   tablespoons chopped fresh parsley

1   teaspoon dried thyme

Dash of ground nutmeg

1   teaspoon salt

¼   teaspoon Worcestershire sauce

3   cups cooked long-grain white or brown rice

3   cups grated cheddar cheese

2   packages (10 ounces each) frozen chopped spinach, thawed and squeezed dry

PREHEAT oven to 350°F. In a large bowl, using a whisk, beat eggs until blended. Add milk, butter, onion, parsley, thyme, nutmeg, salt, and Worcestershire sauce and mix well. Fold in rice, 2 cups of the cheese, and spinach. Turn the mixture into a 4-quart casserole dish or baking dish lightly coated with cooking spray or oil.

BAKE, uncovered, until bubbly, about 45 minutes. Sprinkle remaining 1 cup cheese evenly over top and bake, uncovered, until cheese melts, about 5 minutes longer.

SERVES 8

nice rice with cashews

This makes a large quantity and is a wonderful complementary dish to serve with most meats and seafood. The cashews add a pleasant nutty flavor and extra crunch.

½ cup (1 stick) butter or margarine

12 ounces mushrooms, sliced

6 green onions, including some tender green tops, sliced

2 large cloves garlic, minced

2 cups brown rice

½ teaspoon dried thyme

1 teaspoon salt

Freshly ground pepper to taste

1½ cups coarsely chopped cashews

6 cups Rich Chicken Stock (page 23) or canned low-sodium chicken broth

¼ cup chopped fresh parsley

Whole cashews for garnish

PREHEAT oven to 400°F. In a Dutch oven, melt butter over medium heat. Add mushrooms, onions, and garlic and sauté until tender, about 5 minutes. Add rice and stir about 1 minute. Add seasonings and chopped cashews and stir. Add stock, stir, and bring to a boil.

COVER and bake until rice is tender and liquid is absorbed, about 1¼ hours. Transfer to a large decorative serving dish if desired. Sprinkle with parsley and garnish with whole cashews.

SERVES 10 TO 12

artichoke-rice casserole

Tender, meaty artichoke hearts add variety and flavor to this easy-to-make casserole. Serve as a side dish with chicken or turkey.

2 tablespoons butter or margarine

1 cup chopped yellow onion

1 clove garlic, minced

1 cup long-grain white rice

2 cups Rich Chicken Stock (page 23) or canned low-sodium chicken broth

2 tablespoons dry white wine

¼ teaspoon dried basil

Salt and freshly ground pepper to taste

1 can (14½ ounces) artichoke hearts, drained

¼ cup freshly grated Parmesan cheese

PREHEAT oven to 350°F. In a medium skillet, melt butter over medium heat and sauté onion and garlic until tender, about 5 minutes. Add rice and stir to coat. Add stock, wine, basil, salt, and pepper. Stir, and bring to a boil. Transfer to a 2½-quart casserole dish lightly coated with cooking spray or oil.

STIR in artichokes, cover, and bake until liquid is absorbed, about 45 minutes. Remove lid, fluff with a fork, and sprinkle with Parmesan cheese. Bake until cheese melts, about 5 minutes longer.

SERVES 4 TO 6   **233**

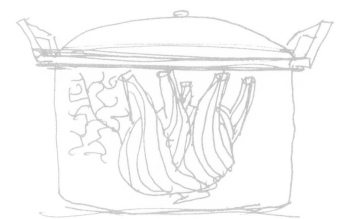

rice verde

Serve this fresh-tasting, green-flecked rice as an accompaniment to Salmon and Peas (page 48) or other seafood. Other combinations of greens can be used with this basic rice recipe.

4 parsley sprigs

6 fresh basil leaves, torn

6 green onions, including some tender green tops, sliced

2 cups firmly packed fresh spinach leaves, stems removed

2¼ cups Rich Chicken Stock (page 23), canned low-sodium chicken broth, or water

½ teaspoon salt

Freshly ground pepper to taste

1 cup long-grain white rice

1 to 2 tablespoons butter or margarine

PREHEAT oven to 350°F. Place parsley, basil, onions, and spinach in a food processor and process until chunky.

IN a medium saucepan over high heat, bring stock, salt, pepper, and rice to a boil. Add greens mixture and mix well. Transfer to a 2½-quart casserole dish lightly coated with cooking spray or oil.

COVER and bake until liquid is absorbed, 45 to 50 minutes. Stir in butter.

SERVES 4 TO 6

beer rice

Beer and peanuts give flavor and crunch to this dish—besides, it makes for good conversation. Serve with burgers or hot dogs and chips.

1 cup brown rice

1 cup beer, allowed to go flat

1¼ cups Rich Chicken Stock (page 23) or canned low-sodium chicken broth

1 tablespoon butter or margarine

¼ cup salted peanuts, coarsely chopped

½ teaspoon salt

Freshly ground pepper to taste

PREHEAT oven to 350°F. Place all ingredients in a 2½-quart casserole dish lightly coated with cooking spray or oil. Cover and bake until liquid is absorbed, about 1¼ hours.

SERVES 4

235

curried rice

Curry powder is a blend of spices used to flavor chicken, lamb, and rice in Indian dishes. In this recipe, apples and raisins are included for extra texture and flavor.

1 cup long-grain white rice

2 cups Rich Chicken Stock (page 23) or canned low-sodium chicken broth

1 teaspoon curry powder, or more to taste

¼ teaspoon salt

1 apple, unpeeled, diced

¼ cup golden raisins (optional)

PREHEAT oven to 350°F. In a 2½-quart casserole dish lightly coated with cooking spray or oil, stir together rice, stock, curry powder, and salt.

COVER and bake until liquid is absorbed, about 45 minutes. Stir in apple and raisins and bake, uncovered, 10 minutes longer.

SERVES 4 TO 6

salsa rice

This simple combination of rice and salsa makes a lively side dish to serve with Mexican food.

2 cups Rich Chicken Stock (page 23) or canned low-sodium chicken broth

1 cup long-grain white rice

1 cup commercially prepared salsa

1 small tomato, seeded, chopped, and drained

3 tablespoons chopped fresh cilantro or parsley

PREHEAT oven to 350°F. In a medium saucepan over medium heat, bring stock to a boil. Stir in rice, salsa, and tomato. Transfer to a 2½-quart casserole dish lightly coated with cooking spray or oil.

COVER and bake until liquid is absorbed, about 45 minutes. Sprinkle with cilantro or parsley.

SERVES 4

sesame rice

I like to serve this side dish with a teriyaki steak or beef kabobs for a summer patio barbecue. Round out the meal with corn on the cob, a loaf of warm garlic bread, and homemade ice cream.

3 tablespoons sesame seeds

3 tablespoons butter or margarine

½ cup sliced celery

¼ cup chopped yellow onion

1 clove garlic, minced

1 cup long-grain white rice

2 cups Beef Stock (page 22) or canned beef broth

2 tablespoons soy sauce

PREHEAT oven to 350°F. Put sesame seeds in a medium nonstick skillet over medium heat. Stir until toasted, about 2 minutes. Transfer to a small bowl and set aside.

IN the same skillet over medium heat, melt butter. Add celery, onion, and garlic and sauté until tender, about 5 minutes. Add rice and stir to coat. Stir in stock and soy sauce and bring to a boil. Transfer to a 2½-quart casserole dish lightly coated with cooking spray or oil.

COVER and bake until liquid is absorbed and rice is tender, about 45 minutes. Stir in sesame seeds.

SERVES 4

238

baked risotto

Risotto is a creamy, delectable Italian rice dish that calls for a short-grain rice such as arborio. It is made by gradually stirring hot broth, half a cup at a time, into the rice and stirring constantly. In this recipe, part of this labor-intensive procedure is reduced by baking the rice in the oven, with the same good results. Other ingredients, such as cooked chicken, vegetables, or shellfish can be included.

2½ cups Rich Chicken Stock (page 23) or canned low-sodium chicken broth

1½ tablespoons butter or margarine

1 cup chopped yellow onion

½ cup chopped red bell pepper

1 clove garlic, minced

¾ cup arborio rice

¼ teaspoon salt

Freshly ground pepper to taste

1 tablespoon dry white wine (optional)

⅓ cup chopped fresh parsley

¼ cup freshly grated Parmesan cheese

PREHEAT oven to 350°F. In a medium saucepan over medium heat, warm stock.

IN another medium saucepan over medium heat, melt butter. Add onion, red bell pepper, and garlic and sauté until tender, about 5 minutes. Add rice, salt, pepper, and wine and stir to coat. Add ½ cup hot stock and stir continuously until liquid is absorbed, about 5 minutes. Add all the remaining broth at once, stir and bring to a boil. Transfer rice mixture and broth to a 2½-quart casserole dish lightly coated with cooking spray or oil.

COVER and bake until all broth is absorbed, about 50 minutes, stirring several times. Stir in parsley. Sprinkle with Parmesan cheese and cook, uncovered, until rice is tender and creamy and cheese is melted, about 10 minutes longer.

SERVES 4 TO 6

spicy peach pilaf
This sweet, spicy rice dish complements chicken, pork, or lamb. If fresh peaches are not in season, use canned drained peaches.

2 cups Rich Chicken Stock (page 23) or canned low-sodium chicken broth

½ teaspoon salt

1 cup long-grain white rice

¼ teaspoon ground cinnamon

¼ teaspoon ground ginger

¼ teaspoon ground nutmeg

⅛ teaspoon ground cloves

1 tablespoon honey

2 tablespoons butter or margarine

2 large peaches, peeled (see page 9), pitted, and cut into bite-size pieces

¼ cup toasted slivered almonds (see page 11)

PREHEAT oven to 350°F. In a medium saucepan, bring stock and salt to a boil. Add rice and return to a boil. Transfer to a 2½-quart casserole dish lightly coated with cooking spray or oil. Add spices, honey, butter, peaches, and nuts and mix well.

COVER and bake until rice is tender and liquid is absorbed, about 45 minutes.

SERVES 6

240

asian rice

Fresh sugar snap peas and red bell pepper add color and flavor to this dish. Serve with a marinated flank steak.

2 teaspoons vegetable oil

½ cup chopped green onions, including some tender green tops

½ cup chopped red bell pepper

¾ cup chopped celery

1 cup long-grain white rice

2 cups Rich Chicken Stock (page 23) or canned low-sodium chicken broth

¼ teaspoon salt

Freshly ground pepper to taste

3 tablespoons soy sauce, or more to taste

1 cup sugar snap peas, trimmed

¼ cup toasted slivered almonds (see page 11)

PREHEAT oven to 350°F. In a medium saucepan over medium heat, warm oil. Sauté onions, bell pepper, and celery until tender, about 5 minutes. Stir in rice. Add stock, seasonings, and soy sauce and bring to a boil.

TRANSFER mixture to a 2½-quart casserole dish lightly coated with cooking spray or oil. Cover and bake 40 minutes. Stir in peas and almonds and cook, covered, until rice is tender and liquid is absorbed, about 10 minutes longer.

SERVES 6

brown and white rice—hazelnut pilaf

Brown rice is the entire rice grain with only the outer husk removed. It has a nutlike flavor, a chewy texture, and is highly nutritious. When paired with white rice and spiked with hazelnuts, it makes an interesting combination.

1 tablespoon butter or margarine

½ cup chopped yellow onion

¼ cup chopped toasted hazelnuts (see page 11)

1 cup brown rice

½ cup long-grain white rice

3 cups Rich Chicken Stock (page 23) or canned low-sodium chicken broth

1 teaspoon Worcestershire sauce

2 drops Tabasco sauce

¼ teaspoon salt

Freshly ground pepper to taste

¼ cup chopped fresh parsley

PREHEAT oven to 350°F. In a medium skillet over medium heat, melt butter. Add onion and sauté until soft, about 5 minutes. Add nuts and sauté 2 minutes longer. Stir in rices and mix well to coat. Add remaining ingredients, stir, and bring to a boil.

TRANSFER to a 2½-quart casserole dish lightly coated with cooking spray or oil. Bake, covered, until all liquid is absorbed, about 1 hour and 10 minutes.

SERVES 6

barley-rice pilaf

There are several kinds of this hearty grain, but the most common is pearl barley. It should be washed and drained thoroughly. With its mixture of barley and brown rice, this dish appeals to the health conscious.

2 tablespoons butter or margarine

¼ cup chopped almonds

1 yellow onion, chopped

1 clove garlic, minced

⅔ cup brown rice

⅓ cup pearl barley, rinsed well and drained

2¼ cups Rich Chicken Stock (page 23), Vegetable Stock (page 24) or canned low-sodium chicken or vegetable broth

¼ cup dry white wine

¼ teaspoon dried basil

¼ teaspoon dried oregano

¼ teaspoon salt

Freshly ground pepper to taste

¼ cup chopped fresh parsley

PREHEAT oven to 350°F. In a medium skillet over medium heat, melt butter. Add almonds and stir until lightly browned, about 2 minutes. Add onion and garlic and sauté until tender, about 5 minutes. Stir in rice and barley. Add stock, wine, seasonings, and parsley. Stir and bring to a boil.

TRANSFER to a 2½-quart casserole dish lightly coated with cooking spray or oil. Cover and bake until rice and barley are tender and liquid is absorbed, about 1 hour and 15 minutes.

243

SERVES 4

golden pilaf

Pasta and rice together make an interesting combination in this easy-to-prepare dish. Serve with grilled pork chops or other meats.

3 tablespoons butter or margarine

½ cup broken (in about ½-inch lengths) vermicelli

1 cup long-grain white rice

2 cups Rich Chicken Stock (page 23) or canned low-sodium chicken broth

PREHEAT oven to 350°F. In a medium saucepan over medium heat, melt butter. Add vermicelli and sauté until golden, about 4 minutes. Add rice and stir until kernels are coated, about 1 minute. Add stock and bring to a boil.

TRANSFER to a 2½-quart casserole dish lightly coated with cooking spray or oil. Cover and bake until liquid is absorbed and rice and pasta are tender, 40 to 45 minutes.

SERVES 6

barley-zucchini pilaf
Barley is paired with zucchini and carrots for a vegetable-and-starch side dish. Rinse barley several times under cold water before using.

2 teaspoons vegetable oil

½ cup chopped yellow onion

1 clove garlic, minced

2½ cups Rich Chicken Stock (page 23), canned low-sodium chicken broth, or water

1 teaspoon dried thyme

½ teaspoon salt

Freshly ground pepper to taste

1 cup pearl barley, rinsed well and drained

1 carrot, peeled and grated

2 zucchini, unpeeled, grated, and blotted dry with a paper towel

¼ cup chopped fresh parsley

PREHEAT oven to 350°F. In a medium skillet over medium heat, warm oil. Add onion and garlic and sauté until tender, about 5 minutes. Add stock, thyme, salt, pepper, and barley. Stir and bring to a boil.

TRANSFER barley mixture to a 2½-quart casserole dish lightly coated with cooking spray or oil. Stir in carrots.

COVER and bake 40 minutes. Stir in zucchini and parsley. Cover and bake until liquid is absorbed and zucchini is tender, 25 to 30 minutes longer.

SERVES 4

bulgur pilaf

Bulgur, sometimes called cracked wheat, is a nutritional staple in the Middle East. It has a tender, chewy texture and is wonderful in pilafs or salads.

1   tablespoon butter or margarine

4   green onions, including some tender green tops, sliced; or 2 shallots, chopped

1   cup bulgur

2   cups Rich Chicken Stock (page 23) or canned low-sodium chicken broth

½   teaspoon salt

Freshly ground pepper to taste

¼   cup sliced pimiento-stuffed green olives

2   tablespoons chopped fresh parsley

PREHEAT oven to 350°F. In a medium saucepan over medium heat, melt butter. Sauté onions until tender, about 5 minutes. Stir in bulgur. Add stock, salt, pepper, and olives. Stir and bring to a boil. Transfer to a 2½-quart casserole dish lightly coated with cooking spray or oil.

BAKE, covered, until liquid is absorbed, 45 to 50 minutes. Add parsley and fluff with a fork.

SERVES 4 TO 6

spicy baked black beans and toppings

Black beans, also called turtle beans, are popular in Mexico and South America. They are available dried or canned. Serve with Festive Chicken Casserole (page 100). The toppings add variety and flavor.

3   cans (15 ounces each) black beans, rinsed and drained

¼   teaspoon dried oregano

¼   teaspoon ground cumin

¼   teaspoon salt

Freshly ground pepper to taste

¼   cup chopped fresh cilantro or parsley

3   tablespoons Fresh Tomato Salsa (page 17), or commercially prepared salsa

1   tablespoon red wine vinegar

2   tablespoons water

TOPPINGS

2   hard-cooked eggs, chopped

2   tomatoes, seeded, diced, and drained

6   green onions, including some tender green tops, chopped

Light sour cream

Grated cheddar cheese

2   avocados, peeled and cubed

PREHEAT oven to 350°F. Mix all ingredients in a large bowl and place in a 2½-quart casserole lightly coated with cooking spray or oil.

COVER and bake until heated through, about 30 minutes. Serve with toppings.

SERVES 6

easy baked beans

This old standby casserole of assorted canned beans is popular for summer barbecues. Other beans such as lima, garbanzo, or butter beans may be substituted for kidney and black beans.

1   small yellow onion, chopped

1   clove garlic, minced

2   cans (16 ounces each) pork and beans, including sauce

1   can (15¼ ounces) kidney beans, rinsed and drained

1   can (15 ounces) black beans, rinsed and drained

2   tablespoons brown sugar

1   teaspoon Worcestershire sauce

½   cup catsup

2   teaspoons commercially prepared yellow mustard

½   teaspoon salt

½   teaspoon chili powder

1   tablespoon cider vinegar

¼   teaspoon freshly ground pepper

PREHEAT oven to 350°F. Stir together all ingredients in a 3- or 4-quart casserole dish lightly coated with cooking spray or oil.

COVER and bake 30 minutes. Uncover and bake until bubbly, 30 to 40 minutes longer.

SERVES 8 TO 10

black bean chili bake

Dried beans may be used, but for convenience and quick preparation, canned black beans are perfect.

1 tablespoon vegetable oil

1 cup chopped yellow onion

3 cloves garlic, minced

½ cup chopped green bell pepper

3 cans (15 ounces each) black beans, rinsed and drained; or 2 cups dried beans, soaked and cooked (see page 10)

1 can (14½ ounces) whole tomatoes, chopped, juice from can included

1 can (8 ounces) tomato sauce

1 cup beer, allowed to go flat

1 jalapeño chile pepper, seeded and diced; or 2 tablespoons canned diced green chiles

1 tablespoon chili powder

½ teaspoon dried oregano

½ teaspoon ground cumin

½ teaspoon salt

Freshly ground pepper to taste

TOPPINGS

Light sour cream or yogurt

Grated cheddar or Monterey Jack cheese

Chopped onions

Lime wedges for garnish

PREHEAT oven to 350°F. In a Dutch oven over medium heat, warm oil. Add onion, garlic, and bell pepper and sauté until tender, about 5 minutes. Add beans, tomatoes, tomato sauce, beer, chile, and seasonings and mix well.

COVER and bake until flavors are blended, at least 1 hour, stirring once.

SERVES 6

249

THE BIG BOOK OF CASSEROLES

border beans

A variety of beans are combined for this savory side dish, ideal for a barbecue or picnic. Bacon or ham is added for extra flavor, but it is optional.

1 can (15 ounces) garbanzo beans, rinsed and drained

1 can (15 ounces) pinto beans, rinsed and drained

1 can (15 ounces) kidney beans, rinsed and drained

1 cup chopped yellow onion

5 or 6 slices bacon, cooked and crumbled; or 1 cup cubed, cooked ham (optional)

1 can (4 ounces) diced green chilies

¾ cup beer, allowed to go flat

¼ cup catsup

¼ cup chili sauce

¼ cup molasses

1 teaspoon chili powder

PREHEAT oven to 350°F. In a 2½-quart casserole dish or bean pot lightly coated with cooking spray or oil, combine all ingredients and mix well.

BAKE, uncovered, stirring occasionally until flavors have blended and desired consistency is reached, about 1½ hours.

SERVES 8

fiesta casserole

Credit for this filling casserole goes to my daughter, Julie, who came up with this vegetarian dish to feed her three hungry teenagers. In fact, it is so easy to prepare, they all can make it.

1 tablespoon vegetable oil

1 yellow onion, chopped

2 large eggs, beaten

1 cup low-fat cottage cheese

1 can (4 ounces) diced green chiles, drained

2 tablespoons chopped fresh cilantro or parsley (kids prefer parsley)

¼ teaspoon ground cumin

¼ teaspoon salt

Freshly ground pepper to taste

1 package (12) corn tortillas, cut into ⅜-inch strips

1 can (16 ounces) refried beans

3 medium tomatoes, seeded, sliced, and drained

2 cups grated Monterey Jack cheese

2 cups grated cheddar cheese

TOPPINGS

Chopped pitted black olives

Sliced green onions

Light sour cream

PREHEAT oven to 350°F. In a small skillet over medium heat, warm oil. Add onion and sauté until tender, about 5 minutes. Set aside.

IN a medium bowl, combine eggs, cottage cheese, chiles, cilantro, seasonings, and cooked onion.

IN a 9-by-13-inch baking dish lightly coated with cooking spray or oil, add half of each of the following in layers: the tortillas, cottage cheese mixture, beans, tomatoes, and the combined Monterey Jack and cheddar. Repeat the layers.

BAKE, uncovered, until bubbly, 30 to 40 minutes. Let stand 10 minutes before serving. Pass the toppings.

SERVES 6 TO 8

251

tuscan beans

Here is a short-cut version of the classic Italian bean dish. Serve with a mixed green salad with Italian dressing.

½ cup diced pancetta, or
4 strips bacon, coarsely
chopped

1 teaspoon olive oil
(optional)

½ cup chopped yellow onion

1 clove garlic, minced

2 cans (15 ounces each)
cannellini (white kidney
beans), rinsed and drained

1 can (15 ounces) ready-cut,
peeled tomatoes, juice from
can included

1 teaspoon dried sage

¼ teaspoon salt

Freshly ground pepper to taste

2 teaspoons balsamic vinegar
or red wine vinegar

2 tablespoons chopped fresh
parsley

Freshly grated Parmesan
cheese for sprinkling on top

PREHEAT oven to 350°F. In a small skillet over medium heat, cook pancetta 4 minutes. Add oil if needed (bacon will not need oil). Add onion and garlic and sauté until vegetables are tender and pancetta is crisp, about 5 minutes longer. Set aside.

IN a 2½-quart casserole dish lightly coated with cooking spray or oil, add beans, tomatoes, seasonings, and pancetta-onion mixture and mix well.

BAKE, uncovered, until bubbly, about 35 minutes. Stir in vinegar and sprinkle with parsley and Parmesan cheese before serving.

SERVES 4

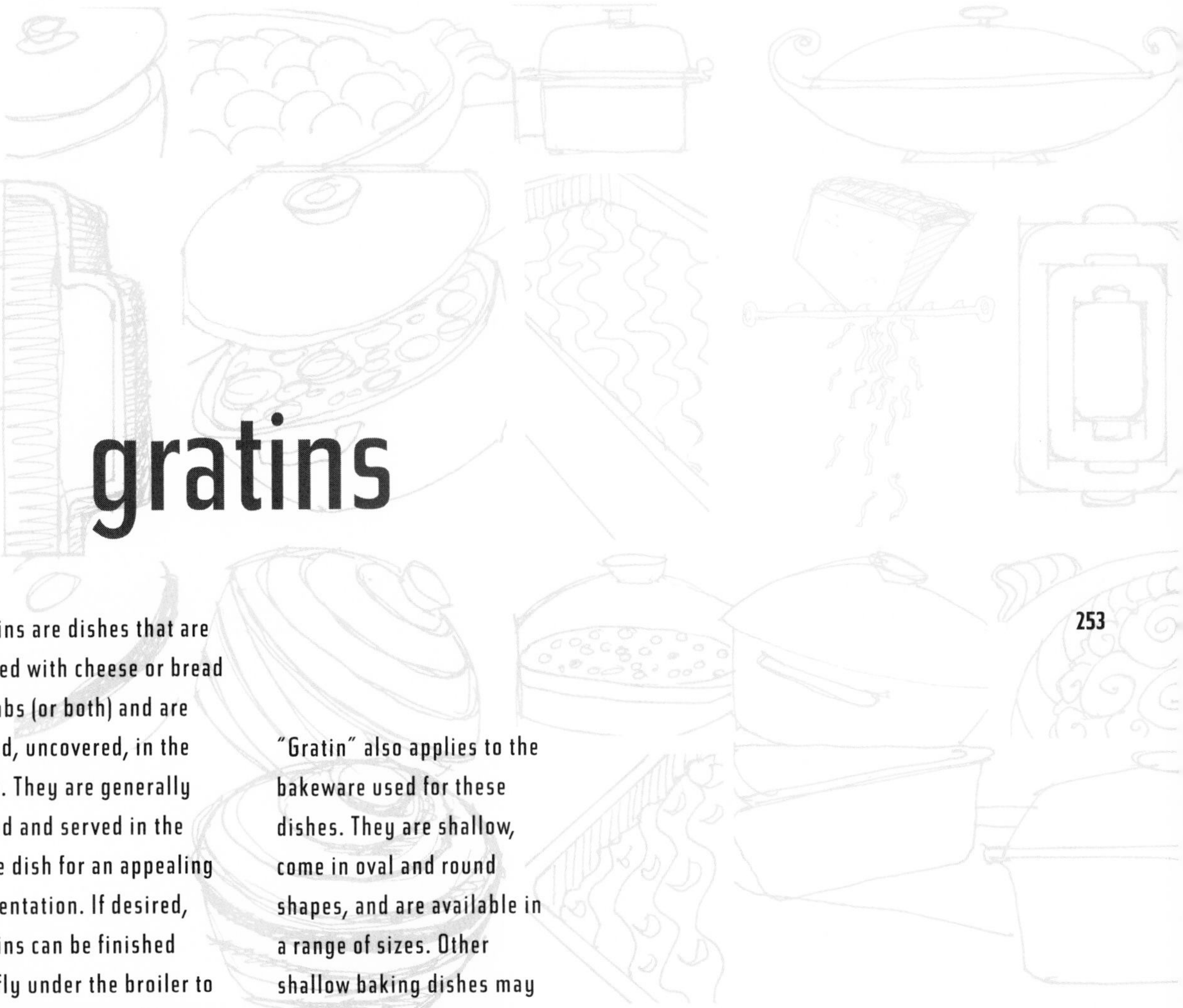

gratins

Gratins are dishes that are topped with cheese or bread crumbs (or both) and are baked, uncovered, in the oven. They are generally baked and served in the same dish for an appealing presentation. If desired, gratins can be finished briefly under the broiler to achieve a crispy-golden top.

"Gratin" also applies to the bakeware used for these dishes. They are shallow, come in oval and round shapes, and are available in a range of sizes. Other shallow baking dishes may also be used. Individual gratin dishes are popular for serving company dinners.

chicken breasts, prosciutto, and asparagus

Chicken breasts are baked in individual gratin dishes and topped with prosciutto, fresh asparagus, and cheese for a delightful spring entrée. Serve a rhubarb crisp for dessert.

1 tablespoon butter or margarine

1 tablespoon vegetable oil

4 skinned and boned chicken breast halves

Salt and freshly ground pepper to taste

12 asparagus spears, tough ends removed

4 thin slices prosciutto

1 cup grated Monterey Jack cheese

PREHEAT oven to 375°F. In a large skillet over medium heat, melt butter with oil. Brown chicken about 5 minutes on each side. Season with salt and pepper on both sides.

IN a wide skillet over medium heat, add asparagus and water to cover. Cook, uncovered, until tender-crisp, about 5 minutes. Drain under cold water.

TRANSFER chicken to 4 individual 4-by-6-inch gratin dishes lightly coated with cooking spray or oil. Lay prosciutto on top of each chicken breast. Place 3 asparagus spears on top of prosciutto. Sprinkle with cheese.

BAKE, uncovered, until heated through and bubbly, about 30 minutes.

SERVES 4

tarragon chicken breasts and mushrooms

Each guest has his own individual entrée in this delicious company gratin. Serve with sweet, fresh corn kernels seasoned with fresh basil and for dessert, a chocolate mousse.

2   tablespoons butter or margarine

1   tablespoon vegetable oil

6   skinned and boned chicken breast halves

Salt and freshly ground pepper to taste

½   teaspoon dried tarragon

¼   cup finely chopped yellow onion

8   ounces mushrooms, sliced

1   clove garlic, minced

1   tablespoon tomato paste

1   tablespoon all-purpose flour

1   cup Rich Chicken Stock (page 23) or canned low-sodium chicken broth

2   tablespoons dry white wine

½   cup light sour cream

¼   cup slivered almonds

PREHEAT oven to 350°F. In a large skillet over medium heat, melt 1 tablespoon of the butter with oil. Brown chicken breasts about 5 minutes on each side. Season both sides with salt, pepper, and tarragon. Transfer to 6 individual 4-by-6-inch gratin dishes lightly coated with cooking spray or oil.

ADD remaining butter to skillet over medium heat and sauté onion, mushrooms, and garlic until tender, about 5 minutes. Add tomato paste and flour and stir to blend. Add stock and wine and stir until thickened, about 2 minutes. Add sour cream and stir until smooth. Pour equally over chicken breasts. Sprinkle with nuts.

BAKE, uncovered, until bubbly and chicken is no longer pink in the center, about 30 minutes.

SERVES 6

layered turkey and broccoli gratin
A good "after the holidays" dish made with a simple cheese sauce in place of condensed soup for improved flavor and taste.

2   tablespoons butter or margarine

2   tablespoons all-purpose flour

1   teaspoon salt

⅛   teaspoon white pepper

1½ cups milk

1   cup grated Swiss cheese

2   cups chopped cooked broccoli

2   cups cubed cooked turkey

1   cup dry bread crumbs (see page 5)

2   tablespoons freshly grated Parmesan cheese

PREHEAT oven to 350°F. In a medium saucepan over medium heat, melt butter. Add flour, salt, and pepper and stir until bubbly. Add milk and stir until thickened, about 2 minutes. Add Swiss cheese and stir until cheese melts and sauce is smooth.

IN an 8-by-8-inch baking dish or gratin dish lightly coated with cooking spray or oil, layer half of the broccoli and then half of the turkey. Repeat the layers and pour sauce over all. Sprinkle with bread crumbs and Parmesan cheese.

BAKE, uncovered, until bubbly, about 25 minutes.

SERVES 6

oysters gratin

My husband, Reed, gives this recipe four stars. We discovered this dish years ago in a small San Francisco restaurant. The restaurant baked the oysters in a large brick oven, but your home oven or covered grill will work just fine. Even if you aren't an oyster fan, this dish is so good, you just might become a convert! Serve with slices of sourdough bread for dipping in the sauce. This recipe appeared in one of my earlier books, but it is worth repeating.

1   pound extra small or small shucked oysters (or larger ones, cut in half), drained

¾   teaspoon dried oregano

1   teaspoon dried basil

½   teaspoon salt

¼   teaspoon pepper

1   teaspoon minced garlic

2   tablespoons fresh lemon juice

1   tablespoon chopped fresh parsley

6   tablespoons butter or margarine, melted

⅓   cup dry bread crumbs (see page 5) or finely crushed saltines

Sourdough bread slices for dipping

PREHEAT oven to 450°F. Place oysters in a strainer and rinse under cold running water. Drain well.

DIVIDE oysters equally among 6 individual 4-by-4-by-6-inch gratin dishes. Sprinkle herbs, salt, pepper, garlic, lemon juice, and parsley evenly over the tops, then drizzle with butter. Add a light layer of crumbs.

BAKE until bubbly, 10 to 12 minutes.

SERVES 6 AS A FIRST COURSE

seafood gratin

Another four-star recipe, according to Reed. This outstanding dish is made with a combination of fresh seafoods, topped with Hollandaise Sauce (recipe follows). It is rich and expensive, but perfect for a special occasion. Serve with a salad of greens, pears, and walnuts with a raspberry vinaigrette dressing.

6   small sole fillets (about 4 ounces each)

12   ounces scallops, cut in half if large

12   ounces cooked small shrimp

8   ounces cooked Dungeness crabmeat, flaked

1½   cups grated Monterey Jack cheese

2   cups Hollandaise Sauce (recipe follows)

1   cup (about 10) finely crushed saltine crackers, for topping

Paprika for sprinkling on top

Chopped fresh parsley for garnish

PREHEAT oven to 425°F. Lightly coat with cooking spray or oil 6 individual 4-by-6-inch gratin dishes. Arrange a sole fillet on the bottom of each dish. In layers, top each fillet with equal amounts of scallops, shrimp, and crabmeat. Top each dish with ¼ cup cheese and cover with about ⅓ cup Hollandaise Sauce. Sprinkle with a light coating of cracker crumbs and then with paprika.

BAKE, uncovered, until bubbly and tops are lightly browned, 10 to 15 minutes. Watch carefully, as they will burn easily. Sprinkle with parsley and serve.

SERVES 6

hollandaise sauce

Hollandaise is also good on asparagus and broccoli, and it's essential for Eggs Benedict. The sauce must be made in the quantity specified to turn out successfully. Do not try to double the recipe. Using a blender instead of a food processor results in a thicker, smoother sauce.

3 large egg yolks

2 tablespoons fresh lemon juice

Dash of cayenne pepper

¼ teaspoon salt

½ cup (1 stick) butter, melted but not browned

IN a blender, combine egg yolks, lemon juice, cayenne, and salt. Blend at high speed for 3 seconds. With motor still on high, pour in melted butter in a slow, steady stream, continuing to blend until sauce is thick and fluffy, about 30 seconds.

TO keep sauce warm, place in a bowl over a pan of hot water over low heat. Whisk before using.

MAKES 1 CUP

scallops with mushrooms gratin

Scallops and mushrooms pair well in this impressive first-course gratin dish.

1¼ pounds large scallops (cut in half if very large), rinsed and drained

Juice of 1 lemon

1¼ cups water

6 tablespoons butter or margarine

¼ cup sliced green onions, including some tender green tops

8 ounces mushrooms, sliced

3 tablespoons all-purpose flour

½ teaspoon dried thyme

½ teaspoon salt

¼ cup dry white wine

1 cup chopped and drained tomatoes

½ cup dry bread crumbs (see page 5)

PREHEAT oven to 350°F. In a medium saucepan over high heat, place scallops, lemon juice, and water. Bring to a boil. Reduce heat and cook, uncovered, until translucent, about 3 minutes. Drain, reserving 1 cup of the liquid. Transfer scallops to a plate.

IN same pan over medium heat, melt 4 tablespoons of the butter. Add onions and mushrooms and sauté until tender, about 5 minutes. Add flour and stir until bubbly. Add liquid from scallops and seasonings and stir until thickened. Stir in wine, scallops, and tomatoes and cook 1 minute.

TRANSFER to 6 individual 4-by-6-inch gratin dishes lightly coated with cooking spray or oil.

IN a small skillet over medium heat, melt 2 remaining tablespoons butter, and stir in bread crumbs. Sprinkle over scallops.

BAKE, uncovered, until bubbly, 15 to 20 minutes.

SERVES 6

crab and shrimp gratin

Delicate crab and small shrimp bathed in a rich mushroom sauce and baked in individual gratin dishes make a great seafood course.

6 tablespoons butter or margarine

8 ounces mushrooms, sliced

3 tablespoons all-purpose flour

1½ cups half-and-half or milk

¼ cup dry white wine

¼ teaspoon salt

¼ teaspoon white pepper

½ teaspoon Worcestershire sauce

12 ounces small shrimp

12 ounces crabmeat, flaked

1½ cups fresh white bread crumbs (see Note, page 181)

1½ cups grated Swiss cheese

Paprika for sprinkling on top

PREHEAT oven to 350°F. In a large saucepan over medium heat, melt 4 tablespoons butter. Add mushrooms and sauté until tender, about 5 minutes. Stir in flour and blend. Add half-and-half and stir until thickened, about 3 minutes. Add wine, salt, pepper, and Worcestershire sauce. Fold in shrimp and crab. Spoon into 8 individual 4-by-6-inch gratin dishes lightly coated with cooking spray or oil.

IN a small skillet over medium heat, melt remaining butter and stir in bread crumbs. Sprinkle evenly on each serving.

BAKE, uncovered, 15 minutes. Add cheese and paprika and bake until bubbly and cheese melts, about 10 minutes longer.

SERVES 8

baked halibut with cashew-crumb topping

Low in fat, firm in texture, and mild in flavor, halibut is always a popular choice. The cashew topping adds extra flavor and crunch. Serve with Rice Verde (page 234).

2 teaspoons vegetable oil

¾ cup dry bread crumbs

2 tablespoons freshly grated Parmesan cheese

3 tablespoons chopped fresh parsley

2 tablespoons chopped cashew nuts

1 tablespoons fresh snipped tarragon; or ½ teaspoon dried tarragon

1 teaspoon grated lemon zest

½ teaspoon paprika

Freshly ground pepper to taste

4 small halibut steaks or fillets (about 1½ to 2 pounds combined weight)

Lemon wedges for garnish

PREHEAT oven to 425°F. In a small bowl, stir together all ingredients except halibut and lemon wedges. Place fish in 4 individual 4-by-6-inch gratin dishes lightly coated with cooking spray or oil. Spread crumb-nut mixture on top of each fish.

BAKE until fish flakes and top is golden, 10 to 12 minutes. Serve with lemon wedges.

SERVES 4

green bean gratin

Enjoy an updated version of the old "Green Bean Supreme" recipe, which called for canned beans and condensed soup and was topped with onion rings or cornflakes. Here, a simple sour cream sauce and fresh beans are used for a much-improved flavor. This makes a complementary side dish to serve with a holiday dinner.

4   tablespoons butter or margarine

2   tablespoons all-purpose flour

1   cup milk

1   teaspoon sugar

½   teaspoon salt

Freshly ground pepper to taste

2   tablespoons finely chopped yellow onion

1   cup light sour cream

2   pounds fresh green beans, trimmed

¼   cup toasted slivered almonds, (see page 11)

2   cups (about ½ pound) grated Swiss cheese

2   cups dry bread crumbs (preferably sourdough; see page 5)

PREHEAT oven to 350°F. In a medium saucepan over medium heat, melt 2 tablespoons of the butter. Add flour and stir until bubbly. Add milk and stir until thickened, about 2 minutes. Add sugar, salt, pepper, and onion. Fold in sour cream and set aside.

IN a medium pan over medium heat, add beans and ½ cup water. Cover and cook until tender-crisp, about 5 minutes. Drain well.

PLACE beans in a 7½-by-11¾-inch baking dish or gratin dish lightly coated with cooking spray or oil. Add sauce and almonds and mix well. Sprinkle cheese on top. Do not stir.

IN a small skillet over medium heat, melt remaining butter and stir in crumbs. Sprinkle on top of gratin dish.

BAKE, uncovered, until bubbly, 30 to 35 minutes.

SERVES 6 TO 8

263

creamy swiss chard and shallots

Chard is a member of the beet family. It is full of vitamins and minerals—a healthful vegetable to include in your diet. In this recipe, the chard is lightly mixed with sour cream and served as a gratin.

1 tablespoon butter or margarine

2 shallots, peeled and chopped

1 large bunch green chard (about 2½ pounds), ribs removed and coarsely chopped

¼ cup Rich Chicken Stock (page 23) or canned low-sodium chicken broth

½ teaspoon salt

¼ teaspoon freshly ground pepper

½ cup light sour cream

Freshly grated Parmesan cheese for sprinkling on top

¼ cup pine nuts

PREHEAT oven to 375°F. In a large saucepan over medium heat, melt butter. Add shallots and cook until tender, about 5 minutes. Add chard, stock, salt, and pepper and cook, covered, until chard is wilted, about 5 minutes longer. Remove from heat and fold in sour cream.

PLACE in a 7½-by-11¾-inch baking dish or gratin dish lightly coated with cooking spray or oil. Sprinkle with cheese and pine nuts, and bake, uncovered, until heated through, about 15 minutes.

SERVES 6

baked fennel, onion, and red bell pepper with gorgonzola

Fennel, sometimes called sweet anise, has a subtle licorice flavor that goes well with onion and red bell pepper. The feathery top can be used as a seasoning or as a garnish.

1 yellow onion, sliced

2 fennel bulbs, stalks and tops removed (save some top for garnish), washed, drained, and sliced

1 red bell pepper, seeded and cut into 1½-inch squares

½ cup Rich Chicken Stock (page 23) or canned low-sodium chicken broth

2 tablespoons olive oil

Salt and freshly ground pepper to taste

½ cup dry bread crumbs (see page 5)

½ cup crumbled gorgonzola cheese

PREHEAT oven to 375°F. Arrange onion slices in an 8-by-8-inch baking dish or gratin dish lightly coated with cooking spray or oil. Layer fennel and red pepper on top of onion slices. Pour stock into dish. Drizzle vegetables with oil and season with salt and pepper.

COVER and bake 30 minutes. Uncover and sprinkle with bread crumbs and cheese. Bake, uncovered, until fennel and peppers are tender and top is lightly browned, about 20 minutes longer. Garnish with fennel tops.

SERVES 4

wild mushroom gratin

You will especially enjoy this gratin if you serve it with roast beef or steak. The combination of mixed wild mushrooms imparts extra flavor, but button mushrooms can be used instead. The recipe can easily be doubled.

4 tablespoons butter or margarine

1 pound mixed wild mushrooms (chanterelle, oyster, or shiitake), cut into uniform slices

6 green onions, including some tender green tops, sliced

½ cup light sour cream

1 tablespoon all-purpose flour

2 tablespoons chopped fresh parsley

¼ teaspoon salt

Freshly ground pepper to taste

1 cup dry bread crumbs (see page 5)

Paprika for sprinkling on top

PREHEAT oven to 350°F. In a large skillet over medium heat, melt 2 tablespoons butter. Add mushrooms and onions and sauté until tender, about 5 minutes. Stir in sour cream, flour, parsley, salt, and pepper.

PLACE mixture in 4 individual 4-by-6-inch gratin dishes lightly coated with cooking spray or oil. In a small skillet over medium heat, melt remaining butter and stir in crumbs. Top the 4 gratin dishes equally with buttered bread crumbs and paprika.

BAKE, uncovered, until bubbly, about 25 minutes.

SERVES 4

creamy spinach gratin

This recipe was sent to me from a friend in Phoenix who got it from a Las Vegas show girl. You can bet on this one!

2 packages (10 ounces each) frozen chopped spinach, thawed

4 tablespoons butter or margarine

1 package (8 ounces) cream cheese, cut into cubes

¼ teaspoon salt

Freshly ground pepper to taste

Dash of ground nutmeg

1 cup dry bread crumbs (see page 5)

Freshly grated Parmesan cheese for sprinkling on top

PREHEAT oven to 350°F. In a medium saucepan over high heat, bring spinach and a small amount of water to a boil. Cook about 30 seconds. (Spinach must be hot to blend with other ingredients.) Drain well and with a spoon, press spinach against the side of a sieve with a spoon to remove excess water.

RETURN spinach to the pan. Add 1 tablespoon of the butter, the cream cheese, salt, pepper, and nutmeg, and mix well.

TRANSFER mixture to an 8-by-8-inch baking dish or gratin dish lightly coated with cooking spray or oil. In a small skillet over medium heat, melt remaining 3 tablespoons butter and stir in crumbs. Top spinach mixture with Parmesan cheese and crumbs.

BAKE, uncovered, until bubbly, about 20 minutes.

SERVES 6

267

parmesan cheese—mashed potato gratin

Potato gratin traditionally calls for sliced potatoes, but this version uses mashed potatoes with cheese and garlic. Serve with baked salmon.

3 pounds (5 or 6) baking potatoes, peeled and quartered

4 cloves garlic, halved

½ cup buttermilk or milk

2 tablespoons butter or margarine

½ cup freshly grated Parmesan cheese

¼ teaspoon salt

⅛ teaspoon white pepper

½ cup chopped green onions, including some tender green tops

⅓ cup dry bread crumbs (see page 5)

Paprika for sprinkling on top

PREHEAT oven to 375°F. In a medium saucepan over high heat, add potatoes, garlic, and water to cover. Bring to a boil. Reduce heat to low, cover, and cook until vegetables are tender, about 20 minutes. Drain well. Add buttermilk, butter, ¼ cup of the cheese, salt, and pepper. With a hand-held electric mixer, beat potatoes until smooth and fluffy. Fold in onions.

TRANSFER to an 8-by-8-inch baking dish or gratin dish lightly coated with cooking spray or oil. Sprinkle with bread crumbs, remaining cheese, and paprika.

BAKE until potatoes are heated through, 30 to 35 minutes.

SERVES 4

NOTE: For a crispier, golden top, place under broiler for 2 minutes.

swiss potatoes gratin

In this elegant dish, the potatoes are cooked ahead of time. Then they are combined with cheese and sour cream, topped with crumbs, and baked in the oven. Serve with roast beef for a company dinner.

2½ pounds (about 4 large) russet potatoes, peeled and halved

1 cup densely packed grated Swiss cheese

½ cup sliced green onions, including some tender green tops

½ cup chopped red bell pepper

¼ cup chopped fresh parsley

¼ cup toasted slivered almonds (see page 11)

½ teaspoon salt

1 tablespoon fresh dill, or 1 teaspoon dried dill weed

2 cups light sour cream

3 tablespoons butter or margarine, melted

1 cup dry bread crumbs (see page 5)

IN a large saucepan over high heat, add potatoes and water to nearly cover, and bring to a boil. Reduce heat to low, cover, and cook until tender, about 20 minutes. Drain, and when cool enough to handle, slice. (You should have about 7 to 8 cups.)

PREHEAT oven to 375°F. In a large bowl, combine cheese, onions, bell pepper, parsley, almonds, salt, dill, and sour cream. Add potatoes and mix well.

TRANSFER to a 2½ quart casserole dish or gratin dish lightly coated with cooking spray or oil. In a small skillet over medium heat, melt butter and stir in crumbs. Sprinkle buttered crumbs evenly on top of potatoes.

BAKE, uncovered, until crispy on top and bubbly, about 40 minutes.

SERVES 4 TO 6

spinach and tomatoes gratin
Here is a no-fuss gratin that is perfect for a dinner party. It is made ahead, then baked and presented in the same dish. Serve with a seafood entrée.

2   large eggs, beaten

2   packages (10 ounces each) frozen chopped spinach, thawed and squeezed dry

½   cup freshly grated Parmesan cheese plus extra for sprinkling on top

⅓   cup light sour cream

¼   teaspoon dried thyme

¼   teaspoon salt

¼   teaspoon ground nutmeg

1   teaspoon fresh lemon juice

2   teaspoons pine nuts

2   firm tomatoes, seeded, sliced, and drained

Freshly ground pepper to taste

PREHEAT oven to 375°F. In a large bowl, stir together eggs, spinach, ½ cup of the cheese, sour cream, seasonings, lemon juice, and pine nuts. Divide evenly among 4 individual 4-by-6-inch gratin dishes lightly coated with cooking spray or oil. Place 2 tomato slices on top of each one. Season with pepper and sprinkle with Parmesan cheese.

BAKE until heated through, about 12 minutes.

SERVES 4

vegetables gratin

Here is a mixed vegetable side dish to serve for a ham or turkey holiday menu. Make ahead to avoid a last-minute rush on a busy day.

3 tablespoons butter or margarine

1 small green bell pepper, seeded and cut into 1-inch pieces

½ cup chopped yellow onion

1 clove garlic, minced

¼ cup all-purpose flour

⅔ cup whole milk

½ teaspoon salt

¼ teaspoon dried basil

¼ teaspoon dried oregano

Freshly ground pepper to taste

1 can (14½ ounces) whole tomatoes, chopped, juice from can included

1½ cups grated cheddar cheese

1 package (10 ounces) frozen corn, thawed, and drained

1½ cups frozen small whole onions, thawed and drained

PREHEAT oven to 350°F.

IN a large saucepan over medium heat, melt butter. Add bell pepper, yellow onion, and garlic and sauté until tender, about 5 minutes. Add flour and stir until bubbly. Stir in milk and cook until thickened (mixture will be quite thick), about 2 minutes. Add seasonings, tomatoes, ¾ cup of the cheese, corn, and onions and mix well. Stir until cheese is melted, about 1 minute.

TRANSFER to a 2½-quart casserole dish or gratin dish lightly coated with cooking spray or oil. Top with remaining cheese.

BAKE, uncovered, until bubbly and flavors are blended, about 45 minutes.

SERVES 6

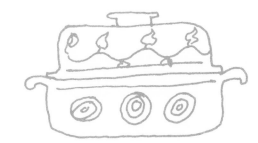

mixed squash with pecans gratin

This recipe is a variation of a southern classic that is often paired with ham or pork.

1 zucchini (about 8 ounces), unpeeled, cut into ½-inch slices

1 crookneck squash (about 8 ounces), unpeeled, cut into ½-inch slices

1 large egg

1 cup grated cheddar cheese

½ cup chopped green onions, including some tender green tops

1 teaspoon dried dill weed

½ teaspoon salt

Freshly ground pepper to taste

2 tablespoons butter

1 cup dry bread crumbs (see page 5)

¼ cup chopped pecans

PREHEAT oven to 350°F. Add some water to a pan fitted with a steamer rack over medium heat. Place squashes on rack and steam over gently boiling water for 10 minutes.

TRANSFER to food processor. With pulses, coarsely chop squash. Add egg, cheese, onions, dill, salt, and pepper. Mix briefly. Turn into a 9-inch glass pie plate or gratin dish lightly coated with cooking spray or oil.

IN a small skillet over medium heat, melt butter. Add crumbs and nuts and stir until toasted, about 3 minutes. Sprinkle on top of squash mixture.

BAKE, uncovered, until puffed up and set, about 30 minutes.

SERVES 4

layered zucchini, mushroom, onion, and tomato gratin

In this gratin, fresh vegetable slices are briefly sautéed, then layered with cheese, topped with sourdough bread crumbs, and baked until crispy. A great side dish for an autumn dinner.

1½ tablespoons vegetable oil

1 large yellow onion, sliced

2 cloves garlic, minced

2 zucchini, unpeeled, cut into ¼-inch slices

4 ounces mushrooms, sliced

2 cups grated cheddar or Monterey Jack cheese or a combination of the two

1 large tomato, seeded, sliced, and drained

Salt and freshly ground pepper to taste

1 tablespoon chopped fresh basil, or 1 teaspoon dried basil

½ cup dry sourdough bread crumbs (see page 5)

PREHEAT oven to 350°F. In a large skillet over medium heat, warm oil. Add onion, garlic, zucchini, and mushrooms. Sauté until slightly tender, 6 to 7 minutes.

IN a 7½-by-11¾-inch baking dish or gratin dish lightly coated with cooking spray or oil, layer half the vegetable mixture, half the cheese, and all the tomato slices. Sprinkle with salt, pepper, and basil. Add remaining vegetables in layers and top with cheese. Sprinkle with bread crumbs.

BAKE, uncovered, until vegetables are tender, about 40 minutes.

SERVES 4 TO 6

swiss cheese and sourdough bread gratin

In this simple but tasty side dish, bread strips dipped in a custard sauce and topped with cheese bake into a crispy, golden gratin.

2   large eggs

½   cup milk

½   cup half-and-half (see Note)

¼   teaspoon dried thyme

⅛   teaspoon white pepper

¼   teaspoon salt

1   tablespoon dry white wine

½   loaf (about 10 ounces) sourdough bread, cut into 1-inch slices and then into 1-by-3-inch strips

1   cup grated Swiss cheese

PREHEAT oven to 350°F. In a medium bowl, beat eggs, milk, half-and-half, thyme, pepper, salt, and wine. Dip bread strips into egg mixture and quickly arrange in an 8-by-8-inch baking dish or gratin dish lightly coated with cooking spray or oil. Pour leftover egg mixture on top. Sprinkle with cheese.

BAKE, uncovered, until center is set and the top is lightly browned, 40 to 45 minutes.

SERVES 4

NOTE: Half-and-half makes a richer dish, but milk may be substituted.

angel-hair pasta with creamy sauce

Angel-hair pasta (*cappellini,* in Italian) is a long, delicate strand that should be mixed with a lightly flavored sauce. This makes a simple but tasty side dish for steaks.

1   cup (8 ounces) ricotta or cottage cheese

½   cup freshly grated Parmesan cheese

¼   cup light sour cream at room temperature

2   cups Rich Chicken Stock (page 23) or canned low-sodium chicken broth

1   clove garlic, minced

3 or 4 parsley sprigs

¼   teaspoon salt

⅛   teaspoon white pepper

8   ounces angel-hair pasta, cooked and drained

Freshly grated Parmesan cheese for sprinkling on top

PREHEAT oven to 350°F. Place cheeses and sour cream in food processor and blend. Add stock, garlic, parsley, salt, and pepper and mix well.

IN a 7½-by-11¾-inch baking dish or gratin dish lightly coated with cooking spray or oil, mix pasta with cheese sauce. Sprinkle Parmesan cheese on top.

BAKE, uncovered, until bubbly, 25 to 30 minutes.

SERVES 6

eggs gratin

For an impressive brunch dish, serve this Eggs Gratin with various toppings. Add a fresh fruit plate and croissants to complete the brunch. This recipe is for one person, but you can make as many as you need.

2   large eggs

½   tablespoon water

Salt and freshly ground pepper
    to taste

TOPPINGS

Diced mushrooms

Diced green bell pepper

Diced green onion

Cooked and crumbled pancetta
    or bacon

Diced cooked ham

Grated Swiss cheese

Grated cheddar cheese

PREHEAT oven to 350°F. Carefully break eggs into a 4-by-6-inch individual gratin dish lightly coated with cooking spray or oil. Sprinkle water over eggs. Season with salt and pepper. Add toppings of your choice.

BAKE until whites are set and cheese is melted, 15 to 18 minutes. Serve immediately. Eggs will stay very hot.

SERVES 1

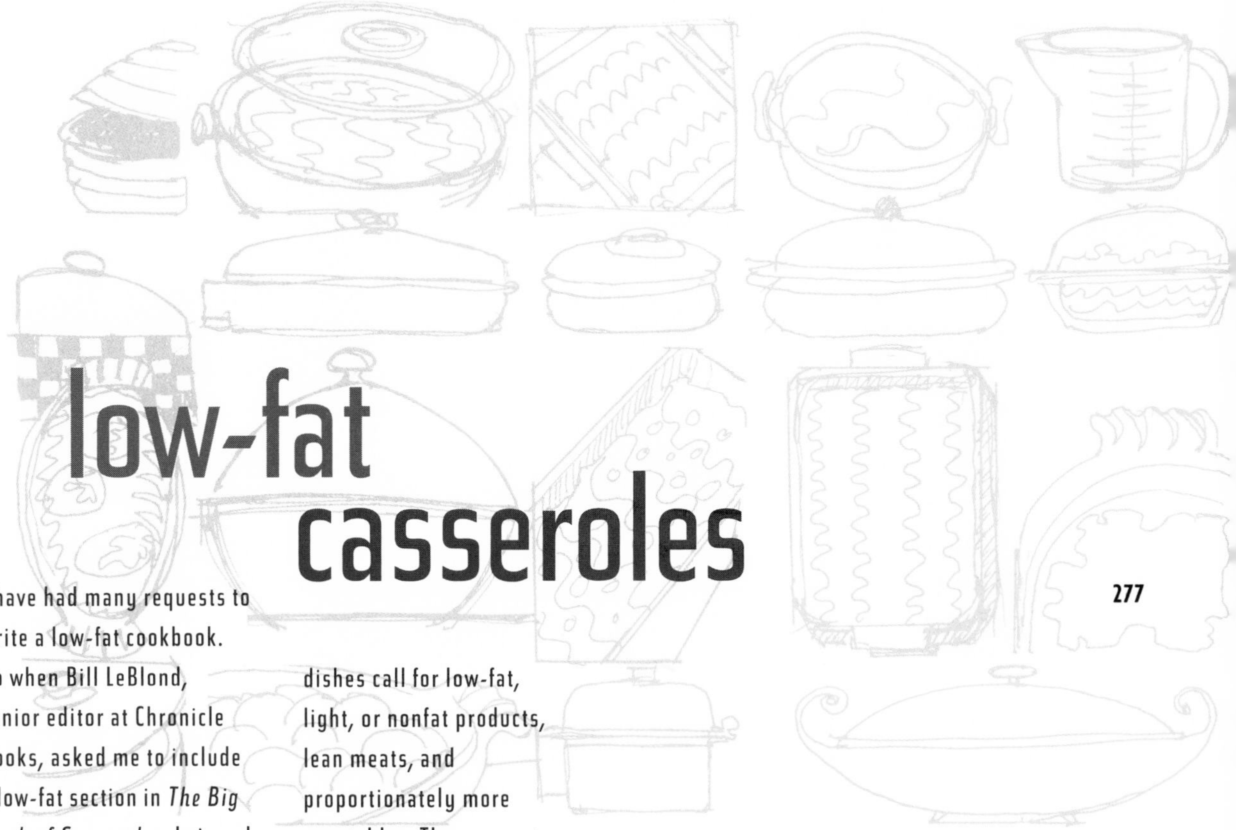

low-fat casseroles

I have had many requests to write a low-fat cookbook. So when Bill LeBlond, senior editor at Chronicle Books, asked me to include a low-fat section in *The Big Book of Casseroles*, I viewed it as my opportunity (and challenge) to develop some tasty, low-fat dishes that are interesting and full of flavor.

All these recipes are tailored for the calorie- and health-conscious. These dishes call for low-fat, light, or nonfat products, lean meats, and proportionately more vegetables. They are not, however, intended to be strict dieting recipes.

Some innovative sauces are included, as well as extra herbs and spices.

Cooking the low-fat way becomes a habit, and it is a healthful way to go.

garden lasagna

Pasta is great for low-fat dishes if other low-fat ingredients are included. This baked lasagna is full of healthy vegetables and part-skim cheeses.

1½ tablespoons olive oil

8 ounces mushrooms, sliced

2 cups chopped unpeeled zucchini (1 large), drained on a paper towel

1 cup chopped yellow onion

½ cup chopped red bell pepper

1 clove garlic, minced

1 can (14½ ounces) whole tomatoes, chopped, juice from can included

1 can (15 ounces) tomato sauce

1 tablespoon chopped fresh basil, or ¾ teaspoon dried basil

½ teaspoon dried oregano

¾ teaspoon salt

Freshly ground pepper to taste

¼ teaspoon sugar

2 bags (6 ounces each) fresh spinach, cooked (see page 7), chopped, and well drained; or 1 package (10 ounces) frozen spinach, thawed, and squeezed dry

1 container (16 ounces) low-fat cottage cheese

1 cup grated part-skim mozzarella cheese

1 cup freshly grated Parmesan cheese

9 lasagna noodles, cooked and drained on a clean towel

IN a large saucepan over medium heat, warm oil. Add mushrooms, zucchini, onion, bell pepper, and garlic and sauté about 10 minutes. Stir in tomatoes, tomato sauce, seasonings, and sugar. Reduce temperature to low and simmer, uncovered, until vegetables are tender-crisp and sauce has thickened slightly, about 10 minutes. Set aside.

PREHEAT oven to 375°F. In a medium bowl, combine spinach, cottage cheese, mozzarella, and ¼ cup of the Parmesan cheese.

SPOON one third of the tomato-vegetable sauce into the bottom of a 9-by-13-inch baking dish lightly coated with cooking spray or oil. In layers, add 3 noodles, half of the spinach-cheese mixture, 3 more noodles, another one-third of the sauce, the remaining spinach-cheese mixture, and the remaining noodles. Top with remaining sauce, and sprinkle with remaining Parmesan cheese.

BAKE, uncovered, until bubbly, 40 to 50 minutes.

SERVES 8

vegetables and noodles with good creamy sauce

Lighten up with this pasta dish, which is almost "guilt-free." Fresh summer fruit goes well with this combination.

8 ounces mushrooms, sliced

1 zucchini, unpeeled, sliced

1 clove garlic, minced

½ cup canned fat free low-sodium chicken broth

1 tablespoon dry white wine (optional)

¼ teaspoon dried thyme

¼ teaspoon salt

Freshly ground pepper to taste

4 ounces (about 2½ cups) egg noodles, cooked and drained

Good Creamy Low-Fat Sauce (recipe follows)

3 tablespoons freshly grated Parmesan cheese

PREHEAT oven to 375°F. In a medium pan over medium heat, place mushrooms, zucchini, garlic, chicken stock, wine, and seasonings. Bring to a boil, reduce heat, and simmer, covered, until vegetables are tender-crisp, about 5 minutes.

TRANSFER to a 2½-quart casserole dish lightly coated with cooking spray or oil. Stir in noodles and sauce. Sprinkle with Parmesan cheese.

BAKE, uncovered, until bubbly, about 30 minutes.

SERVES 4

good creamy low-fat sauce

This sauce can be used with any pasta. It is also good on vegetables.

½ cup low-fat cottage cheese

4 ounces light cream cheese

1 tablespoon skim milk

3 sprigs parsley

2 green onions, including some tender green tops, chopped

PLACE all ingredients in food processor or blender and process until smooth.

MAKES ABOUT 1 CUP

penne, fresh basil, pine nuts, and cheese casserole

A flavorful meatless dish, perfect when served with a tossed green salad and warm bread.

8 ounces (about 3 cups) penne, cooked and drained

2 cans (14½ ounces each) crushed tomatoes in thick purée

2 tablespoons toasted pine nuts (see page 11)

¼ cup slivered fresh basil (see page 9), or 1 teaspoon dried basil

¾ teaspoon salt

Freshly ground pepper to taste

¼ cup chopped fresh parsley

1 cup firmly packed grated Swiss cheese

Freshly grated Parmesan cheese for sprinkling on top

PREHEAT oven to 375°F. Place pasta in a 2½-quart casserole dish lightly coated with cooking spray or oil.

IN a medium saucepan over medium heat, stir together tomatoes, pine nuts, basil, salt, pepper, and parsley. Simmer 2 to 3 minutes. Mix with pasta in casserole, and stir in Swiss cheese. Sprinkle Parmesan cheese on top.

BAKE, uncovered, until bubbly, 35 to 40 minutes. Let stand 10 minutes before serving.

SERVES 6

spinach, parmesan cheese, and rotini with pine nuts

This pasta dish is low-fat, but still flavorful and satisfying. Be sure to use good-quality, freshly grated Parmesan cheese.

1 cup canned fat free low-sodium chicken broth

1 cup chopped yellow onion

2 large cloves garlic, minced

¼ teaspoon salt

Freshly ground pepper to taste

Dash of ground nutmeg

1 package (10 ounces) frozen chopped spinach, thawed and squeezed dry

8 ounces (about 3 cups) rotini or any spiral pasta, cooked and drained

3 tablespoons toasted pine nuts (see page 11)

¼ cup freshly grated Parmesan cheese, plus extra for sprinkling on top

PREHEAT oven to 350°F. In a large saucepan over medium heat, add broth, onion, and garlic and cook, covered, until vegetables are tender-crisp, about 5 minutes. Add salt, pepper, and nutmeg and simmer, uncovered, 1 minute. Add spinach, pasta, nuts, and cheese and mix well. If the mixture seems dry, add a little more broth.

TRANSFER to a 2½-quart casserole dish lightly coated with cooking spray or oil, and sprinkle with Parmesan cheese.

COVER and bake until heated through, about 25 minutes.

SERVES 4

shrimp and scallops with rotelle

Enjoy this low-fat pasta dish with plenty of flavor and without the usual heavy cream and butter. A green salad with a light, lemony dressing will complete the meal.

¾ cup canned fat free low-sodium chicken broth

½ cup chopped yellow onion

¼ cup chopped green bell pepper (optional)

2 cloves garlic, chopped

8 ounces fresh scallops (cut in half if large)

8 ounces large shrimp, shelled and deveined

2 tomatoes, seeded, chopped, and drained

½ cup low-fat cottage cheese

½ cup nonfat plain yogurt or light sour cream

¼ cup slivered fresh basil leaves (see page 9), or ¾ teaspoon dried basil

2 or 3 sprigs fresh parsley

2 tablespoons dry white wine

½ teaspoon salt

Freshly ground pepper to taste

8 ounces (about 3 cups) rotelle, cooked and drained

½ cup grated part-skim mozzarella cheese

2 tablespoons freshly grated Parmesan cheese for topping

PREHEAT oven to 350°F. In a large saucepan over medium heat, stir in broth, onion, bell pepper, and garlic and cook, uncovered, 3 minutes. Add scallops and shrimp, stir, and cook until scallops are translucent and shrimp turn pink, about 2 minutes longer. Drain and place in a 2½-quart casserole dish lightly coated with cooking spray or oil. Add tomato and mix well.

IN food processor, blend together cottage cheese, yogurt, basil, parsley, wine, salt, and pepper. Transfer to casserole dish.

ADD pasta and mozzarella cheese to the casserole and mix well. Sprinkle Parmesan cheese on top.

BAKE, uncovered, until flavors are blended, about 30 minutes.

SERVES 6

sun-dried tomatoes and orzo

The addition of sun-dried tomatoes adds a unique flavor to this colorful side dish. They are easy on the calories, too.

- ¼ cup sun-dried tomatoes (not in oil)
- ¾ cup boiling water
- 1 cup orzo
- 6 green onions, including some tender green tops, sliced
- 1 clove garlic, minced
- 1 cup spicy tomato juice
- 1 cup canned fat free low-sodium chicken broth
- 1 tablespoon red wine vinegar
- 1 tablespoon slivered fresh basil (see page 9), or ¾ teaspoon dried basil
- ¼ teaspoon salt
- Freshly ground pepper to taste
- ¼ cup freshly grated Parmesan cheese

PREHEAT oven to 375°F. Place sun-dried tomatoes in a cup. Add boiling water. Let stand 10 minutes. Drain, and place tomatoes in a 2½-quart casserole dish lightly coated with cooking spray or oil. Add orzo, onions, and garlic. Stir in tomato juice, broth, vinegar, basil, salt, and pepper.

COVER and bake until liquid is absorbed, about 40 minutes. Sprinkle with cheese and bake, uncovered, until cheese melts, 5 minutes longer.

SERVES 4 TO 6

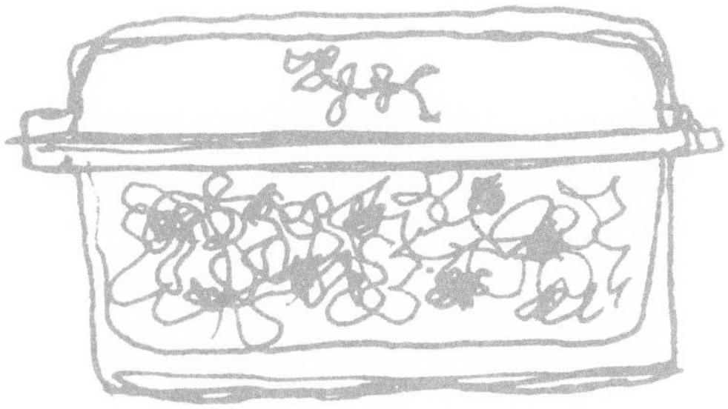

chicken and orzo bake

The creamy texture of orzo mixed with yogurt makes you think you are eating a rich, high-calorie dish. With chicken added, the entrée is complete.

2¼ cups canned fat free low-sodium chicken broth

¼ teaspoon salt

1 cup orzo

½ cup chopped red bell pepper

2 cups cubed cooked chicken (see page 6)

¼ teaspoon dried tarragon

½ teaspoon dried basil

Freshly ground pepper to taste

2 tablespoons dry white wine

¼ cup chopped fresh parsley

½ cup plain nonfat yogurt

½ cup diced green onions, including some tender green tops

PREHEAT oven to 350°F. In a large saucepan over high heat, bring broth to a boil. Add salt, orzo, and bell pepper. Reduce heat to medium and cook, uncovered, stirring occasionally, until orzo and bell pepper are tender, about 12 minutes. Stir in chicken, seasonings, wine, and parsley.

PLACE in a 2½-quart casserole dish lightly coated with cooking spray or oil, and fold in yogurt.

BAKE, covered, until flavors are blended, about 25 minutes. Sprinkle with onions before serving.

SERVES 4

chicken curry, vegetables, and rice
Out-of-town company coming and no time to go to the market. What's on hand? Chicken breasts in the freezer, odds and ends of vegetables, and, of course, rice. This is a simple and quick casserole to prepare for an impromptu luncheon. Serve with a fresh fruit plate.

2¼ cups canned fat free low-sodium chicken broth

¼ cup chopped yellow onion

1 cup (2 stalks) chopped celery

½ cup chopped red bell pepper

4 ounces mushrooms, sliced

1 cup long-grain white rice

1½ to 2 teaspoons curry powder to taste

¼ teaspoon salt

3 cups cubed cooked chicken breast (see page 6)

½ cup unsalted peanuts (optional)

½ cup golden raisins (optional)

PREHEAT oven to 350°F.

IN a medium saucepan over medium-high heat, bring broth to a boil. Add vegetables, reduce heat to medium-low, and cook vegetables until tender-crisp, about 6 minutes. Stir in rice and seasonings, and transfer mixture to a 2½-quart casserole dish lightly coated with cooking spray or oil. Add chicken and mix well.

COVER and bake 45 minutes. Stir in peanuts and raisins, if using, and bake, covered, until liquid is absorbed and rice is tender, about 10 minutes longer.

SERVES 4 TO 6

mexi-corn and rice dish

Light on the calories, but zesty with seasonings, this makes a good companion dish to Mexican food. Use fresh corn if available. Serve with salsa.

1   cup chopped yellow onion

½   cup chopped red bell pepper

¼   cup Vegetable Stock (page 24) or canned fat free low-sodium chicken or vegetable broth

1½   cups cooked long-grain white rice

1½   cups cooked corn (fresh or frozen)

1   can (4 ounces) diced green chiles, drained

½   cup plain nonfat yogurt or light sour cream

¼   teaspoon salt

½   teaspoon chili powder

Freshly ground pepper to taste

¼   cup chopped fresh parsley

1   cup firmly packed grated mozzarella cheese

PREHEAT oven to 350°F. In a medium saucepan over medium heat, cook onion and bell pepper in stock, covered, until tender-crisp, about 5 minutes. Stir in remaining ingredients, but only ½ cup of the cheese, and mix well.

TRANSFER to a 2½-quart casserole dish lightly coated with cooking spray or oil, and sprinkle remaining cheese on top. Bake, uncovered, until bubbly, 35 to 40 minutes.

SERVES 4

brown rice and broccoli
This rice and vegetable dish adds variety to a winter menu. Serve with pork chops and baked apples.

2¼ cups canned fat free low-sodium chicken broth

¼ teaspoon salt

1 cup brown rice

2 cups coarsely chopped broccoli florets

¼ cup chopped yellow onion

1 teaspoon Worcestershire sauce

¼ cup chopped fresh parsley

1 tablespoon butter or margarine (optional)

Freshly ground pepper to taste

PREHEAT oven to 350°F. In a medium saucepan over high heat, bring broth to a boil. Add salt and rice and boil 1 minute. Transfer to a 2½-quart casserole dish lightly coated with cooking spray or oil.

COVER and bake 40 minutes. Add remaining ingredients and mix well. Cover and bake until liquid is absorbed and vegetables are tender, about 20 minutes longer.

SERVES 6

baked lentils and vegetables

Lentils are convenient to use because they require no presoaking or precooking. They contain vitamins and minerals and practically no fat, and are often used as a meat substitute. Combined with vegetables, lentils make a healthful and delicious vegetarian dish.

1	tablespoon olive oil
1	yellow onion, chopped
½	red bell pepper, seeded and chopped
½	green bell pepper, seeded and chopped
2	cloves garlic, minced
1½	cups Vegetable Stock (page 24)
¾	cup brown lentils, picked over (to remove foreign matter) and rinsed
1	can (14½ ounces) whole tomatoes, chopped, juice from can included
¼	teaspoon dried oregano
¼	teaspoon dried basil
¼	teaspoon dried tarragon
¼	teaspoon curry powder, or more to taste
¼	teaspoon salt

Freshly ground pepper to taste

1	package (10 ounces) frozen chopped broccoli, thawed and drained
¼	cup freshly grated Parmesan cheese

PREHEAT oven to 350°F. In a medium saucepan over medium heat, warm oil. Add onion, bell peppers, and garlic and sauté until tender, about 5 minutes. Stir in stock, lentils, tomatoes, seasonings, and broccoli and cook, uncovered, 5 minutes.

TRANSFER to a 2½-quart casserole dish lightly coated with cooking spray or oil. Sprinkle with Parmesan cheese, cover, and bake until liquid is absorbed, about 45 minutes.

SERVES 6 TO 8

THE BIG BOOK OF CASSEROLES

chicken and vegetables

Cutting calories is easy with this one-dish meal because there is no sautéing or browning. Fresh herbs highlight the flavor of the other ingredients. Serve with a platter of refreshing fruit.

2 zucchini, unpeeled, sliced

2 cups cherry tomatoes

1 yellow onion, sliced and rings separated

1 green bell pepper, seeded and cut into chunks

2 tablespoons chopped fresh parsley

2 tablespoons slivered fresh basil (see page 9), or 1 teaspoon dried basil

1 tablespoon chopped fresh oregano, or ¾ teaspoon dried oregano

½ teaspoon salt

Freshly ground pepper to taste

1 teaspoon olive oil (optional)

6 skinned and boned chicken breasts halves (about 3 pounds; see page 7)

½ cup canned fat free low-sodium chicken broth

Freshly grated Parmesan cheese for sprinkling on top

Paprika for sprinkling on top

PREHEAT oven to 350°F. In a large bowl, stir together zucchini, tomatoes, onion, bell pepper, parsley, basil, oregano, salt, pepper, and olive oil, if using.

TRANSFER to a 7½-by-11¾-inch baking dish lightly coated with cooking spray or oil. Arrange chicken on top. Add broth. Sprinkle with Parmesan cheese and paprika.

COVER and bake until chicken is no longer pink in the center and vegetables are tender-crisp, about 40 minutes.

SERVES 4

289

turkey-zucchini casserole
This is a healthful, one-dish casserole that is very filling and satisfying. Leftovers are good the next day.

1   pound ground turkey breast

1   cup chopped yellow onion

1   clove garlic, minced

2   zucchini (about 1 pound combined weight), unpeeled, cut into ¼-inch slices

1   cup chopped celery

1   red bell pepper, seeded and chopped

2   cans (14½ ounces each) ready-cut, peeled tomatoes, including juice

2   tablespoons slivered fresh basil (see page 9), or ¾ teaspoon dried basil

1   teaspoon snipped fresh thyme, or ½ teaspoon dried thyme

¼   cup chopped fresh parsley

½   teaspoon salt

Freshly ground pepper to taste

1   cup dry bread crumbs (see page 5)

⅓   cup freshly grated Parmesan cheese

PREHEAT oven to 350°F. Spray a large nonstick skillet with vegetable cooking spray. Place on medium heat, and add turkey, onion, and garlic and stir, breaking up turkey until it is no longer pink and vegetables are tender-crisp, about 5 minutes. Add zucchini, celery, bell pepper, tomatoes, and seasonings and mix well. Bring to a boil. Stir in bread crumbs.

TRANSFER mixture to a 9-by-13-inch baking dish lightly coated with cooking spray or oil. Cover and bake until vegetables are tender, 45 minutes. Uncover and sprinkle with cheese. Bake, uncovered, about 5 minutes longer. Let stand 5 minutes before serving.

SERVES 6

turkey breast and vegetables
Trim the budget as well as the waistline with this healthful, low-fat, turkey-vegetable casserole baked in broth and wine.

2   carrots, peeled and cut into
    ½-inch slices

1   yellow onion, sliced

3   whole cloves garlic, peeled

1   red bell pepper, seeded and
    cut lengthwise into ½-inch
    strips

2   celery stalks, sliced into
    1-inch pieces

1   boned turkey breast, with
    skin (about 2 pounds)

½   cup canned fat free low-
    sodium chicken broth

¼   cup dry white wine

1   teaspoon salt

½   teaspoon paprika

1   teaspoon dried sage

Freshly ground pepper to taste

1   tablespoon cornstarch

Fresh sage leaves for garnish

PREHEAT oven to 350°F. In a 4-quart casserole dish lightly coated with cooking spray or oil, put carrots, onion, garlic, bell pepper, and celery. Place turkey breast on top.

IN a small saucepan, mix broth, wine, seasonings, and cornstarch. Over medium-high heat, bring to a boil, stirring constantly, until thickened, about 2 minutes. Pour over turkey and vegetables.

COVER and bake until turkey is white in the center and vegetables are tender, about 1½ hours. Garnish with sage leaves.

SERVES 4 TO 6

greek meatballs in tomato-yogurt-mint sauce   Treat

yourself to lamb meatballs baked in a mint-flavored sauce. Serve with rice or bulgur.

1   large egg, beaten

1¼ pounds ground lamb

½   cup plain nonfat yogurt

¼   cup finely chopped yellow onion

2   cloves garlic, minced

¾   cup fresh bread crumbs (see Note, page 181)

¼   teaspoon dried oregano

1   tablespoon chopped fresh parsley

¾   teaspoon salt

Freshly ground pepper to taste

1   can (8 ounces) tomato sauce

1   tablespoon chopped fresh mint

Mint sprigs for garnish

IN a large bowl, combine all ingredients except ¼ cup of the yogurt, tomato sauce, and mint and mix well. Cover and refrigerate for 30 minutes for easier handling.

PREHEAT oven to 400°F. Form lamb mixture into 1-inch balls. Place on a rimmed baking sheet. Bake until browned, about 15 minutes.

REDUCE oven temperature to 350°F. Transfer lamb meatballs to a 2½-quart casserole dish lightly coated with cooking spray or oil.

IN a small bowl whisk together tomato sauce, remaining yogurt, and mint. Pour tomato-yogurt sauce over meatballs.

COVER and bake 30 minutes. Uncover and bake until bubbly, about 10 minutes longer. Garnish with mint leaves.

SERVES 4 TO 6

potatoes and onion casserole

Potatoes and onions bake together for an easy, low-fat version of scalloped potatoes.

4   large new potatoes (about 2 pounds), unpeeled, thinly sliced

1   yellow onion, sliced and rings separated

Salt and freshly ground pepper to taste

¼   cup chopped fresh parsley

1   tablespoon butter or margarine (optional)

½   cup canned fat free low-sodium chicken broth

Freshly grated Parmesan cheese for topping

PREHEAT oven to 375°F. In a 2½-quart casserole dish lightly coated with cooking spray or oil, layer half the potatoes, all of the onions, and the remaining potatoes, sprinkling salt, pepper, and parsely between each layer. Dot with butter, if using. Pour broth over all.

COVER and bake until tender, about 1 hour. Remove lid and sprinkle with Parmesan cheese. Bake, uncovered, until cheese melts, 5 minutes longer.

SERVES 4

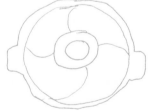

two-potato bake

Sweet and white potatoes bake together in a broth seasoned with caraway seeds for a flavorful and colorful dish. Use a food processor for easy slicing.

2   large baking potatoes (about 1 pound) peeled and cut into ¼-inch slices

2   large sweet potatoes (about 1 pound), peeled and cut into ¼-inch slices

1   yellow onion, sliced and rings separated

3   tablespoons chopped fresh parsley

1   teaspoon caraway seeds

½   teaspoon salt

Freshly ground pepper to taste

½   cup canned fat free low-sodium chicken broth

1   tablespoon butter or margarine, cut up (optional)

PREHEAT oven to 350°F. Place potatoes, onions, parsley, and seasonings in a 2½-quart casserole dish lightly coated with cooking spray or oil and mix well. Pour broth over all. Dot with butter, if using.

COVER and bake until potatoes are tender, about 1 hour.

SERVES 4 TO 6

oven-braised parmesan, celery, and red bell pepper

Though often overlooked as a vegetable in its own right, celery plays a starring role in this low-fat vegetable side dish.

8 or 9 celery stalks cut into 1-inch pieces (about 5 cups)

½ cup chopped red bell pepper

½ cup canned fat free low-sodium chicken broth

1 teaspoon butter or margarine

¼ cup freshly grated Parmesan cheese

¼ teaspoon salt

Freshly ground pepper to taste

PREHEAT oven to 350°F. Place all ingredients in a 2½-quart casserole dish lightly coated with cooking spray or oil, and mix well. Cover and bake until tender, about 40 minutes. Serve with a slotted spoon.

SERVES 4 TO 6

295

spaghetti squash with vegetables

Spaghetti squash is an amazing vegetable. When cooked, it looks like spaghetti but has a slightly sweet, buttery flavor and a crunchy texture. It can be eaten simply with butter, salt, and pepper, or made into a delicious casserole.

1   spaghetti squash (about 3 pounds)

1 to 2 tablespoons olive oil

6   green onions, including some tender green tops, sliced

8   ounces mushrooms, sliced

1   small zucchini, unpeeled, sliced

2   cloves garlic, minced

1   tomato, seeded, diced, and drained

½   cup canned fat free low-sodium chicken broth

1   tablespoon chopped fresh basil, or ½ teaspoon dried basil

½   teaspoon salt

Freshly ground pepper to taste

¼   cup freshly grated Parmesan cheese for sprinkling on top

PREHEAT oven to 350°F. Cut squash in half lengthwise and scoop out seeds and loose strings. On an aluminum foil–lined baking sheet, place squash, cut side down. Bake until tender, about 40 minutes (see Note). Remove from baking sheet and cool. With a fork, scrape out flesh and place in a 2½-quart casserole dish lightly coated with cooking spray or oil.

IN a medium skillet over medium heat, warm 1 tablespoon of the oil. Add onions, mushrooms, zucchini, and garlic and sauté until tender, 6 to 7 minutes. Add more oil, if needed. Stir in tomato, broth, and seasonings and simmer 5 minutes longer.

TRANSFER to a casserole dish containing squash and mix well. Sprinkle Parmesan cheese on top.

BAKE, uncovered, until heated through and flavors are blended, about 40 minutes.

SERVES 8

NOTE: Spaghetti squash may also be cooked in the microwave oven. Cut squash as directed. Place cut side down in a shallow glass dish with ¼ cup water. Cover with plastic wrap. Cook 7 to 8 minutes on high, then proceed as directed.

THE BIG BOOK OF CASSEROLES

index

A

B

C

N

O

P

R

S

T

V